MCSA

Windows Server® 2012 R2

Administration Study Guide

Exam 70-411

MCSA
Windows Server® 2012 R2
Administration Study Guide
Exam 70-411

William Panek

A Wiley Brand

Senior Acquisitions Editor: Jeff Kellum
Development Editor: Gary Schwartz
Technical Editors: Rodney Fournier and Michael Rice
Production Editor: Eric Charbonneau
Copy Editor: Kim Wimpsett
Editorial Manager: Pete Gaughan
Production Manager: Kathleen Wisor
Professional Technology and Strategy Director: Barry Pruett
Associate Publisher: Jim Minatel
Media Project Manager 1: Laura Moss-Hollister
Media Associate Producer: Marilyn Hummel
Media Quality Assurance: Josh Frank
Book Designer: Judy Fung
Proofreader: Josh Chase, Word One New York
Indexer: Ted Laux
Project Coordinator, Cover: Patrick Redmond
Cover Designer: Wiley

This book is dedicated to the three ladies of my life: Crystal, Alexandria, and Paige.

Acknowledgments

I would like to thank my wife and best friend, Crystal. She is always the light at the end of my tunnel. I want to thank my two daughters, Alexandria and Paige, for all of their love and support during the writing of all my books. They make it all worthwhile.

I want to thank my family, and especially my brothers, Rick, Gary, and Rob. They have always been there for me. I want to thank my father, Richard, who helped me become the man I am today, and my mother, Maggie, for all of her love and support.

I would like to thank all of my friends and co-workers especially Vic, Catherine, Jeff, Stephanie, Don, Jason, Doug, Dave, Steve, Pat, Mike (all of them), Tommy, George, Greg, Becca, Deb, Jeri, Lisa, Scotty, and all of the field guys. I want to also thank my team and everyone who works with my group including Moe, Jimmy, Paul, Dana, Dean, Reanna, Todd, and Will F. Because of all your hard work, you make me look good every day and make it a pleasure to go to work. Thanks to all of you for everything you do.

I want to thank everyone on my Sybex team, especially my development editor, Gary Schwartz, who helped me make this the best book possible, and Rodney R. Fournier, who is the technical editor of many of my books. It's always good to have the very best technical guy backing you up.

I want to thank Eric Charbonneau, who was my production editor, and my acquisitions editor, Jeff Kellum, who served as lead for the entire book. He has always been there for me, and it is always great to write for him.

Finally, I want to thank everyone else behind the scenes that helped make this book possible. It's truly an amazing thing to have so many people work on my books to help make them the very best. I can't thank you all enough for your hard work.

About the Author

 **William Panek** holds the following certifications: MCP, MCP+I, MCSA, MCSA+ Security and Messaging, MCSE-NT (3.51 and 4.0), MCSE 2000, 2003, 2012/2012 R2, MCSE+Security and Messaging, MCDBA, MCT, MCTS, MCITP, CCNA, CCDA, and CHFI. Will is also a Microsoft MVP.

After many successful years in the computer industry and a degree in computer programming, Will decided that he could better use his talents and his personality as an instructor. He began teaching for schools such as Boston University and the University of Maryland, just to name a few. He has done consulting and training work for some of the biggest government and corporate companies in the world including the U.S. Secret Service, Cisco, the U.S. Air Force, and the U.S. Army.

In January 2015, Will is now teaching for StormWind (www.stormwind.com). He currently lives in New Hampshire with his wife and two daughters. Will was also a representative in the New Hampshire House of Representatives from 2010 to 2012. In his spare time, he likes to golf, ski, shoot, snowmobiling, and ride his Harley. Will is also a commercially rated helicopter pilot.

Contents at a Glance

Contents

Table of Exercises

Introduction

This book is drawn from more than 20 years of IT experience. I have taken that experience and translated it into a Windows Server 2012 R2 book that will help you not only prepare for the MCSA: Windows Server 2012 R2 exams but also develop a clear understanding of how to install and configure Windows Server 2012 R2 while avoiding all of the possible configuration pitfalls.

Many Microsoft books just explain the Windows operating system, but with *MCSA: Windows Server 2012 R2 Complete Study Guide*, I go a step further by providing many in-depth, step-by-step procedures to support my explanations of how the operating system performs at its best.

Microsoft Windows Server 2012 R2 is the newest version of Microsoft's server operating system software. Microsoft has taken the best of Windows Server 2003, Windows Server 2008/2008 R2, and Windows Server 2012 and combined them into the latest creation, Windows Server 2012 R2.

Windows Server 2012 R2 eliminates many of the problems that plagued the previous versions of Windows Server and it includes a much faster boot time and shutdown. It is also easier to install and configure, and it barely stops to ask the user any questions during installation. In this book, I will show you what features are installed during the automated installation and where you can make changes if you need to be more in charge of your operating system and its features.

This book takes you through all the ins and outs of Windows Server 2012 R2, including installation, configuration, Group Policy objects, auditing, backups, and so much more.

Windows Server 2012 R2 has improved on Microsoft's desktop environment, made networking easier, enhanced searching capability, and improved performance—and that's only scratching the surface.

When all is said and done, this is a technical book for IT professionals who want to take Windows Server 2012 R2 to the next step and get certified. With this book, you will not only learn Windows Server 2012 R2 and ideally pass the exams, but you will also become a Windows Server 2012 R2 expert.

The Microsoft Certification Program

Since the inception of its certification program, Microsoft has certified more than 2 million people. As the computer network industry continues to increase in both size and complexity, this number is sure to grow—and the need for proven ability will also increase. Certifications can help companies verify the skills of prospective employees and contractors.

The Microsoft certification tracks for Windows Server 2012 R2 include the following:

MCSA: Windows Server 2012 R2   The MCSA is now the lowest-level certification you can achieve with Microsoft in relation to Windows Server 2012 R2. It requires passing three exams: 70-410, 70-411, and 70-412. Or, if you qualify, you can take an Upgrading exam: Exam 70-417. This book assists in your preparation for all four exams.

MCSE: Server Infrastructure or MCSE: Desktop Infrastructure   The MCSE certifications, in relation to Windows Server 2012 R2, require that you become an MCSA first and then pass two additional exams. The additional exams will vary depending on which of the two MCSE tracks you choose. For more information, visit Microsoft's website at www.microsoft.com/learning.

MCSM: Directory Services   The MCSM certification takes things to an entirely new level. It requires passing a knowledge exam (in addition to having the MCSE in Windows Server 2012 R2) and a lab exam. This is now the elite-level certification in Windows Server 2012 R2.

How Do You Become Certified on Windows Server 2012 R2?

Attaining Microsoft certification has always been a challenge. In the past, students have been able to acquire detailed exam information—even most of the exam questions—from online "brain dumps" and third-party "cram" books or software products. For the new generation of exams, this is simply not the case.

Microsoft has taken strong steps to protect the security and integrity of its new certification tracks. Now prospective candidates must complete a course of study that develops detailed knowledge about a wide range of topics. It supplies them with the true skills needed, derived from working with the technology being tested.

The new generations of Microsoft certification programs are heavily weighted toward hands-on skills and experience. It is recommended that candidates have troubleshooting skills acquired through hands-on experience and working knowledge.

Fortunately, if you are willing to dedicate the time and effort to learn Windows Server 2012 R2, you can prepare yourself well for the exam by using the proper tools. By working through this book, you can successfully meet the requirements to pass the Windows Server 2012 R2 exams.

MCITP Exam Requirements

Candidates for MCITP certification on Windows Server 2012 R2 must pass one Windows Server 2012 R2 exams. This book will help you get ready for the 70-411: Administering Windows Server 2012 R2 exam.

Microsoft provides exam objectives to give you a general overview of possible areas of coverage on the Microsoft exams. Keep in mind, however, that exam objectives are subject to change at any time without prior notice and at Microsoft's sole discretion. Visit the Microsoft Learning website (www.microsoft.com/learning) for the most current listing of exam objectives. The published objectives and how they map to this book are listed later in this introduction.

 For a more detailed description of the Microsoft certification programs, including a list of all the exams, visit the Microsoft Learning website at www.microsoft.com/learning.

Tips for Taking the Windows Server 2012 R2 Exams

Here are some general tips for achieving success on your certification exam:

- Arrive early at the exam center so that you can relax and review your study materials. During this final review, you can look over tables and lists of exam-related information.

- Read the questions carefully. Do not be tempted to jump to an early conclusion. Make sure you know *exactly* what the question is asking.

- Answer all questions. If you are unsure about a question, mark it for review and come back to it at a later time.

- On simulations, do not change settings that are not directly related to the question. Also, assume the default settings if the question does not specify or imply which settings are used.

- For questions about which you're unsure, use a process of elimination to get rid of the obviously incorrect answers first. This improves your odds of selecting the correct answer when you need to make an educated guess.

Exam Registration

At the time this book was released, Microsoft exams are given at Prometric testing centers (800-755-EXAM (800-755-3926)). As of December 31, 2014, Microsoft will be ending its relationship with Prometric and all exams will be delivered through the more than 1,000 Authorized VUE Testing Centers around the world. For the location of a testing center near you, go to VUE's website at www.vue.com. If you are outside of the United States and Canada, contact your local VUE registration center.

Find out the number of the exam that you want to take, and then register with the Prometric or VUE registration center nearest to you. At this point, you will be asked for advance payment for the exam. The exams are $150 each and you must take them within one year of payment. You can schedule exams up to six weeks in advance or as late as one working day prior to the date of the exam. You can cancel or reschedule your exam if you contact the center at least two working days prior to the exam. Same-day registration is available in some locations, subject to space availability. Where same-day registration is available, you must register a minimum of two hours before test time.

When you schedule the exam, you will be provided with instructions regarding appointment and cancellation procedures, ID requirements, and information about the testing center location. In addition, you will receive a registration and payment confirmation letter from Prometric.

Microsoft requires certification candidates to accept the terms of a nondisclosure agreement before taking certification exams.

Who Should Read This Book?

This book is intended for individuals who want to earn their MCITP by taking exam 70-411: Administering Windows Server 2012 R2.

This book will not only help anyone who is looking to pass the Microsoft exams, it will also help anyone who wants to learn the real ins and outs of the Windows Server 2012 R2 operating system.

What's Inside?

Here is a glance at what's in each chapter:

Chapter 1: Manage and Maintain Servers   In this chapter, I explain the requirements and steps to deploy, manage, and maintain the Windows Server 2012 R2 system.

Chapter 2: Manage File Services   This chapter shows you how to configure file and print services. You will look at how to set up a file server for faster response times, and I will also explain the different ways to set up and configure print services.

Chapter 3: Configure DNS   I take you through the advantages and benefits of Windows Server 2012 R2 Network Services.

Chapter 4: Configure Routing and Remote Access   I will show you how to configure the different types of remote access and Windows routing protocols.

Chapter 5: Configure a Network Policy Server Infrastructure   This chapter takes you through the different ways to create and manage your Windows Server 2012 R2 NPS server.

Chapter 6: Configure and Manage Active Directory   You will see how to configure and manage different types of objects in Active Directory.

Chapter 7: Configure and Manage Group Policy   This chapter will show you how to manage different parts of Windows policies by using the Group Policy Management Console. This chapter will also explain how to install and configure software using GPOs.

What's Included with the Book

This book includes many helpful items intended to prepare you for the MCSA: Windows Server 2012 R2 certification.

Assessment Test   There is an assessment test at the conclusion of the introduction that can be used to evaluate quickly where you are with Windows Server 2012 R2. This test should be taken prior to beginning your work in this book, and it should help you identify areas in which you are either strong or weak. Note that these questions are purposely more simple than the types of questions you may see on the exams.

Objective Map and Opening List of Objectives   Later in this introduction, I include a detailed exam objective map showing you where each of the exam objectives are covered. Each chapter also includes a list of the exam objectives that are covered.

Helpful Exercises   Throughout the book, I have included step-by-step exercises of some of the more important tasks that you should be able to perform. Some of these exercises have corresponding videos that can be downloaded from the book's website. Also, in the following section I have a recommended home lab setup that will be helpful in completing these tasks.

Exam Essentials   The end of each chapter also includes a listing of exam essentials. These are essentially repeats of the objectives, but remember that any objective on the exam blueprint could show up on the exam.

Chapter Review Questions   Each chapter includes review questions. These are used to assess your understanding of the chapter and are taken directly from the chapter. These questions are based on the exam objectives, and they are similar in difficulty to items you might actually receive on the MCSA: Windows Server 2012 R2 exams.

The Sybex Test Engine, flashcards, videos, and glossary can be obtained at www.sybex.com/go/mcsawin2012r2admin.

Sybex Test Engine   Readers can access the Sybex Test Engine, which includes the assessment test and chapter review questions in electronic format. In addition, there is a practice exam included with the Sybex test engine for exam 70-411.

Electronic Flashcards   Flashcards are included for quick reference. They are great tools for learning important facts quickly. You may even consider these as additional simple practice questions, which is essentially what they are.

Videos   Some of the exercises include corresponding videos. These videos show you how I do the exercises. There is also a video that shows you how to set up virtualization so that you can complete the exercises within a virtualized environment. This same video also shows you how to install Windows Server 2012 R2 Datacenter on that virtualized machine.

PDF of Glossary of Terms   There is a glossary included that covers the key terms used in this book.

Recommended Home Lab Setup

To get the most out of this book, you will want to make sure you complete the exercises throughout the chapters. To complete the exercises, you will need one of two setups. First, you can set up a machine with Windows Server 2012 R2 and complete the labs using a regular Windows Server 2012 R2 machine.

The second way to set up Windows Server 2012 R2 (the way I set up Server 2012 R2) is by using virtualization. I set up Windows Server 2012 R2 as a virtual hard disk (VHD), and I did all the labs this way. The advantages of using virtualization are that you can always just wipe out the system and start over without losing a real server. Plus, you can set up multiple virtual servers and create a full lab environment on one machine.

I created a video for this book showing you how to set up a virtual machine and how to install Windows Server 2012 R2 onto that virtual machine.

How to Contact the Author/Sybex

Sybex strives to keep you supplied with the latest tools and information you need for your work. Please check the website at www.sybex.com/go/mcsawin2012r2admin, where I'll post additional content and updates that supplement this book should the need arise.
You can contact me by going to my website at www.willpanek.com.

Certification Objectives Maps

In addition to the book chapters, you will find coverage of exam objectives in the flashcards, practice exams, and videos on the book's companion website: www.sybex.com/go/mcsawin2012r2admin

Exam objectives are subject to change at any time without prior notice and at Microsoft's sole discretion. Please visit Microsoft's website (www.micro soft.com/learning) for the most current listing of exam objectives.

Objectives

Exam 70-411: Administering Windows Server 2012

Deploy and manage server images, Chapter 10

> Install the Windows Deployment Services (WDS) role
>
> Configure and manage boot, install, and discover images
>
> Update images with patches, hotfixes, and drivers
>
> Install features for offline images
>
> Configure driver groups and packages

Implement patch management., Chapter 10

> Install and configure the Windows Server Update Services (WSUS) role
>
> Configure group policies for updates

Configure client-side targeting, Chapter 10

> Configure WSUS synchronization
>
> Configure WSUS groups
>
> Manage patch management in mixed environments Monitor servers.
>
> Configure Data Collector Sets (DCS)
>
> Configure alerts
>
> Monitor real-time performance
>
> Monitor virtual machines (vms)
>
> Monitor events
>
> Configure event subscriptions
>
> Configure network monitoring
>
> Schedule performance monitoring

Configure Distributed File System (DFS), Chapter 11

> Install and configure DFS namespaces
>
> Configure DFS Replication Targets
>
> Configure Replication Scheduling
>
> Configure Remote Differential Compression settings
>
> Configure staging
>
> Configure fault tolerance
>
> Clone a DFS database

Recover DFS databases

Optimize DFS replication

Configure File Server Resource Manager (FSRM), Chapter 11

Install the FSRM role service

Configure quotas

Configure file screens

Configure reports

Configure file management tasks

Configure file and disk encryption, Chapter 11

Configure Bitlocker encryption

Configure the Network Unlock feature

Configure Bitlocker policies

Configure the EFS recovery agent

Manage EFS and Bitlocker certificates including backup and restore

Configure advanced audit policies, Chapter 11

Implement auditing using Group Policy and AuditPol.exe

Create expression-based

Create removable device audit policies

Configure DNS zones, Chapter 12

Configure primary and secondary zones

Configure stub zones

Configure conditional forwards

Configure zone and conditional forward storage in Active Directory

Configure zone delegation

Configure zone transfer settings

Configure notify settings

Configure DNS records, Chapter 12

Create and configure DNS Resource Records (RR) including A, AAAA, PTR, SOA, NS, SRV, CNAME, and MX records

Configure zone scavenging

Configure record options including time to live (ttl) and weight

Configure round robin

Configure secure dynamic updates

Assessment Test

1. You need to stop an application from running in Task Manager. Which tab would you use to stop an application from running?

   A. Performance

   B. Users

   C. Options

   D. Details

2. As a network administrator, you are responsible for all client computers at the central corporate location. Your company has asked you to make sure that all the client computers are secure. You need to use MBSA to scan your client computers, based on IP addresses, for possible security violations, but you need to use the command-line version. Which of the following commands would you use?

   A. `mdsacli.exe /hf -i xxxx.xxxx.xxxx.xxxx`

   B. `mdsacli.exe /ip xxxx.xxxx.xxxx.xxxx`

   C. `mbsa.exe /hf -ip xxxx.xxxx.xxxx.xxxx`

   D. `mbsa.exe /ip xxxx.xxxx.xxxx.xxxx`

3. You are the administrator of a new Windows Server 2012 R2 machine. You need to install DNS and create a primary zone. Which MMC snap-in would you use to install DNS?

   A. Add/Remove Programs

   B. Programs

   C. Server Manager

   D. Administrative Tools

4. You are the administrator for a large company that has purchased a new multifunction printer. You want to publish the printer to Active Directory. Where would you click in order to accomplish this task?

   A. The Sharing tab

   B. The Advanced tab

   C. The Device Settings tab

   D. The Printing Preferences button

5. Crystal is a system administrator for an Active Directory environment that is running in Native mode. Recently, several managers have reported suspicions about user activities and have asked her to increase security in the environment. Specifically, the requirements are as follows:

   - The accessing of certain sensitive files must be logged.

   - Modifications to certain sensitive files must be logged.

- System administrators must be able to provide information about which users accessed sensitive files and when they were accessed.

- All logon attempts for specific shared machines must be recorded.

Which of the following steps should Isabel take to meet these requirements? (Choose all that apply.)

A. Enable auditing with the Computer Management tool.

B. Enable auditing with the Active Directory Users and Computers tool.

C. Enable auditing with the Active Directory Domains and Trusts tool.

D. Enable auditing with the Event Viewer tool.

E. View the audit log using the Event Viewer tool.

F. View auditing information using the Computer Management tool.

G. Enable failure and success auditing settings for specific files stored on NTFS volumes.

H. Enable failure and success auditing settings for logon events on specific computer accounts.

6. You are the network administrator for a large widget distributor. Your company's network has 20 Windows 2012 R2 servers, and all of the clients are running either Windows 8 or Windows 7. All of your end users use laptops to do their work, and many of them work away from the office. What should you configure to help them work on documents when away from the office?

A. Online file access

B. Offline file access

C. Share permissions

D. NTFS permissions

7. Your company has decided to implement an external hard drive. The company IT manager before you always used FAT32 as the system partition. Your company wants to know whether it should move to NTFS. Which of the following are some advantages of NTFS? (Choose all that apply.)

A. Security

B. Quotas

C. Compression

D. Encryption

8. You have been hired by a small company to implement new Windows Server 2012 R2 systems. The company wants you to set up a server for users' home folder locations. What type of server would you be setting up?

A. PDC server

B. Web server

C. Exchange server

D. File server

9. GPOs assigned at which of the following level(s) will override GPO settings at the domain level?

   A. OU

   B. Site

   C. Domain

   D. Both OU and site

10. A system administrator wants to ensure that only the GPOs set at the OU level affect the Group Policy settings for objects within the OU. Which option can they use to do this (assuming that all other GPO settings are the defaults)?

   A. The Enforced option

   B. The Block Policy Inheritance option

   C. The Disable option

   D. The Deny permission

11. Mateo, a system administrator, is planning to implement Group Policy objects in a new Windows Server 2012 R2 Active Directory environment. To meet the needs of the organization, he decides to implement a hierarchical system of Group Policy settings. At which of the following levels is he able to assign Group Policy settings? (Choose all that apply.)

   A. Sites

   B. Domains

   C. Organizational units

   D. Local system

12. Ann is a system administrator for a medium-sized Active Directory environment. She has determined that several new applications that will be deployed throughout the organization use registry-based settings. She would like to do the following:

   ▪ Control these registry settings using Group Policy.

   ▪ Create a standard set of options for these applications and allow other system administrators to modify them using the standard Active Directory tools.

Which of the following options can she use to meet these requirements? (Choose all that apply.)

   A. Implement the inheritance functionality of GPOs.

   B. Implement delegation of specific objects within Active Directory.

   C. Implement the No Override functionality of GPOs.

   D. Create administrative templates.

   E. Provide administrative templates to the system administrators who are responsible for creating Group Policy for the applications.

13. You are the network administrator for your organization. A new company policy has been released wherein if a user enters their password incorrectly three times within 5 minutes, they are locked out for 30 minutes. What three actions do you need to set to comply with this policy? (Choose all that apply.)

    A. Set Account Lockout Duration to 5 minutes.

    B. Set Account Lockout Duration to 30 minutes.

    C. Set the Account Lockout Threshold setting to 3 invalid logon attempts.

    D. Set the Account Lockout Threshold setting to 30 minutes.

    E. Set the Reset Account Lockout Counter setting to 5 minutes.

    F. Set the Reset Account Lockout Counter setting to 3 times.

14. You are teaching a Microsoft Active Directory class, and one of your students asks, "Which of the following folders in the Active Directory Users and Computers tool is used when users from outside the forest are granted access to resources within a domain?" What answer would you give your student?

    A. Users

    B. Computers

    C. Domain Controllers

    D. Foreign Security Principals

15. Your manager has decided that your organization needs to use an Active Directory application data partition. Which command can you use to create and manage application data partitions?

    A. DCPromo.exe

    B. NTDSUtil.exe

    C. ADUtil.exe

    D. ADSI.exe

16. Your network contains an Active Directory domain named Sybex.com. The domain contains a RADIUS server named Server1 that runs Windows Server 2012 R2. You add a VPN server named Server2 to the network. On Server1, you create several network policies. You need to configure Server1 to accept authentication requests from Server2. Which tool should you use on Server1?

    A. Set-RemoteAccessRadius

    B. CMAK

    C. NPS

    D. Routing and Remote Access

17. Your network contains an Active Directory domain named Sybex.com. The domain contains a server named Server1 that runs Windows Server 2012 R2. Server1 has the following role services installed:

    ■ DirectAccess and VPN (RRAS)

    ■ Network Policy Server

Remote users have client computers that run Windows XP, Windows 7, or Windows 8. You need to ensure that only the client computers that run Windows 7 or Windows 8 can establish VPN connections to Server1. What should you configure on Server1?

A. A vendor-specific RADIUS attribute of a Network Policy Server (NPS) connection request policy

B. A condition of a Network Policy Server (NPS) network policy

C. A condition of a Network Policy Server (NPS) connection request policy

D. A constraint of a Network Policy Server (NPS) network policy

18. You are the network administrator for a large organization that contains an Active Directory domain named WillPanek.com. The domain contains a server named Server1 that runs Windows Server 2012 R2. Server1 has the Network Policy and Access Services server role installed. You plan to deploy 802.1x authentication to secure the wireless network. You need to identify which Network Policy Server (NPS) authentication method supports certificate-based mutual authentication for the 802.lx deployment. Which authentication method should you identify?

A. PEAP-MS-CHAP v2

B. MS-CHAP v2

C. EAP-TLS

D. MS-CHAP

19. You have an Active Directory domain named WillPanek.com. The domain contains a server named ServerA that runs Windows Server 2012 R2. ServerA has the Network Policy and Access Services server role installed. Your company's security policy requires that certificate-based authentication must be used by some network services. You need to identify which Network Policy Server (NPS) authentication methods comply with the security policy. Which two authentication methods should you identify? (Choose two.)

A. MS-CHAP

B. PEAP-MS-CHAP v2

C. Chap

D. EAP-TLS

E. MS-CHAP v2

20. You are the network administrator, and you have been asked to set up an accounting system so that each department is responsible for the cost of their use of network services. Your network contains a Network Policy Server (NPS) server named ServerA. The network contains a server named Database1 that has Microsoft SQL server installed. All servers run Windows Server 2012 R2. You configure NPS on ServerA to log accounting data to a database on Database1. You need to ensure that the accounting data is captured if Database1 fails. The solution must minimize cost. What should you do?

A. Implement failover clustering.

B. Implement database mirroring.

C. Run the Accounting Configuration Wizard.

D. Modify the SQL Server Logging properties.

Answers to Assessment Test

1. D. All of the applications that are running on the Windows Server 2012 R2 machine will show up on the Details tab. Right-click the application and end the process.

2. A. If you use MBSA from the command-line utility mdsacli.exe, you can specify several options. You type **mdsacli.exe/hf** (from the folder that contains Mdsacli.exe) and then customize the command execution with an option such as /i*xxxx.xxxx.xxxx.xxxx*, which specifies that the computer with the specified IP address should be scanned.

3. C. Server Manager is the one place where you install all roles and features for a Windows Server 2012 R2 system.

4. A. The Sharing tab contains a check box that you can use to list the printer in Active Directory.

5. B, E, G and H. The Active Directory Users and Computers tool allows system administrators to change auditing options and to choose which actions are audited. At the file system level, Crystal can specify exactly which actions are recorded in the audit log. She can then use Event Viewer to view the recorded information and provide it to the appropriate managers.

6. B. Offline files give you the opportunity to set up files and folders so that users can work on the data while outside the office.

7. A, B, C and D. Improved security, quotas, compression, and encryption are all advantages of using NTFS over FAT32. These features are not available in FAT32. The only security you have in FAT32 is shared folder permissions.

8. D. File servers are used for storage of data, especially for users' home folders. Home folders are folder locations for your users to store data that is important and that needs to be backed up.

9. A. GPOs at the OU level take precedence over GPOs at the domain level. GPOs at the domain level, in turn, take precedence over GPOs at the site level.

10. B. The Block Policy Inheritance option prevents group policies of higher-level Active Directory objects from applying to lower-level objects as long as the Enforced option is not set.

11. A, B, C and D. GPOs can be set at all of the levels listed. You cannot set GPOs on security principals such as users or groups.

12. D and E. Administrative templates are used to specify the options available for setting Group Policy. By creating new administrative templates, Ann can specify which options are available for the new applications. She can then distribute these templates to other system administrators in the environment.

13. B, C and E. The Account Lockout Duration states how long an account will be locked out if the password is entered incorrectly. The Account Lockout Threshold is the number of bad password attempts, and the Account Lockout Counter is the time in which the bad

password attempts are made. Once the Account Lockout Counter reaches 0, the number of bad password attempts returns to 0.

14. D. When resources are made available to users who reside in domains outside the forest, Foreign Security Principal objects are automatically created. These new objects are stored within the Foreign Security Principals folder.

15. B. The primary method by which systems administrators create and manage application data partitions is through the ntdsutil tool.

16. C. The NPS snap-in allows you to set up RADIUS servers and designate which RADIUS server will accept authentication from other RADIUS servers. You can do your entire RADIUS configuration through the NPS snap-in.

17. C. NPS allows you to set up policies on how your users could log into the network. NPS allows you to set up policies that systems need to follow, and if they don't follow these policies or rules, they will not have access to the full network.

18. C. Windows Server 2012 R2 comes with *EAP-Transport Level Security (TLS)*. This EAP type allows you to use public key certificates as an authenticator. TLS is similar to the familiar Secure Sockets Layer (SSL) protocol used for web browsers and 802.1x authentication. When EAP-TLS is turned on, the client and server send TLS-encrypted messages back and forth. EAP-TLS is the strongest authentication method you can use; as a bonus, it supports smart cards. However, EAP-TLS requires your NPS server to be part of the Windows Server 2012 R2 domain.

19. B and D. PEAP-MS-CHAP v2 is an EAP type protocol that is easier to deploy than Extensible Authentication Protocol with Transport Level Security (EAP-TLS). It is easier because user authentication is accomplished by using password-based credentials (username and password) instead of digital certificates or smart cards. Both PEAP and EAP use certificates with their protocols.

20. C. One advantage of NPS is that you can use the accounting part of NPS so that you can keep track of what each department does on your NPS server. This way, departments pay for the amount of time they use the SQL server database.

Chapter

1

Manage and Maintain Servers

THE FOLLOWING 70-411 EXAM OBJECTIVES ARE COVERED IN THIS CHAPTER:

✓ **Deploy and manage server images**

- Install the Windows Deployment Services (WDS) role
- Configure and manage boot, install, and discover images
- Update images with patches, hotfixes, and drivers
- Install features for offline images
- Configure driver groups and packages

✓ **Implement patch management**

- Install and configure the Windows Server Update Services (WSUS) role
- Configure group policies for updates

✓ **Configure client-side targeting**

- Configure WSUS synchronization
- Configure WSUS groups
- Manage patch management in mixed environments

✓ **Monitor servers**

- Configure Data Collector Sets (DCS)
- Configure alerts
- Monitor real-time performance
- Monitor virtual machines (vms)
- Monitor events
- Configure event subscriptions
- Configure network monitoring
- Schedule performance monitoring

We have already discussed how to set up clients on a network and how to keep their systems running on that network. In this chapter, we will start the Windows Deployment Services. We will then turn the discussion to keeping your systems updated using Windows Server Update Services (WSUS).

Another important task of an IT team is to keep the network up and running quickly and efficiently. Keeping your network running at its peak performance is one way to make sure your end users continue to use the network and its resources without problems or interruptions. Remember, everyone has clients—salespeople have theirs, accountants have theirs, and so do we as system administrators. Our clients are the end users, and it's our job to make sure that our clients can do their jobs.

When you are working with servers, it is important you make sure that your system's information is safely backed up. Backups become useful when you lose data because of system failures, file corruptions, or accidental modifications of information. As consultants, we can tell you from experience that backups are among the most important tasks that an IT person performs daily.

Sometimes, performance optimization can feel like a luxury, especially if you can't get your domain controllers to the point where they are actually performing the services for which you intended them, such as servicing printers or allowing users to share and work on files. The Windows Server 2012 R2 operating system has been specifically designed to provide high-availability services solely intended to keep your mission-critical applications and data accessible, even in times of disaster. Occasionally, however, you might experience intermittent server crashes on one or more of the domain controllers or other computers in your environment.

The most common cause of such problems is a hardware configuration issue. Poorly written device drivers and unsupported hardware can cause problems with system stability. Failed hardware components (such as system memory) may do so as well. Memory chips can be faulty, electrostatic discharge can ruin them, and other hardware issues can occur. No matter what, a problem with your memory chip spells disaster for your server.

Third-party hardware vendors usually provide utility programs with their computers that can be used for performing hardware diagnostics on machines to help you find problems. These utilities are a good first step in resolving intermittent server crashes. When these utility programs are used in combination with the troubleshooting tips provided in this and other chapters of this book, you should be able to pinpoint most network-related problems that might occur.

In this chapter, I'll cover the tools and methods used for measuring performance and troubleshooting failures in Windows Server 2012 R2. Before you dive into the technical details, however, you should thoroughly understand what you're trying to accomplish and how you'll meet this goal.

Knowing How to Locate and Isolate Problems

In a book such as this, it would be almost impossible to cover everything that could go wrong with your Windows Server 2012 R2 system. This book covers many of the most common issues that you might come across, but almost anything is possible. Make sure you focus on the methodology used and the steps required to locate and isolate a problem—even if you are not 100 percent sure about the cause of the problem. Use online resources to help you locate and troubleshoot the problem, but don't believe everything you read (some things that are posted online can be wrong or misleading). Test your changes in a lab environment, and try to read multiple sources. Always use Microsoft Support (http://support.microsoft.com/) as one of your sources because this site is most likely the right source for information. You won't be able to find and fix everything, but knowing where to find critical information that will help you in your efforts never hurts. One of the tools that many of us in the industry use is *Microsoft TechNet*. The full version of TechNet (a paid subscription) is a resource that will help you find and fix many real-world issues.

Using Windows Deployment Services

In this section, you will look at how to install and configure *Windows Deployment Services (WDS)*. WDS is a utility that allows an administrator to deploy an operating system remotely. The client machine that is receiving the operating system needs to use a set of disks (WDS client disks) that will automatically initiate a network card, connect to the WDS server, and download the operating system.

WDS allows an IT administrator to install a Windows operating system without using a CD or DVD installation disc. Using WDS allows you to deploy the operating system through a network installation. WDS can deploy Windows XP, Windows Server 2003, Windows Vista, Windows 7, Windows 8, Windows Server 2008, Windows Server 2008 R2, Microsoft Windows 2012, and Microsoft Windows Server 2012 R2.

The following are some of the advantages of using WDS for automated installation:

- You can remotely install Windows 7 or Windows 8.

- The procedure simplifies management of the server image by allowing you to access Windows 7 or Windows 8 distribution files from a distribution server.

- You can quickly recover the operating system in the event of a computer failure.

Here are the basic steps of the WDS process from a PXE-enabled WDS client:

1. The WDS client initiates a special boot process through the PXE network adapter (and the computer's BIOS configured for a network boot). On a PXE client, the user presses F12 to start the PXE boot process and to indicate that they want to perform a WDS installation.

2. A list of available Windows PE boot images is displayed. The user should select the appropriate Windows PE boot image from the boot menu.

3. The Windows Welcome screen is displayed. The user should click the Next button.

4. The WDS user is prompted to enter credentials for accessing and installing images from the WDS server.

5. A list of available operating system images is displayed. The user should select the appropriate image file to install.

6. The WDS user is prompted to enter the product key for the selected image.

7. The Partition And Configure The Disk screen is displayed. This screen provides the ability to install a mass storage device driver, if needed, by pressing F6.

8. The image copy process is initiated, and the selected image is copied to the WDS client computer.

The following sections describe how to set up the WDS server and the WDS clients and how to install Windows 7 or Windows 8 through WDS.

Windows Server 2012 R2 WDS Functionality

Windows Server 2012 R2 allows you to use many new and improved features of WDS. Table 1.1 shows some of the highpoints of what WDS can do when installed onto a Windows Server 2012 or Windows Server 2012 R2 system.

Preparing the WDS Server

With the WDS server, you can manage and distribute Windows 7 or Windows 8 operating system images to WDS client computers. The WDS server contains any files necessary for PXE booting, Windows PE boot images, and the Windows 7 or Windows 8 images to be deployed.

The following steps for preparing the WDS server are discussed in the upcoming sections:

1. Make sure that the server meets the requirements for running WDS.

2. Install WDS.

3. Configure and start WDS.

4. Configure the WDS server to respond to client computers (if this was not configured when WDS was installed).

For WDS to work, the server on which you will install WDS must meet the requirements for WDS and be able to access the required network services.

WDS Server Requirements

WDS needs some services and requirements installed before it will work properly:

- Active Directory Domain Services must be present for WDS to function properly. The WDS server must be a domain controller or a member of the Active Directory domain.

- At least one partition on the server must be formatted as NTFS.

- The operating system must be Windows Server 2003, Windows Server 2008/2008 R2, Windows Server 2012, or Windows Server 2012 R2.

TABLE 1.1 WDS functionality with Windows Server 2012 R2

Feature	Description
OS deployed using WDS	Windows XP, Windows Server 2003, Windows Vista SP1, Windows Server 2008, Windows 7, Windows Server 2008 R2, Windows Server 2012, Windows 8, Windows 8.1, Windows Server 2012 R2.
Image types deployed	.wim and .vhd images are both supported. .vhd images can now be managed via the WDS management snap-in in addition to the command line. Also, .vhdx files, the new file format available since Windows Server 2012, are supported directly and over multicast.
Boot environment	Windows PE.
Administration options	MMC snap-in and WDSUTIL. Windows PowerShell cmdlets added in Windows Server 2012 R2.
Multicasting	IPv6 and DHCPv6 support for TFTP and multicasting along with improved multicast deployments.
Driver provisioning	Drivers are automatically detected and installed. Because of this, duplicate driver packages are prevented from being installed into the driver store.
PowerShell cmdlet scripting	Supported on Windows Server 2012 R2 only.

Network Services

Besides the server requirements, some networking requirements need to be installed for WDS. The following network services must be running on the WDS server or be accessible to the WDS server from another network server:

- TCP/IP installed and configured.
- A DHCP server, which is used to assign DHCP addresses to WDS clients. (Make sure your DHCP scope has enough addresses to accommodate all of the WDS clients that will need IP addresses.)
- A DNS server, which is used to locate the Active Directory controller.
- Active Directory, which is used to locate WDS servers and WDS clients as well as authorize WDS clients and manage WDS configuration settings and client installation options.

Installing the WDS Server Components

You can configure WDS on a Windows Server 2003/2008/2008 R2, Windows Server 2012, or Windows Server 2012 R2 computer by using the Windows Deployment Services Configuration Wizard or by using the WDSUTIL command-line utility. Table 1.2 describes the WDSUTIL command-line options.

TABLE 1.2   WDSUTIL command-line options

WDSUTIL option	Description
/initialize-server	Initializes the configuration of the WDS server
/uninitialized -server	Undoes any changes made during the initialization of the WDS server
/add	Adds images and devices to the WDS server
/convert-ripimage	Converts Remote Installation Preparation (RIPrep) images to WIM images
/remove	Removes images from the server
/set	Sets information in images, image groups, WDS servers, and WDS devices
/get	Gets information from images, image groups, WDS servers, and WDS devices
/new	Creates new capture images or discover images
/copy- image	Copies images from the image store
/export-image	Exports to WIM files images contained within the image store
/start	Starts WDS services
/stop	Stops WDS services
/disable	Disables WDS services
/enable	Enables WDS services
/approve-autoadddevices	Approves Auto-Add devices
/reject-autoadddevices	Rejects Auto-Add devices
/delete-autoadddevices	Deletes records from the Auto-Add database
/update	Uses a known good resource to update a server resource

The first step in setting up WDS to deploy operating systems to the clients is to install the WDS role. You do this by using Server Manager.

One of the advantages of using the Windows deployment server is that WDS can work with Windows image (`.wim`) files. Windows image files can be created through the use of the Windows Sysprep utility.

One component to which you need to pay attention when using the Windows deployment server is *Preboot Execution Environment (PXE)* network devices. PXE boot devices are network interface cards (NICs) that can talk to a network without the need for an operating system. PXE boot NIC adapters are network adapters that have a set of preboot commands within the boot firmware.

This is important when using WDS because PXE boot adapters connect to a WDS server and request the data needed to load the operating system remotely. Remember, most of these machines for which you are using WDS do not have an operating system on the computer. You need NIC adapters that can connect to a network without the need for an operating system for WDS to work properly.

For the same reason, you must set up DHCP to accept PXE machines. Those machines need a valid TCP/IP address so that they can connect to the WDS server.

Installing the WDS Services Using PowerShell

As we have stated multiple times throughout this book, we will show you how to do many of these tasks using the Windows PowerShell commands. Table 1.3 describes many of the WDS cmdlets that you can use in Windows Server 2012 R2.

 This table comes directly from Microsoft TechNet at `http://technet` `.microsoft.com/library/dn283416.aspx`.

TABLE 1.3 WDSUTIL command-line options

Cmdlet	Description
Add-WdsDriverPackage	Adds an existing driver package to a driver group or injects it into a boot image
Approve-WdsClient	Approves clients
Copy-WdsInstallImage	Copies install images within an image group
Deny-WdsClient	Denies approval for clients
Disable-WdsBootImage	Disables a boot image

TABLE 1.3   WDSUTIL command-line options *(continued)*

Cmdlet	Description
Disable-WdsDriverPackage	Disables a driver package in the Windows Deployment Services driver store
Disable-WdsInstallImage	Disables an install image
Disconnect-WdsMulticastClient	Disconnects a multicast client from a transmission or namespace
Enable-WdsBootImage	Enables a boot image
Enable-WdsDriverPackage	Enables a driver package in the Windows Deployment Services driver store
Enable-WdsInstallImage	Enables an install image
Export-WdsBootImage	Exports an existing boot image from an image store
Export-WdsInstallImage	Exports an existing install image from an image store
Get-WdsBootImage	Gets properties of boot images from the image store
Get-WdsClient	Gets client devices from the pending device database, or pre-staged devices from Active Directory or the standalone server device database.
Get-WdsDriverPackage	Gets properties of driver packages from the Windows Deployment Services driver store
Get-WdsInstallImage	Gets properties of install images from an image store
Get-WdsInstallImageGroup	Gets properties of install image groups
Get-WdsMulticastClient	Gets a list of clients connected to a multicast transmission or namespace
Import-WdsBootImage	Imports a boot image to the image store
Import-WdsDriverPackage	Imports a driver package into the Windows Deployment Services driver store
Import-WdsInstallImage	Imports an install image to an image store
New-WdsClient	Creates a prestaged client

`New-WdsInstallImageGroup`	Creates an install image group
`Remove-WdsBootImage`	Removes a boot image from the image store
`Remove-WdsClient`	Removes a prestaged client from AD DS or the stand-alone server device database or clears the Pending Devices database
`Remove-WdsDriverPackage`	Removes a driver package from a driver group or removes it from all driver groups and deletes it
`Remove-WdsInstallImage`	Removes an install image from an image store
`Remove-WdsInstallImageGroup`	Removes an install image group
`Set-WdsBootImage`	Modifies settings of a boot image
`Set-WdsClient`	Modifies a prestaged client device
`Set-WdsInstallImage`	Modifies the properties of an install image
`Set-WdsInstallImageGroup`	Modifies the name and access permissions of an install image group

Preparing the WDS Client

The WDS client is the computer on which Windows 7 or Windows 8 will be installed. WDS clients rely on PXE technology, which allows the client computer to remotely boot and connect to a WDS server.

To act as a WDS client, the computer must meet all of the hardware requirements for Windows 7 or Windows 8 and have a PXE-capable network adapter installed. In addition, a WDS server must be present on the network. Furthermore, the user account used to install the image must be a member of the Domain Users group in Active Directory.

After the WDS server has been installed and configured, you can install Windows 7 or Windows 8 on a WDS client that uses a PXE-compliant network card.

To install Windows 7 or Windows 8 on the WDS client, follow these steps:

1. Start the computer. When prompted, press F12 for a network service boot. The Windows PE appears.
2. The Windows Welcome screen appears. Click the Next button to start the installation process.
3. Enter the username and password of an account that has permissions to access and install images from the WDS server.

4. A list of available operating system images stored on the WDS server appears. Select the image to install and click Next.

5. Enter the product key for the selected Windows 7 or Windows 8 image and click Next.

6. The Partition And Configure The Disk screen appears. Select the desired disk-partitioning options or click OK to use the default options.

7. Click Next to initiate the image-copying process. The Windows Setup process will begin after the image is copied to the WDS client computer.

Configuring Windows Server Update Services

To keep your Windows operating systems up-to-date and secure, you can use Windows Update, Automatic Updates, WSUS, and the Microsoft Baseline Security Analyzer.

Windows Update   This utility attaches to the Microsoft website through a user-initiated process, and it allows Windows users to update their operating systems by downloading updated files (critical and noncritical software updates).

Automatic Updates   This utility extends the functionality of Windows Update by automating the process of updating critical files. With Automatic Updates, you can specify whether you want updates to be downloaded and installed automatically or whether you just want to be notified when updates are available.

Windows Server Update Services (WSUS)   This utility is used to deploy a limited version of Windows Update to a corporate server, which in turn provides the Windows updates to client computers within the corporate network. This allows clients that are limited to what they can access through a firewall to be able to keep their Windows operating systems up-to-date.

Microsoft Baseline Security Analyzer (MBSA)   You can download this utility from the Microsoft website to ensure you have the most current security updates.

In the following sections, you will learn how to use these tools.

Windows Update

Windows Update is available through the Microsoft website, and it is used to provide the most current files for Windows operating systems. Examples of updates include security fixes, critical updates, updated help files, and updated drivers.

You can download Windows Update through the Help And Support page on the Microsoft website. Once it's installed, click the Scan For Updates link on the Welcome To Windows Update screen to search for new updates.

The results of the Windows Update search will be displayed on the left side of the Windows Update screen. You will see the following options:

Pick Updates To Install   This lists what updates are available for your computer, and it includes the following categories:

- Critical Updates And Service Packs
- Windows Server 2012 R2 Family
- Driver Updates

Review And Install Updates   This allows you to view all of the updates that you have selected to install, and it installs the updates.

View Installation History   This allows you to track all of the updates that you have applied to your server.

Personalize Windows Update   This customizes what you see when you use Windows Update.

Get Help And Support   This displays help and support information about Windows Update.

Sometimes the updates that are installed require the computer to be restarted before they can take effect. In this event, Windows Update uses a technology called *chained installation*. With chained installation, all updates that require a computer restart are applied before the computer is restarted. This eliminates the need to restart the computer more than once.

The information that is collected by Windows Update includes the operating system and version number, the Internet Explorer version, the software version information for any software that can be updated through Windows Update, the Plug and Play ID numbers for installed hardware, and the region and language settings. Windows Update will also collect the product ID and product key to confirm that you are running a licensed copy of Windows, but this information is retained only during the Windows Update session and it is not stored. No personal information that can be used to identify users of the Windows Update service is collected.

Windows Automatic Updates

The *Automatic Updates* application extends the functionality of Windows Update by automating the update process. With Automatic Updates, Windows Server 2012 R2 recognizes when you have an Internet connection and will automatically search for any updates for your computer from the Windows Update website.

If any updates are identified, they will be downloaded using *Background Intelligent Transfer Services (BITS)*. BITS is a bandwidth-throttling technology that allows downloads to occur using idle bandwidth only. This means that downloading automatic updates will not interfere with any other Internet traffic.

If Automatic Updates detects any updates for your computer, you will see an update icon in the notification area of the taskbar.

> To configure Automatic Updates, you must have local administrative rights to the computer on which Automatic Updates is being configured. Requiring administrative rights prevents users from specifying that critical security updates not be installed. In addition, Microsoft must digitally sign any updates that are downloaded.

You configure Automatic Updates by selecting Start ➤ Control Panel ➤ Windows Update. You will see the Check For Updates button shown in Figure 1.1.

FIGURE 1.1   Windows Update control panel

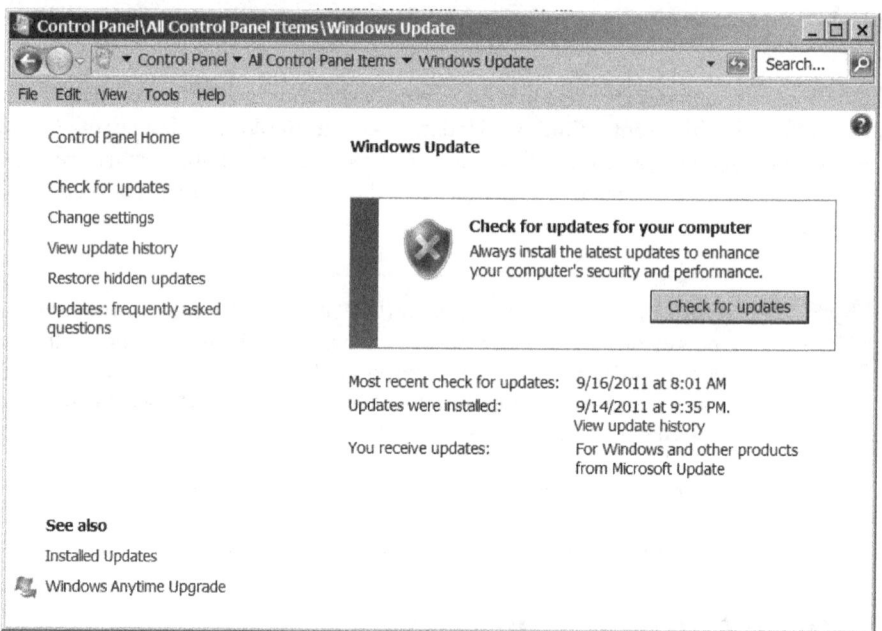

You enable Automatic Updates by clicking the Change Settings link. With this setting enabled, Windows Update software may be automatically updated prior to applying any other updates (see Figure 1.2).

FIGURE 1.2   Change Settings window of the Windows Update control panel

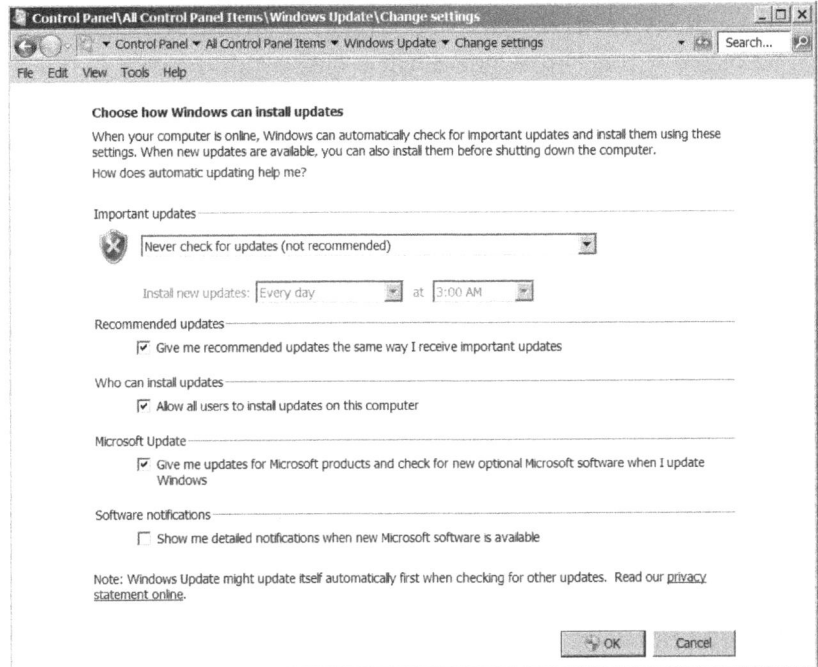

Using Windows Server Update Services

Windows Server Update Services (WSUS), formerly known as Software Update Services (SUS), is used to leverage the features of Windows Update within a corporate environment. WSUS downloads Windows updates to a corporate server, which in turn provides the updates to the internal corporate clients. This allows administrators to test and have full control over what updates are deployed within the corporate environment. WSUS is designed to work in medium-sized corporate networks that are not using System Center Essentials 2012 R2.

Advantages of Using WSUS

Using WSUS has many advantages:

- It allows an internal server within a private intranet to act as a virtual Windows Update server.

- Administrators have selective control over what updates are posted and deployed from the public Windows Update site. No updates are deployed to client computers unless an administrator first approves them.

- Administrators can control the synchronization of updates from the public Windows Update site to the WSUS server either manually or automatically.

- Administrators can configure Automatic Updates on client computers to access the local WSUS server as opposed to the public Windows Update site.

- WSUS checks each update to verify that Microsoft has digitally signed it. Any updates that are not digitally signed are discarded.

- Administrators can selectively specify whether clients can access updated files from the intranet or from Microsoft's public Windows Update site, which is used to support remote clients.

- Administrators can deploy updates to clients in multiple languages.

- Administrators can configure client-side targeting to help client machines get updates. Client-side targeting allows your organization's computers to automatically add themselves to the computer groups that were created in the WSUS console.

- Administrators can configure a WSUS statistics server to log update access, which allows them to track which clients have installed updates. The WSUS server and the WSUS statistics server can coexist on the same computer.

- Administrators can manage WSUS servers remotely using HTTP or HTTPS if their web browser is Internet Explorer 6.0 or newer.

WSUS Server Requirements

To act as a WSUS server, the server must meet the following requirements:

- It must be running Windows 2000 Server with Service Pack 4 or newer, Windows Server 2003 SP1 or greater, Windows Vista, Windows 7, Windows 8, Windows Server 2008, Windows Server 2008 R2, Windows Server 2012, or Windows Server 2012 R2.

- It must have all of the most current security patches applied.

- It must be running Internet Information Services (IIS) 6.0 or newer.

- It must be connected to the network.

- It must have an NTFS partition with 100MB free disk space to install the WSUS server software, and it must have 6GB of free space to store all of the update files.

- It must use BITS version 2.0.

- It must use Microsoft Management Console 3.0.

- It must use Microsoft Report Viewer Redistributable 2008.

If your WSUS server meets the following system requirements, it can support up to 15,000 WSUS clients:

- Pentium III 700MHz processor

- 512MB of RAM

Installing the WSUS Server

WSUS should run on a dedicated server, meaning that the server will not run any other applications except IIS, which is required. Microsoft recommends that you install a clean or new version of Windows Server 2003 SP1 or newer, Windows Server 2008, Windows Server 2008 R2, Windows Server 2012, or Windows Server 2012 R2 and apply any service packs or security-related patches.

Exercise 1.1 walks you through the installation process for WSUS.

EXERCISE 1.1

Installing a WSUS Server

1. Choose Server Manager by clicking the Server Manager icon on the taskbar.

2. Click option number 2, Add Roles And Features.

3. Choose role-based or featured-based installation and click Next.

4. Choose your server and click Next.

5. Choose Windows Server Update Service. Click the Add Features button when the dialog box appears. Then click Next.

6. At the Select features screen, just click Next.

7. At the Windows Server Update Services screen, click Next.

8. At the Select Role Services screen, make sure that WID Database and WSUS Services are both checked. Click Next.

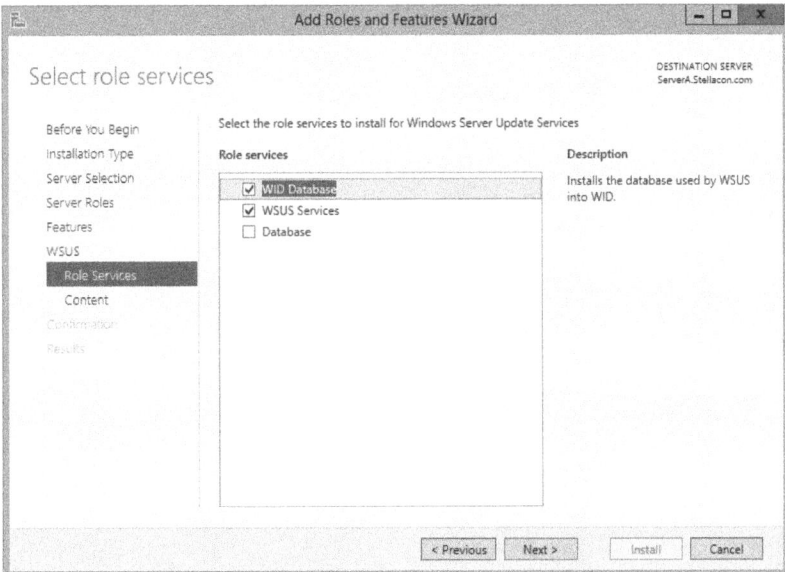

9. At the Content Location Selection screen, uncheck the box Store Updates In The Following Location and click Next. When you uncheck this box, updates are not stored locally. They are downloaded from Microsoft only once they are approved. This will help save hard drive space.

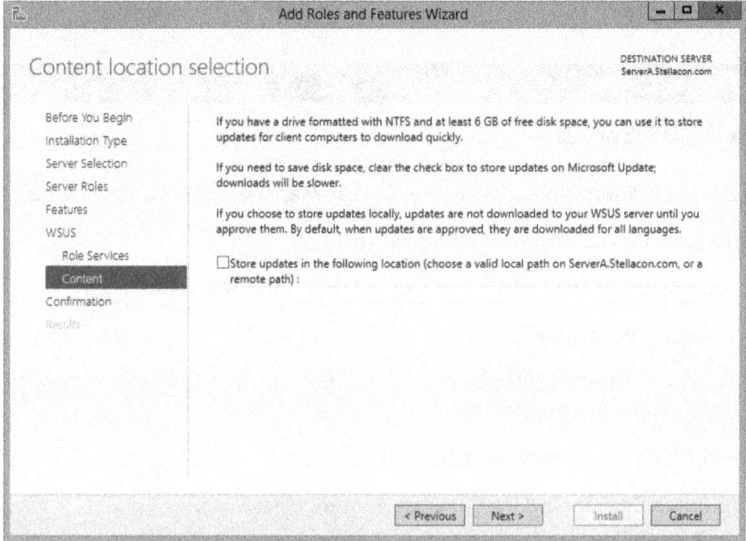

10. At the Confirmation screen, click the Install button.

11. The installation will begin, and you will see the progress. Once the installation is complete, click Close.

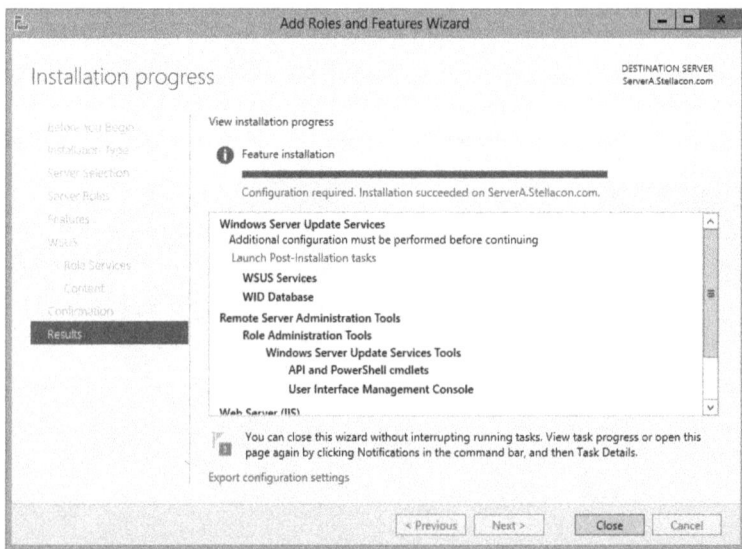

12. In Server Manager, click the WSUS link on the left side. Then click the More link next to Configuration Required For Windows Server Update Services.

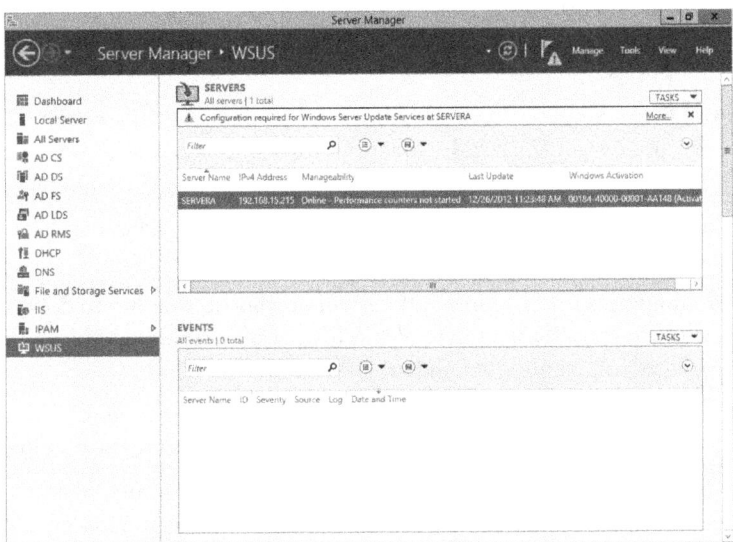

13. At the All Servers Task Details And Notifications screen, click the Launch Post-Installation Tasks link.

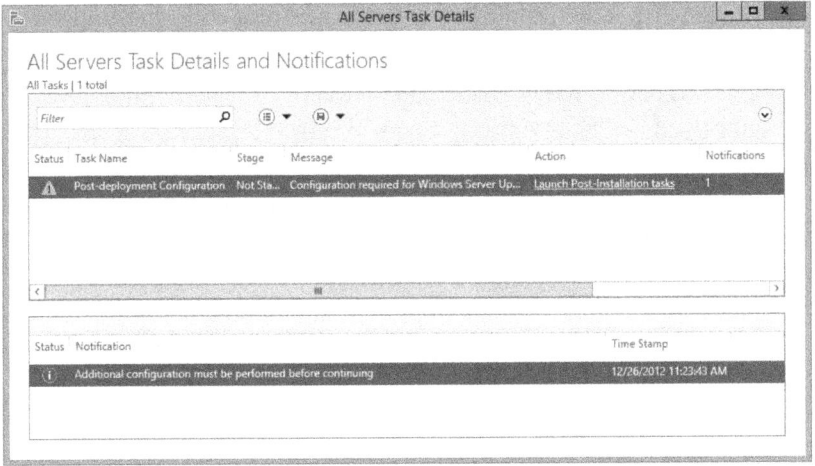

14. The installation process will automatically continue. Once it is finished, you will see Complete under Stage. Close the All Servers Task Details And Notifications screen.

15. Close Server Manager.

16. If a WSUS Configure Options box appears, just close it. You will set options in the next exercise.

Configuring a WSUS Server

Configuring a WSUS machine is a straightforward process. The easiest way to do it is to use the WSUS Server Configuration Wizard. This wizard walks you through the WSUS setup process, and it makes it easy to configure WSUS. When in the WSUS snap-in, you can configure different options.

Update Source And Proxy Server   This option allows you to configure whether this WSUS server synchronizes either from Microsoft Update or from another WSUS server on your network.

Products And Classifications   This option allows you to select the products for which you want to get updates and the type of updates that you want to receive.

Update Files And Languages   This option allows you to choose whether to download update files and where to store these update files. This option also allows you to choose which update languages you want downloaded.

Automatic Approvals   This option allows you to specify how to approve installation of updates automatically for selected groups and how to approve revisions to existing updates.

Synchronization Schedule   This option allows you to configure how and when you synchronize your updates. Administrators can choose to synchronize manually or to set up a schedule for daily automatic synchronization.

Computers   This option allows you to set computers to groups or use Group Policy or registry settings on the computer to receive updates.

Server Cleanup Wizard   This option allows you to clean out old computers, updates, and update files from your server.

Reporting Rollup   This option allows you to choose whether to have replica downstream servers roll up computer and update status to this WSUS server.

Email Notifications   This option allows you to set up email notifications for WSUS. You can be notified when new updates are synchronized, or you can get email status reports. This option also allows you to set up the email server's information on your WSUS server.

Microsoft Update Improvement Program   This option allows you to choose whether you want to participate in the Microsoft Update Improvement program. When you choose to participate in this program, your WSUS server will automatically send information to Microsoft about the quality of your updates. This following information is included:

- How many computers are in the organization
- How many computers successfully installed each update
- How many computers failed to install each update

Personalization   This option allows you to personalize the way that information is displayed for this server. This option also allows you to set up a to-do list for WSUS.

WSUS Server Configuration Wizard   This option allows you to set up many of the preceding options by just using this one setup wizard.

In Exercise 1.2, you will learn how to set up some of the WSUS server options. To complete this exercise, you need to have an Internet connection that can communicate with Microsoft.

EXERCISE 1.2

Setting WSUS Server Options

1. Open the Windows Server Update Services snap-in from Administrative Tools by pressing the Windows key on the keyboard and then choosing Administrative Tools. The Windows Server Update Services snap-in will be at the bottom of the list alphabetically.

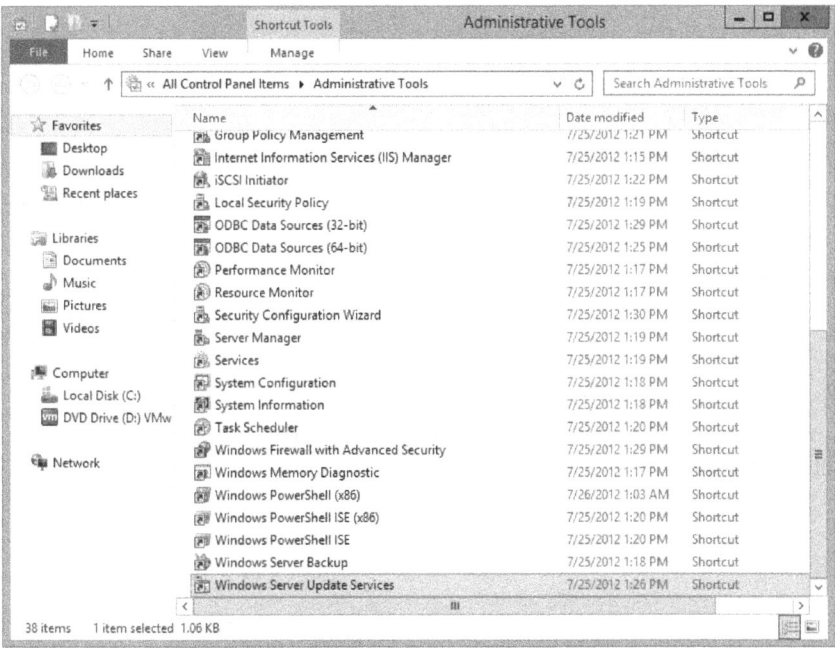

2. On the left side, click the name of your server. Then, in the middle section under To Do, click the Options link.

EXERCISE 1.2 *(continued)*

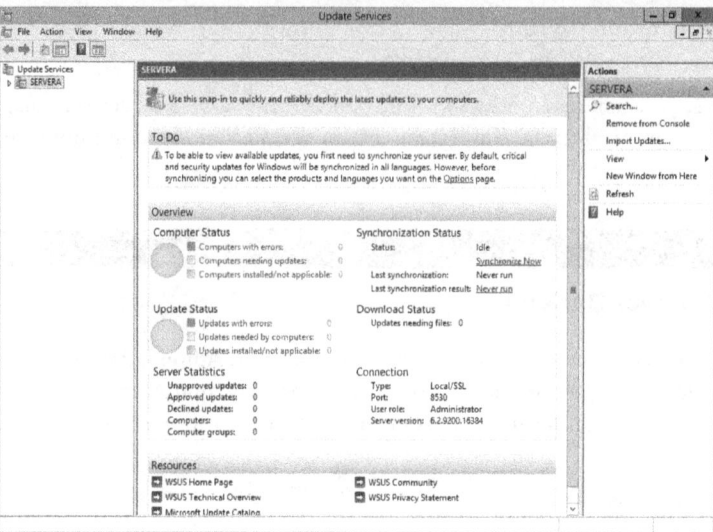

3. A WSUS Server Configuration Wizard appears at the bottom of the options list. Click this link.

4. Click Next at the Before You Begin screen.

5. At the Join Microsoft Update Improvement Program screen, uncheck the Yes box and click Next.

6. At the Choose Upstream Server screen, choose Synchronize From Microsoft Update and click Next.

7. Fill in the information at the Specify Proxy Server screen if you need to use a proxy server. If you do not need a proxy server, just click Next.

8. At the Connect To Upstream Server screen, click the Start Connecting button. This step can take a few minutes depending on your connection speed. Once it's finished connecting, click Next.

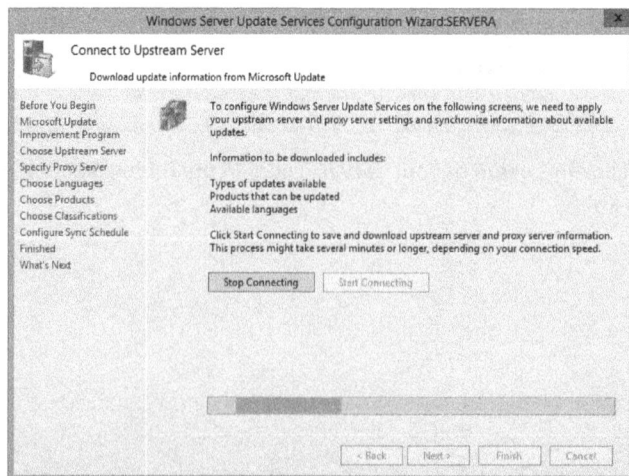

9. At the Choose Products screen, scroll down and choose the products for which you want to receive updates. Then click Next.

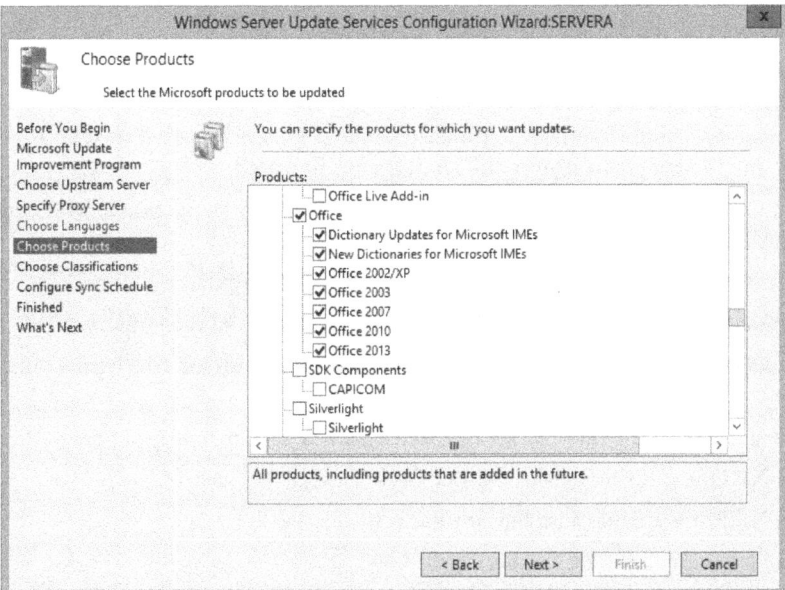

10. At the Choose Classifications screen, choose the classifications of updates you would like and click Next.

11. The Set Sync Schedule screen will appear next. At this screen, you can choose whether you want manual or automatic synchronizations. For this exercise, choose Synchronize Manually and click Next.

12. At the Finish screen, you can click Begin Initial Synchronization and click Finish. Be advised, this initial sync can take some time to finish. So if you don't have time to complete it now, you can always synchronize later.

13. Close WSUS.

Testing and Approving Updates

The administrator should test and approve updates before they are deployed to WSUS clients. The testing should be done on a test machine that is not used for daily tasks.

To approve updates, from the welcome screen, click Updates on the site's toolbar. Make your settings on the Updates page that appears.

Viewing the Synchronization Log

To view the synchronization log, click the Reports button on the site's toolbar from the welcome screen. The Reports page will appear. Click Synchronization Results to view the results.

Configuring a Disconnected Network

You have the ability to use WSUS on a disconnected network. To do so, you download the updates to the Internet-connected WSUS server. After the download is complete, you can export the updates and then import the updates to the disconnected network.

WSUS Client Requirements

WSUS clients run a special version of Automatic Updates that is designed to support WSUS. The following enhancements to Automatic Updates are included:

- Clients can receive updates from a WSUS server as opposed to the public Microsoft Windows Update site.

- The administrator can schedule when the downloading of updated files will occur.

- Clients can be configured via Group Policy or through editing the registry.

- Updates can occur when an administrative account or nonadministrative account is logged on.

   The following client platforms are the only ones that WSUS currently supports:

- Windows XP Home Edition (with Service Pack 3)

- Windows XP Professional (with Service Pack 3)

- Windows Server 2003 (SP1 or newer)

- Windows Vista (all platforms)

- Windows 7 (all platforms)

- Windows 8 (all platforms)

- Windows Server 2008 and 2008 R2 (all platforms)

- Windows Server 2012 R2 (all platforms)

Configuring the WSUS Clients

You can configure WSUS clients in two ways. The method you use depends on whether you use Active Directory in your network.

   In a nonenterprise network (not running Active Directory), you would configure Automatic Updates through the Control Panel using the same process that was defined in the section "Windows Automatic Updates" earlier in this chapter. Each client's registry would then be edited to reflect the location of the server providing the automatic updates.

   Within an enterprise network, using Active Directory, you would typically see Automatic Updates configured through Group Policy. Group Policy is used to manage configuration and security settings via Active Directory. Group Policy is also used to specify what server a client will use for Automatic Updates. If Automatic Updates is configured through Group Policy, the user will not be able to change Automatic Updates settings by choosing Control Panel ➢ System (for XP) or Windows Update (for Windows 8, Windows 7, Windows Vista, Windows Server 2008, Windows Server 2008 R2, Windows Server 2012, and Windows Server 2012 R2).

Configuring a Client in a Non–Active Directory Network

The easiest way to configure the client to use Automatic Updates is through the control panel. However, you can also configure Automatic Updates through the registry. The registry is a database of all your server settings. You can access it by choosing Start ➢ Run and typing **regedit** in the Run dialog box. Automatic Updates settings are defined through HKEY_LOCAL_MACHINE\Software\Policies\Microsoft\Windows\WindowsUpdate\AU.

Table 1.4 lists some of the registry options that you can configure for Automatic Updates.

TABLE 1.4 Selected registry keys and values for Automatic Updates

Registry key	Options for values
NoAutoUpdate	0: Automatic Updates are enabled (default).
	1: Automatic Updates are disabled.
	2: Notify of download and installation.
	3: Autodownload and notify of installation.
	4: Autodownload and schedule installation.
	5: Automatic Updates is required, but end users can configure.
ScheduledInstallDay	1: Sunday.
	2: Monday.
	3: Tuesday.
	4: Wednesday.
	5: Thursday.
	6: Friday.
	7: Saturday.
UseWUServer	0: Use public Microsoft Windows Update site.
	1: Use server specified in WUServer entry.

To specify what server will be used as the Windows Update server, you edit two registry keys, which are found here:

`HKEY_LOCAL_MACHINE\Software\Policies\Microsoft\Windows\WindowsUpdate`

- The WUServer key sets the Windows Update server using the server's HTTP name—for example, `http://intranetSUS`.
- The WUStatusServer key sets the Windows Update intranet WSUS statistics server by using the server's HTTP name—for example, `http://intranetSUS`.

Configuring a Client in an Active Directory Network

If the WSUS client is part of an enterprise network using Active Directory, you would configure the client via Group Policy. In Exercise 1.3, we will walk you through the steps needed to configure the Group Policy object (GPO) for WSUS clients. The *Group Policy Management Console (GPMC)* needs to be installed to complete this exercise. If you don't have the GPMC installed, you can install it using the Server Manager utility.

EXERCISE 1.3

Configuring a GPO for WSUS

1. Open the GPMC by pressing the Windows key and selecting Administrative Tools ➢ Group Policy Management.

2. Expand the forest, domains, and your domain name. Under your domain name, click Default Domain Policy. Right-click and choose Edit.

3. Under the Computer Configuration section, expand Policies ➢ Administrative Templates ➢ Windows Components ➢ Windows Update.

4. In the right pane, double-click the Configure Automatic Updates option. The Configure Automatic Updates Properties dialog box appears. Click the Enabled button. Then, in the drop-down list, choose Auto Download And Notify For Install. Click OK.

5. Double-click Specify Intranet Microsoft Update Service Location Properties. This setting allows you to specify the server from which the clients will get the updates. Click Enabled. In the two server name boxes, enter **//servername** (the name of the server on which you installed WSUS in Exercise 1.1). Click OK.

6. To configure the rescheduling of automatic updates, double-click Reschedule Automatic Updates Scheduled Installations. You can enable and schedule the amount of time that Automatic Updates waits after system startup before it attempts to proceed with a scheduled installation that was previously missed. Click Enabled. Enter **10** in the Startup (Minutes) box. Click OK.

7. To configure auto-restart for scheduled Automatic Updates installations, double-click No Auto-Restart For Scheduled Automatic Updates Installations. When you enable this option, the computer is not required to restart after an update. Enable this option and click OK.

8. Close the GPMC.

Configuring Client-Side Targeting

Administrators can use a GPO to enable client-side targeting. Client machines can be automatically added into the proper computer group once the client computer connects to the WSUS server. Client-side targeting can be a very useful tool when an administrator has multiple client computers and the administrator needs to automate the process of assigning those computers to computer groups.

Administrators can enable client-side targeting on the WSUS server by clicking the Use Group Policy or registry settings on client computers option on the Computers Options page.

1. On the WSUS console toolbar, click Options and then click Computer Options.
2. In Computer Options, choose one of the following options:
   - If an administrator wants to create groups and assign computers through the WSUS console (server-side targeting), click Use The Move Computers Task In Windows Server Update Services.
   - If an administrator wants to create groups and assign computers by using Group Policy settings on the client computer (client-side targeting), click Use Group Policy Or Registry Settings On Computers.
3. Under Tasks, click the Save Settings button and then click OK.

Overview of Windows Server 2012 R2 Performance Monitoring

The first step in any performance optimization strategy is to measure performance accurately and consistently. The insight that you'll gain from monitoring factors such as network and system utilization will be extremely useful when you measure the effects of any changes.

The overall performance monitoring process usually involves the following steps:

1. Establish a baseline of current performance.
2. Identify the bottlenecks.
3. Plan for and implement changes.
4. Measure the effects of the changes.
5. Repeat the process based on business needs.

Note that the performance optimization process is never really finished because you can always try to gain more performance from your system by modifying settings and applying other well-known tweaks. Before you get discouraged, realize that you'll reach some level of performance that you and your network and system users consider acceptable and that it's not worth the additional effort it will take to optimize performance any further. Also note that as your network and system load increases (more users or users doing more), so too will the need to reiterate this process. By continuing to monitor, measure, and optimize, you will keep ahead of the pack and keep your end users happy.

Now that you have an idea of the overall process, let's focus on how changes should be made. It's important to keep in mind the following ideas when monitoring performance:

Plan Changes Carefully   Here's a rule of thumb that you should always try to follow: An hour of planning can save a week of work. When you are working in an easy-to-use GUI-based operating system like Windows Server 2012 R2, it's tempting to remove a check mark here or there and then retest the performance. You should resist the urge to do this because some changes can cause large decreases in performance or can impact functionality. Before you make haphazard changes (especially on production servers), take the time to learn about, plan for, and test your changes. Plan for outages and testing accordingly.

Utilize a Test Environment   Test in a test lab that simulates a production environment. Do not make changes on production environments without first giving warning. Ideally, change production environments in off-hours when fewer network and system users will be affected. Making haphazard changes in a production environment can cause serious problems. These problems will likely outweigh any benefits that you may receive from making performance tweaks.

Make Only One Change at a Time   The golden rule of scientific experiments is that you should always keep track of as many variables as possible. When the topic is server optimization, this roughly translates into making only one change at a time.

One of the problems with making multiple system changes is that although you may have improved overall performance, it's hard to determine exactly *which* change created the positive effects. It's also possible, for example, that changing one parameter increased performance greatly while changing another decreased it only slightly. Although the overall result was an increase in performance, you should identify the second, performance-reducing option so that the same mistake is not made again. To reduce the chance of obtaining misleading results, always try to make only one change at a time.

The main reason to make one change at a time, however, is that if you do make a mistake or create an unexpected issue, you can easily "back out" of the change. If you make two or three changes at the same time and are not sure which one created the problem, you will have to undo all of the changes and then make one alteration at a time to find the problem. If you make only one change at a time and follow that methodology every time, you won't find yourself in this situation.

It's important to remember that many changes (such as registry changes) take place immediately; they do not need to be applied explicitly. Once the change is made, it's live. Be careful to plan your changes wisely.

Ensure Consistency in Measurements   When you are monitoring performance, consistency is extremely important. You should strive to have repeatable and accurate measurements. Controlling variables, such as system load at various times during the day, can help.

Assume, for instance, that you want to measure the number of transactions that you can simulate on the accounting database server within an hour. The results would be widely different if you ran the test during the month-end accounting close than if you ran the test on a Sunday morning. By running the same tests when the server is under a relatively static load, you will be able to get more accurate measurements.

Maintain a Performance History   In the introduction to this chapter, I mentioned that the performance optimization cycle is a continuous improvement process. Because many changes may be made over time, it is important to keep track of the changes that have been made and the results you have experienced. Documenting this knowledge will help solve similar problems if they arise. I understand that many IT professionals do not like to document, but documentation can make life much easier in the long run.

As you can see, you need to keep a lot of factors in mind when optimizing performance. Although this might seem like a lot to digest and remember, do not fear. As a system administrator, you will learn some of the rules you need to know to keep your system running optimally. Fortunately, the tools included with Windows Server 2012 R2 can help you organize the process and take measurements. Now that you have a good overview of the process, let's move on to look at the tools that can be used to set it in motion.

Using Windows Server 2012 R2 Performance Tools

Because performance monitoring and optimization are vital functions in network environments of any size, Windows Server 2012 R2 includes several performance-related tools.

Introducing Performance Monitor

The first and most useful tool is the Windows Server 2012 R2 *Performance Monitor*, which was designed to allow users and system administrators to monitor performance statistics for various operating system parameters. Specifically, you can collect, store, and analyze information about CPU, memory, disk, and network resources using this tool, and these are only a handful of the things that you can monitor. By collecting and analyzing performance values, system administrators can identify many potential problems.

You can use the Performance Monitor in the following ways:

Performance Monitor ActiveX Control   The Windows Server 2012 R2 Performance Monitor is an ActiveX control that you can place within other applications. Examples of applications that can host the Performance Monitor control include web browsers and client programs such as Microsoft Word or Microsoft Excel. This functionality can make it easy for applications developers and system administrators to incorporate the Performance Monitor into their own tools and applications.

Performance Monitor MMC   For more common performance monitoring functions, you'll want to use the built-in Microsoft Management Console (MMC) version of the Performance Monitor.

System Stability Index   The *System Stability Index* is a numerical value from 1 (least stable) to 10 (most stable) that represents the stability of your network. Performance Monitor calculates and creates the System Stability Index. You can view a graph of this index value. The graph can help a network administrator identify when the network started encountering problems. The System Stability Index also offers side-by-side comparisons. An administrator can view when system changes occurred (installing applications, devices, or drivers) and when system problems started to occur. This way, you can determine whether any system changes caused the problems that you are encountering.

Data Collector Sets   Windows Server 2012 R2 Performance Monitor includes the Data Collector Set. This tool works with performance logs, telling Performance Monitor where the logs are stored and when the log needs to run. The Data Collector Sets also define the credentials used to run the set.

To access the Performance Monitor MMC, you open Administrative Tools and then choose Performance Monitor. This launches the Performance MMC and loads and initializes Performance Monitor with a handful of default counters.

You can choose from many different methods of monitoring performance when you are using Performance Monitor. A couple of examples are listed here:

- You can look at a snapshot of current activity for a few of the most important counters. This allows you to find areas of potential bottlenecks and monitor the load on your servers at a certain point in time.

- You can save information to a log file for historical reporting and later analysis. This type of information is useful, for example, if you want to compare the load on your servers from three months ago to the current load.

You'll get to take a closer look at this method and many others as you examine Performance Monitor in more detail.

In the following sections, you'll learn about the basics of working with the Windows Server 2012 R2 Performance Monitor and other performance tools. Then you'll apply these tools and techniques when you monitor the performance of your network.

Your Performance Monitor grows as your system grows, and whenever you add services to Windows Server 2012 R2 (such as installing Exchange Server 2010), you also add to what you can monitor. You should make sure that, as you install services, you take a look at what it is you can monitor.

Deciding What to Monitor

The first step in monitoring performance is to decide *what* you want to monitor. In Windows Server 2012 R2, the operating system and related services include hundreds of performance statistics that you can track easily. For example, you may want to monitor IPsec by monitoring connection security rules. This is just one of many items that can be monitored. All performance statistics fall into three main categories that you can choose to measure:

Performance Objects   A *performance object* within Performance Monitor is a collection of various performance statistics that you can monitor. Performance objects are based on various areas of system resources. For example, there are performance objects for the processor and memory as well as for specific services such as web services.

Counters   *Counters* are the actual parameters measured by Performance Monitor. They are specific items that are grouped within performance objects. For example, within the Processor performance object, there is a counter for % Processor Time. This counter displays one type of detailed information about the Processor performance object (specifically, the amount of total CPU time all of the processes on the system are using). Another set of counters you can use will allow you to monitor print servers.

Instances   Some counters will have instances. An *instance* further identifies which performance parameter the counter is measuring. A simple example is a server with two CPUs. If you decide you want to monitor processor usage (using the Processor performance object)—specifically, utilization (the % Total Utilization counter)—you must still specify *which* CPU(s) you want to measure. In this example, you would have the choice of monitoring either of the two CPUs or a total value for both (using the Total instance).

To specify which performance objects, counters, and instances you want to monitor, you add them to Performance Monitor using the Add Counters dialog box. Figure 1.3 shows the various options that are available when you add new counters to monitor using Performance Monitor.

FIGURE 1.3   Adding a new Performance Monitor counter

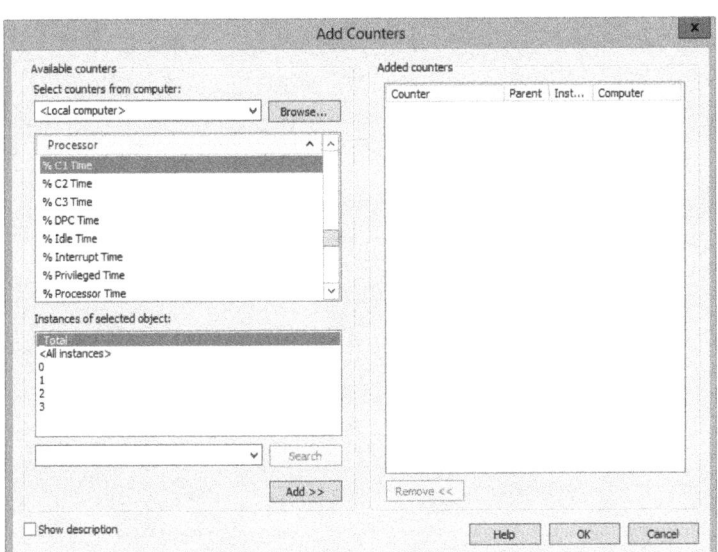

The items that you will be able to monitor will be based on your hardware and software configuration. For example, if you have not installed and configured the IIS, the options available within the Web Server performance object will not be available. Or, if you have multiple network adapters or CPUs in the server, you will have the option of viewing each instance separately or as part of the total value.

Viewing Performance Information   The Windows Server 2012 R2 Performance Monitor was designed to show information in a clear and easy-to-understand format. Performance objects, counters, and instances may be displayed in each of three views. This flexibility allows system administrators to define quickly and easily the information they want to see once and then choose how it will be displayed based on specific needs. Most likely, you will use only one view, but it's helpful to know what other views are available depending on what it is you are trying to assess.

You can use the following main views to review statistics and information on performance:

Graph View   The *Graph view* is the default display that is presented when you first access the Windows Server 2012 R2 Performance Monitor. The chart displays values using the vertical axis and displays time using the horizontal axis. This view is useful if you want to display values over a period of time or see the changes in these values over that time period. Each point that is plotted on the graph is based on an average value calculated during the sample interval for the measurement being made. For example, you may notice overall CPU utilization starting at a low value at the beginning of the chart and then becoming much higher during later measurements. This indicates that the server has become busier (specifically, with CPU-intensive processes). Figure 1.4 provides an example of the Graph view.

FIGURE 1.4   Viewing information in Performance Monitor Graph view

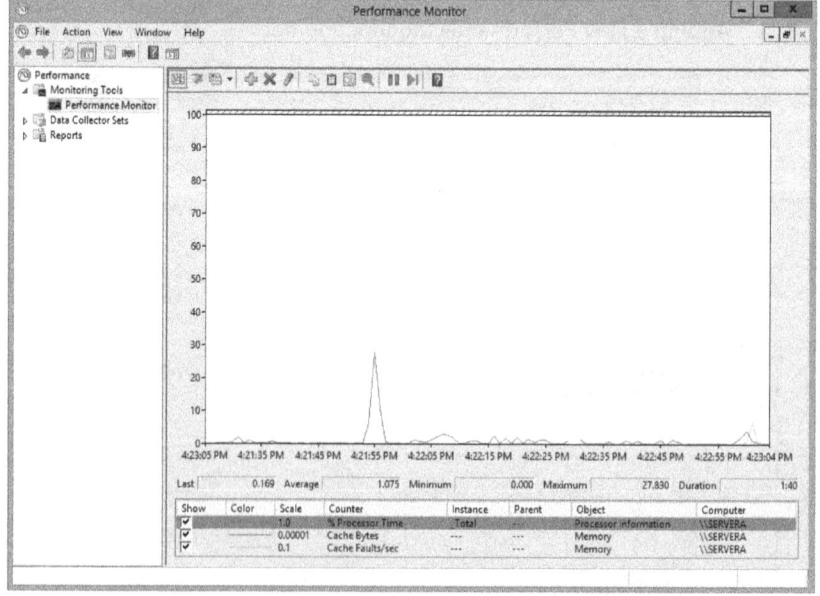

Histogram View   The *Histogram view* shows performance statistics and information using a set of relative bar charts. This view is useful if you want to see a snapshot of the latest value for a given counter. For example, if you were interested in viewing a snapshot of current system performance statistics during each refresh interval, the length of each of the bars in the display would give you a visual representation of each value. It would also allow you to compare measurements visually relative to each other. You can set the histogram to display an average measurement as well as minimum and maximum thresholds. Figure 1.5 shows a typical Histogram view.

FIGURE 1.5   Viewing information in Performance Monitor Histogram view

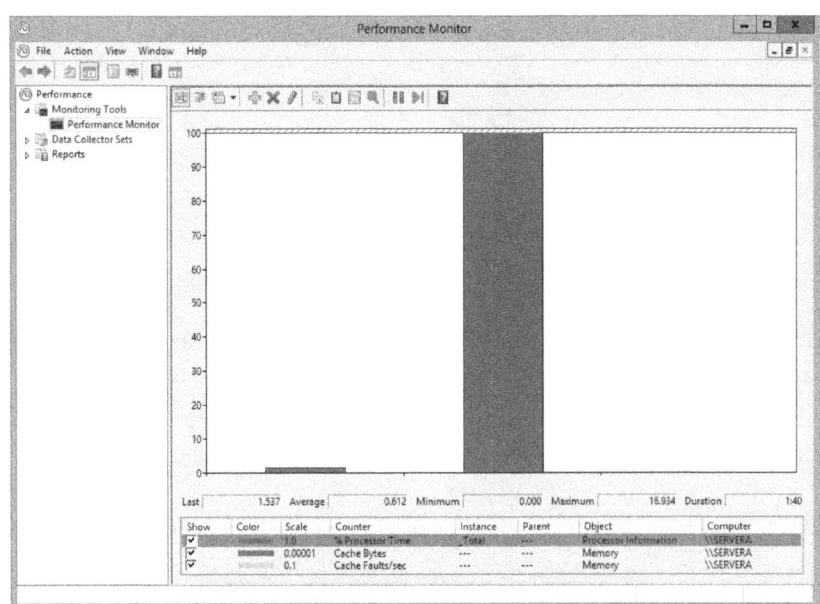

Report View   Like the Histogram view, the *Report view* shows performance statistics based on the latest measurement. You can see an average measurement as well as minimum and maximum thresholds. This view is most useful for determining exact values because it provides information in numeric terms, whereas the Chart and Histogram views provide information graphically. Figure 1.6 provides an example of the type of information you'll see in the Report view.

Managing Performance Monitor Properties

You can specify additional settings for viewing performance information within the properties of Performance Monitor. You can access these options by clicking the Properties button

FIGURE 1.6 Viewing information in Performance Monitor Report view

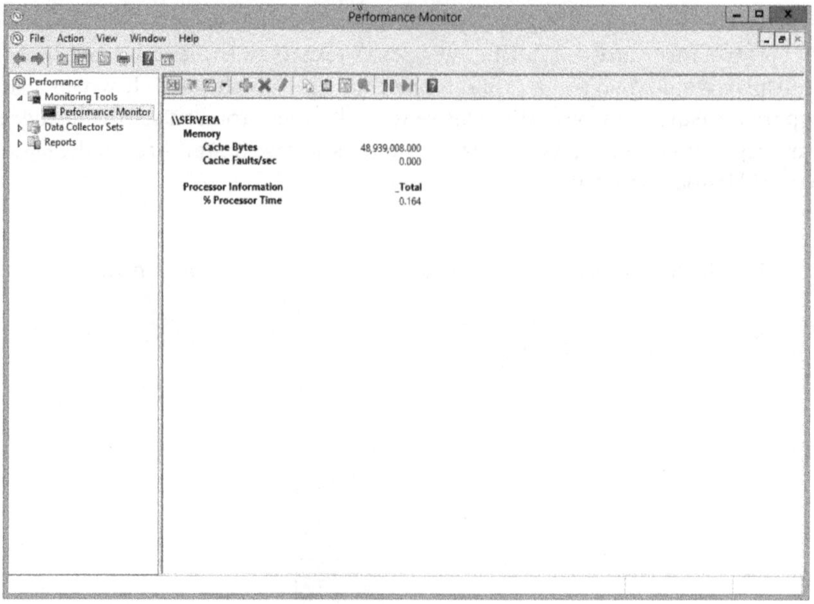

in the taskbar or by right-clicking the Performance Monitor display and selecting Properties. You can change these additional settings by using the following tabs:

General Tab On the General tab (shown in Figure 1.7), you can specify several options that relate to Performance Monitor views:

FIGURE 1.7 General tab of the Performance Monitor Properties dialog box

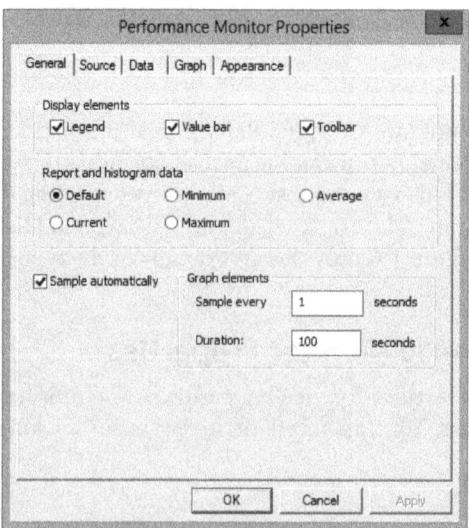

- You can enable or disable legends (which display information about the various counters), the value bar, and the toolbar.

- For the Report and Histogram views, you can choose which type of information is displayed. The options are Default, Current, Minimum, Maximum, and Average. What you see with each of these options depends on the type of data being collected. These options are not available for the Graph view because the Graph view displays an average value over a period of time (the sample interval).

- You can also choose the graph elements. By default, the display will be set to update every second. If you want to update less often, you should increase the number of seconds between updates.

Source Tab   On the Source tab (shown in Figure 1.8), you can specify the source for the performance information you want to view. Options include current activity (the default setting) or data from a log file. If you choose to analyze information from a log file, you can also specify the time range for which you want to view statistics. We'll cover these selections in the next section.

FIGURE 1.8   Source tab of the Performance Monitor Properties dialog box

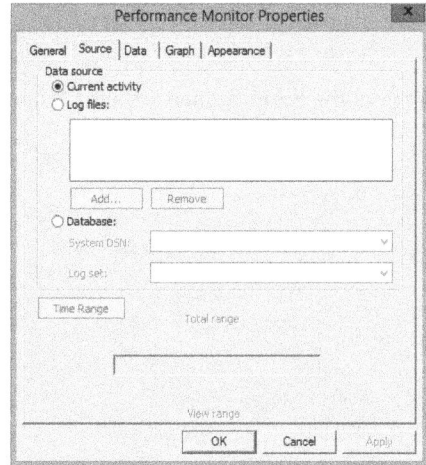

Data Tab   The Data tab (shown in Figure 1.9) lists the counters that have been added to the Performance Monitor display. These counters apply to the Chart, Histogram, and Report views. Using this interface, you can also add or remove any of the counters and change the properties, such as the width, style, and color of the line and the scale used for display.

Graph Tab   On the Graph tab (shown in Figure 1.10), you can specify certain options that will allow you to customize the display of Performance Monitor views. First you can

FIGURE 1.9 The Data tab of the Performance Monitor Properties dialog box

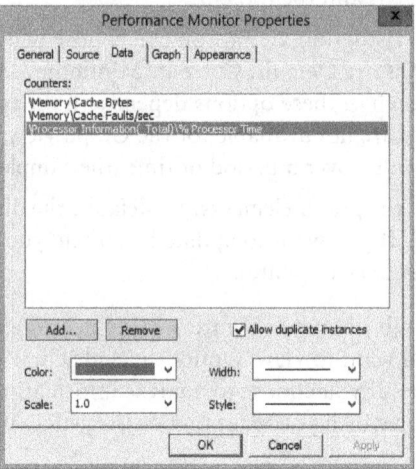

specify what type of view you want to see (Line, Histogram, or Report). Then you can add a title for the graph, specify a label for the vertical axis, choose to display grids, and specify the vertical scale range.

FIGURE 1.10 The Graph tab of the Performance Monitor Properties dialog box

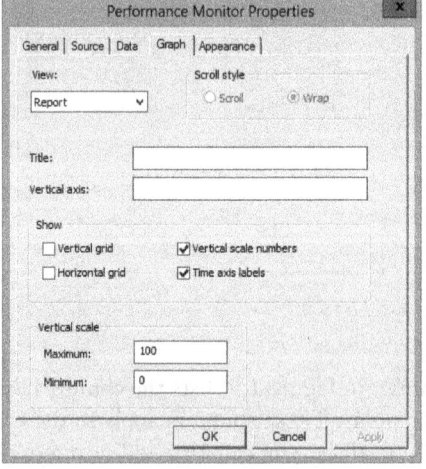

Appearance Tab Using the Appearance tab (see Figure 1.11), you can specify the colors for the areas of the display, such as the background and foreground. You can also specify the fonts that are used to display counter values in Performance Monitor views. You can

FIGURE 1.11   The Appearance tab of the Performance Monitor Properties dialog box

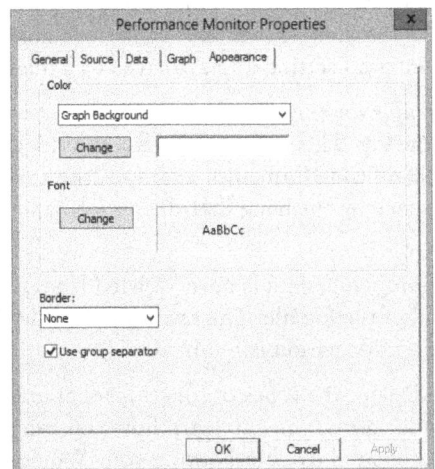

change settings to find a suitable balance between readability and the amount of information shown on one screen. Finally, you can set up the properties for a border.

Now that you have an idea of the types of information Performance Monitor tracks and how this data is displayed, you'll take a look at another feature—saving and analyzing performance data.

Saving and Analyzing Data with Performance Logs and Alerts

One of the most important aspects of monitoring performance is that it should be done over a given period of time (referred to as a *baseline*). So far, I have shown you how you can use Performance Monitor to view statistics in real time. I have, however, also alluded to using Performance Monitor to save data for later analysis. Now let's take a look at how you can do this.

When viewing information in Performance Monitor, you have two main options with respect to the data on display:

View Current Activity   When you first open the Performance icon from the Administrative Tools folder, the default option is to view data obtained from current system information. This method of viewing measures and displays various real-time statistics on the system's performance.

View Log File Data   This option allows you to view information that was previously saved to a log file. Although the performance objects, counters, and instances may appear to be the same as those viewed using the View Current Activity option, the information itself was actually captured at a previous point in time and stored into a log file.

Log files for the View Log File Data option are created in the Performance Logs And Alerts section of the Windows Server 2012 R2 Performance tool.

Three items allow you to customize how the data is collected in the log files:

Counter Logs   *Counter logs* record performance statistics based on the various performance objects, counters, and instances available in Performance Monitor. The values are updated based on a time interval setting and are saved to a file for later analysis.

Circular Logging   In *circular logging*, the data that is stored within a file is overwritten as new data is entered into the log. This is a useful method of logging if you want to record information only for a certain time frame (for example, the past four hours). Circular logging also conserves disk space by ensuring that the performance log file will not continue to grow over certain limits.

Linear Logging   In *linear logging*, data is never deleted from the log files, and new information is added to the end of the log file. The result is a log file that continually grows. The benefit is that all historical information is retained.

Now that you have an idea of the types of functions that are supported by the Windows Server 2012 R2 Performance tools, you can learn how you can apply this information to the task at hand—monitoring and troubleshooting your Windows network.

 Real World Scenario

Real-World Performance Monitoring

In our daily jobs as system engineers and administrators, we come across systems that are in need of our help...and may even ask for it. You, of course, check your Event Viewer and Performance Monitor and perform other tasks that help you troubleshoot. But what is really the most common problem that occurs? From my experience, I'd say that you suffer performance problems many times if your Windows Server 2012 R2 operating system is installed on a subpar system. Either the server hardware isn't enterprise class or the minimum hardware requirements weren't addressed. Most production servers suffer from slow response times, lagging, and so on, because money wasn't spent where it should have been in the first place—on the server's hardware requirements.

Using Other Performance-Monitoring Tools

Performance Monitor allows you to monitor different parameters of the Windows Server 2012 R2 operating system and associated services and applications. However, you can also use three other tools to monitor performance in Windows Server 2012 R2. They are Network Monitor, Task Manager, and Event Viewer. All three of these tools are useful for monitoring different areas of overall system performance and for examining details related to specific system events. In the following sections, you'll take a quick look at these tools and how you can best use them.

The Network Monitor

Although Performance Monitor is a great tool for viewing overall network performance statistics, it isn't equipped for packet-level analysis and doesn't give you much insight into what types of network traffic are traveling on the wire. That's where the Network Monitor tool comes in. *Network Monitor* has two main components: the Network Monitor Agent and the Network Monitor tool.

The Network Monitor Agent is available for use with Windows XP, Windows Server 2003, Windows Vista, Windows 7, Windows 8, Windows Server 2008, Windows Server 2008 R2, Windows Server 2012, and Windows Server 2012 R2. The agent allows you to track network packets. When you install the Network Monitor Agent, you will also be able to access the Network Segment System Monitor counter.

On Windows Server 2012 R2 computers, you'll see the Network Monitor icon appear in the Administrative Tools program group. You can use the Network Monitor tool to capture data as it travels on your network.

> A version of Network Monitor is available for free with Windows Server 2012 R2. The full version of Network Monitor is available at Microsoft's download server. For more information, see www.microsoft.com/ downloads/.

Once you have captured the data of interest, you can save it to a capture file or further analyze it using Microsoft Message Analyzer. Experienced network and system administrators can use this information to determine how applications are communicating and the types of data that are being passed via the network.

> For the exam, you don't need to understand the detailed information that Network Monitor displays, but you should be aware of the types of information that you can view and when you should use Network Monitor.

Task Manager

Performance Monitor is designed to allow you to keep track of specific aspects of system performance over time. But what do you do if you want to get a quick snapshot of what the local system is doing? Creating a System Monitor chart, adding counters, and choosing a view is overkill. Fortunately, the Windows Server 2012 R2 Task Manager has been designed to provide a quick overview of important system performance statistics without requiring any configuration. Better yet, it's always readily available.

You can easily access Task Manager in several ways:

- Right-click the Windows taskbar and then click Task Manager.
- Press Ctrl+Alt+Del and then select Task Manager.
- Press Ctrl+Shift+Esc.

Each of these methods allows you to access a snapshot of the current system performance quickly.

Once you access Task Manager, you will see the following five tabs:

Processes Tab The Processes tab shows you all of the processes that are currently running on the local computer. By default, you'll be able to view how much CPU time and memory a particular process is using. By clicking any of the columns, you can quickly sort by the data values in that particular column. This is useful, for example, if you want to find out which processes are using the most memory on your server.

By accessing the performance objects in the View menu, you can add columns to the Processes tab. Figure 1.12 shows a list of the current processes running on a Windows Server 2012 R2 computer.

FIGURE 1.12 Viewing process statistics and information using Task Manager

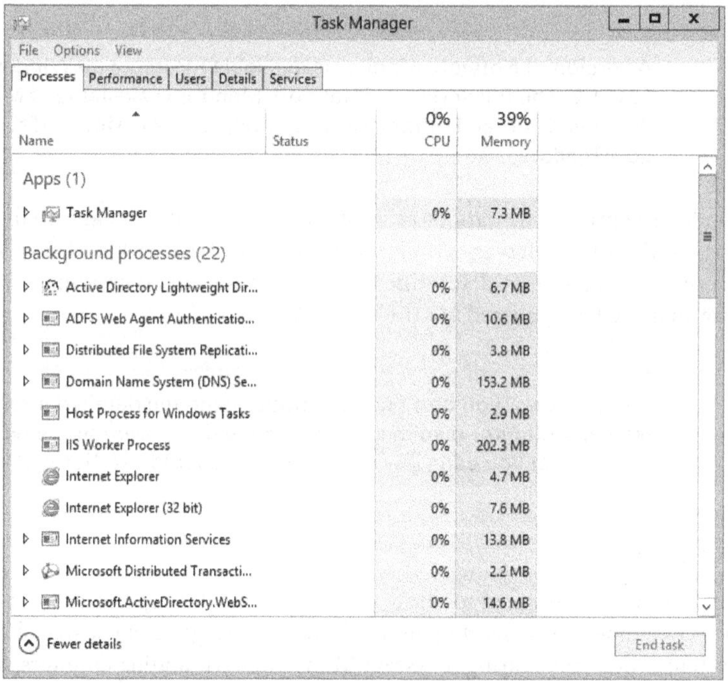

Performance Tab One of the problems with using Performance Monitor to get a quick snapshot of system performance is that you have to add counters to a chart. Most system administrators are too busy to take the time to do this when all they need is basic CPU and memory information. That's where the Performance tab of Task Manager comes in. Using the Performance tab, you can view details about how memory is allocated on the computer and how much of the CPU is utilized (see Figure 1.13).

FIGURE 1.13   Viewing CPU and memory performance information using Task Manager

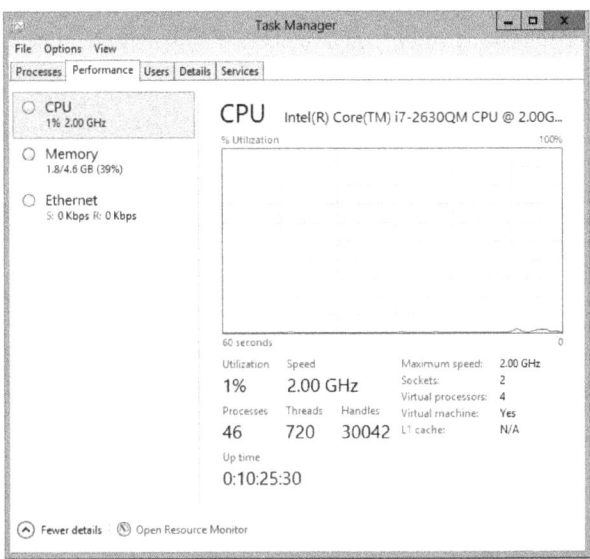

Users Tab   The Users tab (see Figure 1.14) lists the currently active user accounts. This is particularly helpful if you want to see who is online and quickly log off or disconnect users. You can also send a console message to any remote user in the list by clicking the Send Message button. (The button is grayed out in Figure 1.14 because you cannot send a message to yourself. If you select a different user, the button will be available.)

FIGURE 1.14   Viewing user information using Task Manager

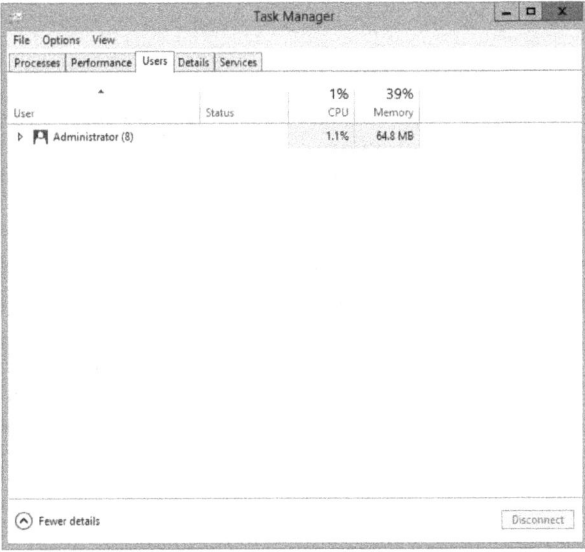

Details Tab   The Details tab (see Figure 1.15) shows you what applications are currently running on the system. From this location, you can stop an application from running by right-clicking the application and choosing Stop. You also have the ability to set your affinity level here. By setting the affinity, you can choose which applications will use which processors on your system.

FIGURE 1.15   Viewing applications that are currently running using Task Manager

Name ▲	PID	Status	User name	CPU	Memory (p...	Description
certsrv.exe	1600	Running	SYSTEM	00	4,940 K	Microsoft® Certifica...
csrss.exe	340	Running	SYSTEM	00	968 K	Client Server Runtim...
csrss.exe	396	Running	SYSTEM	00	1,172 K	Client Server Runtim...
dfsrs.exe	1668	Running	SYSTEM	00	3,924 K	Distributed File Syste...
dfssvc.exe	1176	Running	SYSTEM	00	1,264 K	Windows NT Distrib...
dns.exe	1704	Running	SYSTEM	00	156,836 K	Domain Name Syste...
dsamain.exe	1412	Running	NETWORK...	00	6,880 K	Active Directory Lig...
dwm.exe	852	Running	DWM-1	00	20,300 K	Desktop Window M...
explorer.exe	3188	Running	Administra...	00	21,032 K	Windows Explorer
iexplore.exe	1348	Running	Administra...	00	4,836 K	Internet Explorer
iexplore.exe	3564	Running	Administra...	00	7,744 K	Internet Explorer
ifssvc.exe	2460	Running	SYSTEM	00	10,828 K	ADFS Web Agent Au...
inetinfo.exe	2340	Running	SYSTEM	00	14,160 K	Internet Information...
ismserv.exe	1776	Running	SYSTEM	00	1,040 K	Windows NT Intersit...
lsass.exe	500	Running	SYSTEM	00	15,936 K	Local Security Autho...
Microsoft.ActiveDire...	1456	Running	SYSTEM	00	14,936 K	Microsoft.ActiveDire...
Microsoft.IdentitySer...	3636	Running	NETWORK...	00	251,332 K	Microsoft.IdentitySe...
msdtc.exe	3824	Running	NETWORK...	00	2,292 K	Microsoft Distribute...
services.exe	492	Running	SYSTEM	00	3,816 K	Services and Control...
smss.exe	228	Running	SYSTEM	00	288 K	Windows Session M...
SMSvcHost.exe	1820	Running	LOCAL SE...	00	5,980 K	SMSvcHost.exe
spoolsv.exe	1384	Running	SYSTEM	00	3,784 K	Spooler SubSystem ...
sqlservr.exe	2128	Running	MSSQLSMI...	00	256,052 K	SQL Server Windows...

Services Tab   The Services tab (see Figure 1.16) shows you what services are currently running on the system. From this location, you can stop a service from running by right-clicking the service and choosing Stop. The Open Services link launches the Services MMC.

These tabs can be different on Windows Client machines. For example, Windows 7 has six tabs, not five, and Windows 8 has seven tabs.

As you can see, Task Manager is useful for providing important information about the system quickly. Once you get used to using Task Manager, you won't be able to get by without it!

FIGURE 1.16   Viewing services information using Task Manager

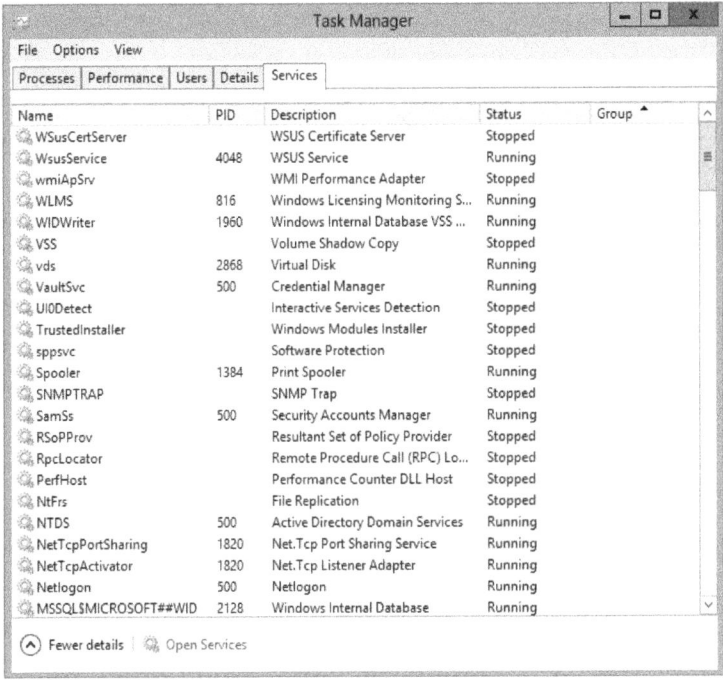

 Make sure that you use Task Manager and familiarize yourself with all that it can do; you can end processes that have become intermittent, kill applications that may hang the system, view NIC performance, and so on. In addition, you can access this tool quickly to get an idea of what could be causing you problems. Event Viewer, Network Monitor, and Performance Monitor are all great tools for getting granular information on potential problems.

Event Viewer

Event Viewer is also useful for monitoring network information. Specifically, you can use the logs to view any information, warnings, or alerts related to the proper functioning of the network. You can access Event Viewer by selecting Administrative Tools ➢ Event Viewer. Clicking any of the items in the left pane displays the various events that have been logged for each item. Figure 1.17 shows the contents of the Directory Service log.

Each event is preceded by a blue *i* icon. That icon designates that these events are informational and do not indicate problems with the network. Rather, they record benign events such as Active Directory startup or a domain controller finding a global catalog server.

FIGURE 1.17 Event Viewer

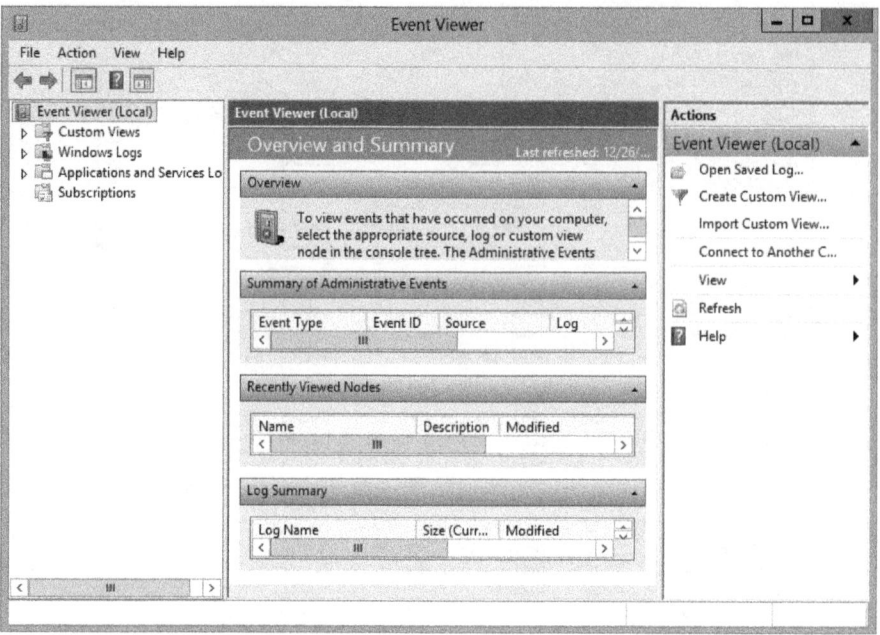

A yellow warning icon or a red error icon, both of which are shown in Figure 1.18, indicate problematic or potentially problematic events. Warnings usually indicate a problem that wouldn't prevent a service from running but might cause undesired effects with the service in question. For example, I was configuring a site with some fictional domain controllers and IP addresses. My local domain controller's IP address wasn't associated with any of the sites, and Event Viewer generated a warning. In this case, the local domain controller could still function as a domain controller, but the site configuration could produce undesirable results.

Error events almost always indicate a failed service, application, or function. For instance, if the dynamic registration of a DNS client fails, Event Viewer will generate an error. As you can see, errors are more severe than warnings because, in this case, the DNS client cannot participate in DNS at all.

Double-clicking any event opens the Event Properties dialog box, as shown in Figure 1.19, which displays a detailed description of the event.

Event Viewer can display thousands of different events, so it would be impossible to list them all here. The important points of which you should be aware are the following:

- Information events are always benign.

- Warnings indicate noncritical problems.

- Errors indicate show-stopping events.

FIGURE 1.18   Information, errors, and warnings in Event Viewer

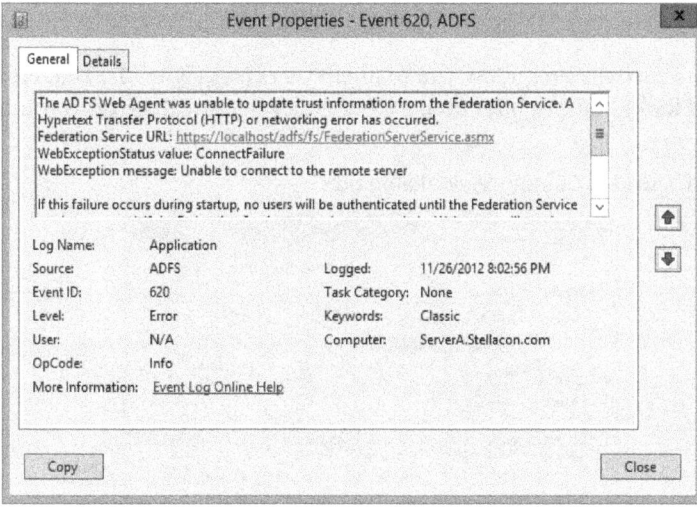

FIGURE 1.19   An Event Properties dialog box

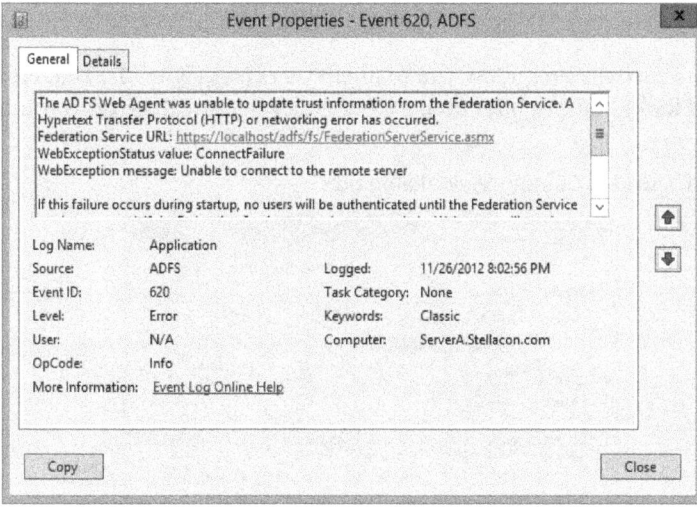

Let's discuss some of the logs and the ways you can view data:

Applications and Services The *applications and services logs* are part of Event Viewer where applications (for example, Exchange) and services (DNS) log their events. DFS events would be logged in this part of Event Viewer. An important log in this section is the DNS Server log (see Figure 1.20). This is where all of your DNS events get stored.

FIGURE 1.20 The applications and services DNS Server log

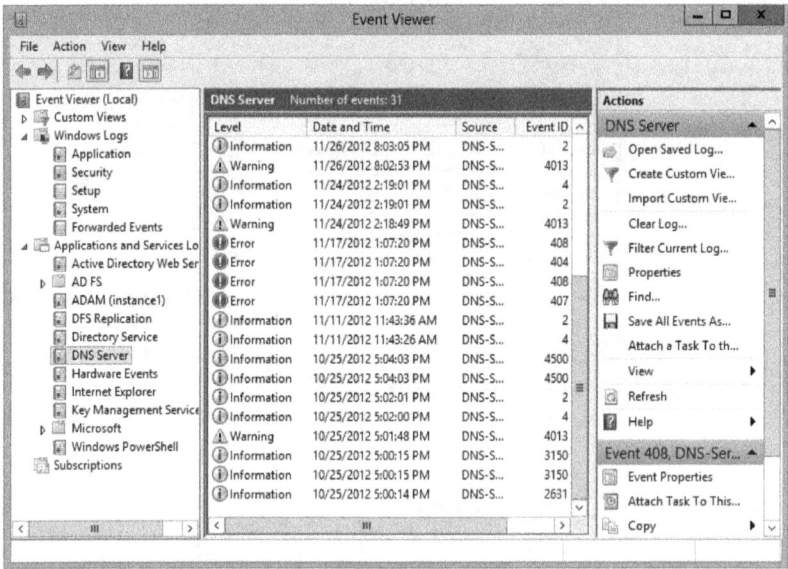

Custom Views *Custom views* allow you to filter events (see Figure 1.21) to create your own customized look. You can filter events by event level (critical, error, warning, and so

FIGURE 1.21 Create Custom View dialog box

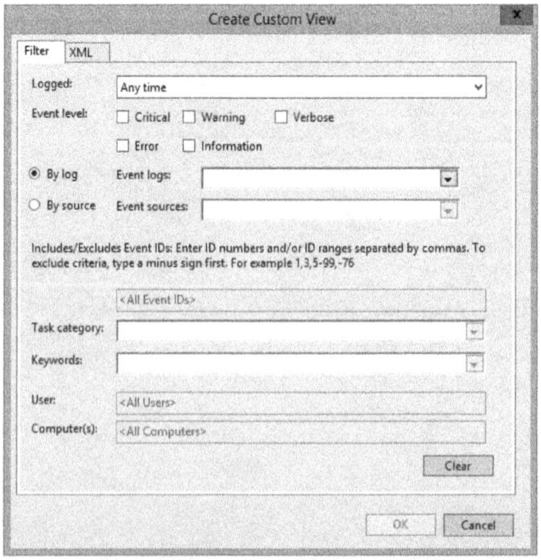

on), by logs, and by source. You also have the ability to view events occurring within a specific timeframe. This allows you to look only at the events that are important to you.

Subscriptions *Subscriptions* allow a user to receive alerts about events that you predefine. In the Subscription Properties dialog box (see Figure 1.22), you can define what type of events you want notifications about and the notification method. The Subscriptions section is an advanced alerting service to help you watch for events.

FIGURE 1.22 Subscription Properties dialog box

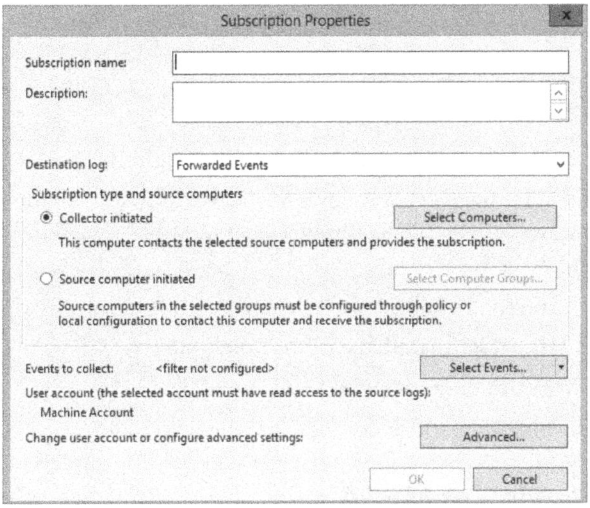

Microsoft Baseline Security Analyzer

The *Microsoft Baseline Security Analyzer (MBSA)* is a security assessment utility that you can download from the Microsoft website at the following location:

www.microsoft.com/en-us/download/details.aspx?id=19892

The filename of the download is mbsasetup.msi. It verifies whether your computer has the latest security updates and whether any common security violation configurations have been applied to your computer. MBSA can scan the following programs and operating systems:

- Windows 2000
- Windows XP
- Windows Vista
- Windows 7

- Windows 8
- Windows Server 2003
- Windows Server 2008
- Windows Server 2008 R2
- Windows Server 2012
- Windows Server 2012 R2
- IIS 5 or newer
- Internet Explorer, versions 6.0 and newer
- SQL Server 7 or newer
- Microsoft Office 2000 or newer
- Windows Media Player, versions 6.4 and newer

To use MBSA, the computer must meet the following requirements:

- It must be running Windows XP, Windows Vista, Windows 7, Windows 8, Windows Server 2003, Windows Server 2008, Windows Server 2008 R2, Windows Server 2012, or Windows Server 2012 R2.
- It must be running Internet Explorer 5.01 or newer.
- It must have an XML parser installed for full functionality.
- It must have the Workstation and Server services enabled.
- It must have Client for Microsoft Networks installed.

Using the GUI Version of MBSA

Once you have installed MBSA, you can access it by using the Windows key and choosing Microsoft Baseline Security Analyzer or by opening the command prompt and executing mbsa.exe. This opens the Baseline Security Analyzer utility. You can select from Scan A Computer, Scan More Than One Computer, and View Existing Security Reports.

When you click Scan A Computer, the Pick A Computer To Scan dialog box appears. You can specify that you want to scan a computer based on a computer name or IP address. You can also specify the name of the security report that will be generated.

The following are options for the security scan:

- Check For Windows Vulnerabilities
- Check For Weak Passwords
- Check For IIS Vulnerabilities
- Check For SQL Vulnerabilities
- Check For Security Updates

If you use the Check For Security Updates option and are using WSUS, you can specify the name of the WSUS server that should be checked for the security updates.

Once you have made your selections, click Start Scan. When the scan is complete, the security report will be automatically displayed. If you have scanned multiple computers, you can sort the security reports based on issue name or score (worst first or best first).

Using the MBSA Command-Line Utility *mbsacli.exe*

After Microsoft Baseline Security Analyzer has been installed, you can use the command-line utility mbsacli.exe. Enter **mbsacli.exe/hf** and then customize the command execution with any of the options defined in Table 1.5.

TABLE 1.5 mbsacli.exe /hf command-line options

Option	Description
-h *host name[, host name, . . .]*	Scans the specified host. You can specify that you want to scan multiple host computers by separating the hostnames with commas.
-fh *filename*	Scans the NetBIOS name of each computer that is to be scanned, and it saves the information as text within a file specified by *filename*.
-i *xxxx.xxxx.xxxx.xxxx [, xxxx.xxxx.xxxx.xxxx, . . .]*	Scans a computer based on the specified IP address. You can scan multiple computers by IP address by separating the IP addresses with commas.
-fip *filename*	Looks in the text file specified by *filename* for IP addresses and scans the computers with those IP addresses. The file can have up to a maximum of 256 IP addresses.
-d *domainname*	Scans the specified domain.
-n	Scans all of the computers on the local network.

Simple Network Management Protocol

The *Simple Network Management Protocol (SNMP)* is a TCP/IP protocol monitor. The SNMP service creates trap messages that are then sent to a trap destination. One way you might use SNMP is to trap messages that don't contain an appropriate hostname for a particular service.

When you set up SNMP, you set up communities. *Communities* are groupings of computers that help monitor each other.

Windows Server 2012 R2 includes SNMP with the operating system. To install the service, you must use Server Manager. In Exercise 1.4, you will walk through the process of installing the SNMP service.

EXERCISE 1.4

Installing SNMP

1. Open Server Manager by clicking the Server Manager icon on the taskbar.

2. Click option number 2, Add Roles And Features.

3. Choose role-based or feature-based installation and click Next.

4. Choose your server and click Next.

5. Click Next at the Select Server Roles screen.

6. When the Select Features window appears, click the SNMP Services check box. If an ADD Features dialog box appears, click the Add Features button. Click Next.

7. The Confirm Installation page appears. Click Install.

8. Click Close. Exit the Server Manager application.

Now that you have installed the SNMP service, you have to set up your community so that you can start trapping messages. As stated earlier, communities are a grouping of computers to help monitor each other. After you have created the initial community, you can add other computer systems to the community.

In Exercise 1.5, you will walk through the steps to set up the SNMP service and also set up your first community name. To complete this exercise, you must have completed Exercise 1.4.

EXERCISE 1.5

Configuring SNMP

1. Open Computer Management by pressing the keyboard's Windows Key and selecting Administrative Tools ➢ Computer Management.

2. Expand Services And Applications. Click Services. In the right pane, double-click SNMP Service.

3. The SNMP Service Properties window will open. Click the Traps tab. In the Community Name box, enter **Community1**. Click the Add To List button.

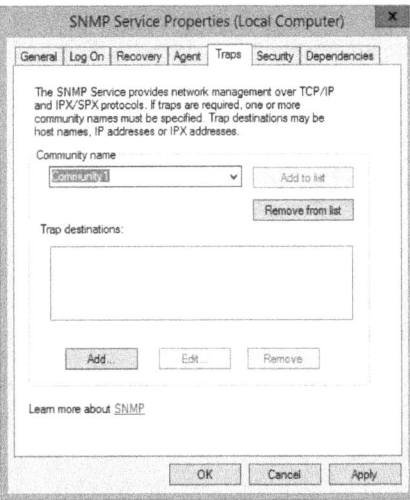

4.   Click the General tab. Click the Start button to start the service. Click OK.

5.   Close Computer Management.

Summary

This chapter began with a discussion of WSUS and what Windows Update can do for your network. You learned why you would want to use a WSUS server instead of having clients manually connect to the Internet to receive their updates.

The chapter also covered file server and print server optimization and reliability, including many tools that can help you monitor and manage your systems and the basics of troubleshooting the network in times of disaster.

Monitoring performance on servers is imperative to rooting out any issues that may affect your network. If your systems are not running at their best, your end users may experience issues such as latency, or worse, you may experience corruption in your network data. Either way, it's important to know how to monitor the performance of your servers. You also looked at ways system administrators can optimize the operations of servers to ensure that end users experience adequate performance.

You also examined how to use the various performance-related tools that are included with Windows Server 2012 R2. Tools such as Performance Monitor, Task Manager, Network Monitor, and Event Viewer can help you diagnose and troubleshoot system performance issues. These tools will help you find typical problems related to memory, disk space, and any other hardware-related issues you may experience. Knowing how to use tools to troubleshoot and test your systems is imperative, not only to passing the exam but also to performing your duties at work. To have a smoothly running network environment, it is vital that you understand the issues related to the reliability and performance of your network servers and domain controllers.

Exam Essentials

Understand WSUS.   Windows Server Update Services is one way to have your end users receive important updates from Microsoft. WSUS gives administrators the ability to download, test, and approve updates before they get released onto the network.

Understand the methodology behind troubleshooting performance.   By following a set of steps that involves making measurements and finding bottlenecks, you can systematically troubleshoot performance problems.

Be familiar with the features and capabilities of the Windows Server 2012 R2 Performance Monitor tool for troubleshooting performance problems.   The Performance Monitor administrative tool is a powerful method for collecting data about all areas of system performance. Through the use of performance objects, counters, and instances, you can choose to collect and record only the data of interest and use this information for pinpointing performance problems.

Know the importance of common performance counters.   Several important performance-related counters deal with general system performance. Know the importance of monitoring memory, print server, CPU, and network usage on a busy server.

Understand the role of other troubleshooting tools.   Windows Task Manager, Network Monitor, SNMP, Baseline Security Analyzer, and Event Viewer can all be used to diagnose and troubleshoot configuration- and performance-related issues.

Understand how to troubleshoot common sources of server reliability problems.   Windows Server 2012 R2 has been designed to be a stable, robust, and reliable operating system. Should you experience intermittent failures, you should know how to troubleshoot device drivers and buggy system-level software.

Review Questions

1. You need to stop an application from running in Task Manager. Which tab would you use to stop an application from running?

    A. Performance

    B. Users

    C. Options

    D. Details

2. You are the network administrator for a Fortune 500 company. You are responsible for all client computers at the central campus. You want to make sure that all of the client computers are secure. You decide to use MBSA to scan your client computers for possible security violations. You want to use the command-line version of MBSA to scan your computers based on IP address. Which of the following commands should you use?

    A. `mdsacli.exe /hf -i xxxx.xxxx.xxxx.xxxx`

    B. `mdsacli.exe /ip xxxx.xxxx.xxxx.xxxx`

    C. `mbsa.exe /hf -ip xxxx.xxxx.xxxx.xxxx`

    D. `mbsa.exe /ip xxxx.xxxx.xxxx.xxxx`

3. You are the network administrator for a Fortune 500 company. You are responsible for all client computers at the central campus. You want to make sure that all of the client computers have the most current software installed for their operating systems, including software in the categories Critical Updates and Service Packs, Windows Server 2012 R2 Family, and Driver Updates. You want to automate the process as much as possible, and you want the client computers to download the updates from a central server that you are managing. You decide to use Windows Server Update Services. The WSUS server software has been installed on a server called *WSUSServer*. You want to test the WSUS server before you set up group policies within the domain. You install Windows 8. Which of the following registry entries needs to be made for the client to specify that the client should use WSUSServer for Windows Update? (Choose all that apply.)

    A. Use `HKEY_LOCAL_MACHINE\Software\Policies\Microsoft\Windows\WindowsUpdate\AU\UseWUServer` and specify 0 data.

    B. Use `HKEY_LOCAL_MACHINE\Software\Policies\Microsoft\Windows\WindowsUpdate\AU\UseWUServer` and specify 1 for data.

    C. Use `HKEY_LOCAL_MACHINE\Software\Policies\Microsoft\Windows\WindowsUpdate\AU\WUServer` and specify `http://WSUSServer`.

    D. Use `HKEY_LOCAL_MACHINE\Software\Policies\Microsoft\Windows\WindowsUpdate\AU\WUServer` and specify WSUSServer.

    E. Use `HKEY_LOCAL_MACHINE\Software\Policies\Microsoft\Windows\WindowsUpdate\WUServer` and specify `http://WSUSServer`.

    F. Use `HKEY_LOCAL_MACHINE\Software\Policies\Microsoft\Windows\WindowsUpdate\WUServer` and specify WSUSServer.

4. You are the administrator of a new Windows Server 2012 R2 machine. You need to install WSUS. From where do you install WSUS?

    A. Add/Remove Programs

    B. Programs

    C. Server Manager

    D. Administrative Tools

5. You are a network administrator for your company. The network consists of a single Active Directory domain. All servers run Windows Server 2012 R2. Windows Server Update Services (WSUS) is installed on two servers, SERVERA and SERVERB. SERVERA receives software updates from Microsoft Windows Update servers. You manually synchronized SERVERB with the Windows Update servers, and now you need to complete the WSUS configuration on SERVERB. Which of the following is *not* a step that you might take to complete the configuration of WSUS on SERVERB?

    A. Approve the current updates.

    B. Set SERVERB to receive updates from SERVERA and automatically synchronize with approved updates on SERVERA.

    C. Set SERVERB to draw updates automatically from whichever sources that SERVERA is set to draw from.

    D. Set SERVERB to receive daily updates automatically at a given time.

6. You are the network administrator for your company. The network consists of a single Active Directory domain. All servers run Windows Server 2012 R2. All client computers run Windows 7. The company has 16 mobile sales representatives who are all members of the Power Users local group on their computers. From 6 p.m. until 7 a.m., the sales representatives' laptops are usually turned off and disconnected from the corporate network. The mobile sales representatives' computers must receive software updates every day with minimal user interaction. While verifying the recent updates on one of the laptops, you notice that the updates from the Windows Update servers were not applied. On the Automatic Updates tab of the System Properties dialog box of the mobile computer, what should you do to make sure that software updates are applied to the computer? (Choose three.)

    A. Set the scheduled time to every day at 12 a.m.

    B. Select the option Automatically Download The Updates, And Install Them On The Schedule That I Specify.

    C. Select the option Notify Me Before Downloading Any Updates And Notify Me Again Before Installing Them On My Computer.

    D. Select the Keep My Computer Up To Date check box.

    E. Select the option Download The Updates Automatically And Notify Me When They Are Ready To Be Installed.

    F. Set the scheduled time to every day at 12 p.m.

7. You are responsible for managing several Windows Server 2012 R2 domain controller computers in your environment. Recently, a single hard disk on one of these machines failed, and the Active Directory database was lost. You want to perform the following tasks:

- Determine which partitions on the server are still accessible.

- Restore as much of the system configuration (including the Active Directory database) as possible.

Which of the following could be used to help meet these requirements?

A. Event Viewer

B. Performance Monitor

C. A hard disk from another server that is not configured as a domain controller

D. A valid system state backup from the server

8. You have been hired as a consultant to research a network-related problem at a small organization. The environment supports many custom-developed applications that are not well documented. A manager suspects that some computers on the network are generating excessive traffic and bogging down the network. You want to do the following:

- Determine which computers are causing the problems.

- Record and examine network packets that are coming to/from specific machines.

- View data related only to specific types of network packets.

What tool should you use to accomplish all of the requirements?

A. Task Manager

B. Performance Monitor

C. Event Viewer

D. Network Monitor

9. You need to install Microsoft Baseline Security Analyzer. How do you need to do the install?

A. Download MBSA from Microsoft's website.

B. Install from Server Manager.

C. Use Add/Remove Programs.

D. Install from Programs.

10. While setting up WSUS, you need to configure the server from which you will be getting your Microsoft updates. Under which option would you set this up?

A. Products And Classifications

B. Update Files and Languages

C. Update Source And Proxy Server

D. Synchronization Schedule

Chapter

2

Manage File Services

THE FOLLOWING 70-411 EXAM OBJECTIVES ARE COVERED IN THIS CHAPTER:

✓ **Configure Distributed File System (DFS)**

- Install and configure DFS namespaces
- Configure DFS Replication Targets
- Configure Replication Scheduling
- Configure Remote Differential Compression settings
- Configure staging
- Configure fault tolerance
- Clone a DFS database
- Recover DFS databases
- Optimize DFS replication

✓ **Configure File Server Resource Manager (FSRM)**

- Install the FSRM role service
- Configure quotas
- Configure file screens
- Configure reports
- Configure file management tasks

✓ **Configure file and disk encryption**

- Configure Bitlocker encryption
- Configure the Network Unlock feature
- Configure Bitlocker policies
- Configure the EFS recovery agent
- Manage EFS and Bitlocker certificates including backup and restore

✓ **Configure advanced audit policies**

- Implement auditing using Group Policy and AuditPol.exe
- Create expression-based
- Create removable device audit policies

In this chapter, I will show you how to set up one of the more important server types: a file server. File servers are important because you need storage allocation where you can store files on your server.

Microsoft Windows Server 2012 R2 is used for all the server types in this chapter. Although other operating systems can be used, this chapter refers only to Windows Server 2012 R2.

Configuring File Server Resource Manager

As an administrator, when you need to control and manage the amount and type of data stored on your servers, Microsoft delivers the tools to help you do just that. The *File Server Resource Manager (FSRM)* is a suite of tools that allows an administrator to place quotas on folders or volumes, filter file types, and create detailed storage reports. These tools allow an administrator to properly plan and implement policies on data as needed.

FSRM Features

Many of the advantages of using FSRM come from all of the included features, which allow administrators to manage the data that is stored on their file servers. Some of the advantages included with FSRM are as follows:

Configure File Management Tasks   FSRM allows an administrator to apply a policy or action to data files. Some of the actions that can be performed include the ability to encrypt files or run a custom command.

Configure Quotas   Quotas give an administrator the ability to limit how much disk space a user can use on a file server. Administrators have the ability to limit space to an entire volume or to specific folders.

File Classification Infrastructure   Administrators can set file classifications and then manage the data more effectively by using these classifications. Classifying files, and then setting policies to those classifications, allows an administrator to set policies on those classifications. These policies include restricting file access, file encryption, and file expirations.

Configure File Screens Administrators can set file screening on a server and limit the types of files that are being stored on that server. For example, an administrator can set a file screen on a server so that any file ending in .bmp gets rejected.

Configure Reports Administrators can create reports that show them how data is classified and accessed. They also have the ability to see which users are trying to save unauthorized file extensions.

Installing the FSRM Role Service

Installing FSRM is easy when using either Server Manager or PowerShell. To install using Server Manager, you go into Add Roles And Features and choose File And Storage Services ➢ File Services ➢ File Server Resource Manager. To install FSRM using PowerShell, you use the following command:

```
Install-WindowsFeature -Name FS-Resource-Manager -IncludeManagementTools
```

Configuring FSRM using the Windows GUI version is straightforward, but setting up FSRM using PowerShell is a bit more challenging. Table 2.1 describes some of the PowerShell commands for FSRM.

TABLE 2.1 PowerShell commands for FSRM

PowerShell cmdlet	Description
Get-FsrmAutoQuota	Gets auto-apply quotas on a server
Get-FsrmClassification	Gets the status of the running file classification
Get-FsrmClassificationRule	Gets classification rules
Get-FsrmFileGroup	Gets file groups
Get-FsrmFileScreen	Gets file screens
Get-FsrmFileScreenException	Gets file screen exceptions
Get-FsrmQuota	Gets quotas on the server
Get-FsrmSetting	Gets the current FSRM settings
Get-FsrmStorageReport	Gets storage reports
New-FsrmAutoQuota	Creates an auto-apply quota
New-FsrmFileGroup	Creates a file group
New-FsrmFileScreen	Creates a file screen

TABLE 2.1   PowerShell commands for FSRM *(continued)*

PowerShell cmdlet	Description
New-FsrmQuota	Creates an FSRM quota
New-FsrmQuotaTemplate	Creates a quota template
Remove-FsrmClassificationRule	Removes classification rules
Remove-FsrmFileScreen	Removes a file screen
Remove-FsrmQuota	Removes an FSRM quota from the server
Set-FsrmFileScreen	Changes the configuration settings of a file screen
Set-FsrmQuota	Changes the configuration settings for an FSRM quota

Configure File and Disk Encryption

Hardware and software encryption are some of the most important actions you can take as an administrator. You must make sure that if anyone steals hardware from your company or from your server rooms that the data they are stealing is secured and cannot be used. This is where BitLocker can help.

Using BitLocker Drive Encryption

To prevent individuals from stealing your computer and viewing personal and sensitive data found on your hard disk, some editions of Windows come with a new feature called *BitLocker Drive Encryption.* BitLocker encrypts the entire system drive. New files added to this drive are encrypted automatically, and files moved from this drive to another drive or computers are decrypted automatically.

Only Windows 7 Enterprise, Windows 7 Ultimate, Windows 8 Pro, Windows 8 Enterprise, Windows Server 2008, Windows Server 2008 R2, Windows Server 2012, and Windows Server 2012 R2 include BitLocker Drive Encryption, and only the operating system drive (usually C:) or internal hard drives can be encrypted with BitLocker. Files on other types of drives must be encrypted using BitLocker To Go. BitLocker To Go allows you to put BitLocker on removable media such as external hard disks or USB drives.

BitLocker uses a *Trusted Platform Module (TPM)* version 1.2 or newer to store the security key. A TPM is a chip that is found in newer computers. If you do not have a computer with a TPM, you can store the key on a removable USB drive. The USB drive will be required each time you start the computer so that the system drive can be decrypted.

If the TPM discovers a potential security risk, such as a disk error or changes made to the BIOS, hardware, system files, or startup components, the system drive will not be unlocked until you enter the 48-digit BitLocker recovery password or use a USB drive with a recovery key as a recovery agent.

BitLocker must be set up either within the Local Group Policy editor or through the BitLocker icon in the control panel. One advantage of using BitLocker is that you can prevent any unencrypted data from being copied onto a removable disk, thus protecting the computer.

BitLocker Recovery Password

The BitLocker recovery password is important. Do not lose it, or you may not be able to unlock the drive. Even if you do not have a TPM, be sure to keep your recovery password in case your USB drive becomes lost or corrupted.

BitLocker requires that you have a hard disk with at least two partitions, both formatted with NTFS. One partition will be the system partition that will be encrypted. The other partition will be the active partition that is used to start the computer. This partition will remain unencrypted.

Features of BitLocker

As with any version of Windows, Microsoft continues to improve on the technologies used in Windows Server 2012 R2 and Windows 8. The following sections cover some of the features of BitLocker.

BitLocker Provisioning

In previous versions of BitLocker (Windows Vista and Windows 7), BitLocker provisioning (system and data volumes) was completed during the postinstallation of the BitLocker utility. BitLocker provisioning was done through either the command-line interface (CLI) or the control panel. In the Windows 8/Windows Server 2012 R2 version of BitLocker, an administrator can choose to provision BitLocker before the operating system is even installed.

Administrators have the ability to enable BitLocker prior to the operating system deployment from the Windows Preinstallation Environment (WinPE). BitLocker is applied to the formatted volume, and BitLocker encrypts the volume prior to running the Windows setup process.

If an administrator wants to check the status of BitLocker on a particular volume, the administrator can view the status of the drive either in the BitLocker control panel applet or in Windows Explorer.

Used Disk Space–Only Encryption

Windows 7 BitLocker requires that all data and free space on the drive must be encrypted. Because of this requirement, the encryption process can take a long time on larger volumes.

In Windows 8 BitLocker, administrators have the ability to encrypt either the entire volume or just the space being used. When you choose the Used Disk Space Only option, only the section of the drive that contains data will be encrypted. Because of this, encryption is completed much faster.

Standard User PIN and Password Change

One issue that BitLocker has had in the past is that you need to be an administrator to configure BitLocker on operating system drives. This could become an issue in a large organization because deploying TPM + PIN to a large number of computers can be challenging.

Even with the new operating system changes, administrative privileges are still needed to configure BitLocker, but now your users have the ability to change the BitLocker PIN for the operating system or change the password on the data volumes.

When a user gets to choose their own PIN and password, they normally choose something that has meaning to them and something that is easy to remember. That is a good and bad thing at the same time. It's a good thing because when your users choose their own PIN and password, they normally don't need to write it down—they just know it. It's a bad thing because if anyone knows the user well, they can have an easier time figuring out the person's PIN and password. Even when you allow your users to choose their own PIN and password, make sure you set a GPO to require password complexity.

Network Unlock

One of the new features of BitLocker is called Network Unlock. *Network Unlock* allows administrators to easily manage desktop and servers that are configured to use BitLocker. Network Unlock allows an administrator to configure BitLocker to automatically unlock an encrypted hard drive during a system reboot when that hard drive is connected to their trusted corporate environment. For this to function properly on a machine, there has to be a DHCP driver implementation in the system's firmware.

If your operating system volume is also protected by the TPM + PIN protection, the administrator has to be sure to enter the PIN at the time of the reboot. This protection can actually make using Network Unlock more difficult to use, but they can be used in combination.

Support for Encrypted Hard Drives for Windows

One of the new advantages of using BitLocker is *Full Volume Encryption (FVE)*. BitLocker provides built-in encryption for Windows data files and Windows operating system files. The advantage of this type of encryption is that encrypted hard drives that use *Full Disk Encryption (FDE)* get each block of the physical disk space encrypted. Because each physical block gets encrypted, it offers much better encryption. The only downside to this is that because each physical block is encrypted, it degrades the hard drive speed somewhat. So, as an administrator, you have to decide whether you want better speed or better security on your hard disk.

Windows 7 and 2008 R2 vs. Windows 8 and 2012 R2

The real question is what's the difference between Windows 7/Windows 2008 R2 and Windows 8/Windows Server 2012 R2? Table 2.2 shows you many of the common features and how they work then and now.

TABLE 2.2   BitLocker then and now

Feature	Windows 7/Server 2008 R2	Windows 8/Server 2012 R2
Resetting the BitLocker PIN or password	The user's privileges must be set to an administrator if you want to reset the BitLocker PIN on an operating system drive and the password on a fixed or removable data drive.	Standard users now have the ability to reset the BitLocker PIN and password on operating system drives, fixed data drives, and removable data drives.
Disk encryption	When BitLocker is enabled, the entire disk is encrypted.	When BitLocker is enabled, users have the ability to choose whether to encrypt the entire disk or only the used space on the disk.
Hardware-encrypted drive support	Not supported.	If the Windows logo hard drive comes preencrypted from the manufacturer, BitLocker is supported.
Unlocking using a network-based key to provide dual-factor authentication	Not available.	If a computer is rebooted on a trusted corporate wired-network key protector, then this feature allows a key to unlock and skip the PIN entry.
Protection for clusters	Not available.	Windows Server 2012 R2 BitLocker includes the ability to support cluster-shared volumes and failover clusters as long as they are running in a domain that was established by a Windows Server 2012 R2 domain controller with the Kerberos Key Distribution Center Service enabled.
Linking a BitLocker key protector to an Active Directory account	Not available.	BitLocker allows a user, group, or computer account in Active Directory to be tied to a key protector. This key protector allows protected data volumes to be unlocked.

In Exercise 2.1, you will enable BitLocker on the Windows Server 2012 R2 system.

EXERCISE 2.1

Enabling BitLocker in Windows Server 2012 R2

1. Open Server Manager by selecting the Server Manager icon or running servermanager.exe.

2. Select Add Roles And Features from the dashboard.

3. Select Next at the Before you begin pane (if shown).

4. Select Role-based or feature-based installation and select Next to continue.

5. Select the Select a server from the server pool option and click Next.

6. At the Select Server Roles screen, click Next.

7. At the Select features screen, click the BitLocker Drive Encryption check box. When the Add Roles and Features dialog box appears, click the Add Features button. Then click Next.

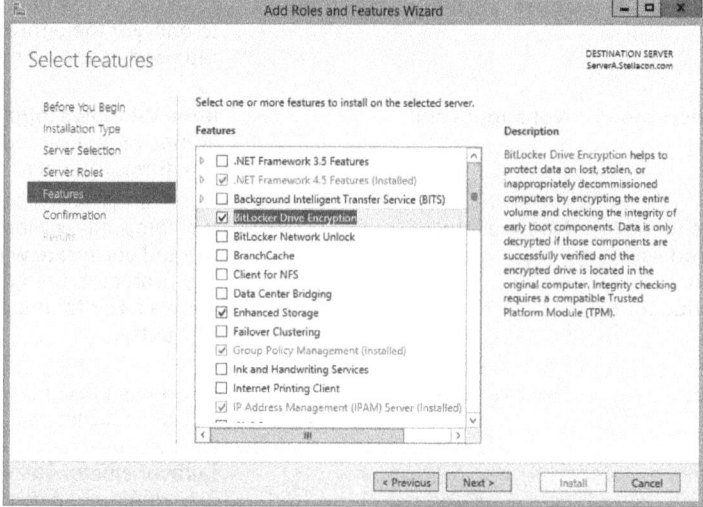

8. Select the Install button on the Confirmation pane of the Add Roles And Features Wizard to begin BitLocker feature installation. The BitLocker feature requires a restart to complete. Selecting the Restart The Destination Server Automatically If Required option in the Confirmation pane will force a restart of the computer after installation is complete.

9. If the Restart The Destination Server Automatically If Required check box is not selected, the Results pane of the Add Roles And Features Wizard will display the success or failure of the BitLocker feature installation. If required, a notification of additional action necessary to complete the feature installation, such as the restart of the computer, will be displayed in the results text.

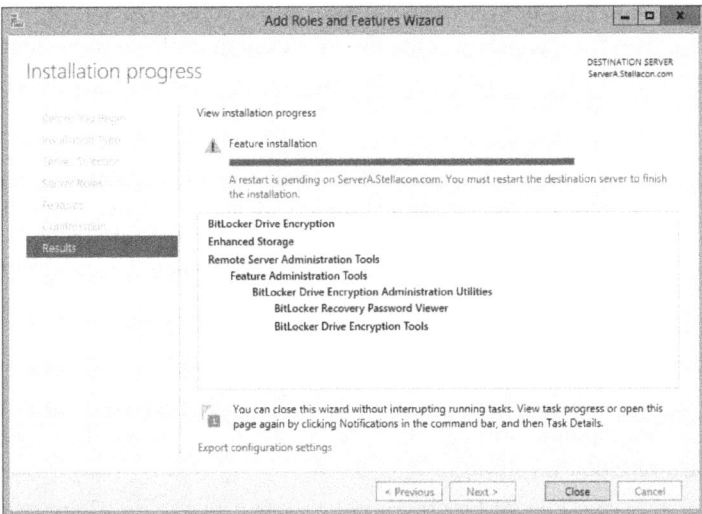

You also can install BitLocker by using the Windows PowerShell utility. To install BitLocker, use the following PowerShell commands:

```
Install-WindowsFeature BitLocker –IncludeAllSubFeature –IncludeManagementTools
–Restart
```

Using EFS Drive Encryption

If you have been in the computer industry long enough, you may remember the days when only servers used NTFS. Years ago, most client systems used FAT or FAT32, but NTFS had some key benefits over FAT/FAT32. The main advantages were NTFS security, quotas, compression, and encryption. Encryption is available on a system because you are using a file structure (for example, NTFS) that allows encryption. Windows Server 2012 R2 NTFS allows administrators to use these four advantages including encryption.

Encrypting File System (EFS) allows a user or administrator to secure files or folders by using encryption. Encryption employs the user's security identification (SID) number to secure the file or folder. Encryption is the strongest protection that Windows provides to help you keep your information secure. Some key features of EFS are as follows:

- Encrypting is simple; just select a check box in the file or folder's properties to turn it on.
- You have control over who can read the files.
- Files are encrypted when you close them but are automatically ready to use when you open them.
- If you change your mind about encrypting a file, clear the check box in the file's properties.

To implement encryption, open the Advanced Attributes dialog box for a folder and check the Encrypt Contents To Secure Data box.

If files are encrypted using EFS and an administrator has to unencrypt the files, there are two ways to do this. You can log in using the user's account (the account that encrypted the files) and unencrypt the files using the Cipher command. Alternatively, you can become a recovery agent and manually unencrypt the files.

If you use EFS, it's best not to delete users immediately when they leave a company. Administrators have the ability to recover encrypted files, but it is much easier to gain access to the user's encrypted files by logging in as the user who left the company and unchecking the encryption box.

Using the Cipher Command

The Cipher command is useful when it comes to EFS. Cipher is a command-line utility that allows you to change and/or configure EFS. When it comes to using the Cipher command, you should be aware of a few things:

- Administrators can decrypt files by running Cipher.exe in the Command Prompt window (advanced users).

- Administrators can use Cipher to modify an EFS-encrypted file.

- Administrators can use Cipher to import EFS certificates and keys.

- Administrators can also use Cipher to back up EFS certificates and keys.

Let's take a look at some of the different switches that you can use with Cipher. Table 2.3 describes many of the different Cipher switches you can use. This table comes from Microsoft's TechNet site. Microsoft continues to add and improve switches, so make sure you check Microsoft's website to see whether there are any changes.

TABLE 2.3 Using the cipher switches

Cipher switch	Description
/e	This switch allows an administrator to encrypt specified folders. With this folder encrypted, any files added to this folder will automatically be encrypted.
/d	This switch allows an administrator to decrypt specified folders.
/s: dir	By using this switch, the operation you are running will be performed in the specified folder and all subfolders.
/i	By default, when an error occurs, Cipher automatically halts. By using this switch, Cipher will continue to operate even after errors occur.
/f	The force switch (/f) will encrypt or decrypt all of the specified objects, even if the files have been modified by using encryption previously. Cipher, by default, does not touch files that have been encrypted or decrypted previously.

/q	This switch shows you a report about the most critical information of the EFS object.
/h	Normally, system or hidden files are not touched by encryption. By using this switch, you can display files with hidden or system attributes.
/k	This switch will create a new file encryption key based on the user currently running the Cipher command.
/?	This shows the Cipher help command.

Configuring Distributed File System

One problem that network administrators have is deciding how to share folders and communicating to end users how to find the shares. For example, if you share a folder called Stellacon Documents on server A, how do you make sure your users will find the folder and the files within it? The users have to know the server name and the share name. This can be a huge problem if you have hundreds of shares on multiple servers. If you want to have multiple copies of the folder called Stellacon Documents for fault tolerance and load balancing, the problem becomes even more complicated.

Distributed File System (DFS) in Windows Server 2012 R2 offers a simplified way for users to access geographically dispersed files. DFS allows you to set up a tree structure of virtual directories that allows users to connect to shared folders throughout the entire network.

Administrators have the ability to take shared folders that are located on different servers and transparently connect them to one or more DFS namespaces—virtual trees of shared folders throughout an organization. The advantage of using DFS is that if one of the folders becomes unavailable, DFS has failover capability that will allow your users to connect to the data on a different server.

Administrators can use the DFS tools to choose which shared folders will appear in the namespace and also to decide how the names of these shared folders will show up in the virtual tree listing.

Advantages of DFS

One of the advantages of DFS is that when a user views this virtual tree, the shared folders appear to be located on a single machine. These are some of the other advantages of DFS:

Simplified Data Migration   DFS gives you the ability to move data from one location to another without the user needing to know the physical location of the data. Because the users do not need to know the physical location of the shared data, administrators can simply move data from one location to another.

Security Integration   Administrators do not need to configure additional security for the DFS shared folders. The shared folders use the NTFS and shared folder permissions that an administrator has already assigned when the share was set up.

Access-Based Enumeration (ABE)   This DFS feature (disabled by default) displays only the files and folders that a user has permissions to access. If a user does not have access to a folder, Windows hides the folder from the user's DFS view. This feature is not active if the user is viewing the files and folders locally.

Types of DFS

The following are types of DFS:

DFS Replication   Administrators have the ability to manage replication scheduling and bandwidth throttling using the DFS management console. Replication is the process of sharing data between multiple machines. As explained earlier in the section, replicated shared folders allow you to balance the load and have fault tolerance. DFS also has read-only replication folders.

DFS Namespace   The DFS Namespace service is the virtual tree listing in the DFS server. An administrator can set up multiple namespaces on the DFS, allowing for multiple virtual trees within DFS. The DFS Namespace service was once known as *Distributed File System* in Windows 2000 Server and Windows Server 2003 (in case you still use Server 2003).

In Exercise 2.2, you will install the DFS Namespace service on the file server. You need to start the installation using the Server Manager MMC.

EXERCISE 2.2

Installing the DFS Namespace Service

1. Open Server Manager by selecting the Server Manager icon or running servermanager.exe.

2. Select Add Roles And Features from the dashboard.

3. Select Next at the Before You Begin pane (if shown).

4. Select Role-Based or Feature-Based installation and select Next to continue.

5. Select the Select A Server From The Server Pool option and click Next.

6. At the Select Server Roles screen, expand File And Storage Services and check the DFS Namespace and DFS Replication check boxes. Then click Next. If a dialog box appears, click the Add Features button.

7. At the Select Features screen, click Next.

8. At the Confirmation screen, click the Install button.

9. After the installation is complete, click the Close button.

10. Close Server Manager.

Once you have installed DFS, it's time to learn how to manage DFS with the DFS Management MMC. The DFS Management console (see Figure 2.1) gives you one place to do all of your DFS configurations. The DFS Management console allows you to set up DFS Replication and DFS Namespace. Another task you can do in the DFS Management console is to add a folder target—a folder that you add to the DFS namespace (the virtual tree) for all your users to share.

FIGURE 2.1 DFS Management console

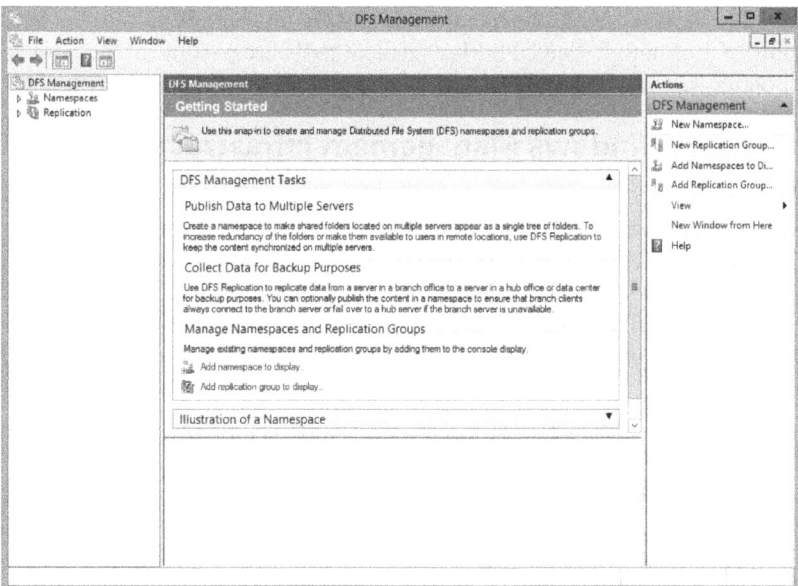

What's New in Windows Server 2012 R2

As with any new version of an operation system, Microsoft is trying to make each version of Windows Server better than the previous ones. This is also true with DFS. Microsoft has added many new features to DFS, and the following are just some of the major changes of Windows Server 2012 R2 DFS.

Windows PowerShell Module for DFS Replication

Windows PowerShell cmdlets for DFS replication modules can help administrators perform the majority of their DFS replication tasks. Administrators can use Windows PowerShell cmdlets to perform common administrative tasks such as creating, modifying, and removing DFS replication settings by using Window PowerShell scripts.

One of the nice new advantages of using Windows PowerShell for DFS is the ability to clone DFS replication databases and also to have the ability to restore those DFS databases in the event of an issue or crash.

Administrators have the ability to manage DFS management and replication through the use of the DNS Management and DFS Replication command-line utilities. Administrators who use the command-line tools are not doing anything incorrectly, but it is an inefficient way to do these tasks as well as being extremely time-consuming.

Administrators can use Windows PowerShell instead of command-line utilities and run hundreds of scripted commands, thus making their jobs easier and more efficient.

For an administrator who wants to use the Windows PowerShell cmdlets, the computer system installed with the DFS Management tools must be running Windows Server 2012 R2 or Windows 8.1 or newer. The DFS Management tools are part of the Remote Server Administration tools.

DFS Replication Windows Management Infrastructure Provider

In this book, I have spoken many times about using Windows Remote Management (WinRM) and how WinRM can help you administer a server remotely.

Introduced to Windows Server 2012 R2, the Windows Management Infrastructure (referred to as WMI v2) allows an administrator, using a properly configured firewall, to provide functionality and which provides programmatic access to manage DFS Replication.

Database Cloning

For the first time ever in DFS, Windows Server 2012 R2 includes a new DFS database cloning function. This new feature allows administrators to accelerate replication when creating folders, servers, or recovery systems.

Administrators will now have the ability to extract the DFS database from a single DFS server and then clone that database to multiple DFS servers.

Administrators can use PowerShell and the Export-DfsrClone cmdlet to export the volume that contains the DFS database and configuration .xml file settings. When executing this PowerShell cmdlet, a trigger is engaged that exports the DFS service, and the system will not proceed until the service is completed. Administrators would then use the PowerShell cmdlet Import-DfsrClone to import the data to a specific volume. The service will then validate that the replication was transferred completely.

Recovering a DFS Database

Windows Server 2012 R2 DFS database recovery is a feature that allows DFS to detect a corrupted database, thus allowing DFS to rebuild the database automatically and continue with normal operations of DFS replication. One advantage to this is that when DFS detects and fixes a corrupt database, it does so with no file conflicts.

Prior to this new feature, if a DFS database were determined to be corrupt, DFS Replication would delete the database and start again with an initial nonauthoritative sync process. This would cause newer file versions to be overwritten by older data causing real data loss.

DFS in Windows Server 2012 R2 uses local files and an update sequence number (USN) to fix a corrupt database, allowing for no loss of data.

Optimizing DFS

Windows Server 2012 R2 DFS allows an administrator to configure variable file staging sizes on individual DFS servers. This allows an administrator to set a minimum file size for a file to stage. This increases the staging size of files, and that in turn increases the performance of the replication.

Prior to Windows Server 2012 R2, DFS Replication used a hard-coded 256KB file size to determine staging requirements. If a file size were larger than 256KB, that file would be staged before it replicated. The more file staging that you have, the longer replication takes on a DFS system.

Remote Differential Compression

One issue that can arise occurs when files are changed. There has to be some mechanism that helps files stay accurate. That's where the *Remote Differential Compression (RDC)* feature comes into play. RDC is a group of application programming interfaces (APIs) that programs can use to determine whether files have changed. Once RDC determines that there has been a change, RDC then helps to detect which portions of the files contain the changes. RDC has the ability to detect insertions, removals, and rearrangements of data in files. This feature becomes helpful with limited-bandwidth networks when they replicate changes.

To install the RDC feature, use Server Manager and then run the Add Features Wizard, or type the following command at an elevated command prompt:

```
Servermanagercmd -Install Rdc
```

Implementing an Audit Policy

One of the most important aspects of controlling security in networked environments is ensuring that only authorized users are able to access specific resources. Although system administrators often spend much time managing security permissions, it is almost always possible for a security problem to occur.

Sometimes the best way to find possible security breaches is actually to record the actions that specific users take. Then, in the case of a security breach (the unauthorized shutdown of a server, for example), system administrators can examine the log to find the cause of the problem.

The Windows Server 2012 R2 operating system and Active Directory offer you the ability to audit a wide range of actions. In the following sections, you'll see how to implement auditing for Active Directory.

Overview of Auditing

The act of *auditing* relates to recording specific actions. From a security standpoint, auditing is used to detect any possible misuse of network resources. Although auditing does not necessarily prevent resources from being misused, it does help determine when security violations have occurred (or were attempted). Furthermore, just the fact that others know that you have implemented auditing may prevent them from attempting to circumvent security.

You need to complete several steps in order to implement auditing using Windows Server 2012 R2:

1.   Configure the size and storage settings for the audit logs.

2.   Enable categories of events to audit.

3.   Specify which objects and actions should be recorded in the audit log.

Note that there are trade-offs to implementing auditing. First, recording auditing information can consume system resources. This can decrease overall system performance and use up valuable disk space. Second, auditing many events can make the audit log impractical to view. If too much detail is provided, system administrators are unlikely to scrutinize all of the recorded events. For these reasons, you should always be sure to find a balance between the level of auditing detail provided and the performance-management implications of these settings.

Implementing Auditing

Auditing is not an all-or-none type of process. As is the case with security in general, system administrators must choose specifically which objects and actions they want to audit.

The main categories for auditing include the following:

- Audit account logon events
- Audit account management
- Audit directory service access
- Audit logon events
- Audit object access
- Audit policy change
- Audit privilege use
- Audit process tracking
- Audit system events

In this list of categories, many of the categories are related to Active Directory. Let's discuss these auditing categories in more detail.

Audit Account Logon Events   You enable this auditing event if you want to audit when a user authenticates with a domain controller and logs onto the domain. This event is logged in the security log on the domain controller.

Audit Account Management   This auditing event is used when you want to watch what changes are being made to Active Directory accounts. For example, when another administrator creates or deletes a user account, it would be an audited event.

Audit Directory Service Access   This auditing event occurs whenever a user or administrator accesses Active Directory objects. Let's say an administrator opens Active Directory and clicks a user account; even if nothing is changed on that account, an event is logged.

Audit Logon Events   Account logon events are created for domain account activity. For example, you have a user who logs on to a server so that they can access files; the act of logging onto the server creates this audit event.

Audit Object Access   Audit object access allows you to audit objects within your network such as folders, files, and printers. If you suspect someone is trying to hack into an object (for example, the finance folder), this is the type of auditing that you would use. You still would need to enable auditing on the actual object (for example, the finance folder).

Audit Policy Change   Audit policy change allows you to audit changes to user rights assignment policies, audit policies, or trust policies. This auditing allows you to see whether anyone changes any of the other audit policies.

Audit Privilege Use   Setting the audit privilege use allows an administrator to audit each instance of a user exercising a user right. For example, if a user changes the system time on a machine, this is a user right. Log on locally is another common user right.

To audit access to objects stored within Active Directory, you must enable the Audit Directory Service Access option. Then you must specify which objects and actions should be tracked.

Exercise 2.3 walks through the steps you must take to implement auditing of Active Directory objects on domain controllers.

EXERCISE 2.3

Enabling Auditing of Active Directory Objects

1. Open the Local Security Policy tool (located in the Administrative Tools program group).

2. Expand Local Policies ➢ Audit Policy.

3. Double-click the setting for Audit Directory Service Access.

4. In the Audit Directory Service Access Properties dialog box, place check marks next to Success and Failure. Click OK to save the settings.

5. Close the Local Security Policy tool.

Viewing Auditing Information

One of the most important aspects of auditing is regularly monitoring the audit logs. If this step is ignored, as it often is in poorly managed environments, the act of auditing is useless. Fortunately, Windows Server 2012 R2 includes the *Event Viewer* tool, which allows system administrators to view audited events quickly and easily. Using the filtering capabilities of Event Viewer, they can find specific events of interest.

Exercise 2.4 walks you through the steps that you must take to generate some auditing events and to examine the data collected for these actions. In this exercise, you will perform some actions that will be audited, and then you will view the information recorded within the audit logs. To complete this exercise, you must first have completed the steps in Exercise 2.1 and Exercise 2.3.

EXERCISE 2.4

Generating and Viewing Audit Logs

1. Open the Active Directory Users and Computers tool.

2. Within the Engineering OU, right-click any user account and select Properties.

3. On the user's Properties dialog box, add the middle initial *A* for this user account and specify **Software Developer** in the Description box. Click OK to save the changes.

4. Within the Engineering OU, right-click the Robert Admin user account and select Properties.

5. In the Robert Properties dialog box, add the description **Engineering IT Admin** and click OK.

6. Close the Active Directory Users and Computers tool.

7. Open the Event Viewer tool from the Administrative Tools program group. Select the Security item under Windows Logs. You will see a list of audited events categorized under Directory Service Access. Note that you can obtain more details about a specific item by double-clicking it.

8. When you have finished viewing the security log, close the Event Viewer tool.

Using the *Auditpol.exe* Command

There may be a time when you need to look at your actual auditing policies set on a user or a system. This is where an administrator can use the Auditpol.exe command. *Auditpol* gives administrators the ability not only to view an audit policy but it also allows an administrator to set, configure, modify, restore, and even remove an audit policy. Auditpol is a command-line utility, and there are multiple switches that can be used with Auditpol. The following is the syntax used with Auditpol.

```
Auditpol command [<sub-command><options>]
```

Here's an example of using the command:

```
Auditpol /get /user:wpanek /category:"Detailed Tracking" /r
```

Table 2.4 describes some of the switches.

TABLE 2.4   Auditpol commands

Command	Description
/backup	Allows an administrator to save the audit policy to a file
/clear	Allows an administrator to clear an audit policy
/get	Gives administrators the ability to view the current audit policy
/list	Allows you to view selectable policy elements
/remove	Removes all per-user audit policy settings and disables all system audit policy settings
/restore	Allows an administrator to restore an audit policy from a file that was previously created using auditpol /backup
/set	Gives an administrator the ability to set an audit policy
/?	Displays help

Windows Server 2012 R2 Auditing Features

Auditing in Windows Server 2012 R2 and Windows 8 has been enhanced in many ways. Microsoft has increased the level of detail in the security auditing logs. Microsoft has also simplified the deployment and management of auditing policies. The following list includes some of the major enhancements:

Global Object Access Auditing   Administrators using Windows Server 2012 R2 and Windows 8 now have the ability to define computer-wide system access control lists (SACLs). Administrators can define SACLs for either the file system or the registry. After the specified SACL is defined, the SACL is then applied automatically to every single object of that type. This can be helpful to administrators in verifying that all critical files, folders, and registry settings on a computer are protected. This is also helpful for identifying when an issue occurs with a system resource.

"Reason for Access" Reporting   When an administrator is performing auditing in Windows Server 2012 R2 and Windows 8, they can now see the reason why an operation was successful or unsuccessful. Previously, they lacked the ability to see the reason why an operation succeeded or failed.

Advanced Audit Policy Settings   In Windows Server 2012 R2, there are hundreds of Advanced Audit Policy settings that can be used in place of the nine basic auditing settings. These advanced audit settings also help eliminate the unnecessary auditing activities that can make audit logs difficult to manage and decipher.

Expression-Based Audit Policies   Administrators have the ability, because of Dynamic Access Control, to create targeted audit policies by using expressions based on user, computer, and resource claims. For example, an administrator has the ability to create an audit policy that tracks all Read and Write operations for files that are considered high-business impact. Expression-based audit policies can be directly created on a file or folder or created through the use of a Group Policy.

Removable Storage Device Auditing   Administrators have the ability to monitor attempts to use a removable storage device on your network. If an administrator decides to implement this policy, an audit event is created every time one of your users attempts to copy, move, or save a network resource onto a removable storage device.

Making Active Directory Objects Available to Users

If you have been reading this book from the start, then this section will be familiar. But if you started this book with only exam 70-411 in mind, then you are about to learn how to make resources available to your users through the use of Active Directory.

With Active Directory, a system administrator can control which objects users can see. The act of making an Active Directory object available is known as *publishing*. The two main publishable objects are Printer objects and Shared Folder objects.

The general process for creating server shares and shared printers has remained unchanged from previous versions of Windows. You create the various objects (printers or file system folders) and then enable them for sharing.

To make these resources available via Active Directory, however, there's an additional step; you must publish the resources. Once an object has been published in Active Directory, clients will be able to find it.

When you publish objects in Active Directory, you should know the server name and share name of the resource. This information, however, doesn't matter to your users. A system administrator can change the resource to which an object points without having to reconfigure or even notify clients. For example, if you move a share from one server to another, all you need to do is update the Shared Folder object's properties to point to the new location. Active Directory clients still refer to the resource with the same path and name that they used previously.

Exercise 2.5 will walk you through the steps required for sharing and publishing a folder for use on your network.

EXERCISE 2.5

Creating and Publishing a Shared Network Folder

1. Create a new folder in the root directory of your C: partition and name it **Test Share**.

2. Right-click the Test Share folder and choose Share With ➢ Specific People.

3. In the File Sharing dialog box, enter the names of users with whom you want to share this folder. In the upper box, enter **Everyone** and then click Add. Note that Everyone appears in the lower box. Click in the Permission Level column next to Everyone and choose Read/Write from the drop-down menu. Then click Share.

4. You see a message that your folder has been shared. Click Done.

5. Open the Active Directory Users and Computers tool. Expand the current domain and right-click RD OU. Select New ➢ Shared Folder.

6. In the New Object – Shared Folder dialog box, type **Shared Folder Test** for the name of the folder. Then type the UNC path to the share (for example, **\\serverA\ Test Share**). Click OK to create the share.

One of the main benefits of having all of your resource information in Active Directory is that you can easily find the information you're seeking using the Find dialog box. When setting up objects in Active Directory, I recommend that you always enter as much information as possible for the objects you are creating. The extra effort will pay off when your users start doing searches for these objects. The more information you enter, the more that will be available for users to search to find the appropriate resource they need.

Configuring Offline Folders

If you have been in this industry long enough, you have seen a major change in end-user computers. Years ago, only a few select users had laptops. They were big and bulky, and they weighed almost as much as today's desktop computers.

The pendulum has swung in the opposite direction. It probably seems like every one of your end users now has a laptop. As an IT administrator, this gives you a whole new set of challenges and problems to address. One challenge that you have to address is how users can work on files while outside of the office. If you have a user who wants to work at home, how do you give them the files they need to get their work done? The answer is *offline folders*. These folders contain data that can be worked on by users while outside the office. An IT administrator can set up offline folders through the use of *Group Policy objects (GPOs)*.

When you decide to make folders available for offline use, these folders need to synchronize with the laptops so that all of the data matches between both systems. As an administrator, one decision that you will need to make is when the offline folders will be synchronized.

You can set up any combination of these three synchronization options in the GPO:

- When you select Synchronize All Offline Files Before Logging Off, offline folders are synchronized when the user logs off the network.

- When you select Synchronize All Offline Files When Logging On, offline folders are synchronized when the user logs on to the network.

- When you select Synchronize Offline Files Before Suspend, offline folders are synchronized before the user does a system suspend.

In Exercise 2.6, you will configure offline folder options by using a GPO. This exercise uses the Group Policy Management Console (GPMC). If your GPMC is not installed, use the Server Manager MMC (under Features) to install it.

EXERCISE 2.6

Configuring Offline Folder Options

1. Open the Group Policy Management Console.

2. In the left pane, expand your forest and then your domain. Under your domain name, there should be a default domain policy.

3. Right-click the default domain policy and choose Edit.

4. In the User Configuration section, expand Policies ➤ Administrative Templates ➤ Network and then click Offline Files.

5. Right-click Synchronize All Offline Files Before Logging Off and choose Edit. The GPO setting dialog box appears. Choose the Enabled option and click OK.

6. Right-click Synchronize All Offline Files When Logging On and choose Edit. The GPO setting dialog box appears. Choose the Enabled option and click OK.

7. Right-click Synchronize Offline Files Before Suspend and choose Edit. The GPO setting dialog box appears. Choose the Enabled option. In the Action drop-down box, make sure Quick is selected. Click OK.

8. Close the GPMC.

Now that you have set up a GPO for synchronization, it's time to share a folder for offline usage. In Exercise 2.7, you will set up a folder for offline access. You must complete Exercise 2.5 before doing this exercise.

EXERCISE 2.7

Configuring a Shared Network Folder for Offline Access

1. Right-click the Test Share folder you created in Exercise 2.5 and choose Properties.

2. Click the Sharing tab and then click the Advanced Sharing button.

3. When the Advanced Sharing dialog box appears, click the Caching button.

4. When the Offline Settings dialog box appears, choose the All Files And Programs That Users Open From The Shares Will Be Automatically Available Offline option. Click OK.

5. Click OK twice more to close the Properties dialog box.

Summary

This chapter took you through the use of many server tools and utilities such as DFS, BitLocker, and auditing. Distributed File System allows an administrator to set up a tree structure of virtual directories that allow users to connect to a shared folder anywhere throughout the entire network. You also looked at the new changes that have taken place with DFS in Windows Server 2012 R2.

You also learned about EFS and how to use Cipher to modify or configure EFS in a command window. Cipher is the best way to change encrypted directories and files.

This chapter also covered auditing. You looked at what needs to be audited if you are watching Active Directory and its objects. You looked at Auditpol and many of the switches that you would use when configuring Auditpol.

Finally, you learned how to publish share folders to Active Directory. By doing this, your users can search Active Directory to find resources they are looking for.

Exam Essentials

Know How to Configure DFS   Distributed File System in Windows Server 2012 R2 offers a simplified way for users to access geographically dispersed files. The DFS Namespace service allows you to set up a tree structure of virtual directories that lets users connect to shared folders throughout the entire network.

Understand EFS and Cipher   Users can encrypt their directories and files by using EFS. Understand how Cipher can help an administrator configure or modify an EFS object while in the command prompt.

Understand the Purpose and Function of Auditing   Auditing helps determine the cause of security violations and helps troubleshoot permissions-related problems.

Review Questions

1. The company for which you work has a multilevel administrative team that is segmented by departments and locations. There are four major locations, and you are in the Northeast group. You have been assigned to the administrative group that is responsible for creating and maintaining network shares for files and printers in your region. The last place you worked was a large Windows Server 2008 network, where you had a much wider range of responsibilities. You are excited about the chance to learn more about Windows Server 2012 R2.

   For your first task, you have been given a list of file and printer shares that need to be created for the users in your region. You ask how to create them in Windows Server 2012 R2, and you are told that the process of creating a share is the same as with Windows Server 2008. You create the shares and use NETUSE to test them. Everything appears to work fine, so you send a message that the shares are available. The next day, you start receiving calls from users who say they cannot see any of resources you created. What is the most likely reason for the calls from the users?

   A. You forgot to enable NetBIOS for the shares.

   B. You need to force replication for the shares to appear in the directory.

   C. You need to publish the shares in the directory.

   D. The shares will appear within the normal replication period.

2. You want to publish a printer to Active Directory. Where would you click in order to accomplish this task?

   A. The Sharing tab

   B. The Advanced tab

   C. The Device Settings tab

   D. The Printing Preferences button

3. Isabel is a system administrator for an Active Directory environment that is running in Native mode. Recently, several managers have reported suspicions about user activities and have asked her to increase security in the environment. Specifically, the requirements are as follows:

   - The accessing of certain sensitive files must be logged.

   - Modifications to certain sensitive files must be logged.

   - System administrators must be able to provide information about which users accessed sensitive files and when they were accessed.

   - All logon attempts for specific shared machines must be recorded.

   Which of the following steps should Isabel take to meet these requirements? (Choose all that apply.)

   A. Enable auditing with the Computer Management tool.

   B. Enable auditing with the Active Directory Users and Computers tool.

   C. Enable auditing with the Active Directory Domains and Trusts tool.

   D. Enable auditing with the Event Viewer tool.

   E. View the audit log using the Event Viewer tool.

   F. View auditing information using the Computer Management tool.

   G. Enable failure and success auditing settings for specific files stored on NTFS volumes.

   H. Enable failure and success auditing settings for logon events on specific computer accounts.

4. You are the network administrator for a midsize coffee bean distributor. Your company's network has four Windows 2012 servers, and all of the clients are running either Windows 8 or Windows 7. Most of your end users use laptops to do their work, and many of them work away from the office. What should you configure to help them work on documents when away from the office?

   A. Online file access

   B. Offline file access

   C. Share permissions

   D. NTFS permissions

5. Your company has decided to implement an external hard drive. The company IT manager before you always used FAT32 as the system partition. Your company wants to know whether it should move to NTFS. Which of the following are some advantages of NTFS? (Choose all that apply.)

   A. Security

   B. Quotas

   C. Compression

   D. Encryption

6. You are the administrator for a large organization that uses Windows Server 2012 R2. You have been asked by your manager to help protect his folders on his Windows 7 NTFS machine. Your manager wants to make sure he is the only person that can open his files. How do you protect his files?

   A. Use EFS.

   B. Use CDMA.

   C. Use FAT32 Security.

   D. Use the `Convert:FAT32/Encrypt` command.

7. You are the administrator of your network, which consists of two Windows Server 2012 R2 systems. One of the servers is a domain controller, and the other server is a file server for data storage. The hard drive of the file server is starting to fill up. You do not have the ability to install another hard drive, so you decide to limit the amount of space everyone gets on the hard drive. What do you need to implement to solve your problem?

   A. Disk spacing

   B. Disk quotas

   C. Disk hardening

   D. Disk limitations

8. You are the administrator for a large communications company. Your company uses Windows Server 2012 R2, and your user's files are encrypted using EFS. What command-line command would you use to change or modify the EFS files?

    A. Convert

    B. Cipher

    C. Gopher

    D. Encrypt

9. You are the administrator for a large organization. You have multiple Windows Server 2012 R2 systems that all contain files that need to be shared for all users. The files and folders constantly move among servers, and users are having a hard time finding files they need. What can you implement to help your users out?

    A. Encrypting File System (EFS)

    B. Distributed File System (DFS)

    C. Shared File System (SFS)

    D. Published File System (PFS)

10. You have been hired by a small company to implement new Windows Server 2012 R2 systems. The company wants you to set up a server for users' home folder locations. What type of server would you be setting up?

    A. PDC server

    B. Web server

    C. Exchange server

    D. File server

Chapter

3

Configure DNS

THE FOLLOWING 70-411 EXAM OBJECTIVES ARE COVERED IN THIS CHAPTER:

✓ **Configure DNS zones**

  ▪ Configure primary and secondary zones

  ▪ Configure stub zones

  ▪ Configure conditional forwards

  ▪ Configure zone and conditional forward storage in Active Directory

  ▪ Configure zone delegation

  ▪ Configure zone transfer settings

  ▪ Configure notify settings

✓ **Configure DNS records**

  ▪ Create and configure DNS Resource Records (RR) including A, AAAA, PTR, SOA, NS, SRV, CNAME, and MX records

  ▪ Configure zone scavenging

  ▪ Configure record options including time to live (TTL) and weight

  ▪ Configure round robin

  ▪ Configure secure dynamic updates

The Domain Name System (DNS) is one of the most important networking services that you can put on your network, and it's also one of the key topics that you'll need to understand if you plan to take any of the Microsoft Windows Server 2012 R2 exams.

By the end of this chapter, you should have a deeper understanding of how DNS works, how to set it up properly, how to configure DNS, proper management of the DNS server, and how to troubleshoot DNS issues quickly and easily in Microsoft Windows Server 2012 R2.

Introducing DNS

The *Domain Name System (DNS)* is a service that allows you to resolve a hostname to an Internet Protocol (IP) address. One of the inherent complexities of operating in networked environments is working with multiple protocols and network addresses. Owing largely to the tremendous rise in the popularity of the Internet, however, most environments have transitioned to use *Transmission Control Protocol/Internet Protocol (TCP/IP)* as their primary networking protocol. Microsoft is no exception when it comes to supporting TCP/IP in its workstation and server products. All current versions of Microsoft's operating systems support TCP/IP, as do most other modern operating systems.

An easy way to understand DNS is to think about making a telephone call. If you wanted to call Microsoft and did not know the phone number, you could call information, tell the operator the name (Microsoft), and get the telephone number. You would then make the call. Now think about trying to connect to Server1. You don't know the TCP/IP number (the computer's telephone number), so your computer asks DNS (information) for the number of Server1. DNS returns the number, and your system makes the connection (call). DNS is your network's 411, or information, and it returns the TCP/IP data for your network.

TCP/IP is actually a collection of different technologies (protocols and services) that allow computers to function together on a single, large, and heterogeneous network. Some of the major advantages of this protocol include widespread support for hardware, software, and network devices; reliance on a system of standards; and scalability. TCP handles tasks such as sequenced acknowledgments. IP involves many jobs, such as logical subnet assignment and routing.

The Form of an IP Address

To understand DNS, you must first understand how TCP/IP addresses are formed. Because DNS is strictly on a network to support TCP/IP, understanding the basics of TCP/IP is extremely important.

An *IP address* is a logical number that uniquely identifies a computer on a TCP/IP network. TCP/IP allows a computer packet to reach the correct host. Windows Server 2012 R2 works with two versions of TCP/IP: IPv4 and IPv6. An IPv4 address takes the form of four octets (eight binary bits), each of which is represented by a decimal number between 0 and 255. The four numbers are separated by decimal points. For example, all of the following are valid IP addresses:

- 128.45.23.17

- 230.212.43.100

- 10.1.1.1

The dotted decimal notation was created to make it easier for users to deal with IP addresses, but this idea did not go far enough. As a result, another abstraction layer was developed, which used names to represent the dotted decimal notation—the domain name. For example, the IP address 11000000 10101000 00000001 00010101 maps to 192.168.1.21, which in turn might map to `server1.company.org`, which is how the computer's address is usually presented to the user or application.

As stated earlier, IPv4 addresses are made up of octets, or the decimal (base 10) representation of 8 bits. It takes four octets to add up to the 32 bits required. IPv6 expands the address space to 128 bits. The address is usually represented in hexadecimal notation as follows:

2001:0DB8:0000:0000:1234:0000:A9FE:133E

You can tell that the implementation of DNS would make life a lot easier for everyone; even those of us who like to use alphanumeric values. (For example, some of us enjoy pinging the address in lieu of the name.) Fortunately, DNS already has the ability to handle IPv6 addresses using an AAAA record. An A record in IPv4's addressing space is 32 bits, and an AAAA record (4 *A*s) in IPv6's is 128 bits.

Nowadays, most computer users are quite familiar with navigating to DNS-based resources, such as `www.microsoft.com`. To resolve these "friendly" names to TCP/IP addresses that the network stack can use, you need a method for mapping them. Originally, ASCII flat files (often called *HOSTS files*, as shown in Figure 3.1) were used for this purpose. In some cases, they are still used today in small networks, and they can be useful in helping to troubleshoot name resolution problems.

FIGURE 3.1 HOSTS file

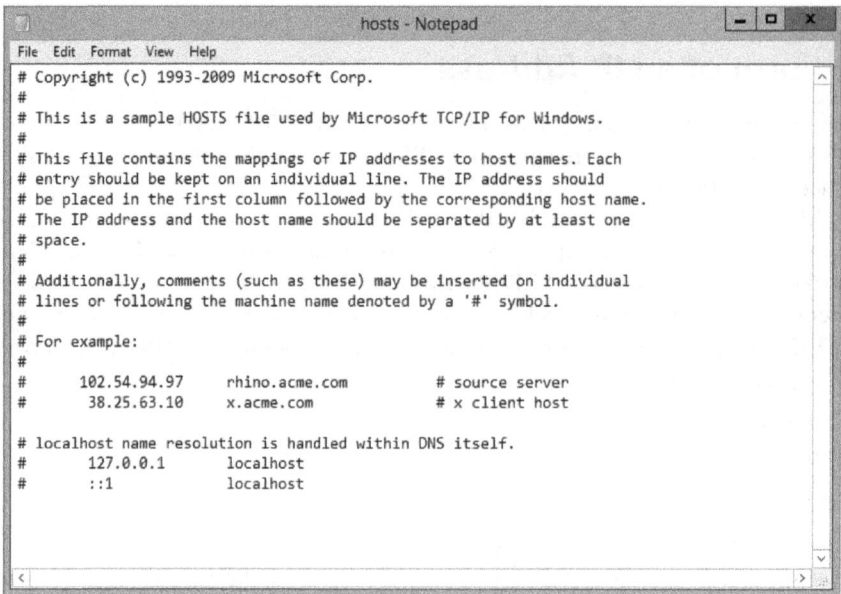

As the number of machines and network devices grew, it became unwieldy for administrators to manage all of the manual updates required to enter new mappings to a master HOSTS file and distribute it. Clearly, a better system was needed.

As you can see from the sample HOSTS file in Figure 3.1, you can conduct a quick test of the email server's name resolution as follows:

1. Open the HOSTS file: C:\Windows\Systems32\drivers\etc.

2. Add the IP-address-to-hostname mapping.

3. Try to ping the server using the hostname to verify that you can reach it using an easy-to-remember name.

Following these steps should drive home the concept of DNS for you because you can see it working to make your life easier. Now you don't have to remember 10.0.0.10; you only need to remember exchange03. However, you can also see how this method can become unwieldy if you have many hosts that want to use easy-to-remember names instead of IP addresses to locate resources on your network.

When dealing with large networks, users and network administrators must be able to locate the resources they require with minimal searching. Users don't care about the actual physical or logical network address of the machine; they just want to be able to connect to it using a simple name that they can remember.

From a network administrator's standpoint, however, each machine must have its own logical address that makes it part of the network on which it resides. Therefore, some scalable and easy-to-manage method for resolving a machine's logical name to an IP address and then to a domain name is required. DNS was created just for this purpose.

DNS is a hierarchically distributed database. In other words, its layers are arranged in a definite order, and its data is distributed across a wide range of machines, each of which can exert control over a portion of the database. DNS is a standard set of protocols that defines the following:

- A mechanism for querying and updating address information in the database
- A mechanism for replicating the information in the database among servers
- A schema of the database

 DNS is defined by a number of requests for comments (RFCs), though primarily by RFC 1034 and RFC 1035.

DNS was originally developed in the early days of the Internet (called ARPAnet at the time) when it was a small network created by the Department of Defense for research purposes. Before DNS, computer names, or hostnames, were manually entered into a HOSTS file located on a centrally administered server. Each site that needed to resolve hostnames outside of its organization had to download this file. As the number of computers on the Internet grew, so did the size of this HOSTS file—and along with it the problems of its management. The need for a new system that would offer features such as scalability, decentralized administration, and support for various data types became more and more obvious. DNS, introduced in 1984, became this new system.

With DNS, the hostnames reside in a database that can be distributed among multiple servers, decreasing the load on any one server and providing the ability to administer this naming system on a per-partition basis. DNS supports hierarchical names and allows for the registration of various data types in addition to the hostname-to-IP-address mapping used in HOSTS files. Database performance is ensured through its distributed nature as well as through caching.

The DNS distributed database establishes an inverted logical tree structure called the *domain namespace*. Each node, or domain, in that space has a unique name. At the top of the tree is the root. This may not sound quite right, which is why the DNS hierarchical model is described as being an inverted tree, with the root at the top. The root is represented by the null set: "". When written, the root node is represented by a single dot (.).

Each node in the DNS can branch out to any number of nodes below it. For example, below the root node are a number of other nodes, commonly referred to as *top-level domains (TLDs)*. These are the familiar .com, .net, .org, .gov, .edu, and other such names. Table 3.1 lists some of these TLDs.

TABLE 3.1   Common top-level DNS domains

Domain name	Type of organization
com	Commercial (for example, `stellacon.com` for Stellacon Training Corporation)
edu	Educational (for example, `gatech.edu` for the Georgia Institute of Technology)
gov	Government (for example, `whitehouse.gov` for the White House in Washington, D.C.)
int	International organizations (for example, `nato.int` for NATO); this top-level domain is fairly rare
mil	Military organizations (for example, `usmc.mil` for the Marine Corps); there is a separate set of root name servers for this domain
net	Networking organizations and Internet providers (for example, `hiwaay.net` for HiWAAY Information Systems); many commercial organizations have registered names under this domain too
org	Noncommercial organizations (for example, `fidonet.org` for FidoNet)
au	Australia
uk	United Kingdom
ca	Canada
us	United States
jp	Japan

Each of these nodes then branches out into another set of domains, and they combine to form what we refer to as *domain names*, such as microsoft.com. A domain name identifies the domain's position in the logical DNS hierarchy in relation to its parent domain by separating each branch of the tree with a dot. Figure 3.2 shows a few of the top-level domains, where the Microsoft domain fits, and a host called Tigger within the microsoft .com domain. If someone wanted to contact that host, they would use the *fully qualified domain name (FQDN)*, tigger.microsoft.com.

An FQDN includes the trailing dot (.) to indicate the root node, but it's commonly left off in practice.

As previously stated, one of the strengths of DNS is the ability to delegate control over portions of the DNS namespace to multiple organizations. For example, the Internet Corporation for Assigned Names and Numbers (ICANN) assigns the control over TLDs

FIGURE 3.2 The DNS hierarchy

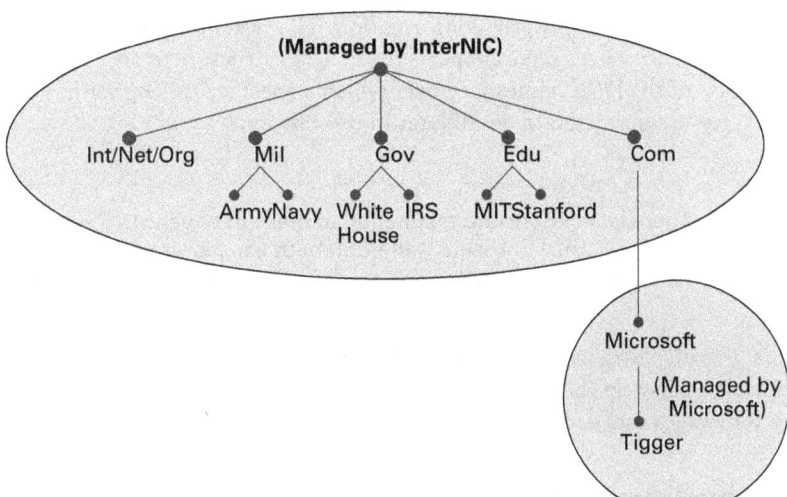

to one or more organizations. In turn, those organizations delegate portions of the DNS namespace to other organizations. For example, when you register a domain name, let's call it example.com, you control the DNS for the portion of the DNS namespace within example.com. The registrar controlling the .com TLD has delegated control over the example.com node in the DNS tree. No other node can be named example directly below the .com within the DNS database.

Within the portion of the domain namespace that you control (example.com), you could create host and other records (more on these later). You could also further subdivide example.com and delegate control over those divisions to other organizations or departments. These divisions are called *subdomains*. For example, you might create subdomains named for the cities in which the company has branch offices and then delegate control over those subdomains to the branch offices. The subdomains might be named losangeles.example.com, chicago.example.com, portsmouth.example.com, and so on.

Each domain (or delegated subdomain) is associated with DNS name servers. In other words, for every node in the DNS, one or more servers can give an authoritative answer to queries about that domain. At the root of the domain namespace are the root servers, which I'll cover later in the chapter.

Domain names and hostnames must contain only characters a to z, A to Z, 0 to 9, and – (hyphen). Other common and useful characters, such as the & (ampersand), / (slash), . (period), and _ (underscore) characters, are not allowed. This is in conflict with NetBIOS's naming restrictions. However, you'll find that Windows Server 2012 R2 is smart enough to take a NetBIOS name, like Server_1, and turn it into a legal DNS name, like server1.example.com.

DNS servers work together to resolve hierarchical names. If a server already has information about a name, it simply fulfills the query for the client. Otherwise, it queries other DNS servers for the appropriate information. The system works well because it distributes the authority over separate parts of the DNS structure to specific servers. A DNS zone is a portion of the DNS namespace over which a specific DNS server has authority. (DNS zone types are discussed in detail later in this chapter.)

> There is an important distinction to make between DNS zones and Active Directory (AD) domains. Although both use hierarchical names and require name resolution, DNS zones do not map directly to AD domains.

Within a given DNS zone, resource records (RRs) contain the hosts and other database information that make up the data for the zone. For example, an RR might contain the host entry for www.example.com, pointing it to the IP address 192.168.1.10.

Understanding Servers, Clients, and Resolvers

You will need to know a few terms and concepts in order to manage a DNS server. Understanding these terms will make it easier to understand how the Windows Server 2012 R2 DNS server works:

DNS Server Any computer providing domain name services is a *DNS name server*. No matter where the server resides in the DNS namespace, it's still a DNS name server. For example, 13 root name servers at the top of the DNS tree are responsible for delegating the TLDs. The *root servers* provide referrals to name servers for the TLDs, which in turn provide referrals to an authoritative name server for a given domain.

> The Berkeley Internet Name Domain (BIND) was originally the only software available for running the root servers on the Internet. However, a few years ago the organizations responsible for the root servers undertook an effort to diversify the software running on these important machines. Today, root servers run multiple types of name server software. BIND is still primarily on Unix-based machines, and it is also the most popular for Internet providers. None of the root servers run Windows DNS.

Any DNS server implementation supporting Service Location Resource Records (see RFC 2782) and Dynamic Updates (RFC 2136) is sufficient to provide the name service for any operating system running Windows 2003 software and newer.

DNS Client A *DNS client* is any machine that issues queries to a DNS server. The client hostname may or may not be registered in a DNS database. Clients issue DNS requests through processes called *resolvers*. You'll sometimes see the terms *client* and *resolver* used synonymously.

Resolver   *Resolvers* are software processes, sometimes implemented in software libraries, which handle the actual process of finding the answers to queries for DNS data. The resolver is also built into many larger pieces of software so that external libraries don't have to be called to make and process DNS queries. Resolvers can be what you'd consider client computers or other DNS servers attempting to resolve an answer on behalf of a client (for example, Internet Explorer).

Query   A *query* is a request for information sent to a DNS server. Three types of queries can be made to a DNS server: recursive, inverse, and iterative. I'll discuss the differences between these query types in the section "DNS Queries" a bit later in the chapter.

Understanding the DNS Process

To help you understand the DNS process, I will start by covering the differences between Dynamic DNS and Non-Dynamic DNS. During this discussion, you will learn how Dynamic DNS populates the DNS database. You'll also see how to implement security for Dynamic DNS. I will then talk about the workings of different types of DNS queries. Finally, I will discuss caching and time to live (TTL). You'll learn how to determine the best setting for your organization.

Dynamic DNS and Non-Dynamic DNS

To understand Dynamic DNS and Non-Dynamic DNS, you must go back in time (here is where the TV screen always used to get wavy). Many years ago when we all worked on NT 3.51 and NT 4.0, most networks used Windows Internet Name Service (WINS) to do their TCP/IP name resolution. Windows versions 95/98 and NT 4.0 Professional were all built on the idea of using WINS. This worked out well for administrators because WINS was dynamic (which meant that once it was installed, it automatically built its own database). Back then, there was no such thing as Dynamic DNS; administrators had to enter DNS records into the server manually. This is important to know even today. If you have clients still running any of these older operating systems (95/98 or NT 4), these clients cannot use Dynamic DNS.

Now let's move forward in time to the release of Windows Server 2000. Microsoft announced that DNS was going to be the name resolution method of choice. Many administrators (me included) did not look forward to the switch. Because there was no such thing as Dynamic DNS, most administrators had nightmares about manually entering records. However, luckily for us, when Microsoft released Windows Server 2000, DNS had the ability to operate dynamically. Now when you're setting up Windows Server 2012 R2 DNS, you can choose what type of dynamic update you would like to use, if any. Let's talk about why you would want to choose one over the other.

The *Dynamic DNS (DDNS) standard*, described in RFC 2136, allows DNS clients to update information in the DNS database files. For example, a Windows Server 2012 R2 DHCP server can automatically tell a DDNS server which IP addresses it has assigned to what machines. Windows 2000, 2003, 2008, XP Pro, Vista, Windows 7, and Windows 8 DHCP clients can do this too. For security reasons, however, it's better to let the DHCP server do it. The result: IP addresses and DNS records stay in sync so that you can use DNS and DHCP together seamlessly. Because DDNS is a proposed Internet standard, you can even use the Windows Server 2012 R2 DDNS-aware parts with Unix/Linux-based DNS servers.

Non-Dynamic DNS (NDDNS) does not automatically populate the DNS database. The client systems do not have the ability to update to DNS. If you decide to use Non-Dynamic DNS, an administrator will need to populate the DNS database manually. Non-Dynamic DNS is a reasonable choice if your organization is small-to-midsize and you do not want extra network traffic (clients updating to the DNS server) or if you need to enter the computer's TCP/IP information manually because of strict security measures.

Dynamic DNS has the ability to be secure, and the chances are slim that a rogue system (a computer that does not belong in your DNS database) could update to a secure DNS server. Nevertheless, some organizations have to follow stricter security measures and are not allowed to have dynamic updates.

The major downside to entering records into DNS manually occurs when the organization is using the *Dynamic Host Configuration Protocol (DHCP)*. When using DHCP, it is possible for users to end up with different TCP/IP addresses every day. This means that an administrator has to update DNS manually each day to keep it accurate.

If you choose to allow Dynamic DNS, you need to decide how you want to set it up. When setting up dynamic updates on your DNS server, you have three choices (see Figure 3.3).

FIGURE 3.3 Setting the Dynamic Updates option

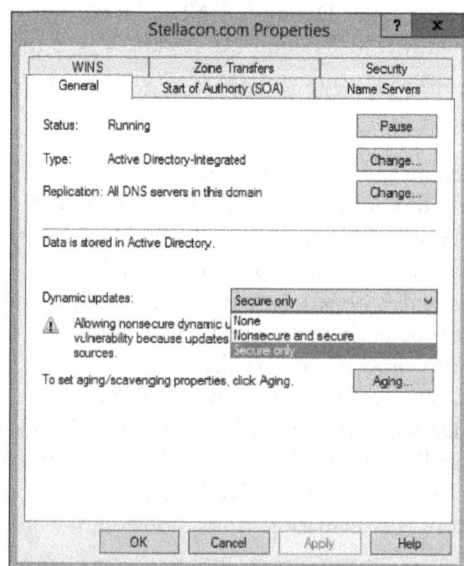

None   This means your DNS server is Non-Dynamic.

Nonsecure and Secure   This means that any machine (even if it does not have a domain account) can register with DNS. Using this setting could allow rogue systems to enter records into your DNS server.

Secure Only   This means that only machines with accounts in Active Directory can register with DNS. Before DNS registers any account in its database, it checks Active Directory to make sure that account is an authorized domain computer.

How Dynamic DNS Populates the DNS Database

TCP/IP is the protocol used for network communications on a Microsoft Windows Server 2012 R2 network. Users have two ways to receive a TCP/IP number:

- Static (administrators manually enter the TCP/IP information)
- Dynamic (using DHCP)

When an administrator sets up TCP/IP, DNS can also be configured.

Once a client gets the address of the DNS server, if that client is allowed to update with DNS, the client sends a registration to DNS or requests DHCP to send the registration. DNS then does one of two things, depending on which Dynamic Updates option is specified:

- Check with Active Directory to see if that computer has an account (Secure Only updates) and, if it does, enter the record into the database.
- Enter the record into its database (nonsecure and secure updates).

What if you have clients that cannot update DNS? Well, there is a solution—DHCP. In the DNS tab of the IPv4 Properties window, check the option labeled "Dynamically update DNS A and PTR records for DHCP clients that do not request updates (for example, clients running Windows NT 4.0)," which is shown in Figure 3.4.

FIGURE 3.4   DHCP settings for DNS

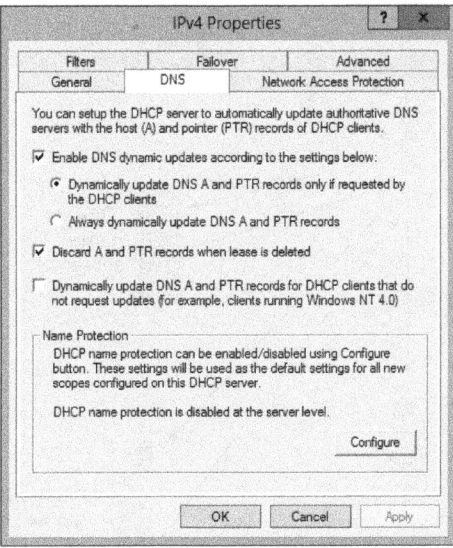

DHCP, along with Dynamic DNS clients, allows an organization to update its DNS database dynamically without the time and effort of having an administrator manually enter DNS records.

DNS Queries

As stated earlier, a client can make three types of queries to a DNS server: recursive, inverse, and iterative. Remember that the client of a DNS server can be a resolver (what you'd normally call a client) or another DNS server.

Iterative Queries

Iterative queries are the easiest to understand: A client asks the DNS server for an answer, and the server returns the best answer. This information likely comes from the server's cache. The server never sends out an additional query in response to an iterative query. If the server doesn't know the answer, it may direct the client to another server through a referral.

Recursive Queries

In a *recursive query*, the client sends a query to a name server, asking it to respond either with the requested answer or with an error message. The error states one of two things:

- The server can't come up with the right answer.
- The domain name doesn't exist.

In a recursive query, the name server isn't allowed to just refer the client to some other name server. Most resolvers use recursive queries. In addition, if your DNS server uses a forwarder, the requests sent by your server to the forwarder will be recursive queries.

Figure 3.5 shows an example of both recursive and iterative queries. In this example, a client within the Microsoft Corporation is querying its DNS server for the IP address for www.whitehouse.gov.

FIGURE 3.5   A sample DNS query

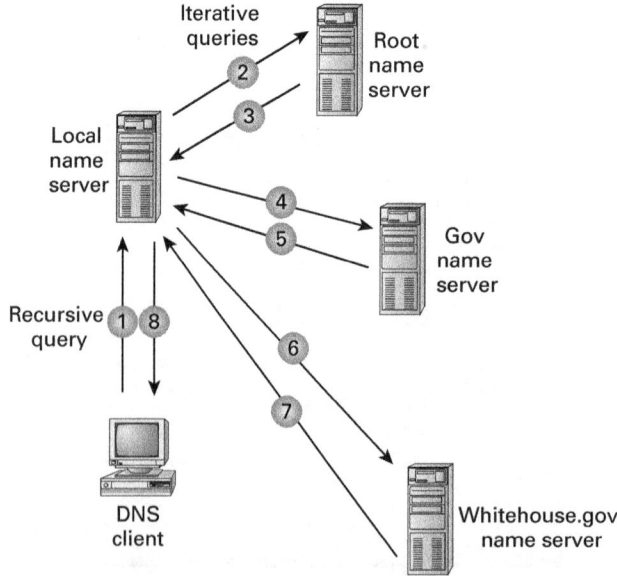

Here's what happens to resolve the request:

1. The resolver sends a recursive DNS query to its local DNS server asking for the IP address of www.whitehouse.gov. The local name server is responsible for resolving the name, and it cannot refer the resolver to another name server.

2. The local name server checks its zones, and it finds no zones corresponding to the requested domain name.

3. The root name server has authority for the root domain and will reply with the IP address of a name server for the .gov top-level domain.

4. The local name server sends an iterative query for www.whitehouse.gov to the Gov name server.

5. The Gov name server replies with the IP address of the name server servicing the whitehouse.gov domain.

6. The local name server sends an iterative query for www.whitehouse.gov to the whitehouse.gov name server.

7. The whitehouse.gov name server replies with the IP address corresponding to www.whitehouse.gov.

8. The local name server sends the IP address of www.whitehouse.gov back to the original resolver.

Inverse Queries

Inverse queries use pointer (PTR) records. Instead of supplying a name and then asking for an IP address, the client first provides the IP address and then asks for the name. Because there's no direct correlation in the DNS namespace between a domain name and its associated IP address, this search would be fruitless without the use of the in-addr.arpa domain. Nodes in the in-addr.arpa domain are named after the numbers in the dotted-octet representation of IP addresses. However, because IP addresses get more specific from left to right and domain names get less specific from left to right, the order of IP address octets must be reversed when building the in-addr.arpa tree. With this arrangement, administration of the lower limbs of the DNS in-addr.arpa tree can be given to companies as they are assigned their Class A, B, or C subnet address or delegated even further down thanks to variable-length subnet masking (VLSM).

Once the domain tree is built into the DNS database, a special PTR record is added to associate the IP addresses with the corresponding hostnames. In other words, to find a hostname for the IP address 206.131.234.1, the resolver would query the DNS server for a PTR record for 1.234.131.206.in-addr.arpa. If this IP address is outside the local domain, the DNS server will start at the root and sequentially resolve the domain nodes until arriving at 234.131.206.in-addr.arpa, which would contain the PTR record for the desired host.

Caching and Time to Live

When a name server is processing a recursive query, it may be required to send out several queries to find the definitive answer. Name servers, acting as resolvers, are allowed to cache all of the received information during this process; each record contains information called *time to live (TTL)*. The TTL specifies how long the record will be held in the local cache until it must be resolved again. If a query comes in that can be satisfied by this cached data, the TTL that's returned with it equals the current amount of time left before the data is flushed.

There is also a negative cache TTL. The *negative cache TTL* is used when an authoritative server responds to a query indicating that the record queried doesn't exist, and it indicates the amount of time that this negative answer may be held. Negative caching is quite helpful in preventing repeated queries for names that don't exist.

The administrator for the DNS zone sets TTL values for the entire zone. The value can be the same across the zone, or the administrator can set a separate TTL for each RR within the zone. Client resolvers also have data caches and honor the TTL value so that they know when to flush.

Choosing Appropriate TTL Values

For zones that you administer, you can choose the TTL values for the entire zone, for negative caching, and for individual records. Choosing an appropriate TTL depends on a number of factors, including the following:

- Amount of change you anticipate for the records within the zone

- Amount of time that you can withstand an outage that might require changing an IP address

- Amount of traffic that you believe the DNS server can handle

Resolvers query the name server every time the TTL expires for a given record. A low TTL, say 60 seconds, can burden the name server, especially for popular DNS records. (DNS queries aren't particularly intensive for a server to handle, but they can add up quickly if you mistakenly use 60 seconds instead of 600 seconds for the TTL on a popular record.) Set a low TTL only when you need to respond quickly to a changing environment.

A high TTL, say 604,800 seconds (that's one week), means that if you need to make a change to the DNS record, clients might not see the change for up to a week. This consideration is especially important when making changes to the network, and it's one that's all too frequently overlooked. I can't count the number of times I've worked with clients who have recently made a DNS change to a new IP for their email or website only to ask why it's not working for some clients. The answer can be found in the TTL value. If the record is being cached, then the only thing that can solve their problem is time.

You should choose a TTL that's appropriate for your environment. Take the following factors into account:

- The amount of time that you can afford to be offline if you need to make a change to a DNS record that's being cached

- The amount of load that a low TTL will cause on the DNS server

In addition, you should plan well ahead of any major infrastructure changes and change the TTL to a lower value to lessen the effect of the downtime by reducing the amount of time that the record(s) can be cached.

Introducing DNS Database Zones

As mentioned earlier in this chapter, a DNS zone is a portion of the DNS namespace over which a specific DNS server has authority. Within a given DNS zone, there are resource records that define the hosts and other types of information that make up the database for the zone. You can choose from several different zone types. Understanding the characteristics of each will help you choose which is right for your organization.

 The DNS zones discussed in this book are all Microsoft Windows Server 2012/2012 R2 zones. Non-Windows (for example, Unix) systems set up their DNS zones differently.

In the following sections, I will discuss the different zone types and their characteristics.

Understanding Primary Zones

When you're learning about zone types, things can get a bit confusing. But it's really not difficult to understand how they work and why you would want to choose one type of zone over another. Zones are databases that store records. By choosing one zone type over another, you are basically just choosing how the database works and how it will be stored on the server.

The primary zone is responsible for maintaining all of the records for the DNS zone. It contains the primary copy of the DNS database. All record updates occur on the primary zone. You will want to create and add primary zones whenever you create a new DNS domain.

There are two types of primary zones:

- Primary zone

- Primary zone with Active Directory Integration (Active Directory DNS)

From this point forward, I refer to a primary zone with Active Directory Integration as an *Active Directory DNS*. When I use only the term *primary zone*, Active Directory is not included.

To install DNS as a primary zone, first you must install DNS using the Server Manager MMC. Once DNS is installed and running, you create a new zone and specify it as a primary zone.

The process of installing DNS and its zones will be discussed later in this chapter. In addition, there will be step-by-step exercises to walk you through how to install these components.

Primary zones have advantages and disadvantages. Knowing the characteristics of a primary zone will help you decide when you need the zone and when it fits into your organization.

Local Database

Primary DNS zones get stored locally in a file (with the suffix .dns) on the server. This allows you to store a primary zone on a domain controller or a member server. In addition, by loading DNS onto a member server, you can help a small organization conserve resources. Such an organization may not have the resources to load DNS on an Active Directory domain controller.

Unfortunately, the local database has many disadvantages:

Lack of Fault Tolerance   Think of a primary zone as a contact list on your smartphone. All of the contacts in the list are the records in your database. The problem is that if you lose your phone or the phone breaks, you lose your contact list. Until your phone gets fixed or you swap out your phone card, the contacts are unavailable.

It works the same way with a primary zone. If the server goes down or you lose the hard drive, DNS records on that machine are unreachable. An administrator can install a secondary zone (explained later in the next section), and that provides temporary fault tolerance. Unfortunately, if the primary zone is down for an extended period of time, the secondary server's information will no longer be valid.

Additional Network Traffic   Let's imagine that you are looking for a contact number for John Smith. John Smith is not listed in your cell phone directory, but he is listed in your partner's cell phone. You have to contact your partner to get the listing. You cannot directly access your partner's cell contacts.

When a resolver sends a request to DNS to get the TCP/IP address for Jsmith (in this case Jsmith is a computer name) and the DNS server does not have an answer, it does not have the ability to check the other server's database directly to get an answer. Thus, it forwards the request to another DNS. When DNS servers are replicating zone databases with other DNS servers, this causes additional network traffic.

No Security Staying with the cell phone example, let's say that you call your partner looking for John Smith's phone number. When your partner gives you the phone number over your wireless phone, someone with a scanner can pick up your conversation. Unfortunately, wireless telephone calls are not very secure.

Now a resolver asks a primary zone for the Jsmith TCP/IP address. If someone on the network has a packet sniffer, they can steal the information in the DNS packets being sent over the network. The packets are not secure unless you implement some form of secondary security. Also, the DNS server has the ability to be dynamic. A primary zone accepts all updates from DNS servers. You cannot set it to accept secure updates only.

Understanding Secondary Zones

In Windows Server 2012 R2 DNS, you have the ability to use secondary DNS zones. Secondary zones are noneditable copies of the DNS database. You use them for *load balancing* (also referred to as *load sharing*), which is a way of managing network overloads on a single server. A secondary zone gets its database from a primary zone.

A *secondary zone* contains a database with all of the same information as the primary zone, and it can be used to resolve DNS requests. Secondary zones have the following advantages:

- A secondary zone provides fault tolerance, so if the primary zone server becomes unavailable, name resolution can still occur using the secondary zone server.

- Secondary DNS servers can also increase network performance by offloading some of the traffic that would otherwise go to the primary server.

Secondary servers are often placed within the parts of an organization that have high-speed network access. This prevents DNS queries from having to run across slow wide area network (WAN) connections. For example, if there are two remote offices within the stellacon.com organization, you may want to place a secondary DNS server in each remote office. This way, when clients require name resolution, they will contact the nearest server for this IP address information, thus preventing unnecessary WAN traffic.

> **NOTE** Having too many secondary zone servers can actually cause an increase in network traffic because of replication (especially if DNS changes are fairly frequent). Therefore, you should always weigh the benefits and drawbacks and properly plan for secondary zone servers.

Configure Zone Delegation

One advantage of DNS is the ability of turning a namespace into one or more zones. These zones can be replicated to each other or other DNS servers. As an administrator, you must decide when you want to break your DNS into multiple zones. When considering this option, there are a few things to think about:

- You want the management of your DNS namespace to be delegated by another location or department in your organization.

- You want to load-balance your traffic among multiple servers by turning a large zone into many smaller zones. This will help improve performance and create redundancy among your DNS servers.

- You have remote offices opening up, and you want to expand your DNS namespace.

To create a new zone delegation, you would complete the following steps:

1. Open the DNS console.

2. In the console tree, right-click the applicable subdomain and then click New Delegation.

3. Follow the instructions provided in the New Delegation Wizard to finish creating the newly delegated domain.

Understanding Active Directory Integrated DNS

Windows Server 2000 introduced *Active Directory Integrated DNS* to the world. This zone type was unique, and it was a separate choice during setup. In Windows Server 2003, this zone type became an add-on to a primary zone. In Windows Server 2012 R2, it works the same way. After choosing to set up a primary zone, you check the box Store The Zone In Active Directory (see Figure 3.6).

FIGURE 3.6   Setting up an Active Directory Integrated zone

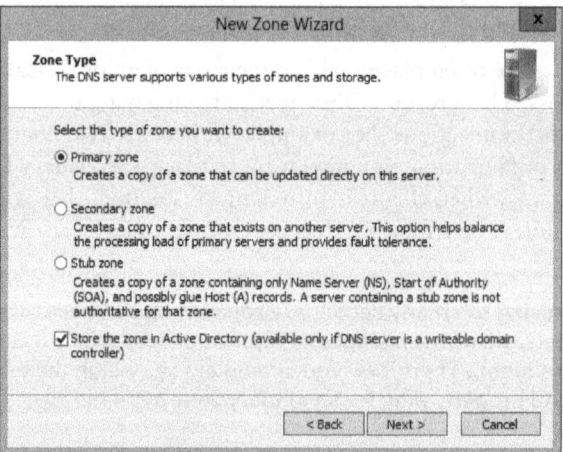

Disadvantages of Active Directory Integrated DNS

The main disadvantage of Active Directory Integrated DNS is that it has to reside on a domain controller because the DNS database is stored in Active Directory. As a result, you cannot load this zone type on a member server, and small organizations might not have the resources to set up a dedicated domain controller.

Advantages of Active Directory Integrated DNS

The advantages of using an Active Directory Integrated DNS zone well outweigh the disadvantages just discussed. The following are some of the major advantages to an Active Directory Integrated zone:

Full Fault Tolerance   Think of an Active Directory Integrated zone as a database on your server that stores contact information for all your clients. If you need to retrieve John Smith's phone number, as long as it was entered, you can look it up on the software.

If John Smith's phone number was stored only on your computer and your computer stopped working, no one could access John Smith's phone number. But since John Smith's phone number is stored in a database to which everyone has access, if your computer stops working, other users can still retrieve John Smith's phone number.

An Active Directory Integrated zone works the same way. Since the DNS database is stored in Active Directory, all Active Directory DNS servers can have access to the same data. If one server goes down or you lose a hard drive, all other Active Directory DNS servers can still retrieve DNS records.

No Additional Network Traffic   As previously discussed, an Active Directory Integrated zone is stored in Active Directory. Since all records are now stored in Active Directory, when a resolver needs a TCP/IP address for Jsmith, any Active Directory DNS server can access Jsmith's address and respond to the resolver.

When you choose an Active Directory Integrated zone, DNS zone data can be replicated automatically to other DNS servers during the normal Active Directory replication process.

DNS Security   An Active Directory Integrated zone has a few security advantages over a primary zone:

- An Active Directory Integrated zone can use secure dynamic updates.
- As explained earlier, the Dynamic DNS standard allows secure-only updates or dynamic updates, not both.
- If you choose secure updates, then only machines with accounts in Active Directory can register with DNS. Before DNS registers any account in its database, it checks Active Directory to make sure that it is an authorized domain computer.
- An Active Directory Integrated zone stores and replicates its database through Active Directory replication. Because of this, the data gets encrypted as it is sent from one DNS server to another.

Background Zone Loading   Background zone loading (discussed in more detail later in this chapter) allows an Active Directory Integrated DNS zone to load in the background. As a result, a DNS server can service client requests while the zone is still loading into memory.

Understanding Stub Zones

Stub zones work a lot like secondary zones—the database is a noneditable copy of a primary zone. The difference is that the stub zone's database contains only the information necessary (three record types) to identify the authoritative DNS servers for a zone (see Figure 3.7). You should not use stub zones to replace secondary zones, nor should you use them for redundancy and load balancing.

FIGURE 3.7   DNS stub zone type

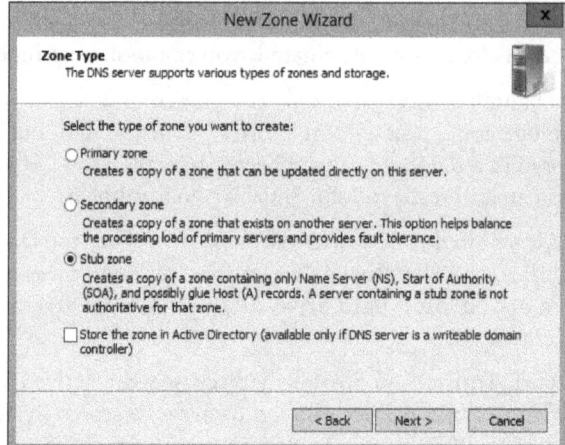

Stub zone databases contain only three record types: name server (NS), start of authority (SOA), and glue host (A) records. Understanding these records will help you on the Microsoft certification exams. Microsoft asks many questions about stub zones on all DNS-related exams.

When to Use Stub Zones

Stub zones become particularly useful in a couple of different scenarios. Consider what happens when two large companies merge: example.com and example.net. In most cases, the DNS zone information from both companies must be available to every employee. You could set up a new zone on each side that acts as a secondary for the other side's primary zone, but administrators tend to be very protective of their DNS databases and probably wouldn't agree to this plan.

A better solution is to add to each side a stub zone that points to the primary server on the other side. When a client in example.com (which you help administer) makes a request for a name in example.net, the stub zone on the example.com DNS server would send the client to the primary DNS server for example.net without actually resolving the name. At this point, it would be up to example.net's primary server to resolve the name.

An added benefit is that, even if the administrators over at example.net change their configuration, you won't have to do anything because the changes will automatically replicate to the stub zone, just as they would for a secondary server.

Stub zones can also be useful when you administer two domains across a slow connection. Let's change the previous example a bit and assume that you have full control over example.com and example.net but they connect through a 56Kbps line. In this case, you wouldn't necessarily mind using secondary zones because you personally administer the entire network. However, it could get messy to replicate an entire zone file across that slow line. Instead, stub zones would refer clients to the appropriate primary server at the other site.

GlobalName Zones

Earlier in this chapter, I talked about organizations using WINS to resolve NetBIOS names (also referred to as *computer names*) to TCP/IP addresses. Even today, many organizations still use WINS along with DNS for name resolution. Unfortunately, WINS is slowly becoming obsolete.

To help organizations move forward with an all-DNS network, Microsoft Windows Server 2012 R2 DNS supports *GlobalName zones*. These use single-label names (DNS names that do not contain a suffix such as .com, .net, and so on). GlobalName zones are not intended to support peer-to-peer networks and workstation name resolution, and they don't support dynamic DNS updates.

GlobalName zones are designed to be used with servers. Because GlobalName zones are not dynamic, an administrator has to enter the records into the zone database manually. In most organizations, the servers have static TCP/IP addresses, and this works well with the GlobalName zone design. GlobalName zones are usually used to map single-label CNAME (alias) resource records to an FQDN.

Zone Transfers and Replication

DNS is such an important part of the network that you should not just use a single DNS server. With a single DNS server, you also have a single point of failure and, in fact, many domain registrars encourage the use of more than two name servers for a domain. Secondary servers or multiple primary Active Directory Integrated servers play an integral role in providing DNS information for an entire domain.

As previously stated, secondary DNS servers receive their zone databases through zone transfers. When you configure a secondary server for the first time, you must specify the primary server that is authoritative for the zone and will send the zone transfer. The primary server must also permit the secondary server to request the zone transfer.

Zone transfers occur in one of two ways: *full zone transfers (AXFR)* and *incremental zone transfers (IXFR)*.

When a new secondary server is configured for the first time, it receives a full zone transfer from the primary DNS server. The full zone transfer contains all of the information in the DNS database. Some DNS implementations always receive full zone transfers.

After the secondary server receives its first full zone transfer, subsequent zone transfers are incremental. The primary name server compares its zone version number with that of the secondary server, and it sends only the changes that have been made in the interim. This significantly reduces network traffic generated by zone transfers.

The secondary server typically initiates zone transfers when the refresh interval time for the zone expires or when the secondary or stub server boots. Alternatively, you can configure notify lists on the primary server that send a message to the secondary or stub servers whenever any changes to the zone database occur.

When you consider your DNS strategy, you must carefully consider the layout of your network. If you have a single domain with offices in separate cities, you want to reduce the number of zone transfers across the potentially slow or expensive WAN links, although this is becoming less of a concern because of continuous increases in bandwidth.

Active Directory Integrated zones do away with traditional zone transfers altogether. Instead, they replicate across Active Directory with all of the other AD information. This replication is secure and encrypted because it uses the Active Directory security.

How DNS Notify Works

Windows Server 2012 R2 supports DNS Notify. *DNS Notify* is a mechanism that allows the process of initiating notifications to secondary servers when zone changes occur (RFC 1996). DNS Notify uses a push mechanism for communicating to a select set of secondary zone servers when their zone information is updated. (DNS Notify does not allow you to configure a notify list for a stub zone.)

After being notified of the changes, secondary servers can then start a pull zone transfer and update their local copies of the database.

Many different mechanisms use the push/pull relationship. Normally, one object pushes information to another, and the second object pulls the information from the first. Most applications push replication on a change value and pull it on a time value. For example, a system can push replication after 10 updates, or it can be pulled every 30 minutes.

To configure the DNS Notify process, you create a list of secondary servers to notify. List the IP address of the server in the primary master's Notify dialog box (see Figure 3.8). The Notify dialog box is located under the Zone Transfers tab, which is located in the zone Properties dialog box (see Figure 3.9).

FIGURE 3.8   DNS Notify dialog box

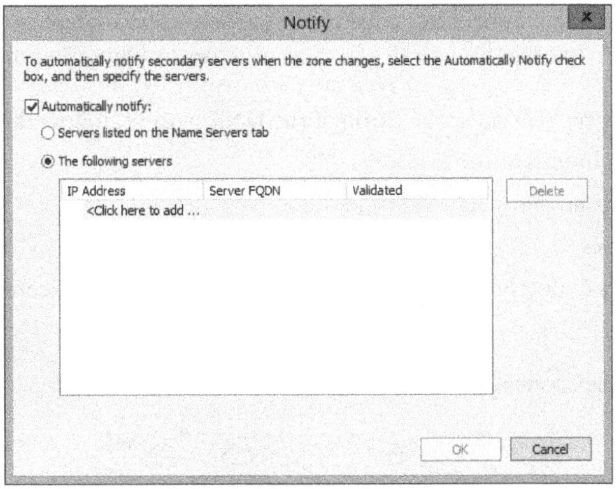

FIGURE 3.9   DNS Zone Transfers tab

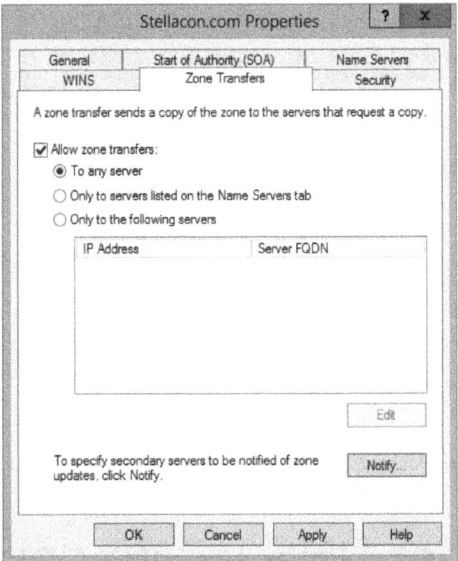

Configuring Stub Zone Transfers with Zone Replication

In the preceding section, I talked about how to configure secondary server zone transfers. What if you wanted to configure settings for stub zone transfers? This is where zone replication scope comes in.

Only Active Directory–integrated primary and stub zones can configure their replication scope. Secondary servers do not have this ability.

You can configure zone replication scope configurations in two ways. An administrator can set configuration options through the DNS snap-in or through a command-line tool called DNSCmd.

To configure zone replication scope through the DNS snap-in, follow these steps:

1. Click Start ➢ Administrative Tools ➢ DNS.

2. Right-click the zone that you want to set up.

3. Choose Properties.

4. In the Properties dialog box, click the Change button next to Replication (see Figure 3.10).

FIGURE 3.10   DNS zone replication scope

5. Choose the replication scope that fits your organization.

Advantages of DNS in Windows Server 2012 R2

DNS in Microsoft Windows Server 2012 R2 has some great advantages over many other versions of Microsoft DNS. Here are some of the improvements of DNS in Windows Server 2012 R2 (some of these became available in Windows Server 2008):

- Background zone loading
- Support for TCP/IP version 6 (IPv6)
- Read-only domain controllers
- GlobalName zone
- DNS socket pools
- DNS cache locking
- DNS Security Extensions (DNSSEC)
- DNS devolution
- Record weighting
- Netmask ordering
- DnsUpdateProxy group

Background Zone Loading

If an organization had to restart a DNS server with an extremely large Active Directory Integrated DNS zones database in the past, DNS had a common problem with an Active Directory Integrated DNS zone. After the DNS restart, it could take hours for DNS data to be retrieved from Active Directory. During this time, the DNS server was unable to service any client requests.

Microsoft Windows Server 2008 DNS addressed this problem by implementing background zone loading, and Windows Server 2012 R2 has taken it a step further. As the DNS restarts, the Active Directory zone data populates the database in the background. This allows the DNS server to service client requests for data from other zones almost immediately after a restart.

Background zone loading accomplishes this task by loading the DNS zone using separate threads. This allows a DNS server to service requests while still loading the rest of the zone. If a client sends a request to the DNS server for a computer that has not yet loaded into memory, the DNS server retrieves the data from Active Directory and updates the record.

Support for IPv6 Addresses

Over the past few years, the Internet has starting running into a problem that was not foreseen when it was first created—it started running out of TCP/IP addresses. As you probably know, when the Internet was created, it was used for government and academic purposes only. Then, seemingly overnight, it grew to be the information superhighway. Nowadays, asking someone for their email address is almost more common as asking for their phone number.

Version 4 (IPv4) was the common version of TCP/IP. The release of TCP/IP version 6 (IPv6) has solved the lack-of-IP-addresses problem. IPv4 addresses are 32 bits long, but IPv6 addresses are 128 bits in length. The longer lengths allow for a much greater number of globally unique TCP/IP addresses.

Microsoft Windows Server 2012 R2 DNS has built-in support to accommodate both IPv4 and IPv6 address records (DNS records are explained later in this chapter). DHCP can also issue IPv6 addresses, which lets administrators allow DHCP to register the client with DNS, or the IPv6 client can register their address with the DNS server.

Support for Read-Only Domain Controllers

Windows Server 2008 introduced a new type of domain controller called the *read-only domain controller (RODC)*. This is a full copy of the Active Directory database without the ability to write to Active Directory. The RODC gives an organization the ability to install a domain controller in a location (onsite or offsite) where security is a concern.

Microsoft Windows Server 2012 R2 DNS has implemented a type of zone to help support an RODC. A primary read-only zone allows a DNS server to receive a copy of the application partition (including ForestDNSZones and DomainDNSZones) that DNS uses. This allows DNS to support an RODC because DNS now has a full copy of all DNS zones stored in Active Directory.

A primary, read-only zone is just what it says—a read-only zone; so to make any changes to it, you have to change the primary zones located on the Active Directory Integrated DNS server.

DNS Socket Pools

If your server is running Windows Server 2012 R2, you will be able to take advantage of DNS socket pools. *DNS socket pools* allow source port randomization to protect against DNS cache-poisoning attacks.

If you choose to use source port randomization, when the DNS service starts, the DNS server will randomly pick a source port from a pool of available sockets. This is an advantage because instead of DNS using a well-known source port when issuing queries, the DNS server uses a random port selected from the socket pool. This helps guard against attacks because a hacker must correctly access the source port of the DNS query. The socket pool is automatically enabled in DNS with the default settings.

When using the DNS socket pool, the default size of the DNS socket pool is 2,500. When configuring the socket pool, you have the ability to choose a size value from 0 to 10,000. The larger the value, the greater the protection you will have against DNS spoofing attacks. If you decide to configure your socket pool size with a zero value, only a single socket for remote DNS queries will be used.

DNS Cache Locking

Windows Server 2012 R2 *DNS cache locking* allows cached DNS records to remain safe for the duration of the record's time to live (TTL) value. This means that the cached DNS records cannot be overwritten or changed. Because of this new DNS feature, it's tougher for hackers to perform cache-poisoning attacks against your DNS server.

DNS administrators can set how long a record will remain safe in cache. The configuration is based on a percent value. For example, if you set your cache locking value to 50 percent, then the cached records cannot be overwritten until half of the TTL has been reached. DNS cache locking is set to 100 percent by default. This means that the cached records never get overwritten.

DNS Security Extensions

One major issue that you must always look at is keeping your DNS safe. Think about it: DNS is a database of computer names and IP addresses. As a hacker, if I control DNS, I can control your company. In organizations that do not support extra security like IPsec, DNS security is even more important. This is where *Domain Name System Security Extensions (DNSSEC)* can help.

Windows Server 2012 R2 can use a suite of extensions that will help add security to DNS, and that suite is called DNSSEC, which was introduced in Windows Server 2008 R2. The DNSSEC protocol allows your DNS servers to be secure by validating DNS responses. DNSSEC secures your DNS resource records by accompanying the records with a digital signature.

To allow your DNS resource records to receive digital signatures, DNSSEC is applied to your DNS server by a procedure called *zone signing*. This process begins when a DNS resolver initiates a DNS query for a resource record in a signed DNS zone. When a response is returned, a digital signature (RRSIG) accompanies the response, and this allows the response to be verified. If the verification is successful, then the DNS resolver knows that the data has not been modified or tampered with in any way.

Once you implement a zone with DNSSEC, all of the records that are contained within that zone get individually signed. Since all of the records in the zone get individually signed, this gives administrators the ability to add, modify, or delete records without re-signing the entire zone. The only requirement is to re-sign any updated records.

Trust Anchors

Trust anchors are an important part of the DNSSEC process because trust anchors allow the DNS servers to validate the DNSKEY resource records. *Trust anchors* are preconfigured public keys that are linked to a DNS zone. For a DNS server to perform validation, one or more trust anchors must be configured. If you are running an Active Directory Integrated zone, trust anchors can be stored in the Active Directory Domain Services directory partition of the forest. If you decide to store the trust anchors in the directory partition, then all DNS servers that reside on a domain controller get a copy of this trust anchor. On DNS servers that reside on stand-alone servers, trust anchors are stored in a file called TrustAnchors.dns.

If your servers are running Windows Server 2012 R2, then you can view trust anchors in the DNS Manager Console tree in the Trust Points container. You can also use Windows PowerShell or Dnscmd.exe to view trust anchors. Windows PowerShell is the recommended command-line method for viewing trust anchors. The following line is a PowerShell command to view the trust anchors for Contoso.com:

```
get-dnsservertrustanchor sec.contoso.com
```

DNSSEC Clients

Windows 7, Windows 8, Windows Server 2008/2008 R2, and Windows Server 2012/2012 R2 are all DNS clients that receive a response to a DNS query, examine the response, and then evaluate whether the response has been validated by a DNS server. The DNS client itself is nonvalidating, and the DNS client relies on the local DNS server to indicate that validation was successful. If the server doesn't perform validation, then the DNS client service can be configured to return no results.

DNS Devolution

Using *DNS devolution*, if a client computer is a member of a child namespace, the client computer will be able to access resources in the parent namespace without the need to explicitly provide the fully qualified domain name of the resource. DNS devolution removes the leftmost label of the namespace to get to the parent suffix. DNS devolution allows the DNS resolver to create the new FQDNs. DNS devolution works by appending the single-label, unqualified domain name with the parent suffix of the primary DNS suffix name.

Record Weighting

Weighting DNS records will allow an administrator to place a value on DNS SRV records. Clients will then randomly choose SRV records proportional to the weight value assigned.

Netmask Ordering

If round robin is enabled, when a client requests name resolution, the first address entered in the database is returned to the resolver, and it is then sent to the end of the list. The next time a client attempts to resolve the name, the DNS server returns the second name in the database (which is now the first name) and then sends it to the end of the list, and so on. Round robin is enabled by default.

Netmask ordering is a part of the round robin process. When an administrator configures netmask ordering, the DNS server will detect the subnet of the querying client. The DNS server will then return a host address available for the same subnet. Netmask ordering is enabled through the DNS Manager console on the Advanced tab of the server Properties dialog box.

DnsUpdateProxy Group

As mentioned previously, the DHCP server can be configured to register host (A) and pointer (PTR) resource records dynamically on behalf of DHCP clients. Because of this, the DNS server can end up with stale resources. To help solve this issue, an administrator can use the built-in security group called *DnsUpdateProxy*.

To use the DnsUpdateProxy group, an administrator must first create a dedicated user account and configure the DHCP servers with its credentials. This will protect against the creation of unsecured records. Also, when you create the dedicated user account, members of the DnsUpdateProxy group will be able to register records in zones that allow only secured dynamic updates. Multiple DHCP servers can use the same credentials of one dedicated user account.

Now that you have learned about some of the new features of Windows Server 2012 R2 DNS, let's take a look at some of the DNS record types.

Introducing DNS Record Types

No matter where your zone information is stored, you can rest assured that it contains a variety of DNS information. Although the DNS snap-in makes it unlikely that you'll ever need to edit these files by hand, it's good to know exactly what data is contained there.

As stated previously, zone files consist of a number of resource records. You need to know about several types of resource records to manage your DNS servers effectively. They are discussed in the following sections.

Part of the resource record is its class. *Classes* define the type of network for the resource record. There are three classes: Internet, Chaosnet, and Hesoid. By far, the Internet class is the most popular. In fact, it's doubtful that you'll see either Chaosnet or Hesoid classes in the wild.

> The following are some of the more important resource records in a DNS database. For a complete listing of records in a Microsoft DNS database, visit Microsoft's website at http://technet.microsoft.com/en-us/library/cc758321(v=WS.10).aspx.

Start of Authority (SOA) Records

The first record in a database file is the *start of authority (SOA) record*. The SOA defines the general parameters for the DNS zone, including the identity of the authoritative server for the zone.

The SOA appears in the following format:

```
@ IN SOA primary_mastercontact_e-mailserial_number
refresh_timeretry_timeexpiration_timetime_to_live
```

Here is a sample SOA from the domain example.com:

```
@ IN SOA win2k3r2.example.com. hostmaster.example.com. (
                    5               ; serial number
                    900             ; refresh
                    600             ; retry
                    86400           ; expire
                    3600        )   ; default TTL
```

Table 3.2 lists the attributes stored in the SOA record.

TABLE 3.2   The SOA record structure

Field	Meaning
Current zone	The current zone for the SOA. This can be represented by an @ symbol to indicate the current zone or by naming the zone itself. In the example, the current zone is example.com. The trailing dot (.com.) indicates the zone's place relative to the root of the DNS.
Class	This will almost always be the letters *IN* for the Internet class.
Type of record	The type of record follows. In this case, it's SOA.
Primary master	The primary master for the zone on which this file is maintained.
Contact email	The Internet email address for the person responsible for this domain's database file. There is no @ symbol in this contact email address because @ is a special character in zone files. The contact email address is separated by a single dot (.). So, the email address of root@example.com would be represented by root.example.com in a zone file.
Serial number	This is the "version number" of this database file. It increases each time the database file is changed.
Refresh time	The amount of time (in seconds) that a secondary server will wait between checks to its master server to see whether the database file has changed and a zone transfer should be requested.
Retry time	The amount of time (in seconds) that a secondary server will wait before retrying a failed zone transfer.
Expiration time	The amount of time (in seconds) that a secondary server will spend trying to download a zone. Once this time limit expires, the old zone information will be discarded.
Time to live	The amount of time (in seconds) that another DNS server is allowed to cache any resource records from this database file. This is the value that is sent out with all query responses from this zone file when the individual resource record doesn't contain an overriding value.

Name Server Records

Name server (NS) records list the name servers for a domain. This record allows other name servers to look up names in your domain. A zone file may contain more than one name server record. The format of these records is simple:

```
example.com.    IN    NS      Hostname.example.com
```

Table 3.3 explains the attributes stored in the NS record.

TABLE 3.3 The NS record structure

Field	Meaning
Name	The domain that will be serviced by this name server. In this case I used `example.com`.
AddressClass	Internet (IN)
RecordType	Name server (NS)
Name Server Name	The FQDN of the server responsible for the domain

Any domain name in the database file that is not terminated with a period will have the root domain appended to the end. For example, an entry that just has the name *sales* will be expanded by adding the root domain to the end, whereas the entry `sales.example.com.` won't be expanded.

Host Record

A *host record* (also called an *A record* for IPv4 and *AAAA record* for IPv6) is used to associate statically a host's name to its IP addresses. The format is pretty simple:

```
host_nameoptional_TTL IN  A  IP_Address
```

Here's an example from my DNS database:

```
www   IN  A  192.168.0.204
SMTP IN  A  192.168.3.144
```

The A or AAAA record ties a hostname (which is part of an FQDN) to a specific IP address. This makes these records suitable for use when you have devices with statically assigned IP addresses. In this case, you create these records manually using the DNS snap-in. As it turns out, if you enable DDNS, your DHCP server can create these for you. This automatic creation is what enables DDNS to work.

Notice that an optional TTL field is available for each resource record in the DNS. This value is used to set a TTL that is different from the default TTL for the domain. For example, if you wanted a 60-second TTL for the www A or AAAA record, it would look like this:

```
www 60 IN  A  192.168.0.204
```

Alias Record

Closely related to the host record is the *alias record*, or *canonical name (CNAME) record*. The syntax of an alias record is as follows:

alias *optional_TTL*   IN   CNAME   *hostname*

Aliases are used to point more than one DNS record toward a host for which an A record already exists. For example, if the hostname of your web server was actually chaos, you would likely have an A record such as this:

```
chaos IN A 192.168.1.10
```

Then you could make an alias or CNAME for the record so that www.example.com would point to chaos:

```
www IN CNAME chaos.example.com.
```

Note the trailing dot (.) on the end of the CNAME record. This means the root domain is not appended to the entry.

Pointer Record

A or AAAA records are probably the most visible component of the DNS database because Internet users depend on them to turn FQDNs like www.microsoft.com into the IP addresses that browsers and other components require to find Internet resources. However, the host record has a lesser-known but still important twin: the *pointer (PTR) record*. The format of a PTR record appears as follows:

```
reversed_address.in-addr.arpa. optional_TTL IN PTR targeted_domain_name
```

The A or AAAA record maps a hostname to an IP address, and the PTR record does just the opposite—mapping an IP address to a hostname through the use of the in-addr.arpa zone.

The PTR record is necessary because IP addresses begin with the least-specific portion first (the network) and end with the most-specific portion (the host), whereas hostnames begin with the most-specific portion at the beginning and the least-specific portion at the end.

Consider the example 192.168.1.10 with a subnet mask 255.255.255.0. The portion 192.168.1 defines the network and the final .10 defines the host, or the most-specific portion of the address. DNS is just the opposite: The hostname www.example.com. defines the most-specific portion, www, at the beginning and then traverses the DNS tree to the least-specific part, the dot (.), at the root of the tree.

Reverse DNS records, therefore, need to be represented in this most-specific-to-least-specific manner. The PTR record for mapping 192.168.1.10 to www.example.com would look like this:

```
10.1.168.192.in-addr.arpa. IN PTR www.example.com.
```

Now a DNS query for that record can follow the logical DNS hierarchy from the root of the DNS tree all the way to the most-specific portion.

Mail Exchanger Record

The *mail exchanger (MX) record* is used to specify which servers accept mail for this domain. Each MX record contains two parameters—a preference and a mail server, as shown in the following example:

```
domain IN MX preference mailserver_host
```

The MX record uses the preference value to specify which server should be used if more than one MX record is present. The preference value is a number. The lower the number, the more preferred the server. Here's an example:

```
example.com.    IN  MX  0  mail.example.com.
example.com.    IN  MX  10 backupmail.example.com.
```

In the example, `mail.example.com` is the default mail server for the domain. If that server goes down for any reason, the `backupmail.example.com` mail server is used by emailers.

Service Record

Windows Server 2012 R2 depends on some other services, like the Lightweight Directory Access Protocol (LDAP) and Kerberos. Using a service record, which is another type of DNS record, a Windows 2000, XP, Vista, Windows 7, or Windows 8 client can query DNS servers for the location of a domain controller. This makes it much easier (for both the client and the administrator) to manage and distribute logon traffic in large-scale networks. For this approach to work, Microsoft has to have some way to register the presence of a service in DNS. Enter the service (SRV) record.

Service (SRV) records tie together the location of a service (like a domain controller) with information about how to contact the service. SRV records provide seven items of information. Let's review an example to help clarify this powerful concept. (Table 3.4 explains the fields in the following example.)

```
ldap.tcp.example.com.  86400 IN SRV  10  100  389  hsv.example.com
ldap.tcp.example.com.  86400 IN SRV  20  100  389  msy.example.com
```

TABLE 3.4   The SRV record structure

Field	Meaning
Domain name	Domain for which this record is valid (`ldap.tcp.example.com.`).
TTL	Time to live (86,400 seconds).
Class	This field is always IN, which stands for Internet.
Record type	Type of record (SRV).
Priority	Specifies a preference, similar to the Preference field in an MX record. The SRV record with the lowest priority is used first (`10`).
Weight	Service records with equal priority are chosen according to their weight (`100`).
Port number	The port where the server is listening for this service (`389`).
Target	The FQDN of the host computer (`hsv.example.com` and `msy.example.com`).

You can define other types of service records. If your applications support them, they can query DNS to find the services they need.

Configuring DNS

In the following sections, you'll begin to learn about the actual DNS server. You will start by installing DNS. Then I will talk about different zone configuration options and what they mean. Finally, you'll complete an exercise that covers configuring Dynamic DNS, delegating zones, and manually entering records.

Installing DNS

Installing DNS is an important part of running a network. Exercise 3.1 walks you through the installation of a DNS server.

 If you are using a Dynamic TCP/IP address, please change your TCP/IP number to static.

EXERCISE 3.1

 Installing and Configuring the DNS Service

1. Open Server Manager.

2. On the Server Manager dashboard, click the Add Roles And Features link.

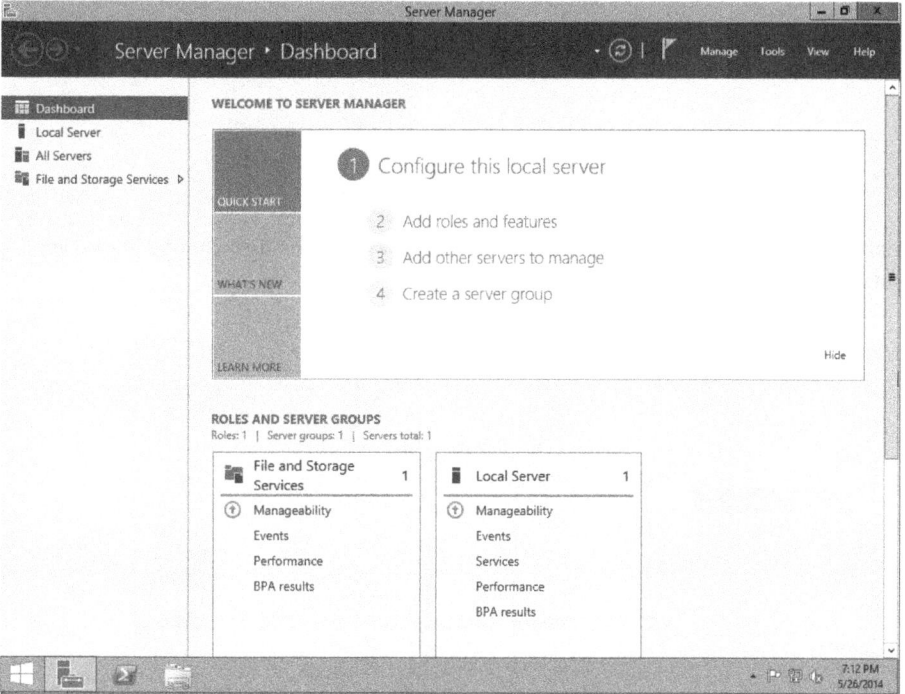

3. If a Before You Begin screen appears, click Next.

4. On the Selection type page, choose Role-Based Or Feature-Based Installation and click Next.

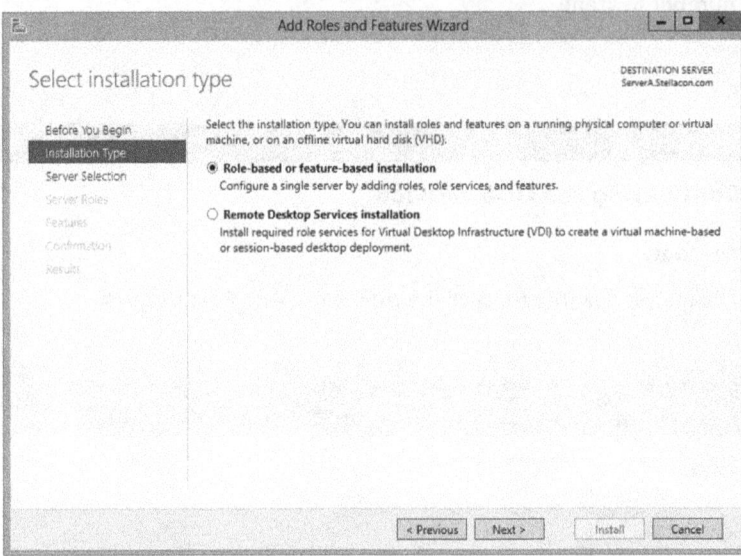

5. Click the Select A Server From The Server Pool radio button and choose the server under the Server Pool section. Click Next.

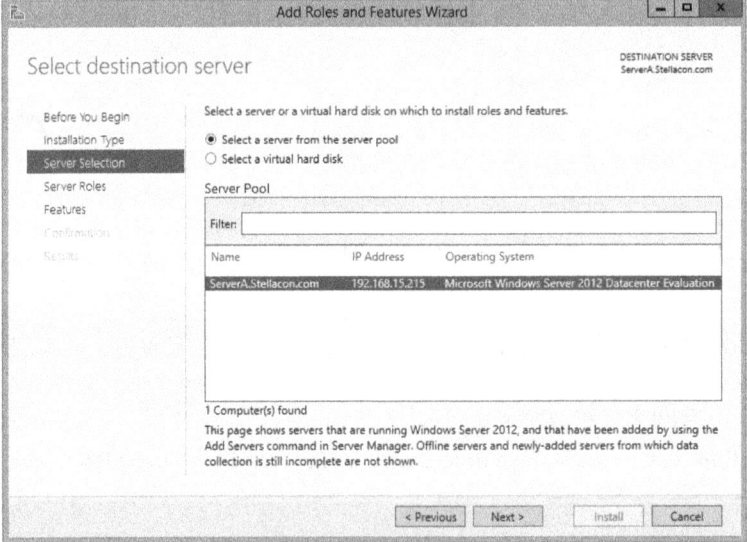

6. Click the DNS Server Item in the Server Role list. If a pop-up window appears telling you that you need to add additional features, click the Add Features button. Click Next to continue.

7. On the Add Features page, just click Next.

8. Click Next on the DNS Server information screen.

9. On the Confirm Installation screen, choose the Restart The Destination Server Automatically If Required check box and then click the Install button.

10. At the Installation progress screen, click Close after the DNS server is installed.

11. Close Server Manager.

Load Balancing with Round Robin

Like other DNS implementations, the Windows Server 2012 R2 implementation of DNS supports load balancing through the use of round robin. Load balancing distributes the network load among multiple network hosts if they are available. You set up round-robin load balancing by creating multiple resource records with the same hostname but different IP addresses for multiple computers. Depending on the options that you select, the DNS server responds with the addresses of one of the host computers.

If round robin is enabled, when a client requests name resolution, the first address entered in the database is returned to the resolver and is then sent to the end of the list. The next time a client attempts to resolve the name, the DNS server returns the second name in the database (which is now the first name) and then sends it to the end of the list, and so on. Round robin is enabled by default.

Configuring a Caching-Only Server

Although all DNS name servers cache queries that they have resolved, caching-only servers are DNS name servers that only perform queries, cache the answers, and return the results. They are not authoritative for any domains, and the information that they contain is limited to what has been cached while resolving queries. Accordingly, they don't have any zone files, and they don't participate in zone transfers. When a caching-only server is first started, it has no information in its cache; the cache is gradually built over time.

Caching-only servers are easy to configure. After installing the DNS service, simply make sure the root hints are configured properly.

1. Right-click your DNS server and choose the Properties command.

2. When the Properties dialog box appears, switch to the Root Hints tab (see Figure 3.11).

3. If your server is connected to the Internet, you should see a list of root hints for the root servers maintained by ICANN and the Internet Assigned Numbers Authority (IANA). If not, click the Add button to add root hints as defined in the cache.dns file.

FIGURE 3.11   The Root Hints tab of the DNS server's Properties dialog box

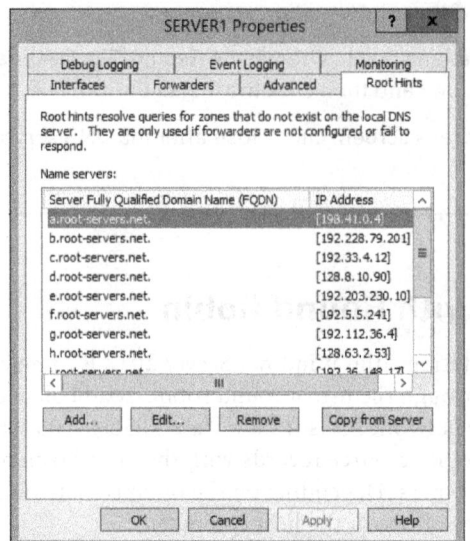

You can obtain current cache·dns files on the Internet by using a search engine. Just search for *cache.dns* and download one. (I always try to get cache·dns files from a university or a company that manages domain names.)

Setting Zone Properties

There are six tabs on the Properties dialog box for a forward or reverse lookup zone. You only use the Security tab to control who can change properties and to make dynamic updates to records on that zone. The other tabs are discussed in the following sections.

Secondary zones don't have a Security tab, and their SOA tab shows you the contents of the master SOA record, which you can't change.

General Tab

The General tab includes the following:

- The Status indicator and the associated Pause button let you see and control whether this zone can be used to answer queries. When the zone is running, the server can use it to answer client queries; when it's paused, the server won't answer any queries it gets for that particular zone.

- The Type indicator and its Change button allow you to select the zone type. The options are Standard Primary, Standard Secondary, and AD-Integrated. (See "Introducing DNS Database Zones" earlier in this chapter.) As you change the type, the controls you see below the horizontal dividing line change too. For primary zones, you'll see a field that lets you select the zone filename; for secondary zones, you'll get controls that allow you to specify the IP addresses of the primary servers. But the most interesting controls are the ones you see for AD Integrated zones. When you change to the AD Integrated zones, you have the ability to make the dynamic zones Secure Only.

- The Replication indicator and its Change button allow you to change the replication scope if the zone is stored in Active Directory. You can choose to replicate the zone data to any of the following:

  - All DNS servers in the Active Directory forest

  - All DNS servers in a specified domain

  - All domain controllers in the Active Directory domain (required if you use Windows 2000 domain controllers in your domain)

  - All domain controllers specified in the replication scope of the application directory partition

- The Dynamic Updates field gives you a way to specify whether you want to support Dynamic DNS updates from compatible DHCP servers. As you learned earlier in the section "Dynamic DNS and Non-Dynamic DNS," the DHCP server or DHCP client must know about and support Dynamic DNS in order to use it, but the DNS server has to participate too. You can turn dynamic updates on or off, or you can require that updates be secured.

Start Of Authority (SOA) Tab

The following options in the Start Of Authority (SOA) tab, shown in Figure 3.12, control the contents of the SOA record for this zone.

FIGURE 3.12 The Start Of Authority (SOA) tab of the zone Properties dialog box

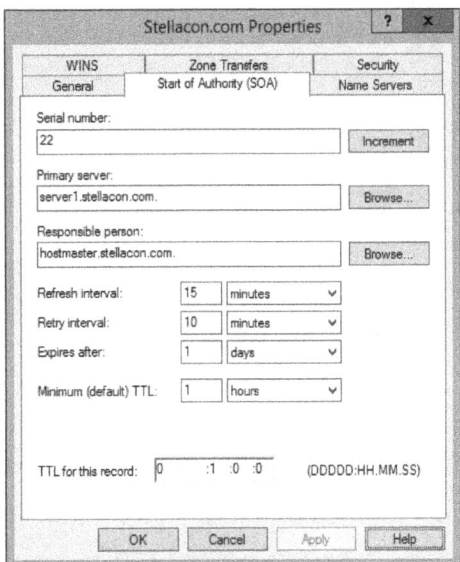

- The Serial Number field indicates which version of the SOA record the server currently holds. Every time you change another field, you should increment the serial number so that other servers will notice the change and get a copy of the updated record.

- The Primary Server and Responsible Person fields indicate the location of the primary name server for this zone and the email address of the administrator responsible for the maintenance of this zone, respectively. The standard username for this is hostmaster.

- The Refresh Interval field controls how often any secondary zones of this zone must contact the primary zone server and get any changes that have been posted since the last update.

- The Retry Interval field controls how long secondary servers will wait after a zone transfer fails before they try again. They'll keep trying at the interval you specify (which should be shorter than the refresh interval) until they eventually succeed in transferring zone data.

- The Expires After field tells the secondary servers when to throw away zone data. The default of 1 day (24 hours) means that a secondary server that hasn't gotten an update in 24 hours will delete its local copy of the zone data.

- The Minimum (Default) TTL field sets the default TTL for all RRs created in the zone. You can assign specific TTLs to individual records if you want.

- The TTL For This Record field controls the TTL for the SOA record itself.

Name Servers Tab

The *name server (NS) record* for a zone indicates which name servers are authoritative for the zone. That normally means the zone primary server and any secondary servers you've configured for the zone. (Remember, secondary servers are authoritative read-only copies of the zone.) You edit the NS record for a zone using the Name Servers tab (see Figure 3.13).

FIGURE 3.13   The Name Servers tab of the zone Properties dialog box

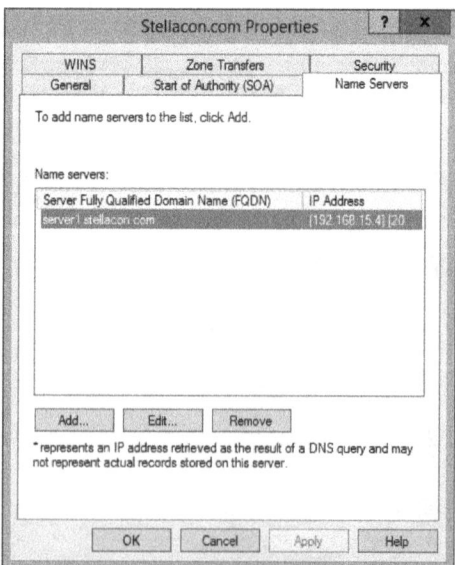

The tab shows you which servers are currently listed, and you use the Add, Edit, and Remove buttons to specify which name servers you want included in the zone's NS record.

WINS Tab

The WINS tab allows you to control whether this zone uses WINS forward lookups or not. These lookups pass on queries that DNS can't resolve to WINS for action. This is a useful setup if you're still using WINS on your network. You must explicitly turn this option on with the Use WINS Forward Lookup check box in the WINS tab for a particular zone.

Zone Transfers Tab

Zone transfers are necessary and useful because they're the mechanism used to propagate zone data between primary and secondary servers. For primary servers (whether AD Integrated or not), you can specify whether your servers will allow zone transfers and, if so, to whom.

You can use the following controls on the Zone Transfers tab to configure these settings per zone:

- The Allow Zone Transfers check box controls whether the server answers zone transfer requests for this zone at all—when it's not checked, no zone data is transferred. The Allow Zone Transfers selections are as follows:
    - To Any Server allows any server anywhere on the Internet to request a copy of your zone data.
    - Only To Servers Listed On The Name Servers Tab (the default) limits transfers to servers you specify. This is a more secure setting than To Any Server because it limits transfers to other servers for the same zone.
    - Only To The Following Servers allows you to specify exactly which servers are allowed to request zone transfers. This list can be larger or smaller than the list specified on the Name Servers tab.
- The Notify button is for setting up automatic notification triggers that are sent to secondary servers for this zone. Those triggers signal the secondary servers that changes have occurred on the primary server so that the secondary servers can request updates sooner than their normally scheduled interval. The options in the Notify dialog box are similar to those in the Zone Transfers tab. You can enable automatic notification and then choose either Servers Listed On The Name Servers Tab or The Following Servers.

Configuring Zones for Dynamic Updates

In Exercise 3.2, you will create and then modify the properties of a forward lookup zone. In addition, you'll configure the zone to allow dynamic updates.

EXERCISE 3.2

Configuring a Zone for Dynamic Updates

1. Open the DNS management snap-in by selecting Server Manager. Once in Server Manager, click DNS on the left side. In the Servers window (center screen), right-click your server name and choose DNS Manager.

2. Click the DNS server to expand it and then click the Forward Lookup Zones folder. Right-click the Forward Lookup Zones folder and choose New Zone.

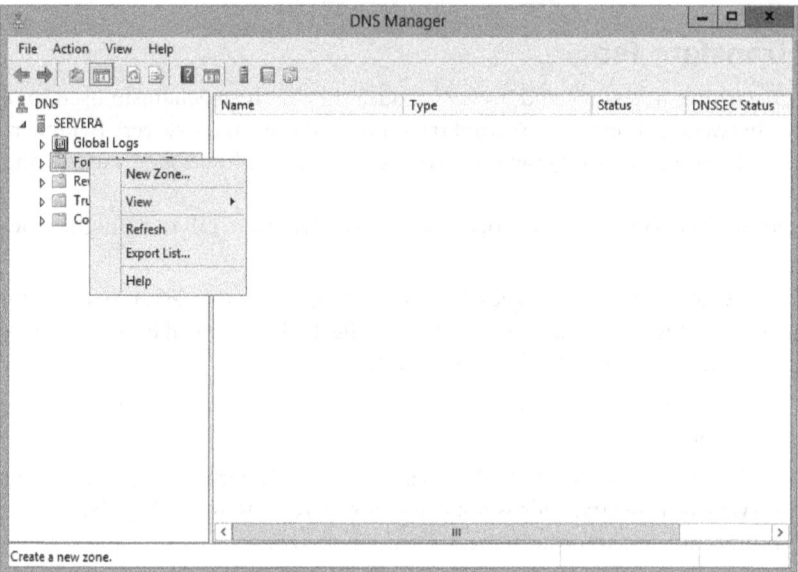

3. At the New Zone Welcome screen, click Next.

4. At the Zone Type screen, choose the Primary Zone option. If your DNS server is also a domain controller, do not check the box to store the zone in Active Directory. Click Next when you are ready.

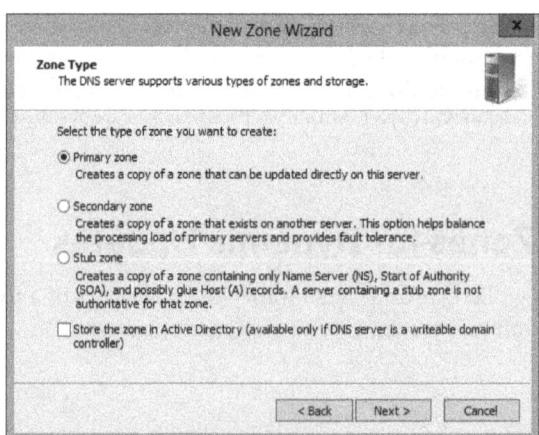

5. Enter a new zone name in the Zone Name field and click Next. (I used my last name— Panek.com.)

6. Leave the default zone filename and click Next.

7. Select the Do Not Allow Dynamic Updates radio button and click Next.

8. Click Finish to end the wizard.

9. Right-click the zone you just created and choose the Properties command.

10. Click the down arrow next to Dynamic Updates. Notice that there are only two options (None and Nonsecure And Secure). The Secure Only option is not available because you are not using Active Directory Integrated. Make sure Nonsecure And Secure is chosen.

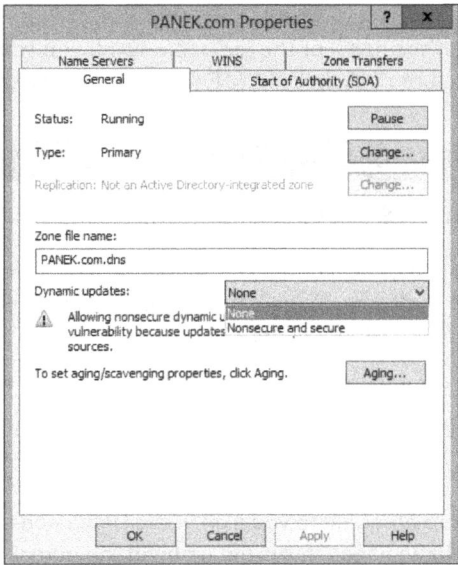

11. Click OK to close the Properties box.

12. Close the DNS management snap-in.

13. Close the Server Manager snap-in.

Delegating Zones for DNS

DNS provides the ability to divide the namespace into one or more zones, which can then be stored, distributed, and replicated to other DNS servers. When deciding whether to divide your DNS namespace to make additional zones, consider the following reasons to use additional zones:

- A need to delegate management of part of your DNS namespace to another location or department within your organization

- A need to divide one large zone into smaller zones for distributing traffic loads among multiple servers, for improving DNS name-resolution performance, or for creating a more fault-tolerant DNS environment

- A need to extend the namespace by adding numerous subdomains at once, such as to accommodate the opening of a new branch or site

Each newly delegated zone requires a primary DNS server just as a regular DNS zone does. When delegating zones within your namespace, be aware that for each new zone you create, you need to place delegation records in other zones that point to the authoritative DNS servers for the new zone. This is necessary both to transfer authority and to provide correct referral to other DNS servers and clients of the new servers being made authoritative for the new zone.

In Exercise 3.3, you'll create a delegated subdomain of the domain you created in Exercise 3.2. Note that the name of the server to which you want to delegate the subdomain must be stored in an A or CNAME record in the parent domain.

EXERCISE 3.3

Creating a Delegated DNS Zone

1. Open the DNS management snap-in by selecting Server Manager. Once in Server Manager, click DNS on the left side. In the Servers window (center screen), right-click your server name and choose DNS Manager.

2. Expand the DNS server and locate the zone you created in Exercise 3.2.

3. Right-click the zone and choose the New Delegation command.

4. The New Delegation Wizard appears. Click Next to dismiss the initial wizard page.

5. Enter **ns1** (or whatever other name you like) in the Delegated Domain field of the Delegated Domain Name page. This is the name of the domain for which you want to delegate authority to another DNS server. It should be a subdomain of the primary domain (for example, to delegate authority for farmington.example.net, you'd enter **farmington** in the Delegated Domain field). Click Next to complete this step.

6. When the Name Servers page appears, click the Add button to add the names and IP addresses of the servers that will be hosting the newly delegated zone. For the purpose of this exercise, enter the server name you used in Exercise 3.2. Click the Resolve button to resolve this domain name's IP address automatically into the IP address field. Click OK when you are finished. Click Next to continue with the wizard.

7. Click the Finish button. The New Delegation Wizard disappears, and you'll see the new zone you just created appear beneath the zone you selected in step 3. The newly delegated zone's folder icon is drawn in gray to indicate that control of the zone is delegated.

DNS Forwarding

If a DNS server does not have an answer to a DNS request, it may be necessary to send that request to another DNS server. This is called *DNS forwarding*. You need to understand the two main types of forwarding:

External Forwarding   When a DNS server forwards an external DNS request to a DNS server outside of your organization, this is considered *external forwarding*. For example, a resolver requests the host www.microsoft.com. Most likely, your internal DNS server is not going to have Microsoft's web address in its DNS database. So, your DNS server is going to send the request to an external DNS (most likely your ISP).

Conditional Forwarding   *Conditional forwarding* is a lot like external forwarding except that you are going to forward requests to specific DNS servers based on a condition. Usually this is an excellent setup for internal DNS resolution. For example, let's say that you have two companies, stellacon.com and stellatest.com. If a request comes in for Stellacon.com, it gets forwarded to the Stellacon DNS server, and any requests for Stellatest.com will get forwarded to the Stellatest DNS server. Requests are forwarded to a specific DNS server depending on the condition that an administrator sets up.

Manually Creating DNS Records

From time to time you may find it necessary to add resource records manually to your Windows Server 2012 R2 DNS servers. Although Dynamic DNS frees you from the need to fiddle with A and PTR records for clients and other such entries, you still have to create other resource types (including MX records, required for the proper flow of SMTP email) manually. You can manually create A, PTR, MX, SRV, and many other record types.

There are only two important things to remember for manually creating DNS records:

- You must right-click the zone and choose either the New Record command or the Other New Records command.

- You must know how to fill in the fields of whatever record type you're using.

  For example, to create an MX record, you need three pieces of information (the domain, the mail server, and the priority). To create an SRV record, however, you need several more pieces of information.

In Exercise 3.4, you will manually create an MX record for a mailtest server in the zone you created in Exercise 3.2.

EXERCISE 3.4

Manually Creating DNS RRs

1. Open the DNS management snap-in by selecting Server Manager. Once in Server Manager, click DNS on the left side. In the Servers window (center screen), right-click your server name and choose DNS Manager.

EXERCISE 3.4 *(continued)*

2. Expand your DNS server, right-click its zone, and choose New Host (A record).

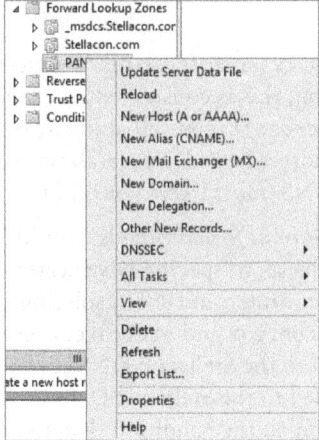

3. Enter **mailtest** in the Name field. Enter a TCP/IP number in the IP Address field. (You can use any number for this exercise, for example, 192.168.1.254.) Click the Add Host button.

4. A dialog box appears stating that the host record was created successfully. Click OK. Click Done.

5. Right-click your zone name and choose New Mail Exchanger (MX).

6. Enter **mailtest** in the Host Or Child Domain field and enter **mailtest.yourDomain.com** (or whatever domain name you used in Exercise 3.2) in the Fully-Qualified Domain Name (FQDN) Of Mail Server field and then click OK. Notice that the new record is already visible.

7. Next create an alias (or CNAME) record to point to the mail server. (It is assumed that you already have an A record for **mailtest** in your zone.) Right-click your zone and choose New Alias (CNAME).

8. Type **mail** into the Alias Name field.

9. Type **mailtest.yourDomain.com** into the Fully-Qualified Domain Name (FQDN) For Target Host field.

10. Click the OK button.

11. Close the DNS management snap-in.

DNS Aging and Scavenging

When using dynamic updates, computers (or DHCP) will register a resource record with DNS. These records get removed when a computer is shut down properly. A major problem in the industry is that laptops are frequently removed from the network without a proper shutdown. Therefore, their resource records continue to live in the DNS database.

Windows Server 2012 R2 DNS supports two features called *DNS aging* and *DNS scavenging*. These features are used to clean up and remove stale resource records. DNS zone or DNS server aging and scavenging flag old resource records that have not been updated in a certain amount of time (determined by the scavenging interval). These stale records will be scavenged at the next cleanup interval. DNS uses time stamps on the resource records to determine how long they have been listed in the DNS database.

Monitoring and Troubleshooting DNS

Now that you have set up and configured your DNS name server and created some resource records, you will want to confirm that it is resolving and replying to client DNS requests. A couple of tools allow you to do some basic monitoring and managing. Once you are able to monitor DNS, you'll want to start troubleshooting.

The simplest test is to use the ping command to make sure that the server is alive. A more thorough test would be to use nslookup to verify that you can actually resolve addresses for items on your DNS server.

In the following sections, you'll look at some of these monitoring and management tools and how to troubleshoot DNS.

Monitoring DNS with the DNS Snap-In

You can use the DNS snap-in to do some basic server testing and monitoring. More important, you use the snap-in to monitor and set logging options. On the Event Logging tab of the server's Properties dialog box (see Figure 3.14), you can pick which events you want logged. The more events you select, the more logging information you'll get. This is useful when you're trying to track what's happening with your servers, but it can result in a very large log file if you're not careful.

FIGURE 3.14 The Event Logging tab of the server's Properties dialog box

The Monitoring tab (see Figure 3.15) gives you some testing tools. When the check box labeled A Simple Query Against This DNS Server is checked, a test is performed that asks for a single record from the local DNS server. It's useful for verifying that the service is running and listening to queries, but not much else. When the check box labeled A Recursive Query To Other DNS Servers is checked, the test is more sophisticated—a recursive query checks whether forwarding is working okay. The Test Now button and the Perform Automatic Testing At The Following Interval check box allow you to run these tests now or later as you require.

FIGURE 3.15 The Monitoring tab of the server's Properties dialog box

SERVER1 Properties	?	x

Interfaces	Forwarders	Advanced	Root Hints
Debug Logging	Event Logging	Monitoring	Security

To verify the configuration of the server, you can perform manual or automatic testing.

Select a test type:

☐ A simple query against this DNS server

☐ A recursive query to other DNS servers

To perform the test immediately, click Test Now.   Test Now

☐ Perform automatic testing at the following interval:

Test interval: 1   minutes ▾

Test results:

Date	Time	Simple Query	Recursive Q...

OK   Cancel   Apply   Help

Another tab in the server's properties that allows you to monitor the activity of the DNS server is the Debug Logging tab. The Debug Logging tab allows you to monitor all outbound and inbound DNS traffic, packet content, packet type, and which transport protocol (TCP or UDP) that you want to monitor on the DNS server.

If the simple query fails, check that the local server contains the zone 1.0.0.127.in-addr.arpa. If the recursive query fails, check that your root hints are correct and that your root servers are running.

In Exercise 3.5, you will enable logging, use the DNS MMC to test the DNS server, and view the contents of the DNS log.

EXERCISE 3.5

Simple DNS Testing

1. Open the DNS management snap-in by selecting Server Manager. Once in Server Manager, click DNS on the left side. In the Servers window (center screen), right-click your server name and choose DNS Manager.

2. Right-click the DNS server name on the top left and select Properties.

3. Switch to the Debug Logging tab, check all the debug logging options except Filter Packets By IP Address and enter a full path and filename in the File Path And Name field. Click the Apply button.

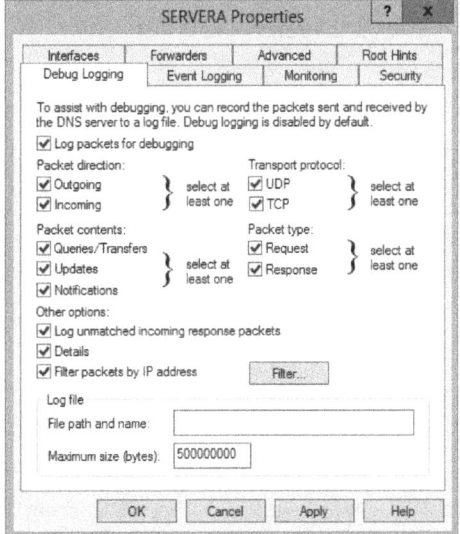

4. Switch to the Monitoring tab and check both A Simple Query Against This DNS Server and A Recursive Query To Other DNS Servers.

5. Click the Test Now button several times and then click OK.

6. Press the Windows key on the keyboard (left side between the Ctrl and Alt keys) and then choose Computer. Navigate to the folder that you specified in step 3 and use Word-Pad or Notepad to view the contents of the log file.

Troubleshooting DNS

When troubleshooting DNS problems, ask yourself the following basic questions:

- What application is failing? What works? What doesn't work?

- Is the problem basic IP connectivity, or is it name resolution? If the problem is name resolution, does the failing application use NetBIOS names, DNS names, or hostnames?

- How are the things that do and don't work related?

- Have the things that don't work ever worked on this computer or network? If so, what has changed since they last worked?

Windows Server 2012 R2 provides several useful tools, discussed in the following sections, which can help you answer these questions:

- Nslookup is used to perform DNS queries and to examine the contents of zone files on local and remote servers.

- DNSLint is a command-line utility used for troubleshooting many common DNS issues.

- Ipconfig allows you to perform the following tasks:

  - View DNS client settings

  - Display and flush the resolver cache

  - Force a dynamic update client to register its DNS records

- The DNS log file monitors certain DNS server events and logs them for your edification.

Using *Nslookup*

Nslookup is a standard command-line tool provided in most DNS server implementations, including Windows Server 2012 R2. Windows Server 2012 R2 gives you the ability to launch nslookup from the DNS snap-in.

 When nslookup is launched from the DNS snap-in, a command prompt window opens automatically. You enter nslookup commands in this window.

Nslookup offers you the ability to perform query testing of DNS servers and to obtain detailed responses at the command prompt. This information can be useful for diagnosing and solving name resolution problems, for verifying that resource records are added or updated correctly in a zone, and for debugging other server-related problems. You can do a number of useful things with nslookup:

- Use it in noninteractive mode to look up a single piece of data

- Enter interactive mode and use the debug feature

- Perform the following from within interactive mode:

  - Set options for your query

  - Look up a name

  - Look up records in a zone

- Perform zone transfers
- Exit `nslookup`

 When you are entering queries, it is generally a good idea to enter FQDNs so that you can control what name is submitted to the server. However, if you want to know which suffixes are added to unqualified names before they are submitted to the server, you can enter **nslookup** in debug mode and then enter an unqualified name.

Using *Nslookup* on the Command Line

To use `nslookup` in plain-old command-line mode, enter the following in the command prompt window:

```
nslookup DNS_name_or_IP_address server_IP_address
```

This command will look up a DNS name or address using a server at the IP address you specify.

Using *Nslookup* in Interactive Mode

Nslookup is a lot more useful in interactive mode because you can enter several commands in sequence. Entering **nslookup** by itself (without specifying a query or server) puts it in interactive mode, where it will stay until you type **exit** and press Enter. Before that point, you can look up lots of useful stuff. The following are some of the tasks that you can perform with nslookup in interactive mode:

Setting Options with the set Command   While in interactive mode, you can use the `set` command to configure how the resolver will carry out queries. Table 3.5 shows a few of the options available with `set`.

TABLE 3.5   Command-line options available with the `set` command

Option	Purpose
set all	Shows all the options available.
set d2	Puts nslookup in debug mode so that you can examine the query and response packets between the resolver and the server.
set domain=*domain name*	Tells the resolver what domain name to append for unqualified queries.
set timeout=*timeout*	Tells the resolver how long to keep trying to contact the server. This option is useful for slow links where queries frequently time out and the wait time must be lengthened.
set type=*record type*	Tells the resolver which type of resource records to search for (for example, A, PTR, or SRV). If you want the resolver to query for all types of resource records, type **settype=all**.

Looking Up a Name While in interactive mode, you can look up a name just by typing it: **stellacon.com**. In this example, stellacon is the owner name for the record for which you are searching, and .com is the server that you want to query.

You can use the wildcard character (*) in your query. For example, if you want to look for all resource records that have *k* as the first letter, just type **k*** as your query.

Looking Up a Record Type If you want to query a particular type of record (for instance, an MX record), use the set type command. The command set type=mx tells nslookup that you're interested only in seeing MX records that meet your search criteria.

Listing the Contents of a Domain To get a list of the contents of an entire domain, use the ls command. To find all the hosts in your domain, you'd type **set type=a** and then type **ls -t yourdomain.com**.

Troubleshooting Zone Transfers You can simulate zone transfers by using the ls command with the -d switch. This can help you determine whether the server you are querying allows zone transfers to your computer. To do this, type the following: **ls -d domain_name**.

Nslookup Responses and Error Messages

A successful nslookup response looks like this:

```
Server: Name_of_DNS_server
Address: IP_address_of_DNS_server
Response_data
```

Nslookup might also return an error message. Some common messages are listed in Table 3.6.

TABLE 3.6 Common nslookup error messages

Error message	Meaning
DNS request timed out. Timeout was *x* seconds. *** Can't find server name for address *IP_Address*: Timed out *** Default servers are not available Default Server: Unknown Address: *IP_address_of_DNS_server*	The resolver did not locate a PTR resource record (containing the hostname) for the server IP address you specified. Nslookup can still query the DNS server, and the DNS server can still answer queries.
*** Request to Server timed-out	A request was not fulfilled in the allotted time. This might happen, for example, if the DNS service was not running on the DNS server that is authoritative for the name.

`*** Server can't find` *`Name_or_IP_`* *`address_queried_for`*`: No response from server`	The server is not receiving requests on User Datagram Protocol (UDP) port 53.
`*** Server can't find` *`Name_or_IP_`* *`address_queried_for:`* `Non-existent domain`	The DNS server was unable to find the name or IP address in the authoritative domain. The authoritative domain might be on the remote DNS server or on another DNS server that this DNS server is unable to reach.
`*** Server can't find` *`Name_or_IP_`* *`address_queried_for`*`: Server failed`	The DNS server is running, but it is not working properly. For example, it might include a corrupted packet, or the zone in which you are querying for a record might be paused. However, this message can also be returned if the client queries for a host in a domain for which the DNS server is not authoritative. You will also receive the error if the DNS server cannot contact its root servers, it is not connected to the Internet, or it has no root hints.

In Exercise 3.6, you'll get some hands-on practice with the nslookup tool.

EXERCISE 3.6

Using the nslookup **Command**

1. Press the Windows key on the keyboard and then choose Computer. Navigate to the C:\ Windows\System32 folder and double-click CMD.exe. (When you get to this file, you can right-click the file and choose Send To Desktop. The shortcut will then always be available on the desktop.)

2. Type **nslookup** and press the Enter key. (For the rest of the exercise, use the Enter key to terminate each command.)

3. Try looking up a well-known address: Type **www.microsoft.com**.

4. Try looking up a nonexistent host: Type **www.example.ccccc**. Notice that your server indicates that it can't find the address and times out. This is normal behavior.

5. Type **Exit** at the prompt. Type **Exit** again to leave the command prompt.

Using *DNSLint*

Microsoft Windows Server 2012 R2 DNS can use the DNSLint command-line utility to help diagnose some common DNS name-resolution issues and to help diagnose potential problems of incorrect delegation. You need to download DNSLint from the Microsoft Download Center.

DNSLint uses three main functions to verify DNS records and to generate a report in HTML:

dnslint /d   This function helps diagnose the reasons for "lame delegation" and other related DNS problems.

dnslint /ql   This function helps verify a user-defined set of DNS records on multiple DNS servers.

dnslint /ad   This function helps verify DNS records pertaining to Active Directory replication.

Here is the syntax for DNSLint:

```
dnslint /d domain_name | /ad [LDAP_IP_address] | /ql input_file
[/c [smtp,pop,imap]] [/no_open] [/r report_name]
[/t] [/test_tcp] [/s DNS_IP_address] [/v] [/y]
```

The following are some sample queries:

```
dnslint /d stellacon.com
dnslint /ad /s 192.168.36.201
dnslint /ql dns_server.txt
dnslint /ql autocreate
dnslint /v /d stellacon.com
dnslint /r newfile /d stellacon.com
dnslint /y /d stellacon.com
dnslint /no_open /d stellacon.com
```

Table 3.7 explains the command options.

TABLE 3.7   DNSLint command options

Command option	Meaning
/d	Domain name that is being tested.
/ad	Resolves DNS records that are used for Active Directory forest replication.
/s	TCP/IP address of host.

/ql	Requests DNS query tests from a list. This switch sends DNS queries specified in an input file.
/v	Turns on verbose mode.
/r *filename*	Allows you to create a report file.
/y	Overwrites an existing report file without being prompted.
/no_open	Prevents a report from opening automatically.

Using *Ipconfig*

You can use the command-line tool ipconfig to view your DNS client settings, to view and reset cached information used locally for resolving DNS name queries, and to register the resource records for a dynamic update client. If you use the ipconfig command with no parameters, it displays DNS information for each adapter, including the domain name and DNS servers used for that adapter. Table 3.8 shows some command-line options available with ipconfig.

TABLE 3.8 Command-line options available for the **ipconfig** command

Command	What it does
ipconfig /all	Displays additional information about DNS, including the FQDN and the DNS suffix search list.
ipconfig /flushdns	Flushes and resets the DNS resolver cache. For more information about this option, see the section "Configuring DNS" earlier in this chapter.
ipconfig /displaydns	Displays the contents of the DNS resolver cache. For more information about this option, see "Configuring DNS" earlier in this chapter.
ipconfig /registerdns	Refreshes all DHCP leases and registers any related DNS names. This option is available only on Windows 2000 and newer computers that run the DHCP client service.

You should know and be comfortable with the ipconfig commands related to DNS for the exam.

Using *DNSCmd*

DNSCmd allows you to display and change the properties of DNS servers, zones, and resource records through the use of command-line commands. The DNSCmd utility allows you to modify, create, and delete resource records and/or zones manually, and it allows you to force replication between two DNS servers.

Table 3.9 lists some of the DNSCmd commands and their explanations.

TABLE 3.9   DNSCmd command-line options

Command	Explanation
dnscmd /clearcache	Clears the DNS server cache
dnscmd /config	Resets DNS server or zone configuration
dnscmd /createdirectorypartition	Creates a DNS application directory partition
dnscmd /deletedirectorypartition	Deletes a DNS application directory partition
dnscmd /enumrecords	Shows the resource records in a zone
dnscmd /exportsettings	Creates a text file of all server configuration information
dnscmd /info	Displays server information
dnscmd /recordadd	Adds a resource record to a zone
dnscmd /recorddelete	Deletes a resource record from a zone
dnscmd /zoneadd	Creates a new DNS zone
dnscmd /zonedelete	Deletes a DNS zone
dnscmd /zoneexport	Creates a text file of all resource records in the zone
dnscmd /zoneinfo	Displays zone information
dnscmd /zonerefresh	Forces replication of the master zone to the secondary zone

Using the DNS Log File

You can configure the DNS server to create a log file that records the following information:

- Queries
- Notification messages from other servers
- Dynamic updates
- Content of the question section for DNS query messages
- Content of the answer section for DNS query messages
- Number of queries this server sends
- Number of queries this server has received
- Number of DNS requests received over a UDP port
- Number of DNS requests received over a TCP port
- Number of full packets sent by the server
- Number of packets written through by the server and back to the zone

The DNS log appears in `systemroot\System32\dns\Dns.log`. Because the log is in RTF format, you must use WordPad or Word to view it.

Once the log file reaches the maximum size, Windows Server 2012 R2 writes over the beginning of the file. You can change the maximum size of the log. If you increase the size value, data persists for a longer time period, but the log file consumes more disk space. If you decrease the value, the log file uses less disk space, but the data persists for a shorter time period.

Do not leave DNS logging turned on during normal operation because it sucks up both processing and hard disk resources. Enable it only when diagnosing and solving DNS problems.

Troubleshooting the .*(root)* Zone

The *DNS root zone* is the top-level DNS zone in the DNS hierarchy. Windows Server 2012 R2-based DNS servers will build a `.(root)` zone when a connection to the Internet can't be found.

Because of this, the `.(root)` zone may prevent access to the Internet. The DNS forwarding option and DNS root hints will not be configurable. If you want your DNS to work as a DNS forwarder or you want to use root hints, you must remove the `.(root)` zone.

Issues with Non-Microsoft DNS Servers

Another troubleshooting problem that you may run into is working with both Microsoft DNS servers and non-Microsoft DNS servers. One of the most common non-Microsoft DNS servers is the Unix-based BIND DNS server.

If you need to complete a zone transfer from Microsoft DNS to a BIND DNS server, you need to enable BIND Secondaries on the Microsoft DNS server (see Figure 3.16).

FIGURE 3.16 Enabling BIND Secondaries

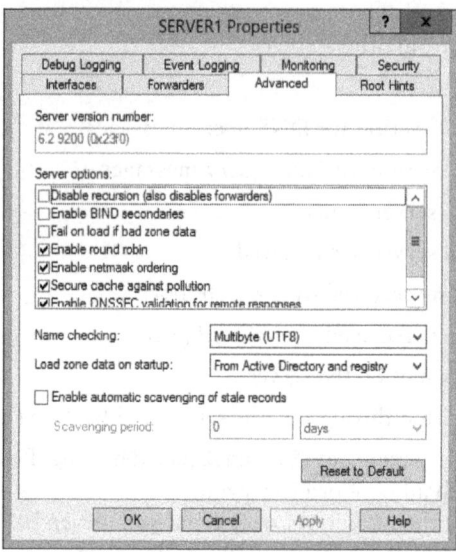

If you need to enable Bind Secondaries, complete the following steps:

1. Open DNS management.
2. Right-click the server name and choose Properties.
3. Click the Advanced tab.
4. Check the Enable BIND Secondaries box.
5. Click OK.

Integrating Dynamic DNS and IPv4 DHCP

DHCP integration with Dynamic DNS is a simple concept but powerful in action. By setting up this integration, you can pass addresses to DHCP clients while still maintaining the integrity of your DNS services.

The DNS server can be updated in two ways. One way is for the DHCP client to tell the DNS server its address. Another way is for the DHCP server to tell the DNS server when it registers a new client.

Neither of these updates will take place, however, unless you configure the DNS server to use Dynamic DNS. You can make this change in two ways:

- If you change it at the scope level, it will apply only to the scope.

- If you change it at the server level, it will apply to all scopes and superscopes served by the server.

Which of these options you choose depends on how widely you want to support Dynamic DNS; most of the sites I visit have enabled DNS updates at the server level.

To update the settings at either the server or scope level, you need to open the scope or server properties by right-clicking the appropriate object and choosing Properties. The DNS tab of the Properties dialog box includes the following options:

Enable DNS Dynamic Updates According To The Settings Below   This check box controls whether this DHCP server will attempt to register lease information with a DNS server. It must be checked to enable Dynamic DNS.

> **Dynamically Update DNS A And PTR Records Only If Requested By The DHCP Clients**   This radio button (which is on by default) tells the DHCP server to register the update only if the DHCP client asks for DNS registration. When this button is active, DHCP clients that aren't hip to DDNS won't have their DNS records updated. However, Windows 2000, XP, Vista, Windows 7, Windows 8, Server 2003, Server 2008/2008 R2, and Server 2012/2012 R2 DHCP clients are smart enough to ask for the updates.

> **Always Dynamically Update DNS A And PTR Records**   This radio button forces the DHCP server to register any client to which it issues a lease. This setting may add DNS registrations for DHCP-enabled devices that don't really need them, such as print servers. However, it allows other clients (such as Mac OS, Windows NT, and Linux machines) to have their DNS information automatically updated.

Discard A And PTR Records When Lease Is Deleted   This check box has a long name but a simple function. When a DHCP lease expires, what should happen to the DNS registration? Obviously, it would be nice if the DNS record associated with a lease vanished when the lease expired. When this check box is checked (as it is by default), that's exactly what happens. If you uncheck this box, your DNS will contain entries for expired leases that are no longer valid. When a particular IP address is reissued on a new lease, the DNS will be updated, but in between leases you'll have incorrect data in your DNS—something that's always best to avoid.

Dynamically Update DNS A And PTR Records For DHCP Clients That Do Not Request Updates   This check box lets you handle these older clients graciously by making the updates using a separate mechanism.

In Exercise 3.7, you will enable a scope to participate in Dynamic DNS updates.

EXERCISE 3.7

Enabling DHCP-DNS Integration

1. Open the DHCP snap-in by selecting Administrative Tools ➤ DHCP.

2. Right-click the IPv4 item, and select Properties.

3. The Server Properties dialog box appears. Click the DNS tab.

EXERCISE 3.7 *(continued)*

4. Verify that the check box labeled Enable DNS Dynamic Updates According To The Settings Below is checked, and verify that the radio button labeled Dynamically Update DNS A And PTR Records Only If Requested By The DHCP Clients is selected.

5. Verify that the check box labeled Discard A And PTR Records When Lease Is Deleted is checked. If not, then check it.

6. Click the OK button to apply your changes and close the Server Properties dialog box.

Summary

DNS was designed to be a robust, scalable, and high-performance system for resolving friendly names to TCP/IP host addresses. This chapter presented an overview of the basics of DNS and how DNS names are generated. You then looked at the many new features available in the Microsoft Windows Server 2012 R2 version of DNS, and you learned how to install, configure, and manage the necessary services. Microsoft's DNS is based on a widely accepted set of industry standards. Because of this, Microsoft's DNS can work with both Windows- and non-Windows-based networks.

Exam Essentials

Understand the purpose of DNS. DNS is a standard set of protocols that defines a mechanism for querying and updating address information in the database, a mechanism for replicating the information in the database among servers, and a schema of the database.

Understand the different parts of the DNS database. The SOA record defines the general parameters for the DNS zone, including who is the authoritative server. NS records list the name servers for a domain; they allow other name servers to look up names in your domain. A host record (also called an address record or an A record) statically associates a host's name with its IP addresses. Pointer records (PTRs) map an IP address to a hostname, making it possible to do reverse lookups. Alias records allow you to use more than one name to point to a single host. The MX record tells you which servers can accept mail bound for a domain. SRV records tie together the location of a service (like a domain controller) with information about how to contact the service.

Know how DNS resolves names. With iterative queries, a client asks the DNS server for an answer, and the client, or resolver, returns the best kind of answer it has. In a recursive query, the client sends a query to one name server, asking it to respond either with the requested answer or with an error. The error states either that the server can't come up with the right answer or that the domain name doesn't exist. With inverse queries, instead of supplying a name and then asking for an IP address, the client first provides the IP address and then asks for the name.

Understand the differences among DNS servers, clients, and resolvers. Any computer providing domain name services is a DNS server. A DNS client is any machine issuing queries to a DNS server. A resolver handles the process of mapping a symbolic name to an actual network address.

Know how to install and configure DNS. DNS can be installed before, during, or after installing the Active Directory service. When you install the DNS server, the DNS snap-in is installed too. Configuring a DNS server ranges from easy to difficult, depending on what you're trying to make it do. In the simplest configuration, for a caching-only server, you don't have to do anything except to make sure that the server's root hints are set correctly. You can also configure a root server, a normal forward lookup server, and a reverse lookup server.

Know how to create new forward and reverse lookup zones. You can use the New Zone Wizard to create a new forward or reverse lookup zone. The process is basically the same for both types, but the specific steps and wizard pages differ somewhat. The wizard walks you through the steps, such as specifying a name for the zone (in the case of forward lookup zones) or the network ID portion of the network that the zone covers (in the case of reverse lookup zones).

Know how to configure zones for dynamic updates. The DNS service allows dynamic updates to be enabled or disabled on a per-zone basis at each server. This is easily done in the DNS snap-in.

Know how to delegate zones for DNS. DNS provides the ability to divide the namespace into one or more zones; these can then be stored, distributed, and replicated to other DNS servers. When delegating zones within your namespace, be aware that for each new zone you create, you need delegation records in other zones that point to the authoritative DNS servers for the new zone.

Understand the tools that are available for monitoring and troubleshooting DNS. You can use the DNS snap-in to do some basic server testing and monitoring. More important, you use the snap-in to monitor and set logging options. Windows Server 2012 R2 automatically logs DNS events in the event log under a distinct DNS server heading. Nslookup offers the ability to perform query testing of DNS servers and to obtain detailed responses at the command prompt. You can use the command-line tool ipconfig to view your DNS client settings, to view and reset cached information used locally for resolving DNS name queries, and to register the resource records for a dynamic update client. Finally, you can configure the DNS server to create a log file that records queries, notification messages, dynamic updates, and various other DNS information.

Review Questions

1. You are the network administrator for the ABC Company. Your network consists of two DNS servers named *DNS1* and *DNS2*. The users who are configured to use DNS2 complain because they are unable to connect to Internet websites. The following table shows the configuration of both servers:

DNS1	DNS2
_msdcs.abc.comabc.com	.(root)_msdcs.abc.comabc.com

The users who are connected to DNS2 need to be able to access the Internet. What needs to be done?

   A. Build a new Active Directory Integrated zone on DNS2.

   B. Delete the .(root) zone from DNS2 and configure conditional forwarding on DNS2.

   C. Delete the current cache.dns file.

   D. Update your cache.dns file and root hints.

2. You are the network administrator for a large company that has one main site and one branch office. Your company has a single Active Directory forest, ABC.com. You have a single domain controller (ServerA) in the main site that has the DNS role installed. ServerA is configured as a primary DNS zone. You have decided to place a domain controller (ServerB) in the remote site and implement the DNS role on that server. You want to configure DNS so that if the WAN link fails, users in both sites can still update records and resolve any DNS queries. How should you configure the DNS servers?

   A. Configure ServerB as a secondary DNS server. Set replication to occur every 5 minutes.

   B. Configure ServerB as a stub zone.

   C. Configure ServerB as an Active Directory Integrated zone and convert ServerA to an Active Directory Integrated zone.

   D. Convert ServerA to an Active Directory Integrated zone and configure ServerB as a secondary zone.

3. You are the network administrator for a midsize computer company. You have a single Active Directory forest, and your DNS servers are configured as Active Directory Integrated zones. When you look at the DNS records in Active Directory, you notice that there are many records for computers that do not exist on your domain. You want to make sure that only domain computers register with your DNS servers. What should you do to resolve this issue?

   A. Set dynamic updates to None.

   B. Set dynamic updates to Nonsecure And Secure.

   C. Set dynamic updates to Domain Users Only.

   D. Set dynamic updates to Secure Only.

4.   Your company consists of a single Active Directory forest. You have a Windows Server 2012 R2 domain controller that also has the DNS role installed. You also have a Unix-based DNS server at the same location. You need to configure your Windows DNS server to allow zone transfers to the Unix-based DNS server. What should you do?

   A.   Enable BIND Secondaries.

   B.   Configure the Unix machine as a stub zone.

   C.   Convert the DNS server to Active Directory Integrated.

   D.   Configure the Microsoft DNS server to forward all requests to the Unix DNS server.

5.   You are the network administrator for Stellacon Corporation. Stellacon has two trees in its Active Directory forest, `stellacon.com` and `abc.com`. Company policy does not allow DNS zone transfers between the two trees. You need to make sure that when anyone in `abc.com` tries to access the `stellacon.com` domain, all names are resolved from the `stellacon.com` DNS server. What should you do?

   A.   Create a new secondary zone in `abc.com` for `stellacon.com`.

   B.   Configure conditional forwarding on the `abc.com` DNS server for `stellacon.com`.

   C.   Create a new secondary zone in `stellacon.com` for `abc.com`.

   D.   Configure conditional forwarding on the `stellacon.com` DNS server for `abc.com`.

6.   You are the network administrator for your organization. A new company policy states that all inbound DNS queries need to be recorded. What can you do to verify that the IT department is compliant with this new policy?

   A.   Enable Server Auditing – Object Access.

   B.   Enable DNS debug logging.

   C.   Enable server database query logging.

   D.   Enable DNS Auditing – Object Access.

7.   You are the network administrator for a small company with two DNS servers: DNS1 and DNS2. Both DNS servers reside on domain controllers. DNS1 is set up as a standard primary zone, and DNS2 is set up as a secondary zone. A new security policy was written stating that all DNS zone transfers must be encrypted. How can you implement the new security policy?

   A.   Enable the Secure Only setting on DNS1.

   B.   Enable the Secure Only setting on DNS2.

   C.   Configure Secure Only on the Zone Transfers tab for both servers.

   D.   Delete the secondary zone on DNS2. Convert both DNS servers to use Active Directory Integrated zones.

8. You are responsible for DNS in your organization. You look at the DNS database and see a large number of older records on the server. These records are no longer valid. What should you do?

A. In the zone properties, enable Zone Aging and Scavenging.

B. In the server properties, enable Zone Aging and Scavenging.

C. Manually delete all of the old records.

D. Set Dynamic Updates to None.

9. Your IT team has been informed by the compliance team that they need copies of the DNS Active Directory Integrated zones for security reasons. You need to give the Compliance department a copy of the DNS zone. How should you accomplish this goal?

A. Run **dnscmd /zonecopy**.

B. Run **dnscmd /zoneinfo**.

C. Run **dnscmd /zoneexport**.

D. Run **dnscmd /zonefile**.

10. You are the network administrator for a Windows Server 2012 R2 network. You have multiple remote locations connected to your main office by slow satellite links. You want to install DNS into these offices so that clients can locate authoritative DNS servers in the main location. What type of DNS servers should be installed in the remote locations?

A. Primary DNS zones

B. Secondary DNS zones

C. Active Directory Integrated zones

D. Stub zones

Chapter

4

Configure Routing and Remote Access

THE FOLLOWING 70-411 EXAM OBJECTIVES ARE COVERED IN THIS CHAPTER:

✓ **Configure VPN and routing**

- Install and configure the Remote Access role
- Implement Network Address Translation (NAT)
- Configure VPN settings
- Configure remote dial-in settings for users
- Configure routing
- Configure Web Application proxy in passthrough mode

✓ **Configure DirectAccess**

- Implement server requirements
- Implement client configuration
- Configure DNS for DirectAccess
- Configure certificates for DirectAccess

Now that you understand how routing works, it's time to discuss how clients connect using remote access. *Routing and Remote Access Services (RRAS)* includes some security features necessary to provide remote access effectively. For example, you'll probably want the ability to restrict user dial-up access by group membership, time of day, or other factors. You'll also need a way to specify the various callback, authentication, and encryption options that the protocols support.

In this chapter, you'll learn about *virtual private networks (VPNs)*, which provide remote access to private networks across public connections. That is, using the Internet, clients can dial in to an Internet service provider (ISP) and connect to your private network. The main benefit of VPNs is reduced cost because it means that long-distance calls are unnecessary. VPNs are becoming more popular because of the increased popularity of high-speed Internet connections, such as cable and digital subscriber line (DSL) connections.

Many of the features included in Windows Server 2012 R2 are simply carried over from Windows Server 2008, with a few minor additions. This is the case with the Routing and Remote Access console.

Before I can get into the details of what these features do and how to configure them to provide remote access for your network, you need to understand some of the terms and concepts specific to RRAS. That's where you'll begin in this chapter, and then you'll move on to learning about the features and configuration settings that you need to understand to meet the exam objectives.

Overview of Dial-Up Networking

LANs provide relatively high-speed connectivity to attached machines, but where does that leave those of us who work from home, who travel, or who need to access data on a remote computer? Until wireless access is available worldwide, we have the option of using dial-up networking in which the client computer uses a modem to dial in and connect to a remote server. Once the connection is established, a variety of protocols and services make it possible for us to view web pages, transfer files and email, and do pretty much anything we could do with a hardwired LAN connection, albeit at a reduced speed.

In the following sections, you will learn more about what dial-up networking does and how it works by examining the specific technologies and protocols associated with remote access.

What DUN Does

At this point in the book, you should understand that Windows Server 2012 R2 network protocols are actually implemented as drivers. These drivers normally work with hardware network interfaces to get data from point A to point B. How do dial-up connections fit in? Many people may read this and say, "Who still uses dial-up?" Well, as a person who lives in New Hampshire, I can tell you that we still have many areas that can't get broadband or even satellite access.

Think back to the OSI model. Each layer has a function, and each layer serves as an intermediary between the layer above it and the one below it. By substituting one driver for another at some level in the stack, you can dramatically change how things work. That's exactly what the Windows Server 2012 R2's *Dial-Up Networking (DUN)* subsystem does. It makes the dial-up connection appear to be just another network adapter.

The DUN driver takes care of the task of making a slow asynchronous modem appear to work just like a fast LAN interface. Applications and services that use TCP/IP on your DUN connection never know the difference. In fact, you can configure Windows Server 2012 R2 to use your primary connection first and then to pass traffic over a secondary connection (such as a dial-up link) if the primary connection is down. This does not affect the applications with which you're working (except that they might run more slowly).

On the server side, DUN allows you to host one or more network users who dial into your Windows Server 2012 R2 machine. Windows XP Professional, Windows Vista, Windows 7, and Windows 8 all allow up to 10 concurrent dial-up connections, and Windows Server 2012 R2 allows up to 255. (Be aware that by the time you allow 255 concurrent connections, you'll probably be overloading your server.)

Depending on how you configure the DUN server, users who dial in can see the whole network or only specific resources on the server. You also get to control who can log on, when they can log on, and what they can do once they've logged on. As far as Windows Server 2012 R2 is concerned, a user connected via DUN is no different from one using resources over your LAN, so all the access controls and permissions you apply remain in force for DUN users.

How DUN Works

A lot of pieces are required to complete a dial-up call successfully from your computer to a server at another physical location. Understanding what these pieces are, how they work, and what they do for you is important. The following sections will cover the DUN infrastructure, how the *Point-to-Point Protocol (PPP)* helps with this connection, the relationship between PPP and the network protocols, and how multilink can be used to increase the speed and efficiency of your remote connections.

The DUN Infrastructure

This section covers the physical layer that underlies voice and data calls. Most of the following material will be familiar to anyone who has ever used a modem, but you should still understand the details you may not have considered before.

Plain Old Telephone Service

Plain Old Telephone Service (POTS) connections offer a theoretical maximum speed of 56Kbps; in practice, many users routinely get connections at 51Kbps or 52Kbps.

The word *modem* is actually short for *modulator-demodulator*. The original Bell System modems took digital data and modulated it into screechy analog audio tones suitable for use on regular phone lines. Because phone lines are purposely designed to pass only the low end of the audible frequency range that most can hear, the amount of data was limited. However, in the early 1990s, an engineer discovered that you could communicate much faster when the path between the sender and receiver was all digital.

An all-digital path doesn't have any analog components that induce signal loss, so it preserves the original signal quality faithfully. This in turn makes it possible to put more information into the original signal. As it happens, phone companies nationwide were in the process of making major upgrades to replace their analog equipment with newer and better digital equivalents. These upgrades made it possible for people in most areas to get almost 56Kbps speeds without changing any of the wiring in their homes or offices. The connection between the house and the phone office was still analog, but the connections between phone offices were digital, ensuring high-quality connections.

Integrated Services Digital Network

In the mid-1970s, *Integrated Services Digital Network (ISDN)* was designed. At the time, no one had any idea that you'd be able to get 56Kbps speeds out of an ordinary phone line. ISDN speeds of up to 128Kbps over a single pair of copper wires seemed pretty revolutionary. In addition, ISDN had features such as call forwarding, caller ID, and multiple directory numbers (so you could have more than one number, perhaps with different ringing patterns, associated with a single line).

Unfortunately, ISDN requires an all-digital signal path. It also requires special equipment on both ends of the connection. The phone companies were slow to promote ISDN as a faster alternative to regular dial-up service, so customers avoided it.

ISDN still has some advantages, though. Because it's all digital, call setup times are much shorter than they are for analog modems—it takes only about half a second to establish a new ISDN call. Modern ISDN adapters and ISDN-capable routers can seamlessly stitch together multiple ISDN channels to deliver bandwidth in 64Kbps increments. Because you can use ISDN lines for regular analog voice, data, and fax traffic, you can make a single ISDN act like two voice lines, a single 128Kbps data line, or a 64Kbps data line plus a voice line.

NOTE ISDN is quickly being replaced by faster broadband services such as DSL and cable modems. In fact, you should resort to ISDN only if these other solutions are not available in your area. Note that DSL (a misnomer because they are all digital) and cable modems do not use PPP (discussed later), so they are technically not considered dial-up connections.

Other Connection Methods

Any other on-demand connection that's established using the Point-to-Point Protocol can be thought of as a dial-up connection, and Windows Server 2012 R2 doesn't make any distinction between POTS, ISDN, and other dial-ups—they're all treated identically.

Connecting with PPP

The Point-to-Point Protocol enables any two devices to establish a TCP/IP connection over a serial link. That usually means a dial-up modem connection, but it could just as easily be a direct serial cable connection, an infrared connection, or any other type of serial connection. When one machine dials another, the machine that initiates the connection is referred to as a *client*, and the machine that receives the call is referred to as a *server*—even though PPP itself makes no such distinction.

PPP negotiation involves three phases that are required to establish a remote access connection. Actually, at least six distinct protocols run on top of PPP. Understanding what they do helps to make the actual PPP negotiation process clearer. These protocols are as follows:

The Link Control Protocol   The *Link Control Protocol (LCP)* handles the details of establishing and configuring the lowest-level PPP link. In that regard, you can think of LCP as if it were almost part of the Physical layer. When one PPP device calls another, the devices use LCP to agree that they want to establish a PPP connection.

The Challenge Handshake Authentication Protocol   *The Challenge Handshake Authentication Protocol (CHAP)*—as well as MS-CHAPv2 and PAP—allow the client to authenticate itself to the server. This authentication functions much like a regular network logon; once the client presents its logon credentials, the server can figure out what access to grant.

The Callback Control Protocol   The *Callback Control Protocol (CBCP)* is used to negotiate whether a callback is required, whether it's permitted, and when it happens. Once the client has authenticated itself, the server can decide whether it should hang up and call the client back. The client can also request a callback at a number it provides. Although this isn't as secure as having the server place a call to a predetermined number, it provides some additional flexibility. If a callback occurs, the connection is reestablished and reauthenticated, but the CBCP stage is skipped.

The Compression Control Protocol   The *Compression Control Protocol (CCP)* allows the two sides of the connection to determine what kind of compression, if any, they want to use on the network data. Because PPP traffic actually consists of wrapped-up IP datagrams and because IP datagram headers tend to be fairly compressible, negotiating effective compression can significantly improve overall PPP throughput.

The IP Control Protocol   At this point in the call, the two sides have agreed to authentication, compression, and a callback. They haven't yet agreed on what IP parameters to use for the connection. These parameters, which include the maximum packet size to be sent over the link (the *maximum transmission unit*, or *MTU*), have a great impact on the overall link performance, so the client and server use the *IP Control Protocol (IPCP)* to negotiate them based on the traffic they expect to be passed.

The Internet Protocol   Once the IPCP negotiation has been completed, each end has complete knowledge of how to communicate with its peer. That knowledge allows the two sides to begin exchanging Internet Protocol (IP) datagrams over the link, just as they would over a standard LAN connection.

The Relationship Between PPP and Network Protocols

Usually, when you hear about network communication, you hear about using TCP/IP on a hardwired LAN. How does this protocol fit in with PPP? In the case of TCP/IP, that's an easy question to answer: The client routes all (or some) of its outgoing TCP/IP traffic to its PPP peer, which can then inspect the IP datagrams it gets back from the PPP stack to analyze and route them properly.

Windows Server 2012 R2 supports only TCP/IP, so consider what has to happen when a client using AppleTalk needs to connect via dial-up. Because the server will not use those other protocols, it will drop the call or cause the client to warn its user (that's what Windows Server 2012 R2 does). After the other PPP setup steps are finished, the client and server can wrap other types of network traffic inside an IP datagram. This process, called *encapsulation*, allows the client to take a packet with some kind of private content, wrap it inside an IP datagram, and send it to the server. The server, in turn, processes the IP datagram, routing real datagrams normally and handling any encapsulated packets with the appropriate protocol. At that point, the client can communicate with the server without knowing that its non-TCP/IP packets are being encapsulated in any way—that detail is hidden deep in the layers of the OSI model.

Understanding the Benefits of Multilink

Many parts of the world don't have high-speed broadband access yet. In fact, many places don't have ISDN or even phone lines that support 56Kbps modems. The *multilink extensions* to the Point-to-Point Protocol provide a way to take several independent PPP connections and make them look like one line so that they act as a single connection.

For example, if you use two phone lines and modems to place a two-line multilink call to your ISP, instead of getting the usual 48Kbps connection, you would end up with an apparent bandwidth of 96Kbps. The multilink PPP software on your Windows Server 2012 R2 machine and on the ISP's router takes care of stringing all of the packets together to make this process seamless. Windows Server 2012's RRAS supports multilink PPP for inbound and outbound calls.

   The primary drawback to multilink calls is that they take up more than one phone line apiece.

Overview of Virtual Private Networks

Private networks offer superior security. You own the wires, so you have control over what they're used for, who can use them, and what kind of data passes over them. However, they're not very flexible because they require you to configure and manage costly leased lines between remote locations. To make things worse, most private networks face a dilemma: Implementing enough capacity to handle peak loads almost guarantees that much of that capacity will remain idle much of the time, even though it still has to be paid for.

One way to work around this problem is to maintain private dial-up services. Such services allow, for example, a field rep in Chicago to dial into the home office in Boston. But dial-ups are expensive, and they have the same excess capacity problem as truly private networks. As an added detriment, someone has to pay long-distance or toll-free number charges.

Virtual private networks (VPNs) offer a solution. You get the security of a true private network with the flexibility, ubiquity, and low cost of the Internet. In the following sections, I will cover VPNs, including what they are used for and how they work (in general and with Windows Server 2012).

What VPNs Do

At any time, two parties can create a connection over the Internet. The idea behind a VPN is that you can use these connections to let two parties establish an *encrypted tunnel* between them using the Internet as a transportation medium. The VPN software on each end takes care of encrypting the VPN packets as they go; when the packets leave one end of the tunnel, their payloads are encrypted and encapsulated inside regular IP packets that cause them to be delivered to the remote machine. Figure 4.1 shows one way to conceptualize this process.

FIGURE 4.1   Drilling a tunnel through the Internet

As an example, let's say you're in the field at a client site. As long as you're somewhere that your ISP serves, you can dial into the client's local point of presence and get connected to the Internet. At that point, you can open a VPN connection back to the servers at your office and do whatever you could do when sitting in front of a regular desktop machine.

VPNs and Windows Server 2012 R2

Windows Server 2012 R2 includes support for Microsoft's proprietary *Point-to-Point Tunneling Protocol* and Layer 2 Tunneling Protocol. *Layer 2 Tunneling Protocol (L2TP)* provides a more generic tunneling mechanism than PPTP, and when combined with IPsec, L2TP also allows you to establish VPNs using a wide range of Microsoft or non-Microsoft hardware and software products, including routers and access devices from companies such as Cisco, Red Creek, and Nortel.

Windows Server 2012 R2's VPN support includes the following worthwhile features:

- You can set up account lockout policies for dial-up and VPN users. This capacity has existed for network and console users for some time.

- The *Extensible Authentication Protocol (EAP)* allows Microsoft or third parties to write modules that implement new authentication methods and retrofit them to servers. One example is the EAP-TLS module, which implements access control based on smart cards and certificates for VPN and dial-up users.

How you enable VPN support on your Windows Server 2012 R2 machine depends on whether you're using a server or a client (Windows XP, Windows Vista, Windows 7, Windows 8, and so on).

Client configuration is easy. Just install the Dial-Up Networking service and then use the Make New Connection Wizard to create a new VPN connection. On the server side, you'll need to install and configure RRAS and then enable it to accept incoming VPN connections.

How VPNs Work

The VPN client assumes that the VPN server is already connected to the Internet in some way. Here's how the VPN connection process works:

1. The client establishes a connection to the Internet. Dial-up networking or any other connection method can be used for this connection. The client must be able to send packets to the Internet.

2. The client sends a VPN connection request to the server. The exact format of the request varies, depending on whether the VPN is using PPTP, L2TP, or SSTP.

3. The client authenticates itself to the server. Again, the exact process varies according to the VPN protocol in use. If the client can't provide valid credentials, the connection is terminated.

4. The client and server negotiate parameters for the VPN session. This negotiation allows the two ends to agree on an encryption algorithm and strength.

5. The client and server go through the PPP negotiation process because both L2TP and PPTP depend on the lower-level PPP.

Because the contents of data passed around in step 2 and step 3 vary according to the tunneling protocol in use, I'll explain the differences. First, though, you should understand encapsulation and how VPNs use it to wrap one kind of data inside another.

An Encapsulation Primer

Most of yesterday's networks could carry only one kind of data. Each network vendor had its own protocol, and most of the time there was no way to intermingle data using different protocols on the same line. Over time, vendors began to find ways to allow a single network to carry many different types of traffic, resulting in the current assortment of traffic types found on most large networks. However, the Internet works only with IP, which is why it's called *Internet Protocol*. If you need to send other types of traffic, such as AppleTalk, across the Internet, you can encapsulate it within IP.

How does encapsulation work? Software at each level of the OSI model has to see header information to figure out where a packet is coming from and where it's going. However, the payload contents aren't important to most of those components, and the payload is what's encapsulated. By fabricating the right kind of header and prepending it for whatever you want in the payload, you can route foreign traffic types through IP networks with no trouble.

VPNs depend on encapsulation because their security method depends on being able to keep the payload information encrypted. The following steps demonstrate what happens to a typical packet as it goes from being a regular IP datagram to a PPTP packet (see Figure 4.2).

FIGURE 4.2   The encapsulation process

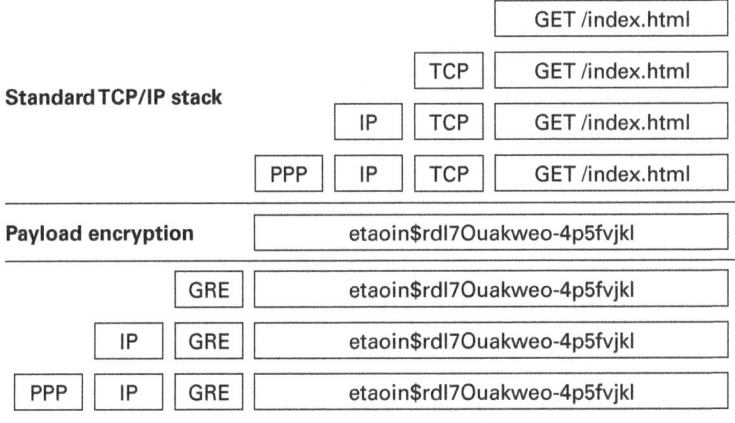

1. An application creates a block of data bound for a remote host. In this case, it's a web browser.

2. The client-side IP stack takes the application's data and turns it into an IP packet, first by adding a TCP header and then by adding an IP header. This is called the *IP datagram* because it contains all of the necessary addressing information to be delivered by IP.

3. The client is connected via PPP, so it adds a PPP header to the IP datagram. This PPP+IP combination is called a *PPP frame.*

4. If you are using PPP instead of a VPN protocol, the packet goes across the PPP link without further modification. When you are using a VPN (as in this example), the next step is for the VPN to encrypt the PPP frame, turning it into unreadable information to be transported over the Internet.

5. A *Generic Routing Encapsulation (GRE) header* is combined with the encrypted payload. GRE really is generic; in this case, the protocol ID field in the GRE header says that this is an encapsulated PPTP packet.

6. Now that there is a tag to tell you what's in the payload, the PPTP stack can add an IP header (specifying the destination address of the VPN server) and a PPP header.

7. Now the packet can be sent out over your PPP connection. The IP header specifies that it should be routed to the VPN server.

8. When the packet arrives at the VPN server, the server reverses steps 1 through 6 to extract the payload.

Encapsulation allows the use of VPN data inside ordinary-looking IP datagrams, which is part of what makes VPNs so powerful—you don't have to change any of your applications, routers, or network components (unless they have to be configured to recognize and pass GRE packets).

PPTP Tunneling

PPTP is a pretty straightforward protocol. It works by encapsulating packets using the mechanism described in the previous section, "An Encapsulation Primer," and performs encryption (step 4) using the *Microsoft Point-to-Point Encryption (MPPE) algorithm.* The encryption keys used to encrypt the packets are generated dynamically for each connection; in fact, the keys can be changed periodically during the connection.

When the client and server have successfully established a PPTP tunnel, the authorization process begins. This process is an exchange of credentials that allows the server to decide whether the client is permitted to connect:

1. The server sends a challenge message to the client.

2. The client answers with an encrypted response.

3. The server checks the response to see whether the answer is right. The challenge-response process allows the server to determine which account is trying to make a connection.

4. The server determines whether the user account is authorized to make a connection.

5. If the account is authorized, the server accepts the inbound connection; any access controls or remote access restrictions still apply.

L2TP/IPsec Tunneling

L2TP is much more flexible than PPTP, but it's also more complicated. It was designed to be a general-purpose tunneling protocol not limited to VPN use.

L2TP itself doesn't offer any kind of security. When you use L2TP, you're setting up an unencrypted, unauthenticated tunnel. Using L2TP by itself over the Internet, therefore, would be dangerous because anyone who wanted to could read your traffic.

The overall flow of an L2TP/IPsec tunnel session looks a little different from that of a PPTP session because IPsec security is different. Here's how the L2TP/IPsec combination works:

1. The client and server establish an IPsec security association using the ISAKMP and Oakley protocols. At this point, the two machines have an encrypted channel between them.

2. The client builds a new L2TP tunnel to the server. Because this happens after the channel has been encrypted, there's no security risk.

3. The server sends an authentication challenge to the client.

4. The client encrypts its answer to the challenge and returns it to the server.

5. The server checks the challenge response to see whether it's valid; if so, the server can determine which account is connecting. At this point, the server can accept the inbound connection, subject to whatever access policies you've put in place.

Note that steps 3 through 5 mirror the steps described for PPTP tunneling. This is because the authorization process is a function of the remote access server, not the VPN stack. All the VPN does is to provide a secure communications channel, and something else has to decide who gets to use it.

SSTP Tunneling

The *Secure Sockets Tunneling Protocol (SSTS)* is a secure way to make a VPN connection using the Secure Sockets Layer v.3 (SSL) port 443. The following steps show how SSTP operates and functions:

1. The client connects to the server through the Internet using port 443.

2. During the TCP session, SSL negotiation takes place.

3. During the SSL authentication phase, the client machine receives the server certificate.

4. The client machine will send HTTPS requests on top of the encrypted SSL session.

5. The client machine will then also send SSTP control packets on top of the HTTPS session.

6. PPP negotiation now takes place on both ends of the connection.

7. After PPP is finished, both ends are ready to send IP packets to each other.

Configuring Your Remote Access Server

Most of the configuration necessary for a remote access server happens at the server level. You use the server's Properties dialog box to control whether the server allows remote connections, what protocols and options it supports, and so forth. Because all of the protocols are carried via PPP, you can set some generic PPP options as well. I will cover these options in the following sections. You also have to configure settings for your users, which you'll read about in the next section, and you will install and configure the Remote Access role for the server in the first exercise.

Configuring PPP Options

You can use the PPP tab of the RRAS server's Properties dialog box (see Figure 4.3) to control the PPP layer options available to clients that call in. The settings you specify here control whether the related PPP options are available to clients; you can use remote access policies to control whether individual connections can use them.

FIGURE 4.3   The PPP tab of the RRAS server's Properties dialog box

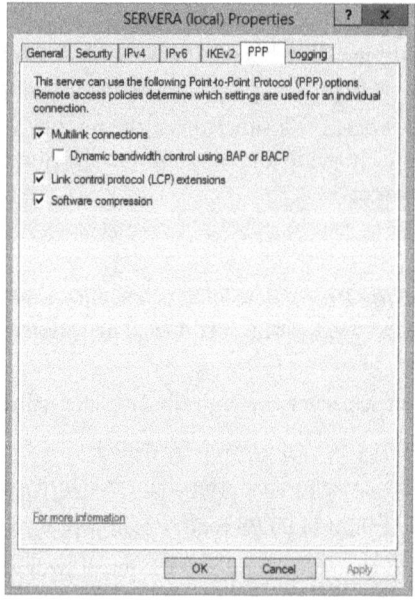

This tab has four check boxes:

- The Multilink Connections check box, which is selected by default, controls whether the server will allow clients to establish multilink connections when they call in.

- The Dynamic Bandwidth Control Using BAP Or BACP check box determines whether clients and servers are allowed to add or remove links dynamically during a multilink session. If you enable this feature, you can throttle the amount of available bandwidth up or down on demand. It's available only when the Multilink Connections check box is selected. (BAP stands for Bandwidth Allocation Protocol, and BACP stands for Bandwidth Allocation Control Protocol.)

- The Link Control Protocol (LCP) is used to establish a PPP link and negotiate its settings. A variety of LCP extensions are defined in various RFCs; these extensions allow a client and server to agree dynamically about which protocols are being passed back and forth, among other things. The Link Control Protocol (LCP) Extensions check box controls whether these extensions are available. Windows 9*x*, NT, 2000, Vista, XP, Windows 7, and Windows 8 clients depend on the LCP extensions, so you should leave this check box selected.

- The Software Compression check box controls whether RRAS will allow a remote client to use the Compression Control Protocol (CCP) to compress PPP traffic. In some cases, hardware compression at the modem level is more efficient, but not everyone has a compression-capable modem. You should leave this check box selected as well.

Configuring IP-Based Connections

TCP/IP is far and away the most commonly used remote access protocol; coincidentally, it's also the most configurable of the protocols that Windows Server 2012 R2 supports. Both of these facts are reflected in the IPv4 and IPv6 tabs of the server's Properties dialog box. Figure 4.4 shows the IPv4 tab.

FIGURE 4.4   The IPv4 tab of the RRAS server's Properties dialog box

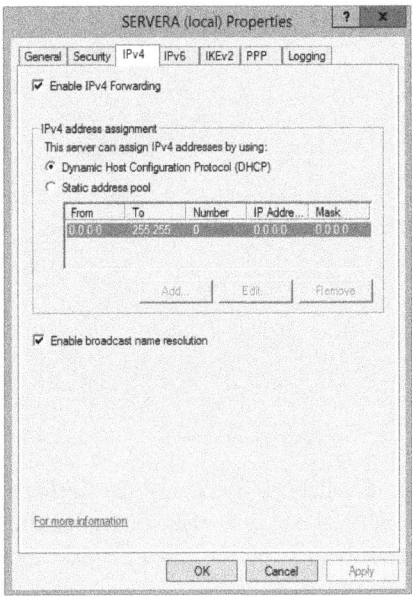

The controls on the IPv4 tab do the following:

- The Enable IPv4 Forwarding check box controls whether RRAS will route IPv4 packets between the remote client and other interfaces on your RRAS server. When this box is checked, as it is by default, remote clients' packets can go to the RRAS server or to any other host to which the RRAS server has a route. To allow clients to access resources on the RRAS server only, uncheck this box.

- The IP Address Assignment control group lets you specify how you want remote clients to get their IP addresses. The default settings here depend on what you told the RRAS Setup Wizard during setup:

  - If you want to use a DHCP server on your network as the source of IP addresses for remote clients, select the Dynamic Host Configuration Protocol (DHCP) radio button and make sure that you have the DHCP relay agent installed and running.

  - If you'd rather use static address allocation, select the Static Address Pool radio button. Then, in the list below, specify which IP address ranges you want issued to clients.

  - The Enable Broadcast Name Resolution option allows remote clients to resolve TCP/IP names without the use of a WINS or DNS server. This feature is enabled by default, and it is new for Windows Server 2012.

Figure 4.5 shows the IPv6 tab of the RRAS server's Properties dialog box. The controls on the IPv6 tab do the following:

FIGURE 4.5   The IPv6 tab of the RRAS Server's Properties dialog box

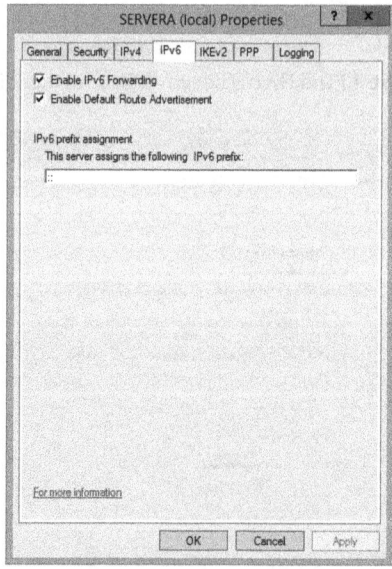

- The Enable IPv6 Forwarding check box controls whether RRAS will route IPv6 packets between the remote client and other interfaces on your RRAS server. When this box is checked, as it is by default, remote clients' packets can go to the RRAS server

or to any other host to which the RRAS server has a route. To allow clients to access resources on the RRAS server only, uncheck this box.

- The Enable Default Route Advertisement check box (enabled by default) makes the *Border Gateway Protocol (BGP)* routing protocol available. BGP can exchange routing information between Windows Server 2012 R2 routers. When this box is checked, your Windows Server 2012 R2 router can announce its route to other routers.

- On the IPv6 tab, you can also set up your IPv6 prefix assignment.

In Exercise 4.1, I will show you how to install and configure the Remote Access role onto your server. Just like many of our installations, you will use Server Manager to install the Remote Access role. This role also installs the DirectAccess role onto your server.

EXERCISE 4.1

Installing the Remote Access Role

1. Open Server Manager.

2. On the Server Manager dashboard, click the Add Roles And Features link (number 2).

3. If a Before You Begin screen appears, click Next.

4. On the Selection type page, choose a role-based or feature-based installation and click Next.

5. Click the top radio button, Select A Server From The Server Pool, and choose the server in the Server Pool section. Click Next.

6. On the Select Server Roles screen, click the Remote Access check box. If a pop-up window appears telling you that you need to add features, click the Add Features button. Click Next.

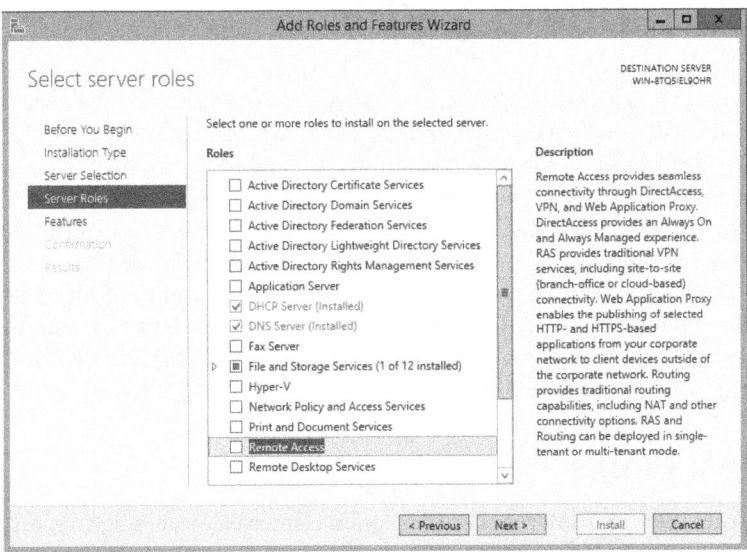

7. On the Add Features page, click Next.

8. On the Remote Access page, click Next.

9. On the Select role services page, choose the first two check boxes: DirectAccess and VPN (RAS) and Routing. If a pop-up window appears telling you that you need to add additional features, click the Add Features button. Click Next.

10. At the Web Server Role (IIS) page, click Next.

11. At the Select Role Services page, click Next.

12. At the Confirmation screen, click the Install button.

13. Open the Routing and Remote Access MMC in Administrative Tools.

14. Right-click your server name and choose Configure And Enable Routing And Remote Access.

15. At the Welcome Screen, click Next.

16. Choose the Custom Configuration radio button. Click Next.

17. Choose VPN access. Click Next.

18. Click Finish at the Completing screen.

19. Click the Start Service button.

Understanding a VPN

Conventional dial-up access works well, but as you saw earlier, it can be expensive to implement, painful to manage, and extremely slow by today's standards. VPNs offer a way around these problems by providing low initial and ongoing costs, easy management, and excellent speeds (depending on your connection). Windows Server 2012's RRAS component includes two complete VPN implementations: one using Microsoft's PPTP and one using a combination of the Internet-standard IPsec protocol and L2TP or SSTP.

The basic process of setting up a VPN is simple, but you need to think some things through before plunging ahead. Getting the VPN installation right may require small hardware or networking changes plus proper configuration of the VPN service. You will look at this process in the following sections.

How VPN Works

A VPN sits between your internal network and the Internet, accepting connections from clients in the outside world. In Figure 4.6, clients 1 and 2 are using different ISPs (probably because they're at different physical locations). For example, a packet from client 1 goes from its computer to its ISP and then through some route, unknown to you, that eventually delivers it to the VPN server, which transforms it into a packet suitable for use on the internal network.

Imagine a line around the internal network, and think of it as a security boundary. In general, you'll want your VPN server to be outside any firewalls or network security measures that you have in place. The most common configuration is to use two NICs: one connects to the Internet, and the other connects either to the private network or to an

FIGURE 4.6   VPNs provide private connections between clients and servers across the Internet

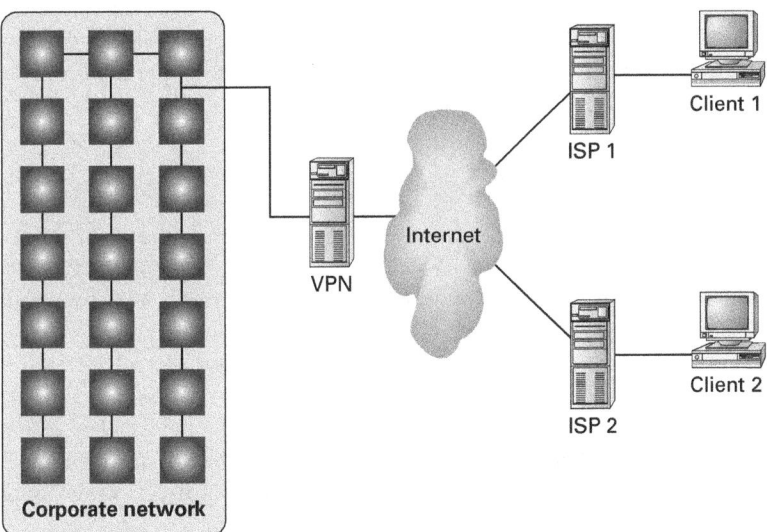

intermediate network that itself connects to the private network. Of course, you can use any type of Internet connection you want for the VPN server, such as cable modem, DSL, T1, satellite, or whatever.

The point behind giving the VPN its own network adapter is that your VPN clients need a public IP address to which they can connect, and you probably don't want them calling directly into your internal network. That also means that things will be easiest for your VPN users if the IP address for your VPN server's external interface is statically assigned so that it won't be changing on them when they least expect it.

Enabling RRAS as a VPN

If you're already using RRAS for IP routing or remote access, you can enable it as a VPN server without reinstalling.

The General tab of the server's Properties dialog box allows you to specify whether your RRAS server is a router, a remote access server, or both. The first step in converting your existing RRAS server to handle VPN traffic is to make sure that the IPv4 Remote Access Server or IPv6 Remote Access Server check box is selected on this tab.

Making this change requires you to stop and restart the RRAS service, but that's OK because the snap-in will do it for you. Then you must configure VPN ports, as shown in the following sections.

Configuring a VPN

VPN configuration is extremely simple, at least for PPTP. Either a server can accept VPN calls or it can't. If it can, it will have a certain number of VPN ports, all of which are configured identically. You don't have to change or tweak much to get a VPN server set up, but you can adjust a few things as you like.

Configuring VPN Ports

The biggest opportunity to configure your VPN server is to adjust the number and kind of VPN ports available for clients to use. You can enable or disable either PPTP or L2TP, depending on what you want your remote users to be able to access. You accomplish this through the Ports Properties dialog box.

For conventional remote access servers, this dialog box shows you a list of hardware ports, but for servers that support VPN connections, there are two WAN Miniport device selections: one for PPTP and one for L2TP. (These aren't really devices; they're actually virtual ports maintained by RRAS for accepting VPN connections.) You configure these ports by selecting one and clicking the Configure button, which displays the Configure Device – WAN Miniport (PPTP) dialog box (see Figure 4.7).

FIGURE 4.7   The Configure Device – WAN Miniport (PPTP) dialog box

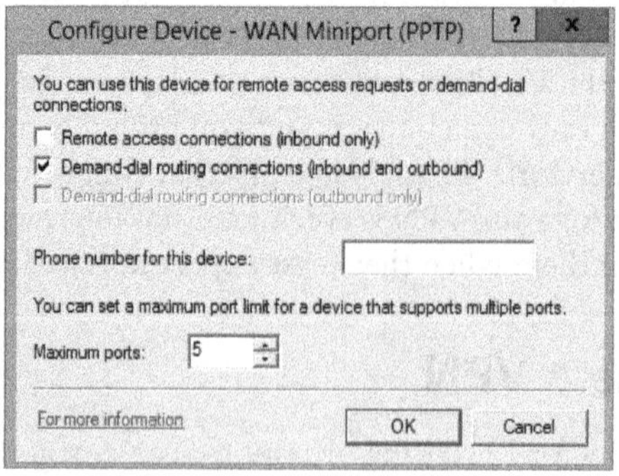

Three controls are pertinent to a VPN configuration:

- The Remote Access Connections (Inbound Only) check box must be activated in order to accept VPN connections with this port type. To disable a VPN type (for instance, if you want to turn off L2TP), uncheck this box.

- The Demand-Dial Routing Connections (Inbound And Outbound) check box controls whether this VPN type can be used for demand-dial connections. By default, this box is checked; you'll need to uncheck it if you don't want to use VPN connections to link your network with other networks.

- The Maximum Ports control lets you set the number of inbound connections that this port type will support. By default, you get 5 PPTP and 5 L2TP ports when you install RRAS; you can use from 0 to 250 ports of each type by adjusting the number here.

You can also use the Phone Number For This Device field to enter the IP address of the public interface to which VPN clients connect. You might want to do this if your remote access policies accept or reject connections based on the number called by the client. Because you can assign multiple IP addresses to a single adapter, you can control VPN traffic by throttling which clients can connect to which addresses through a policy.

Troubleshooting VPNs

The two primary problems you might encounter with VPN are as follows:

- Inability to establish a connection at all

- Inability to reach some needed resource once connected

There's a lot of common ground between the process of troubleshooting a VPN connection and the process of troubleshooting an ordinary remote access connection.

The following are some extremely simple—but sometimes overlooked—things to check when your VPN clients can't connect. First, make sure your clients can make the underlying connection to their ISP; then, check the following:

- Is RRAS installed and configured on the server?

  - Is the server configured to allow remote access? Check the General tab of the server's Properties dialog box.

  - Is the server configured to allow VPN traffic? Check the Ports Properties dialog box to make sure that the appropriate VPN protocol is enabled and that the number of ports for that protocol is greater than 0.

  - Are there any available VPN ports? If you have 10 L2TP ports allocated, the 11th caller will not be able to connect.

- Do the client and server match?

  - Is the VPN protocol used by the client enabled on the server? Windows 2000 and newer clients will try L2TP first and switch to PPTP as a second choice. However, clients on other OSs (including Windows NT) can normally expect L2TP, PPTP, or SSTP (2008 or higher).

- Are the client and server authenticated correctly?
    - Are the username and password correct?
    - Does the user account in question have remote access permissions, either directly on the account or through a policy?
    - Do the authentication settings in the server's policies (if any) match the supported set of authentication protocols?

If you check all of the simple stuff and find nothing wrong, it's time to move on to checking more complex issues. These tend to affect more than one user, as opposed to the simple (and generally user-specific) issues just outlined. The problems include the following:

Policy Problems If you're using a native-mode Windows Server 2012 R2 domain and you're using policies, those policies may cause some subtle problems that show up under some circumstances:

- Are there any policies whose Allow or Deny settings conflict with each other? Remember that all conditions of all policies must match to gain user access; if any condition of any policy fails or if there are any policies that deny access, the connection will be denied.
- Does the user match all of the necessary conditions that are in place, such as time and date?

Network Problems If you're using dynamic IP addressing, are there any addresses left in the pool? If the VPN server can't assign an address, it won't accept the connection.

Domain Problems Windows Server 2012 R2 RRAS servers can coexist with Windows NT RRAS servers, and both of them can interoperate with RADIUS servers from Microsoft and other vendors. Sometimes, though, this interoperation doesn't work exactly as you'd expect. Here are some questions to ask:

- Is the RRAS server's domain membership correct? Your RRAS servers don't have to be domain members unless you want to use native-mode features such as remote access policies.
- If you're in a domain, are the server's group memberships correct? The server account must be a member of the RAS group and Internet Authentication Servers security group.

Managing Your Remote Access Server

RRAS server management is generally pretty easy because, in most cases, there's not much to manage. You set up the server, and it answers calls. You'll probably find it necessary to monitor the server's ongoing activity, however, and you may find it necessary to log activity for accounting or security purposes.

You can monitor your server's activity in a number of ways, including having the server keep local copies of its logs or having it send logging data to a remote RADIUS server. In addition, you can monitor the current status of any of the ports on your system.

Microsoft's documentation distinguishes between event logging, which records significant things that happen such as the RRAS service starting up and shutting down, and authentication and accounting logging, which tracks things like when a user logged on and logged off. The settings for both types of logging are intermingled in the RRAS snap-in.

Managing Remote Users with a RADIUS Server

Remote Authentication Dial-In User Service (RADIUS) allows for maintaining and managing your remote users. A RADIUS server allows Remote Access Service (RAS) clients and dial-up routers to be authenticated.

Network Policy Server (NPS) is Microsoft's implementation of a RADIUS server in Windows Server 2012. NPS is replacing Windows Server 2003 Internet Authentication Service (IAS). NPS, working as a RADIUS server, allows for authentication, authorization, and accounting for wireless and VPN networks.

NPS allows a server to perform the duties of a RADIUS proxy. A RADIUS proxy allows the routing of RADIUS messages between RADIUS clients (RAS) and RADIUS servers. NPS also gives you the ability to record information about forwarded messages in an accounting log.

Monitoring Overall Activity

The Server Status node in the RRAS snap-in shows you a summary of all the RRAS servers known to the system. When you select the Server Status item, the right pane of the MMC will list each known RRAS server. Each entry in the list tells you whether the server is up, what kind of server it is, how many ports it has, how many ports are currently in use, and how long the server has been up. You can right-click any Windows Server 2012 R2 RRAS server in this view to start, stop, restart, pause, or resume its RRAS service; disable RRAS on the server; or remove the server's advertisement from Active Directory (provided, of course, that you're using Active Directory).

Controlling Remote Access Logging

A standard RRAS installation will always log some data locally, but that's pretty useless unless you know what gets logged and where it goes. Each RRAS server on your network has its own set of logs, which you manage through the Remote Access Logging folder. Within that folder, you'll usually see a single item labeled *Local File*, which is the log file stored on that particular server.

If you don't have Windows accounting or Windows authentication turned on, you won't have a local log file. Depending on whether you're using RADIUS accounting and logging, you may see additional entries.

Setting Server Logging Properties

You can control server logging at the server level. You use the Logging tab to control what level of detail you want in the server's event log.

 These controls regulate all logging by RRAS, not just remote access log entries.

You have four choices for the level of logged detail:

- The Log Errors Only radio button instructs the server to log errors and nothing else. This gives you an adequate indication of problems after they happen, but it doesn't point out potential problems noted by warning messages.

- The Log Errors And Warnings radio button is the default choice. This forces the server to log error and warning messages to the event log, giving you a nice balance between information content and log volume.

- The Log All Events radio button causes the RRAS service to log mass quantities of messages, literally covering everything the server does. Although this voluminous output is useful for troubleshooting (or even for getting a better understanding of how remote access works), it's overkill for everyday use.

- The Do Not Log Any Events radio button turns off all event logging for RRAS.

 Don't use the Do Not Log Any Events option. The service's logs are important in case of a problem.

The Log Additional Routing And Remote Access Information check box allows you to turn on the logging of all PPP negotiations and connections. This can provide valuable information when you're trying to figure out what's wrong, but it adds a lot of unnecessary bulk to your log files. Don't turn it on unless you're trying to pin down a problem.

Setting Log File Properties

By selecting an individual log file in the snap-in, you can change what events will be logged in that file. The Local Log File Properties dialog box has two tabs:

- The Settings tab controls what gets logged in the file:
    - Accounting Requests governs whether events related to the service will be logged (as well as accounting data). You should always leave this checked.

- Authentication Requests adjusts whether successful and failed logon requests are logged. You should always leave this checked.

- Periodic Status controls whether interim accounting packets are permanently stored on disk. You should usually leave this checked.

- Periodic Authentication Requests adjusts whether successful and failed logon requests are periodically logged. You should always leave this checked.

- The Log File tab (see Figure 4.8) controls the format of the file, specifically, how the log file is written to disk. You use this tab to designate three things:

  - The Directory field shows where the log file is stored. By default, each server logs its data in *systemroot*\system32\LogFiles. You can change this location to wherever you want.

  - The Format controls determine the format of the log file. By default, Windows Server 2000, 2003, 2008/2008 R2, and 2012/2012 R2 use the database-compatible file format. This format makes it easy for you to take log data and store it in a database, enabling more sophisticated postprocessing for things such as billing and chargebacks.

  - The Create A New Log File controls determine how often new log files are created. For example, some administrators prefer to start a new log file each week or each month, whereas others are content to let the log file grow without end. You can choose to have RRAS start new log files every day, week, month, never, or when the log file reaches a certain size.

FIGURE 4.8 The Log File tab

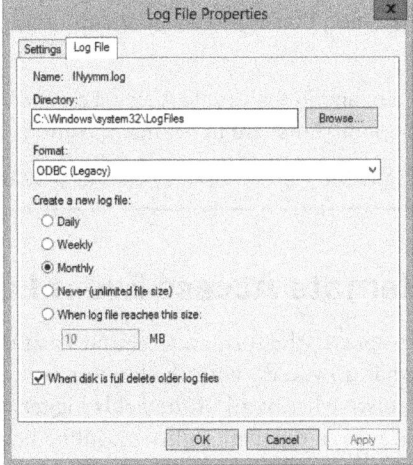

Having correct accounting and authorization data is critical to maintaining a good level of security. Exercise 4.2 walks you through configuring remote access logging.

EXERCISE 4.2

Changing Remote Access Logging Settings

1. Open the RRAS MMC snap-in by pressing the Windows key and selecting Administrative Tools ➢ Routing And Remote Access.

2. Navigate to the Remote Access Logging and Policies folder. Right-click the folder and select Launch NPS.

3. On the left pane, click Accounting. On the right side, click Change Log File Properties.

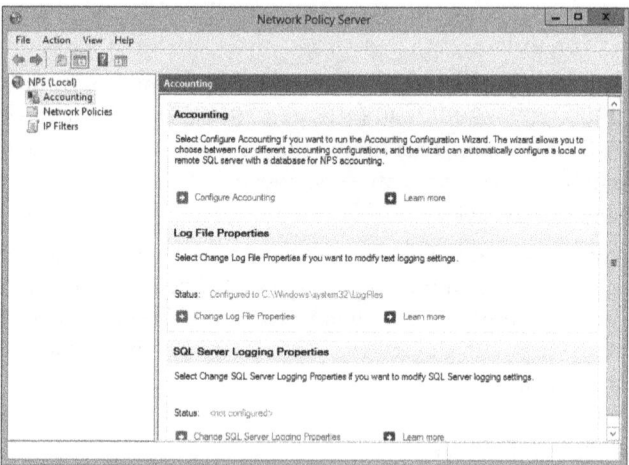

4. The Local File Logging dialog box appears. On the Settings tab, make sure that all check boxes are marked.

5. Switch to the Log File tab, and in the Create A New Log File controls, select the When Log File Reaches This Size option. Enter **50** to set the maximum size of the log file to 50MB.

6. Click the OK button. Close the Network Policy Server window.

Reviewing the Remote Access Event Log

You use the Log File tab to specify the format, size, and location of the log file. Once you have a log file, however, what do you do with the log information? Windows Server 2012 R2 online help has an exhaustive list of all of the fields logged for each connection attempt and accounting record. Because of the availability of online help, you don't need to have all of those fields memorized, and you don't have to remember exactly how to make sense of the log entries.

Why bother reviewing the logs? One nice feature is that each entry in the authentication log indicates which remote access policy was applied (either to accept or to reject the connection). This is a good way to identify problems with policies because sometimes multiple policies can combine to have an effect that you didn't expect.

Furthermore, if it's desirable in your environment, you can use the logged data to generate accounting reports to tell you things such as the average utilization of your dial-in ports, the top 10 users of dial-in connect time, or how much online time accounts or certain Windows groups use.

Monitoring Ports and Port Activity

You can monitor port status and activity from the RRAS snap-in. The Ports folder under the server contains one entry for each defined port. When you select the Ports folder, you'll see a list of the ports and their current status. The list indicates whether each port is a dial-in or VPN port and whether it's active, so you can get a quick summary of your server's workload at any time.

Double-clicking an individual port displays the Port Status dialog box (see Figure 4.9). This dialog box shows information such as a port's line speed (Line BPS), the amount of transmitted and received data (Bytes In and Bytes Out), and the network address for each protocol being carried on the port. This is a useful tool for verifying whether a port is in active use, and it gives you a count of the number of transmission and reception errors on the port.

FIGURE 4.9 The Port Status dialog box

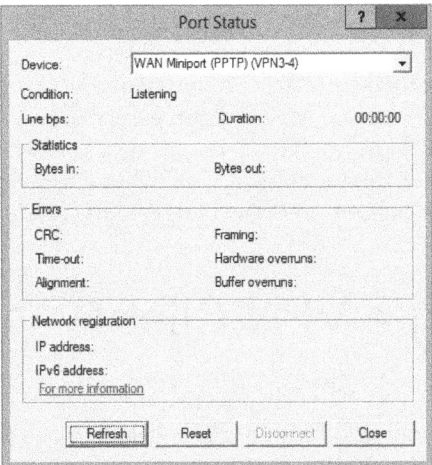

Network Address Translation

Network Address Translation (NAT) provides an advantage with routing and tunneling. NAT (also referred to as network masquerading) allows a router to translate one IP address to another across the tunnel. This allows you to use private IP addressing internally but use pubic addresses between the tunnels.

The huge advantage of NAT is the ability for you to share a single public IP address and single Internet connection between multiple locations using private IP addressing schemes. The nodes on the private network use nonroutable private addresses. NAT maps the private addresses to the public address.

Implementing NAT

Implementing NAT is an easy process. I am going to show you the steps needed to implement NAT, but I am not going to do it as an exercise. To set up NAT in an exercise without a tunnel or without multiple networks is not always an easy thing to do. So, I will just show you how to implement NAT in case you need to do it at work. To run these steps, you must be a member of at least the local Administrators group or higher. The following steps show you how to implement NAT:

1. Start the Routing and Remote Access MMC snap-in (under Administrative Tools). Right-click your server name and choose Configure And Enable Routing And Remote Access.

2. At the Welcome Screen, click Next.

3. Choose the Custom Configuration radio button. Click Next.

4. Click NAT and click Next.

5. Start Service.

6. Expand your server name.

7. Expand IPv4.

At this point, you can configure NAT. If you need to install NAT, you must have a system with multiple NIC devices or a demand-dial setup.

NAT is also commonly used for Internet connections, but this is done through your firewall or router. For example, let's say you have an Internet service provider that issues you only four valid Internet TCP/IP addresses for you to use on your network. You can set up NAT and program it to use those four valid addresses. Then, when a user from the network wants to access the Internet, NAT swaps the user's internal IP address for one of the valid IP addresses.

Configuring a VPN Client

Dial-up RAS clients and VPN clients are similar. Almost all of the options that are available when you set up a RAS client are also available when you set up a VPN client. The main differences are as follows:

- VPN clients specify the server's IP address, whereas RAS clients specify the server's phone number.

- VPN clients require an underlying connection to the Internet.

Client configuration is not a focus of the exam, so in this chapter you will learn how to configure a VPN client but not a RAS client. Just remember that the RAS client configuration is extremely similar and that RAS clients are slowly fading away. Thus, here I will focus on VPN settings only.

VPN connections are almost always created on client workstations, so this section describes the settings in Windows 7 and Windows 8.

When you establish a virtual private network connection, you're actually building an encrypted tunnel between you and some other machine. The tunneled data is carried over an insecure network, such as the Internet.

Once you've created a connection, you can change its properties at any time by opening its Properties dialog box. The Dial-Up Connection Properties dialog box has a total of five tabs that you can use to adjust all of the pertinent settings for each connection.

Don't confuse these settings with the ones in the Local Area Connection Properties dialog box; they serve entirely different purposes.

The General Tab

The General tab of the Connection Properties dialog box (the box is called Dial-Up Connections or VPN Connections, depending on whether you're configuring dial-up RAS or VPN) is where you specify either the IP address of the VPN server or the modem and phone number to use with this particular connection. Some fields have been filled in already from when you used the Network Connection Wizard. Figure 4.10 shows the VPN settings.

FIGURE 4.10   General tab of the VPN Connection Properties dialog box

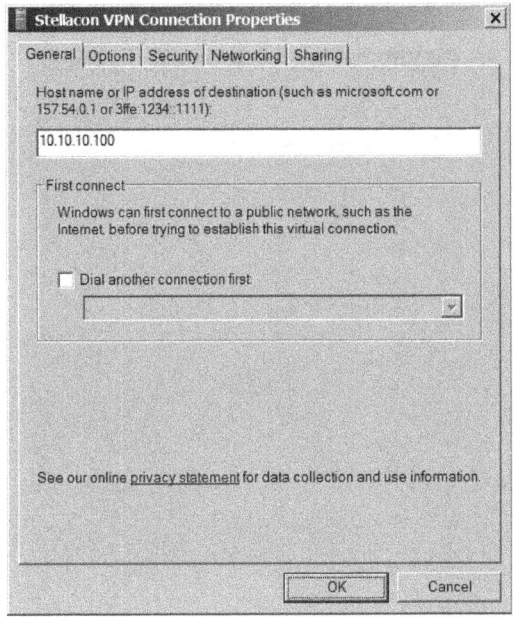

The General tab has a field where you enter the VPN server address or hostname. The First Connect group lets you specify which dial-up connection, if any, you want brought up before the VPN connection is established.

With the General tab, you can also do the following:

- Set VPN options:
  - Enter the VPN server address or hostname.
  - Specify whether to dial another connection automatically first and then specify the connection to dial.
- Set RAS options:
  - Change the modem this connection uses, or the settings for the modem you already have, with the Configure button.

 When configuring dial-up, you can also use the Phone And Modem Options control panel to adjust a broader range of modem settings.

The Options Tab

The Options tab holds settings that control how DUN dials and redials the connection. The controls in this dialog box are segregated into two groups. The Dialing Options group holds controls that govern DUN's interface behavior while dialing, and the Redialing Options group controls whether and how DUN will redial if it doesn't immediately connect (see Figure 4.11).

FIGURE 4.11   Options tab of the VPN Connection Properties dialog box

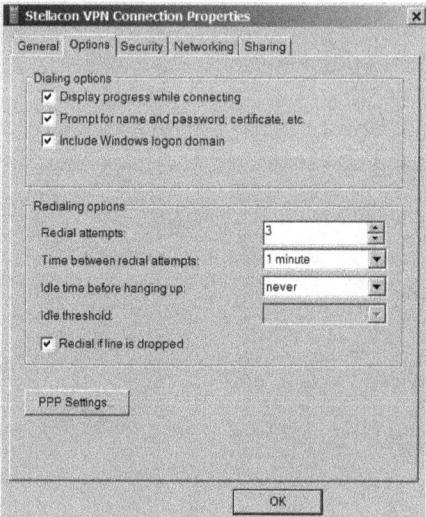

Dialing Options

Four dialing options are available in the Dialing Options group:

- The Display Progress While Connecting check box (selected by default) instructs DUN to keep you updated on its progress as it attempts to raise the connection.

- The Prompt For Name And Password, Certificate, Etc. check box is also selected by default. When it's on, Windows will prompt you for any credentials it needs to authenticate your connection to the remote server. This may be a username, a password, a public key certificate, or some combination of the three, depending on what the remote end requires.

- The Include Windows Logon Domain check box is unchecked by default. It forces DUN to include the domain name of the domain to which you're logged on as part of the authentication credential. Leave this unchecked unless you're dialing into a Windows NT/2000 network that has a trust relationship with your logon domain.

- For RAS connections, a Prompt For Phone Number check box tells DUN to display the phone number in the connection dialog box. This box is checked by default. This gives you a chance to edit the phone number before dialing; you may want to uncheck it if you (or your users) are prone to making accidental changes.

Redialing Options

The settings in the Redialing Options group control how DUN will attempt to redial the specified number if the remote end is busy or doesn't answer with a recognizable carrier tone. These settings are as follows:

- The Redial Attempts field controls how many attempts DUN will make to raise the other end before giving up. The default value is 3, but you can set any value from 0 (meaning that DUN won't attempt to redial) to 999,999,999.

- The Time Between Redial Attempts drop-down menu controls how long DUN will wait after each failed call before it tries again. Values in the drop-down menu range from 1 second all the way up to 10 minutes, with various increments in between.

- The Idle Time Before Hanging Up drop-down menu lets you specify an inactivity timer. If your connection is idle for longer than the specified period, your client will terminate the call. Note that the remote end may drop the call sooner than your client, depending on how it's configured. By default, this drop-down menu is set to Never, meaning that your client will never drop a call. If you want an inactivity timer, you can pick values ranging from 1 minute to 24 hours.

- The Redial If Line Is Dropped check box automatically redials the number if you are disconnected.

The Security Tab

How useful you find the Security tab will depend on whom you're calling. The default settings it provides will work fine with most Internet service providers and corporate dial-up facilities, but Windows 7 and Windows 8 have a broad range of security settings that you can change if you require. The Security Options group contains controls that directly affect the security of your connection. The Advanced (Custom Settings) radio button controls settings such as encryption and authentication protocols.

Security Options

The controls in the Security Options group are pretty straightforward. The security settings in effect for this connection are governed by your choice between the Typical (Recommended Settings) and Advanced (Custom Settings) radio buttons (see Figure 4.12).

FIGURE 4.12   Security tab of the VPN Connection Properties dialog box

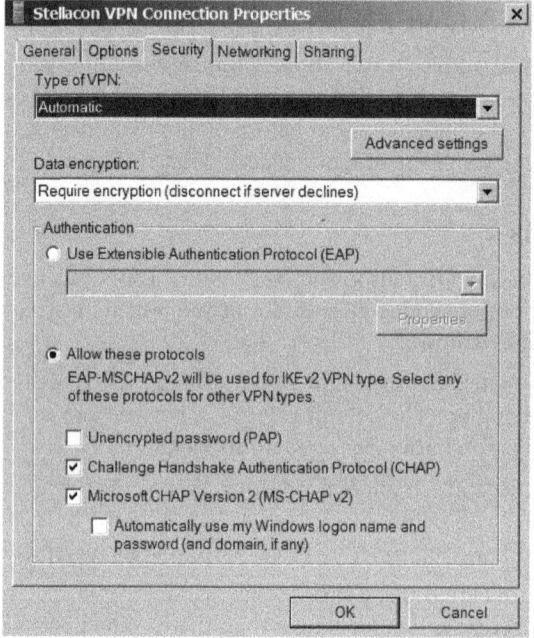

Typical (Recommended Settings)

Usually, it's best to stick with the Typical (Recommended Settings) option and use its subordinate controls to pick a canned setting that matches your needs. These subordinate controls are as follows:

- The Validate My Identity As Follows drop-down menu lets you choose among the following authentication methods:
    - Unsecured passwords (the default, and the only type of authentication that most networks support)

- Secured passwords
- Smart card authentication (useful only when calling another Windows 2000, 2003, 2008/2008 R2, or 2012/2012 R2 network)

- If you choose to require a secured password, the Automatically Use My Windows Logon Name And Password (And Domain If Any) check box instructs DUN to offer to the remote end the logon credentials you used to log on to the computer or domain. This is useful only if you're dialing into a network that has access to your domain authentication information.

- If you require a secured password or smart card authentication, the Require Encryption (Disconnect If None) check box allows you to have either an encrypted connection or none at all. If you check this box, your client and the remote server will attempt to negotiate a common encryption method. If they can't (perhaps because the remote end doesn't offer encryption), your client will hang up.

Advanced (Custom Settings)

If you select the Advanced (Custom Settings) radio button and then click the Settings button, you'll see the Advanced Security Settings dialog box. Its controls are more complex than the ones on the Security tab.

The first field is the Data Encryption drop-down menu. Windows 8 offers you the opportunity to encrypt both sides of network connections using IPsec. This capability extends to dial-up connections too. The drop-down menu gives you the following four choices:

- No Encryption Allowed means that the server will drop your call if it requires encryption because you can't provide it.

- Optional Encryption tells the client to request encryption but to continue the call if it's not available.

- Require Encryption tells the client to request encryption and to refuse to communicate with servers that don't support it.

- Maximum Strength Encryption tells the client to communicate only with servers that offer the same strength encryption it does. For example, with this setting in force, a North American Windows Server 2008 R2 machine running 3DES won't communicate with a French Windows XP machine because the French machine uses the weaker exportable encryption routines.

The Authentication section controls which authentication protocols this client can use. The default setting, Use Extensible Authentication Protocol (EAP), is for standard Windows authentication (using the MD5-Challenge method) or certificate-based authentication (using the Smart Card Or Other Certificate choice in the drop-down menu).

The Allow These Protocols radio button is followed by a long list of authentication protocols. Although the specifics of how they work are different, the basic idea behind all of these protocols is the same. Each provides a secure way for a client to prove its identity to a server. By selecting the appropriate check boxes, you can make your client use the same protocols as the remote end.

The Networking Tab

You use the Networking tab (see Figure 4.13) to control which protocols your client will attempt to use when communicating with other servers.

FIGURE 4.13   Networking tab of the VPN Connection Properties dialog box

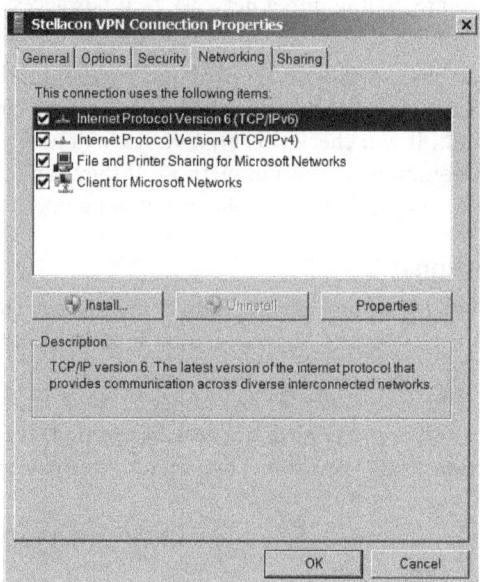

The list box in the middle of the tab shows the network protocols installed on the client. Protocols marked with a check are available for use with this connection. Usually, when configuring RAS, you'll see TCP/IP and Client For Microsoft Networks marked, which indicates that those two protocols can be used over the connection.

The Install, Uninstall, and Properties buttons work just as they do in the Local Area Connection Properties dialog box. By using them, you can control which protocols are on your machine and their settings.

It's worth mentioning that selecting Internet Protocol (TCP/IP) in the protocols list and opening its Properties dialog box gives you access to a set of properties that are completely distinct from any TCP/IP settings that may apply to your LAN interfaces. Usually, the dial-up TCP/IP settings are configured to obtain an IP address and DNS information from the remote server, although if you need to, you can override these settings.

The Sharing Tab

Internet Connection Sharing allows other users to connect to the Internet through this machine. The machine on which you enable this feature works like a gateway to the Internet (see Figure 4.14).

FIGURE 4.14   Sharing tab of the VPN Connection Properties dialog box

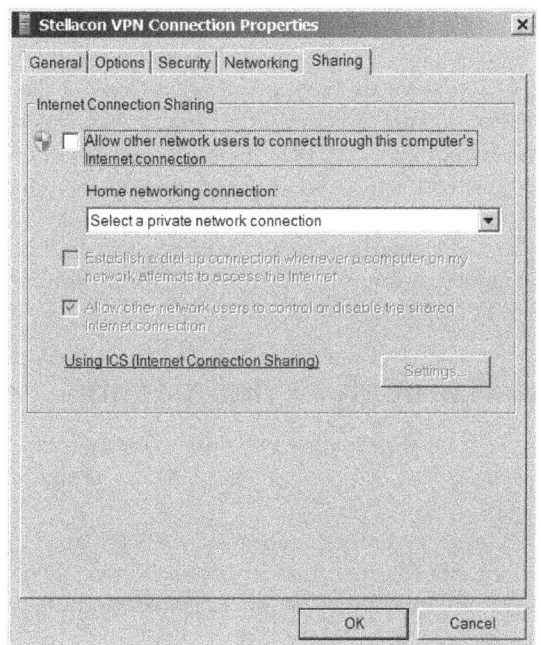

Configuring a Web Application Proxy

One of the new advantages of using the Remote Access role service in Windows Server 2012 R2 is the Web Application Proxy. Normally, your users access applications on the Internet from your corporate network. The *Web Application Proxy* reverses this feature, and it allows your corporate users to access applications from any device outside the network.

Administrators can choose which applications to provide reverse proxy features, and this allows administrators the ability to give access selectively to corporate users for the desired application that you want to set up for the Web Application Proxy service.

The Web Application Proxy feature allows applications running on servers inside the corporate network to be accessed by any device outside the corporate network. The process of allowing an application to be available to users outside of the corporate network is known as *publishing*.

Publishing Applications

One disadvantage to corporate networks are that the machines that access the network are normally devices issued by the organization. That's where Web Application Proxy publishing can help.

Web Application Proxy allows an administrator to publish an organization's applications, thus allowing corporate end users the ability to access the applications from their own devices. This is becoming a big trend in the computer industry called *bring your own device* (BYOD).

In today's technology world, users are buying and using many of their own devices, even for business work. Because of this, the users are comfortable with their own devices. Web Application Proxy allows an organization to set up applications and enable their corporate users to use these applications with the devices the users already own including computers, tablets, and smartphones.

The client side is easy to use as long as the end user has a standard browser or Office client. End users can also use apps from the Microsoft Windows Store that allow the client system to connect to the Web Application Proxy.

Configuring Pass-Through Authentication

Now when setting up the Web Application Proxy so that your users can access applications, you must have some kind of security or everyone with a device would be able to access and use your applications.

Because of this, Active Directory Federation Services (AD FS) must always be deployed with Web Application Proxy. AD FS gives you features such as single sign-on (SSO). *Single sign-on* allows you to log in one time with a set of credentials and use that set of credentials to access the applications over and over.

Pass-through authentication is truly a great benefit for your end users. Think of having a network where a user has to log in every time that user wants to access an application. The more times you make your end users log into an application, the more chances there are that the end user will encounter possible issues. Pass-through authentication works in the following way:

1.   The client enters a URL address on their device, and the client system attempts to access the published web application.

2.   The Web Application Proxy sends the request to the proxy server.

3.   If the backend server needs the user to authenticate, the end user needs to enter their credentials only once.

4.   After the server authenticates the credentials, the client has access to the published web application.

 When an administrators sets up applications to use pass-through pre-authentication, additional features of AD FS will not function. For example, you will not be able to use AD FS Workplace Join, multifactor authentication (MFA), and multifactor access control.

Understanding DirectAccess

DirectAccess was a new technology that was introduced in the Windows Server 2008 R2 and Windows 7 operating systems. DirectAccess has been improved upon, and it is also available for Windows 8 and Windows Server 2012 R2.

DirectAccess allows a remote user to work on their corporate network when they are away from the office without the need for a VPN. As long as the remote user is connected to the Internet, DirectAccess will automatically connect the remote user to the corporate network without the need for any user intervention.

When a user's DirectAccess-enabled laptop is connected to the Internet, a bidirectional connection is automatically established with the user's corporate network. Because the connection is bidirectional, the IT administrator can also remotely manage the Windows 7 or Windows 8 machine while the machine is away from the network.

DirectAccess vs. VPNs

There really is no debate between VPN or DirectAccess—DirectAccess is the better way to go. The downside to DirectAccess is that it requires a great deal of time, resources, and knowledge to set it up properly.

There are a few problems with using VPNs to connect to a network. One issue is that when a user gets disconnected from their VPN connection, they must reestablish the VPN connection.

Another issue with VPNs is that many organizations filter VPN connection traffic. It may not be possible for an organization to open a firewall to allow VPN traffic. Also, if your intranet and your Internet connections are the same as your VPN connections, this can cause your Internet to be slower.

DirectAccess does not face the same limitations of a VPN. DirectAccess allows a laptop or desktop that is configured properly to connect automatically using a bidirectional connection between the client and the server.

To establish this connection, DirectAccess uses Internet Protocol Security (IPsec) and IPv6. IPsec provides a high level of security between the client and the server, and IPv6 is the protocol that the machines use.

Understanding the DirectAccess Process

Before you can set up the features and benefits of DirectAccess, there are some prerequisites that I must first go over. DirectAccess is great way to get your users to access the network from the road, but it is not the easiest thing to set up, and it must be done correctly.

DirectAccess Prerequisites

As with any software package, role, or feature, when you install any one of these, there are always prerequisites that you must deal with. DirectAccess is no different. The following is a list of DirectAccess Server with Advanced Settings prerequisites:

- A public key infrastructure must be deployed.

- ISATAP in the corporate network is not supported. If you are using ISATAP, you should remove it and use native IPv6.

- Computers that are running the following operating systems are supported as DirectAccess clients:
  - Windows Server 2012 R2
  - Windows 8.1 Enterprise
  - Windows Server 2012
  - Windows 8 Enterprise
  - Windows Server 2008 R2
  - Windows 7 Ultimate
  - Windows 7 Enterprise

- Force tunnel configuration is not supported with KerbProxy authentication.

- Changing policies by using a feature other than the DirectAccess management console or Windows PowerShell cmdlets is not supported.

- Separating NAT64/DNS64 and IPHTTPS server roles on another server is not supported.

The following is the list of prerequisites if you want to manage DirectAccess clients remotely:

- Windows Firewall must be enabled on all profiles.

- ISATAP in the corporate network is not supported. If you are using ISATAP, you should remove it and use native IPv6.

- Computers that are running the following operating systems are supported as DirectAccess clients:
  - Windows Server 2012 R2
  - Windows 8.1 Enterprise
  - Windows Server 2012
  - Windows 8 Enterprise
  - Windows Server 2008 R2
  - Windows 7 Ultimate
  - Windows 7 Enterprise

- Changing policies by using a feature other than the DirectAccess management console or Windows PowerShell cmdlets is not supported.

Understanding DirectAccess

To understand DirectAccess better, it helps to understand the process involved with how DirectAccess operates. The following steps, taken from the Microsoft white papers, show how DirectAccess operates.

1. The Windows 8 DirectAccess client determines whether the machine is connected to a network or the Internet.

2. The Windows 8 DirectAccess computer tries to connect to the web server specified during the DirectAccess setup configuration.

3. The Windows 8 DirectAccess client computer connects to the Windows Server 2012 R2 DirectAccess server using IPv6 and IPsec. Because most users connect to the Internet using IPv4, the client establishes an IPv6-over-IPv4 tunnel using 6to4 or Teredo.

4. If an organization has a firewall that prevents the DirectAccess client computer using 6to4 or Teredo from connecting to the DirectAccess server, the Windows 8 client automatically attempts to connect using the IP-HTTPS protocol.

5. As part of establishing the IPsec session, the Windows 8 DirectAccess client and server authenticate each other using computer certificates for authentication.

6. The DirectAccess server uses Active Directory membership, and the DirectAccess server verifies that the computer and user are authorized to connect using DirectAccess.

7. The DirectAccess server begins forwarding traffic from the DirectAccess client to the intranet resources to which the user has been granted access.

Now that you understand how DirectAccess works, let's look at the requirements for setting up DirectAccess on your network.

Knowing the DirectAccess Infrastructure Requirements

To set up DirectAccess, you must make sure that your network infrastructure meets some minimum requirements. The following are the requirements for setting up DirectAccess:

- Windows Server 2012 R2 configured to use DirectAccess. The Windows Server 2012 R2 machine will be set up as a multihomed system. This means your server will need two network adapters so that one adapter is connected directly to the Internet and a second adapter is connected to the intranet. Each network adapter will be configured with its own TCP/IP address.

- Windows 7 or Windows 8 client machines configured to use DirectAccess.

- Minimum of one domain controller and one Domain Name System (DNS) server running Windows Server 2008 SP2, Windows Server 2008 R2, Windows Server 2012, or Windows Server 2012 R2.

- Certificate authority (CA) server that will issue computer certificates, smart card certificates, or health certificates.
- IPsec policies to specify protection for traffic.
- IPv6 on the DirectAccess server that uses ISATAP, Teredo, or 6to4.

Summary

In this chapter, you learned how to install and configure Routing and Remote Access Services to handle dial-in connections, how to configure appropriate encryption and security settings so that communication between the client and server is encrypted and authenticated, how to install RRAS to provide VPN service using the PPTP and L2TP protocols, how to configure VPN services on the server and client, and, finally, how to troubleshoot common problems with VPNs.

Exam Essentials

Know how to install and configure RAS at the server level. The RAS installation process is driven by the Routing and Remote Access Server Setup Wizard, which you use to set up a dial-up server. You can specify whether the server acts as a remote access server, specify what authentication providers and settings you want the server to use, control the settings applied to each protocol you have installed, specify which PPP protocols (including multilink) the clients on this server are allowed to use, and control what level of log detail is kept for incoming connections.

Know how to install and configure a VPN server. If you don't have RRAS installed, you'll need to install it, activate it, and configure it as a VPN server. If you're already using RRAS for IP routing or remote access, you can enable it as a VPN server without reinstalling. VPN configuration is extremely simple, at least for PPTP. Either a server can accept VPN calls or it can't. If it can, it will have a certain number of VPN ports, all of which are configured identically.

Know how to configure an RRAS client. Most client connections are made on Windows 8, Windows 7, Windows Vista, or Windows XP Professional workstations. Dial-in and VPN connections are configured similarly, but when creating a VPN connection, you must substitute an IP address for a phone number.

Review Questions

1. You have a local DHCP server for your dial-in clients, but you also want to use the DHCP relay agent to forward requests to a remote DHCP server if the local server doesn't answer a request. To do this, you must do which of the following?

    A. Add a static route to the remote server.

    B. Adjust the boot threshold on the DHCP relay agent interface for the remote network so that the local server has enough time to respond.

    C. Adjust the DHCP Forwarding Time parameter in the registry.

    D. Adjust the forwarding time in the DHCP Relay Agent Global Properties dialog box.

2. You are considering multilink PPP in order to increase bandwidth available for a dial-up client. Which of the following is not a benefit of multilink?

    A. Multilink can make the client experience faster by combining multiple phone lines and creating one logical PPP connection.

    B. Multilink enables the encryption of data between the client and the server.

    C. Multilink can be relatively low in cost and can utilize existing infrastructure.

    D. Multilink is easy to use and included in Windows Server 2012 R2 for both inbound and outbound calls.

3. Your company has offices in five locations around the country. Most of the users' activity is local to their own network. Occasionally, some of the users in one location need to send confidential information to one of the other four locations or to retrieve information from one of them. The communication between the remote locations is sporadic and relatively infrequent, so you have configured RRAS to use demand-dial lines to set up the connections. Management's only requirement is that any communication between the office locations be appropriately secured. Which of the following steps should you take to ensure compliance with this requirement? (Choose all that apply.)

    A. Configure CHAP on all the RRAS servers.

    B. Configure PAP on all the RRAS servers.

    C. Configure MPPE on all the RRAS servers.

    D. Configure L2TP on all the RRAS servers.

    E. Configure MS-CHAPv2 on all the RRAS servers.

4. Your small financial consulting company has a stand-alone Windows 2012 R2 server that provides a central location for your home-based consultants to upload and download spreadsheet files using Windows 8. A few of the consultants still use Windows XP Professional workstations. You want to set up VPN connections between the consultants and the RRAS server. The RRAS server is connected to a small peer-to-peer network of five Windows XP Professional workstations that use the network for storing files, including the files that the consultants are uploading and downloading. What authentication protocol should you use for the VPN?

   A. CHAP

   B. MS-CHAPv2

   C. EAP-TLS

   D. PAP

5. You recently migrated your company's Windows 2003 network to Windows Server 2012 R2. This migration includes 300 Windows 7 and Windows 8 workstations and 8 Windows Server 2012 R2 servers. Your company has just acquired another company with offices down the street. It has a Windows NT network that needs to be migrated to Windows Server 2012 R2 as well, and you have already begun to move the servers to the new operating system and associated services. Because you have a tight cap on expenses for network additions, you currently can't afford leased lines between the buildings. Until you can get support for them, you are going to create a VPN that is both encrypted and authenticated between the two facilities over the Internet connections that already exist. What do you need to implement to achieve this goal? (Choose all that apply.)

   A. L2TP

   B. PPTP

   C. IPsec

   D. RADIUS

   E. MS-CHAPv2

6. You have implemented VPNs to connect the various locations of your organization. These locations include offices in New York, Sacramento, Memphis, and Omaha, with a significant LAN in each one. The RRAS server is set up such that the users aren't aware of the intricacies of the connections. You are beginning to have problems with the connections between the offices and, as a result, the number of support calls is growing dramatically. What configurations could you use to troubleshoot the communication problems?

   A. L2TP using MPPE

   B. L2TP unencrypted

   C. L2TP using IPsec in transport mode

   D. L2TP using IPsec in tunnel mode

7. Your company's 450 sales reps are finally going to receive laptops so that they can communicate with the corporate office whenever they need information stored on the corporate network. The corporate network is fully upgraded to Windows Server 2012 R2, including the default configuration of the RRAS server for the remote connectivity over VPNs. You have installed Windows 8 with the default configuration on all of the laptops and have added the sales reps to a special group in Active Directory. After you test the laptops, everything appears to work fine. You ship them out and, as they reach the sales reps, you monitor their initial connections. During the next few days, you begin receiving support calls from people complaining they cannot connect to the network. What is the most likely cause of the problem?

A. The Windows 8 clients are not configured to support a VPN.

B. The default RRAS configuration does not support VPNs.

C. The default RRAS configuration does not support enough VPN connections.

D. The default RRAS configuration does not support L2TP.

E. The Windows 8 client default configuration does not support L2TP.

8. You are the network administrator for a company with two offices; one is located on the East Coast and the other is located on the West Coast. Sales information needs to be sent from the East Coast to the West Coast office on a regular basis, and some payroll information and accounting reports need to be sent back to the East Coast. The owner of your company has been reading stories in the press about security problems on the Internet and refuses to allow any company information to travel through the Internet, regardless of how much you talk about securing those transmissions. The communications between the sites occur approximately once a week. What steps would you take to ensure secure authentication and secure transmission while not spending too much money? (Choose all that apply.)

A. Configure PAP as the authentication method between the servers.

B. Install RRAS on a server at each location and keep the line open with an ISDN connection that will always be available for the communication.

C. Install RRAS on a server at each location and configure demand-dial to open the connection each time the transmission occurs.

D. Configure CHAP as the authentication method between the servers.

E. Configure MS-CHAPv2 as the authentication method between the servers.

F. Configure IPsec as the encryption method between the servers.

G. Configure MPPE as the encryption method between the servers.

H. Configure L2TP as the encryption method between the servers.

9. You are using an RRAS server to manage remote access to your small Windows Server 2012 R2 network that serves a single location. RRAS provides access to several remote users and to the people who have machines on the local network but occasionally want to access the network from home or from hotels when on the road. Regardless of the category of user, everyone is authenticated through Active Directory. You haven't spent much time reviewing the use of this remote connectivity since you configured the system, but now there is a concern about unauthorized users as well as intermittent problems that remote users are experiencing when connecting to the network. You've been asked to prepare a report for management describing the extent of these problems in the company. You recall that when you set up the system, you configured the logging to track all connection attempts using local Windows accounting. Where will you find the logging information that you need for preparing your report?

  A. The Performance Monitor log

  B. Active Directory

  C. The *systemroot*\System32\LogFiles folder

  D. The system event log

  E. The RRAS authentication log

10. Your area of responsibility at the All-Terrain Vehicle Rentals Company is to build, deploy, and maintain the remote access system for the Windows Server 2012 R2 network. The system consists of four RRAS servers that serve 200 users across the country. The users often travel from location to location, and they access different servers depending on where they call in. You put together a management station to monitor all of the RRAS servers so that you can keep an eye on this critical aspect of your network. What tool do you use to accomplish this?

  A. The Server Monitor of the RRAS snap-in

  B. The Server Status node of the RRAS snap-in

  C. The System Monitor snap-in

  D. The MMC

Chapter
5

Configure a Network Policy Server Infrastructure

THE FOLLOWING 70-411 EXAM OBJECTIVES ARE COVERED IN THIS CHAPTER:

✓ **Configure Network Policy Server (NPS)**

- Configure a NPS server including RADIUS proxy
- Configure RADIUS clients
- Configure NPS templates
- Configure RADIUS accounting
- Configure certificates

✓ **Configure NPS policies**

- Configure connection request policies
- Configure network policies for VPN clients (multilink and bandwidth allocation, IP filters, encryption, IP addressing)
- Import and export NPS policies

✓ **Configure Network Access Protection (NAP)**

- Configure System Health Validators (SHVs)
- Configure health policies
- Configure NAP enforcement using DHCP and VPN
- Configure isolation and remediation of non-compliant computers using DHCP and VPN
- Configure NAP client settings

In Chapter 4, "Configure Routing and Remote Access," you were introduced to VPNs and RADIUS. In this chapter, I will take that a step further. I will still talk about remote access, but I will get more into the security part of the access. I will talk about how to limit access to your users based on the rules and policies that you preset. When a user logs onto the domain from a remote location, if their system doesn't meet minimum requirements, you can limit how much, if any, access the user has on the network.

I will also cover Network Access Protection (NAP) to show you how to start to protect your network, and you will look into Network Policy Server (NPS). NPS allows you to set policies that your users must follow or get limited-to-no access to the domain.

Overview of Wireless Access

In today's computer world, it seems like everyone has a laptop. We all do a lot of traveling, and at any airport it seems like everyone is working on a laptop while waiting for a plane.

Because laptops have grown in popularity, IT professionals must account for them on their networks. Laptops offer IT administrators a unique set of challenges that must be dealt with on a day-to-day basis.

One major concern for IT administrators is security. Years ago, we never had to worry about users copying documents to a desktop computer and then walking out with the computer. However, today users can copy company documents to laptop computers and then walk out the door with the computer and the documents. So, I will discuss wireless networks, protocols, and security.

Windows 8, Windows 7, Windows Vista, Windows 2008/2008 R2, Windows Server 2012, and Windows Server 2012 R2 have enhanced the IEEE 802.11 wireless support to include some of the following changes:

- Single sign-on
- 802.11 wireless diagnostics
- WPA2 support
- Native Wi-Fi architecture
- User interface improvements for wireless connections
- Wireless Group Policy enhancements
- Changes in wireless auto-configuration
- Integration with Network Access Protection when using 802.1X authentication

- EAP host infrastructure
- Command-line support for configuring wireless settings
- Network location awareness and network profiles
- Next-generation TCP/IP stack enhancements for wireless environments

Configuring Wireless Access

Windows 8, Windows 7, Windows Vista, Windows XP, and Windows Server 2003, 2008/2008 R2, and 2012/2012 R2 provide built-in support for 802.11 wireless LAN networking. Inside the Network Connections folder, an installed 802.11 wireless LAN network adapter appears as a wireless network connection. The following are some of the items you can configure:

Operating Modes   There are two types of operating modes:

Infrastructure Mode   This mode uses at least one wireless access point (WAP) and/or a device that bridges the wireless computers to each other.

Ad Hoc Mode   Using this mode, wireless network computers connect directly to each other without the use of an access point (AP) or bridge.

Wired Equivalent Privacy   All of us (on a laptop) have tried to find a wireless network at one time or another. *Wired Equivalent Privacy (WEP)* is a wireless encryption that was originally defined in 802.11. WEP helps to prevent unauthorized wireless users from accessing your wireless network by the use of a shared secret key:

- If your wireless network is using the infrastructure mode, the WEP key must be configured on the wireless AP and all of the wireless clients.
- If your wireless network is using the ad hoc mode, the WEP key must be configured on all of the wireless clients.

The WEP key can be either 40-bit or 104-bit, depending on what your hardware can accommodate.

Wi-Fi Protected Access   An organization of wireless equipment vendors called the Wi-Fi Alliance created an interim standard called *Wi-Fi Protected Access (WPA)* while the IEEE 802.11i wireless LAN security standard was still being completed. WPA uses a strong encryption method called the *Temporal Key Integrity Protocol (TKIP)* to replace the weaker WEP standard. You have the ability to use the *Advanced Encryption Standard (AES)* for encryption that is provided by WPA.

WPA can be used in two different mode types:

WPA-Personal   This is used for a home office or small company. In the WPA-Personal model, you would use a preshared or passphrase code to gain authorization onto the network.

WPA-Enterprise   This was designed for a midsize to large organization. WPA-Enterprise has all of the same features as WPA-Personal, but it also includes the ability to use a 802.1X RADIUS server.

Wi-Fi Protected Access 2   Wi-Fi Protected Access 2 (WPA2) was officially designed to replace the WEP standard. WPA2 certifies that equipment used in a wireless network is compatible with the IEEE 802.11i standard. This certification is used to help standardize the use of the additional security features of the IEEE 802.11i standard that are not already included in WPA.

WPA2 can be used in two different mode types:

WPA2-Personal   This is used for a home office or small company. In the WPA-Personal model, you would use a preshared or passphrase code to gain authorization onto the network.

WPA2-Enterprise   This was designed for a midsize to large organization. WPA-Enterprise has all of the same features as WPA-Personal, but it also includes the ability to use a 802.1X RADIUS server.

Service Set Identifier   To specify a wireless network by name, you specify the *service set identifier (SSID)*, also known as the *wireless network name*:

Infrastructure Mode   The SSID is configured on the wireless access point.

Ad Hoc Mode   The SSID is configured on the initial wireless client.

To help wireless clients discover and join the wireless network, the wireless AP or the initial wireless client periodically advertises the SSID. (This can be disabled for security.)

Group Policies for Wireless   You have the ability to use Group Policy settings for Vista, Windows 7, Windows 8, Windows 2008/2008 R2, and Windows Server 2012/2012 R2 for WPA2. Group Policy settings allow you to configure WPA2 options at the server for all wireless clients.

Remote Access Security

In the past, remote access was seldom part of most companies' networks. It was too hard to implement, too hard to manage, and too hard to secure. It's reasonably easy to secure your networks from unauthorized physical access, but it was perceived to be much harder to do so for remote access. Recently, a number of security policies, protocols, and technologies have been developed to ease this problem. First I'll discuss the user authentication protocols.

User Authentication

One of the first steps in establishing a secure remote access connection involves allowing the user to present some credentials to the server. You can use any or all of the following authentication protocols that Windows Server 2012 R2 supports:

Password Authentication Protocol   The *Password Authentication Protocol (PAP)* is the simplest authentication protocol. It transmits all authentication information in cleartext with no encryption, which makes it vulnerable to snooping if attackers can put themselves between the modem bank and the remote access server. However, this type of attack is unlikely in most networks. The security risk with PAP is largely overemphasized considering the difficulty of setting up a sniffer in between the modems and the remote access server. If an attacker has the ability to install a sniffer this deep in the network, you have larger problems to address. PAP is the most widely supported authentication protocol, and therefore you may find that you need to leave it enabled.

Microsoft CHAPv2   Microsoft created *Microsoft CHAPv2 (MS-CHAPv2)* as an extension of the CHAP protocol to allow the use of Windows authentication information. Version 2 is more secure than version 1, and version 1 is not supported by Windows Server 2008 and newer. Some other operating systems (besides Microsoft) support MS-CHAP version 1.

Extensible Authentication Protocol   The *Extensible Authentication Protocol (EAP)* doesn't provide any authentication itself. Instead, it relies on external third-party authentication methods that you can retrofit to your existing servers. Instead of hardwiring any one authentication protocol, a client-server pair that understands EAP can negotiate an authentication method. The computer that asks for authentication (the *authenticator*) is free to ask for several pieces of information, making a separate query for each one. This allows the use of almost any authentication method, including smart cards, secure access tokens such as SecurID, one-time password systems such as S/Key, or ordinary username/password systems.

Each authentication scheme supported in EAP is called an *EAP type*. Each EAP type is implemented as a plug-in module. Windows Server 2012 R2 can support any number of EAP types at once; the Routing and Remote Access Services (RRAS) server can use any EAP type to authenticate if you've allowed that module to be used and the client has the module in question.

Windows Server 2012 R2 comes with *EAP-Transport Level Security* (EAP-TLS). This EAP type allows you to use public key certificates as an authenticator. TLS is similar to the familiar Secure Sockets Layer (SSL) protocol used for web browsers. When EAP-TLS is turned on, the client and server send TLS-encrypted messages back and forth. EAP-TLS is the strongest authentication method you can use; as a bonus, it supports smart cards. However, EAP-TLS requires your RRAS server to be part of a Windows 2000, Windows Server 2003, Windows Server 2008/2008 R2, or Windows Server 2012 R2 domain.

EAP-RADIUS is another authentication method included with Windows Server 2012 R2. EAP-RADIUS is a fake EAP type that passes any incoming message to a Remote Authentication Dial-In User Service (RADIUS) server for authentication.

PEAP-MS-CHAP v2   This protocol is founded on the authenticated wireless access design, and it's based on Protected Extensible Authentication Protocol Microsoft Challenge Handshake Authentication Protocol version 2 (PEAP-MS-CHAP v2). This authentication protocol utilizes the user account credentials (username and password) stored in Active Directory Domain Services to authenticate wireless access clients instead of using smart cards or user and computer certificates for client authentication.

PEAP-MS-CHAP v2 is an EAP-type protocol that is easier to deploy than Extensible Authentication Protocol with Transport Level Security (EAP-TLS). It is easier because user authentication is accomplished by using password-based credentials (username and password) instead of digital certificates or smart cards. Only servers running Network Policy Server or PEAP-MS-CHAP v2 are required to have a certificate. The server certificate used by NPS can be issued by your organization's private trusted root CA deployed on your network or by a public CA that is already trusted by the client computer.

 Just in case you missed the very important line above, I will say it again: Servers that are running Network Policy Server or PEAP-MS-CHAP v2 are *required* to have a certificate.

TLS/SSL (Schannel)   *TLS/SSL (Schannel)* implements both the Secure Sockets Layer and Transport Layer Security Internet standard authentication protocols. Administrators can use TLS/SSL to authenticate servers and client computers. Administrators also have the ability to use the protocol to encrypt messages between the authenticated parties (client and server).

The Transport Layer Security protocol, Secure Sockets Layer protocol, Datagram Transport Layer Security (DTLS), and Private Communications Transport (PCT) protocol are all based on the public key cryptography. The Security Channel authentication protocol suite provides these protocols, and this protocol is based on the client-server model.

NTLMv2   *NTLMv2* (Windows NT LAN Manager) helps the authentication process for Windows NT 4 systems or earlier, and it allows for transactions between any two computers running these older systems. Networks that use NTLMv2 are referred to as *mixed mode*.

Kerberos   The *Kerberos authentication protocol* is used to perform Active Directory domain authentication. By default, all computers joined to a Windows Server 2012 R2 domain use the Kerberos authentication protocol. Kerberos allows for single sign-on to network resources on a domain or on a trusted domain. Administrators have the ability to control certain parameters through the Kerberos security settings of the account policies.

802.1X   The IEEE has a standard for wireless authentication called 802.1X. 802.1X allows wireless networks to authenticate onto wired Ethernet networks or wireless 802.11 networks. The IEEE 802.1X standard uses EAP for exchanging messages during the authentication process.

Connection Security

You can use some additional features to provide connection-level security for your remote access clients:

- The *Callback Control Protocol (CBCP)* allows your RRAS servers or clients to negotiate a callback with the other end. When CBCP is enabled, either the client or the server can ask the server at the other end to call the client back at a number supplied by the client or a prearranged number stored on the server.

- You can program the RRAS server to accept or reject calls based on the caller ID or automatic number identification (ANI) information transmitted by the phone company. For example, you can instruct your primary RRAS server to accept calls from only your home analog line. This means you can't call the server when you're on the road, and it also keeps the server from talking to strangers.

- You can specify various types and levels of encryption to protect your connection from interception or tampering.

 Real World Scenario

The Limits of Caller ID

It's risky to rely on ANI information for any type of authentication or caller verification. First, caller ID information can be forged. Therefore, if an attacker knows the telephone numbers from which your network accepted calls, they could make their ANI report as one of those numbers and be authenticated onto the network.

Another problem with relying on ANI for authentication is that not all telephone companies pass ANI information with the call. Therefore, if your users are in remote locations (which is why they'd be dialing in anyway), they might not be able to authenticate. Even when ANI information is sent, some telephone companies pass different pieces of the information, which can also result in authentication failures.

Finally, not all incoming line types support ANI. If your site uses a network access server or modem bank that doesn't receive this information based on the type of T1 connection used for incoming calls, the ANI information might not be there at all.

Access Control

Apart from the connection-level measures that you can use to prohibit outside callers from talking to your servers, you can restrict which users can make remote connections in a number of ways:

- You can allow or disallow remote access from individual user accounts. This is the same limited control you have in Windows NT, but it's just the start for Windows Server 2012 R2.

- You can use network access policies to control whether users can get access.

    Like group policies, network access policies give you an easy way to apply a consistent set of policies to groups of users. However, the policy mechanism is a little different: You create rules that include or exclude the users whom you want in the policy.

Unlike group policies, network access policies are available only in Windows 2000 native, Windows Server 2003, Windows Server 2008, and Windows Server 2008 R2 domain functional level (that is, in domains in which there are no Windows NT domain controllers present). This means you may not have the option to use network access policies until your Windows 2000, Windows Server 2003, Windows Server 2008/2008 R2, and Windows Server 2012 R2 deployment is further along.

In the next sections, you will learn how to configure user access control.

Configuring User Access

Now it's time to determine who can actually use the remote access services. You do this in two ways:

- By setting up remote access profiles on individual accounts
- By creating and managing network access policies that apply to groups of users

This distinction is subtle but important because you manage and apply profiles and policies in different places.

Setting Up User Profiles

Windows Server 2012 R2 stores a lot of information for each user account. Collectively, this information is known as the account's *profile*, and it's normally stored in Active Directory. Some settings in the user's profile are available through one of the two user-management snap-ins:

- If your RRAS server is part of an Active Directory domain, the user profile settings are in the Active Directory Users and Computers snap-in.
- If your RRAS server is *not* part of an Active Directory domain, the user profile settings are in the Local Users and Groups snap-in.

In either case, the interesting part of the profile is the Dial-In tab of the user's Properties dialog box (see Figure 5.1). This tab has a number of controls that regulate how the user account can be used for dial-in access.

These controls include the following:

Network Access Permission Control Group The first, and probably most familiar, controls on this tab are in the Network Access Permission control group. These options control whether the user has dial-in permission. Windows Server 2012 R2 has a feature that, in addition to explicitly allowing or denying access, lets you control access through Network Access Protection.

Verify Caller-ID Check Box RRAS can verify a user's caller ID information and use the results to allow or deny access. When you check the Verify Caller-ID check box and enter

FIGURE 5.1   The Dial-In tab of the user's Properties dialog box

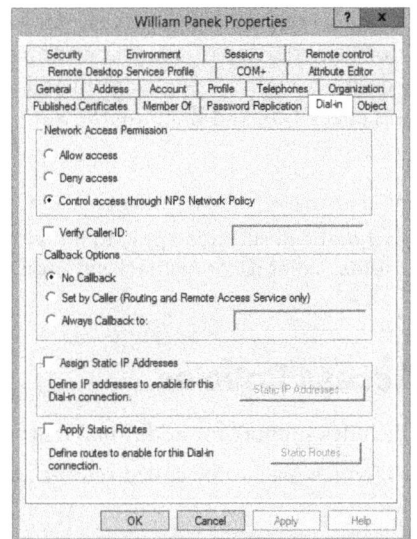

a phone number in the field, you're telling RRAS to reject a call from anyone who provides that username and password but whose caller ID information doesn't match what you enter. This means the user can call in only from a single phone number.

Callback Options Control Group   The Callback Options control group gives you three choices for regulating callback:

No Callback   This is the default setting. It means that the server will never honor callback requests from this account.

Set By Caller   This setting allows the calling system to specify a number at which it wants to be called back. The RRAS server will call the client back at that number.

Always Callback To   This setting allows you to enter a number that the server will call back no matter from where the client is actually calling. This option is less flexible but more secure than the Set By Caller option.

Assign Static IP Addresses Check Box   If you want this user always to get the same static IP address, you can arrange to do so by selecting the Assign Static IP Addresses check box and then entering the desired IP address. This allows you to set up nondynamic DNS records for individual users, guaranteeing that their machines will always have a valid DNS entry. On the other hand, this can be more prone to typographical errors on setup than the dynamic DNS-DHCP combination you could use instead.

Apply Static Routes Check Box   In an ordinary LAN, you don't have to do anything special to clients to enable them to route packets—just configure them with a default gateway, and the gateway handles the rest. For dial-up connections, though, you may want to define a list of static routes that will enable the remote client to reach hosts on your network, or elsewhere, without requiring that packets be sent to a gateway in between. Depending on the remote access server, though, the client may be able to use Address Resolution Protocol (ARP) for local devices too. If you want to define a set of static routes on the client, you'll have to do it manually. If you want to assign static routes on the server, select the Apply Static Routes check box and then use the Static Routes button to add and remove routes as necessary.

Remember that these settings apply to individual users, so you can assign different routes, caller ID, or callback settings to each user.

Using Network Access Policies

Windows Server 2012 R2 includes support for additional configuration systems:

- Network access policies (which used to be called *remote access policy*).
- Remote access profiles.
- Network Policy Server (NPS) is the Microsoft implementation of a Remote Authentication Dial-in User Service (RADIUS) server and proxy in Windows Server 2012. NPS is the replacement for Internet Authentication Service (IAS) in Windows Server 2003.

Policies determine who can and cannot connect; you define rules with conditions that the system evaluates to see whether a particular user can connect.

You can have any number of policies in a native Windows Server 2012 R2 domain; each policy must have exactly one profile associated with it.

Settings in an individual user's profile override settings in a network access policy.

You manage network access policies through the Remote Access Logging & Policies folder in the RRAS snap-in. Policies contain conditions that you pick from a list. When a caller connects, the policy's conditions are evaluated, one by one, to see whether the caller gets in. All of the conditions in the policy must match for the user to gain access. If there are multiple policies, they're evaluated according to an order you specify.

In the following sections, you will see how to create and configure network access policies.

Network Policy Attributes

To create a policy, right-click the Remote Access Logging & Policies folder and select Launch NPS (see Figure 5.2). Then right-click Network Policies and choose New.

FIGURE 5.2   The Launch NPS option in RRAS

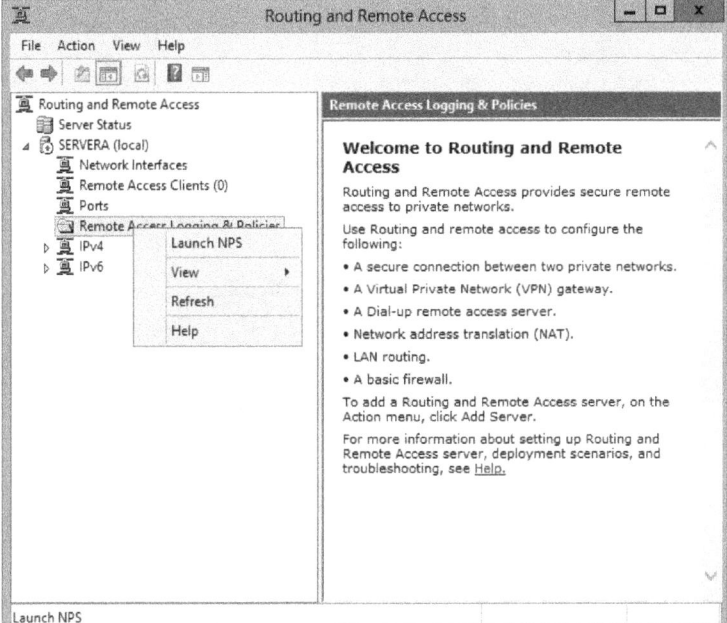

This command starts the New Network Policy Wizard, which uses a series of steps to help you define the policy.

The Select Condition dialog box (see Figure 5.3) is part of the New Network Policy Wizard. It lists the attributes you can evaluate in a policy. Table 5.1 describes the attributes that you can set. These attributes are drawn from the RADIUS standards, so you can (and in some cases, should) intermix your Windows Server 2012 R2 RRAS servers with RADIUS servers.

 When setting up any policies, you must base your policy on company rules and standards. Remember, policies can allow or restrict users from remotely accessing your network. The needs of the organization determine the policy and when to use it.

Once you choose an attribute and click the Add button, its corresponding editor appears. You use the editor to set the value of the attribute. For example, if you select the Day And Time Restrictions attribute, you'll see the Time Of Day Constraints dialog box, which offers a calendar grid that lets you select which days and times are available for logging on.

FIGURE 5.3   Select Condition dialog box of New Network Policy Wizard

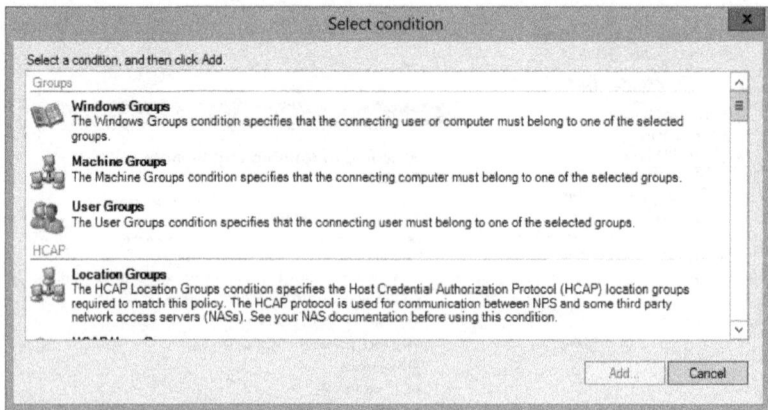

TABLE 5.1   Network access policy attributes

Attribute name	What it specifies
Authentication Type	Specifies the authentication methods required to match this policy.
Allowed EAP Types	Specifies the EAP types required for the client computer authentication method configuration to match this policy.
Called Station Id	Specifies the phone number of the remote access port called by the caller.
Calling Station Id	Specifies the caller's phone number.
Client Friendly Name	Specifies the name of the RADIUS server that's attempting to validate the connection.
Client IP Address (IPv4 and IPv6)	Specifies the IP address of the RADIUS server that's attempting to validate the connection.
Client Vendor	Specifies the vendor of the remote access server that originally accepted the connection. This is used to set different policies for different hardware.
Day And Time Restrictions	Specifies the weekdays and times when connection attempts are accepted or rejected.
Framed Protocol	Specifies the protocol to be used for framing incoming packets (for example, PPP, SLIP, and so on).

HCAP (Host Credential Authorization Protocol) User Groups	Used for communications between NPS and some third-party network access servers (NASs).
Location Groups	Specifies the HCAP location groups required to match this policy. This is used for communications between HCAP and some third-party network access servers (NASs).
MS RAS Vendor	Specifies the vendor identification number of the network access server (NAS) that is requesting authentication.
NAS Identifier	Specifies the friendly name of the remote access server that originally accepted the connection.
NAS IP Address (IPv4 and IPv6)	Specifies the IP address of the remote access server that originally accepted the connection.
NAS Port Type	Specifies the physical connection (for example, ISDN, POTS) used by the caller.
Service Type	Specifies Framed or Async (for PPP) or login (Telnet).
Tunnel Type	Specifies which tunneling protocol should be used (L2TP or PPTP).
Windows Groups	Specifies which Windows groups are allowed access.

After you select an attribute and give it a value, you can add more attributes or move to the next page by clicking the Next button on the Select Condition page.

Once you're finished setting attributes, you arrive at the Specify Access Permission page of the wizard. This page has only two radio buttons: Grant Remote Access Permissions and Deny Remote Access Permissions. These buttons specify whether the policy you create *allows* users to connect or *prevents* users from connecting. The page also includes an Access Is Determined By User Dial-In Properties check box. If this box is checked and there is a conflict between the network policy and user dial-in properties, the user dial-in properties take precedence.

Creating a Network Access Policy

In Exercise 5.1, you'll create an adjunct policy that adds time and day restrictions to the default policy. (An *adjunct policy* is one used in conjunction with another policy.) This exercise requires that you have completed the previous exercises in this chapter.

Creating a Network Access Policy

1. Open the RRAS MMC snap-in by pressing the Windows key and selecting Administrative Tools ➢ Routing And Remote Access.

2. Expand the server you want to configure in the left pane of the MMC.

3. Right-click the Remote Access Logging And Policies folder.

4. Right-click and then select Launch NPS.

5. Once the Network Policy Server page appears, right-click Network Policies and then choose New.

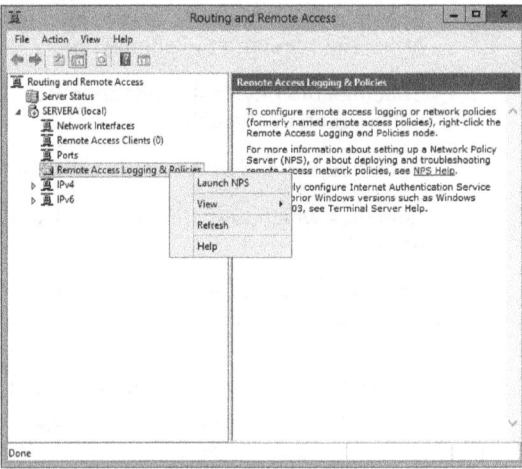

6. The New Network Policy Wizard starts. In the Policy Name box, enter **Test Policy** and then click Next (leave the other settings as they are).

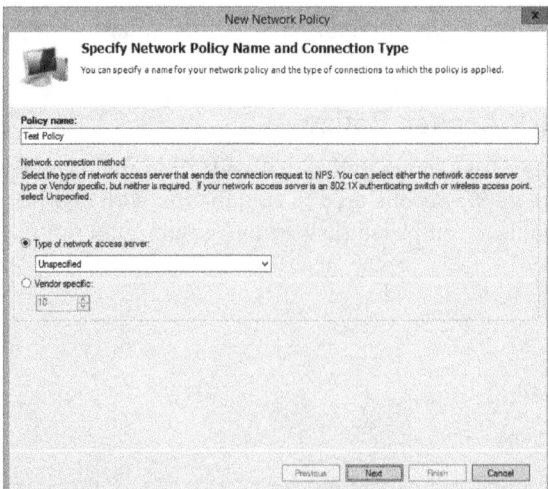

7. On the Specify Conditions page, click the Add button.

8. In the Select Condition dialog box, scroll down and click Day And Time Restrictions. Click Add.

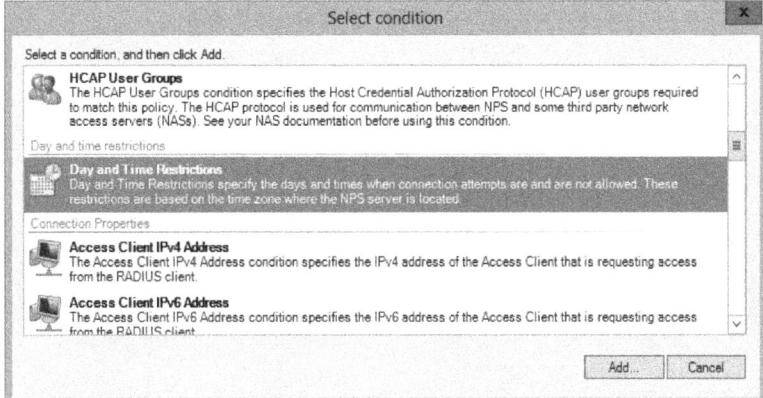

9. The Time Of Day Constraints dialog box appears. Use the calendar controls to allow remote access Monday through Saturday from 7 a.m. to 7 p.m. and then click the OK button.

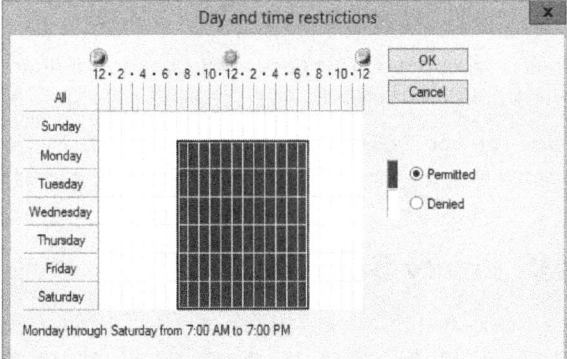

10. The Select Conditions dialog box reappears, this time with the new condition listed. Click the Next button.

11. The Specify Access Permission page appears. Select the Access Granted radio button and click Next to continue.

12. The Configure Authentication Methods page appears next. This page is where you choose which authentication methods will be used for this connection. Make sure that MS-CHAP and MS-CHAPv2 are both checked, along with the check boxes associated with them. Click Next.

13. The Configure Constraints page appears. Under Constraints, click Session Timeout. On the right side, click the Disconnect After The Following Maximum Session Time box, and type **60** in the field (the value represents minutes). Click Next.

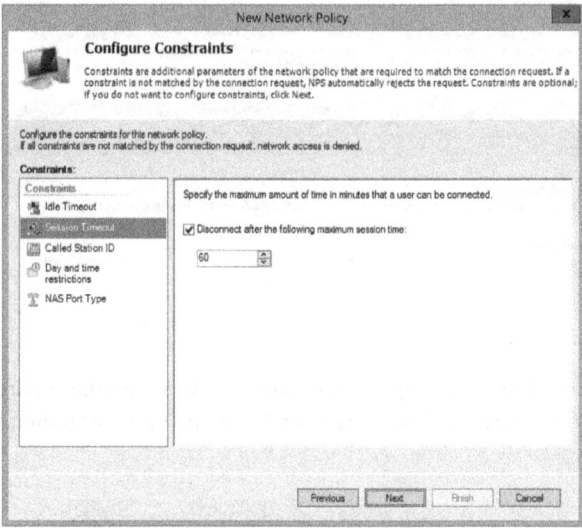

14. The Configure Settings page appears. This page allows you to configure any additional settings for this network policy. Click Next.

15. On the Completing New Network Policy page, click Finish.

NPS as a RADIUS Proxy Server

When a user tries to log into a domain through the use of a RADIUS server, the RADIUS server processes the connection request and helps the user log into the network.

RADIUS proxy servers work in a different way. When a connection request comes into a RADIUS proxy server, the RADIUS proxy server forwards the request to another RADIUS server for authentication onto the network. Servers that are running Network Policy Server can act both as a RADIUS server and as a RADIUS proxy.

When an administrator sets up NPS as a RADIUS server, NPS provides some of the following actions to help the RADIUS server work properly:

- RADIUS clients send an access request to the central authentication and authorization service. NPS uses Active Directory to authenticate the user's credentials. NPS accesses the Active Directories user's dial-in properties and policies to authorize the connection.

- When using NPS, the RADIUS server also records all accounting information on how much the RADIUS server is used. This is helpful when you have to bill other departments for the RADIUS use. Many organizations require that each department pay for its RADIUS use for its users, and using NPS allows an administrator to do this.

When you set up NPS as a RADIUS proxy, NPS provides all of the routing between all of the RADIUS servers and RADIUS clients. NPS is the main switching and routing service when you use RADIUS as a proxy server.

NPS Configuration

Now that you know that NPS can be set up as a RADIUS server, let's take a look at some of those details of how to do it. When an administrator sets up NPS as a RADIUS proxy, network access servers are then configured as the RADIUS clients. The RADIUS proxy server receives requests from the RADIUS clients, and then the RADIUS server forwards those requests to the appropriate servers. Using NPS to set up a RADIUS proxy should be done when the following conditions are needed:

- If you are the administrator of an organization that offers VPN or wireless network access to multiple clients, the RADIUS server can authenticate and authorize the user through their authentication server.

- If you are an administrator of a domain and you want users who are not members of your domain to authenticate into your domain, you can use an NPS server with a RADIUS proxy. To make this situation work, you must set up a two-way trust (two one-way trusts in opposite directions).

- Another great example of when to set up a RADIUS proxy server is when you are using a non-Microsoft-based database. RADIUS servers have the ability to communicate with different types of databases, allowing users still to be authenticated even when it's not a Microsoft authentication database; an example is a Novell Directory Services (NDS) database.

Another configuration that you may need to set when configuring NPS and RADIUS is the priority. The higher the RADIUS priority number, the less that the RADIUS server gets used. For example, if I have two RADIUS servers named Server1 and Server2 and I want Server2 used only when Server1 is unavailable, I would set the RADIUS priority from 1 to 10. This way it will get used only when Server1 is having issues or is unresponsive.

RADIUS Clients

Network access servers that are RADIUS RFC compliant (2865 and 2866) are considered RADIUS clients when used with NPS and a RADIUS server or proxy.

NPS allows an administrator to enable the use of wireless, switches, remote access, or VPN equipment as long as they are heterogeneous or homogenous sets. Network administrators can allow authentication and authorization through the use of NPS network connection requests as long as administrators deploy the following types of network access servers and technologies:

- Wired access with 802.1X-secured and RADIUS-compliant authenticating switches
- Wireless access with 802.1X-secured and RADIUS-compliant wireless access points

NPS Templates

Templates can be a valuable tool when used properly. Templates allow you to create something once and then use that template to create the same thing over and over again.

You can use templates when creating Active Directory users, when setting up GPOs, and now even when setting up NPS. NPS templates allow an administrator to save time and thus also save the cost required to manage and configure NPS on multiple servers. Multiple NPS templates are available in the Templates Management MMC for an administrator to configure:

- Shared Secrets
- RADIUS Clients
- Remote RADIUS Servers
- IP Filters
- Health Policies
- Remediation Server Groups

One advantage of creating a template is that once the template is created, there is no interference with the actual NPS server's performance. Creating templates does not affect an operational NPS server in any way. Once you load the template to the appropriate location, the template becomes active.

Creating Templates

To create a template in the Template Management MMC, right-click the template type you want to create (such as Health Policies) and click New. The New Template dialog box appears, and you just fill in all of your configuration information.

Importing and Exporting NPS Policies

Importing/exporting NPS is a pretty easy thing. It just happens to depend on which version of Windows you are exporting from. In the following examples, I will explain how to export from Windows Server 2008 R2 using the Windows MMC and how to import into Windows Server 2012 R2.

Exporting from Windows Server 2008 R2

To export NPS from Windows Server 2008 R2, follow these steps:

1. On the source server, open Server Manager.
2. In the Server Manager console tree, open Roles\Network Policy and Access Services\ NPS.
3. Right-click NPS and then click Export Configuration.
4. In the dialog box that appears, select the check box I Am Aware That I Am Exporting All Shared Secrets and then click OK.

5. For File Name, type **file.xml**, navigate to the migration store file location, and then click Save.

6. In the console tree, right-click Templates Management and then click Export Templates To A File.

7. For File Name, type **iastemplates.xml**, navigate to the migration store file location, and then click Save.

8. If you have configured SQL logging, you must manually record detailed SQL configuration settings.

   To record these settings, follow these steps:

   a. In the NPS console tree, click Accounting and then click Change SQL Server Logging Properties.

   b. Record the configuration settings on the Settings tab and then click Configure.

   c. Manually record all configuration settings from the Connection and Advanced tabs by copying them into the sql.txt file. Alternatively, you can click the All tab and enter Name and Value settings displayed on each line into the sql.txt file.

9. Copy the file.xml, iastemplates.xml, and sql.txt files to the migration store file location. This information will be required to configure the destination server.

Importing to Windows Server 2012 R2

To import NPS from Windows Server 2012 R2, follow these steps

1. Copy the configuration files file.xml, iastemplates.xml, and sql.txt that were exported to the migration store file location to the destination NPS server. Alternatively, you can import configuration settings directly from the migration store file location by supplying the appropriate path to the file in the import command. If you have custom settings that were recorded using the NPS Server Migration: Appendix A—Data Collection Worksheet, they must be configured manually on the destination server.

2. On the destination server, open Server Manager.

3. In the Server Manager console tree, click All Servers; then, from the list of servers in the right pane, right-click the relevant server and select Network Policy Server.

4. To import template configuration settings, complete the remaining steps in this list. If you do not have template settings, skip to step 7.

5. In the console tree, right-click Templates Management and then click Import Templates from a file.

6. Select the template configuration file iastemplates.xml that you copied from the source server and then click Open.

7. In the console tree, right-click NPS and then click Import Configuration.

8. Select the configuration file file.xml or ias.txt that you copied from the source server and then click Open.

9. Verify that a message appears indicating the import was successful.

10. Configure SQL accounting if required using the sql.txt file and the data collection worksheet. To configure SQL accounting, complete the remaining steps in this list.

11. In the NPS console tree, click Accounting and then click Change SQL Server Logging Properties in the details pane.

12. Modify the properties on the Settings tab if required and then click Configure to enter detailed settings.

13. Using information recorded in the sql.txt file, enter the required settings on the Connection and Advanced tabs and then click OK.

Using Remote Access Profiles

Remote access profiles are an integral part of network access policies. Profiles determine what happens during call setup and completion. Each policy has a profile associated with it; the profile determines what settings will be applied to connections that meet the conditions stated in the policy.

For security reasons, it's usually a good idea to limit access to the administrative accounts on your network. In particular, as a consultant, I usually tell clients to restrict remote access for the administrator account; that way, the potential exposure from a dial-up compromise is reduced. In Exercise 5.2, you will learn how to configure the administrator account's user profile to restrict dial-up access.

EXERCISE 5.2

Restricting a User Profile for Dial-In Access

1. Log on to your computer using an account that has administrative privileges.

2. If you're using an RRAS server that's part of an Active Directory domain, open the Active Directory Users and Computers snap-in by pressing the Windows key and selecting Administrative Tools ➤ Active Directory Users And Computers. If not, open the Local Users and Groups snap-in by pressing the Windows key and selecting Administrative Tools ➤ Computer Management ➤ Local Users And Groups.

3. Expand the tree to the Users folder. Right-click the Administrator account in the right pane and choose Properties. The Administrator Properties dialog box appears.

4. Switch to the Dial-In tab. On machines that participate in Active Directory, make sure the Control Access Through NPS Network Policy option (in the Permissions group) is selected.

5. Click the Deny Access radio button to prevent the use of this account over a dial-in connection.

6. Click the OK button.

You can create one profile for each policy. The profile contains settings that fit into specific areas. Each area has its own link in the profile's Properties dialog box.

The Constraints Tab

The Constraints tab has most of the settings that you think of when you consider dial-in access controls. The controls here allow you to adjust how long the connection can be idle before it gets dropped, how long it can be up, the dates and times for establishing the connection, and what dial-in port and medium can be used to connect.

Authentication Link

In the Authentication Methods pane (see Figure 5.4), you can specify which authentication methods are allowed on this specific policy. Note that these settings, like the other policy settings, will be useful only if the server's settings match. For example, if you turn EAP authentication off in the server's Properties dialog box, turning it on in the Authentication Methods pane of the profile's Properties dialog box will have no effect.

FIGURE 5.4   Authentication Methods settings

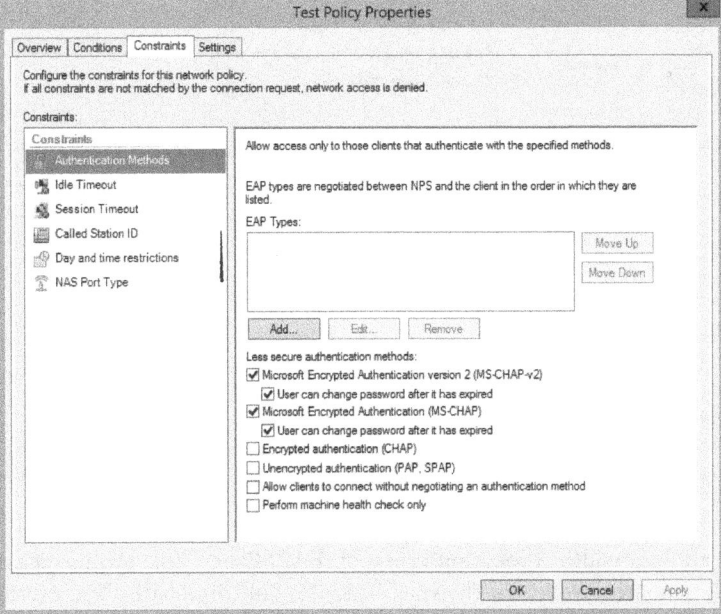

You'll notice that each authentication method has a check box. Check the appropriate boxes to control the protocols that you want this profile to use. If you enable EAP, you can also choose which specific EAP type you want the profile to support. You can also choose to allow totally unauthenticated access (which is unchecked by default).

Settings Tab

The Settings tab of the policy's Properties dialog box has several useful sections, which are described in the following list:

IP Settings Pane   The IP Settings pane (see Figure 5.5) gives you control over the IP-related settings associated with an incoming call. If you think back to the server-specific settings covered earlier, you'll remember that the server preferences include settings for protocols other than IP; this is not so in the network access profile. In this pane, you can specify where the client gets its IP address.

FIGURE 5.5   IP Settings pane of the Settings tab

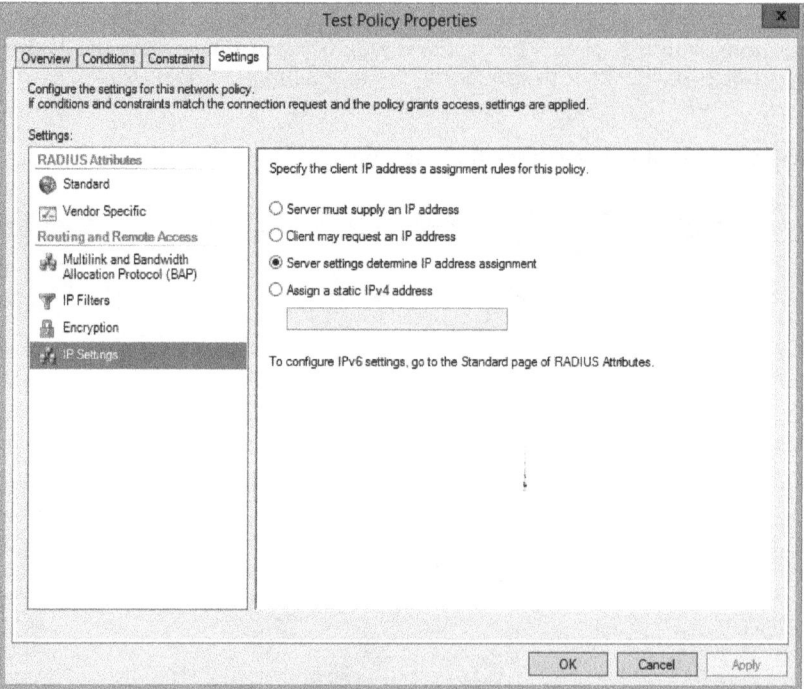

Multilink And Bandwidth Allocation Protocol (BAP) Pane   The profile mechanism gives you a degree of control over how the server handles multilink calls. You exert this control through the Multilink And Bandwidth Allocation Protocol (BAP) pane of the profile Properties dialog box. Your first choice is to decide whether to allow multilink calls at all and, if so, how many ports you want to let a single client use at once. Normally, this setting is configured so that the server-specific settings take precedence, but you can override them.

Bandwidth Allocation Protocol Group   The Bandwidth Allocation Protocol control group gives you a way to control what happens during a multilink call when the bandwidth usage drops below a certain threshold. For example, why tie up three analog lines to provide 168Kbps of bandwidth when the connection is using only 56Kbps? You can tweak the capacity and time thresholds. By default, a multilink call will drop one line every time the bandwidth usage falls to less than 50 percent of the available bandwidth and stays there for two minutes. The Require BAP For Dynamic Multilink Requests check box allows you to refuse calls from clients that don't support BAP. This is an easy way to make sure that no client can hog your multilink bandwidth.

Encryption Pane   The Encryption pane of the Settings tab (see Figure 5.6) controls which type of encryption you want your remote users to be able to access.

FIGURE 5.6   Encryption pane of the Settings tab of the policy's Properties dialog box

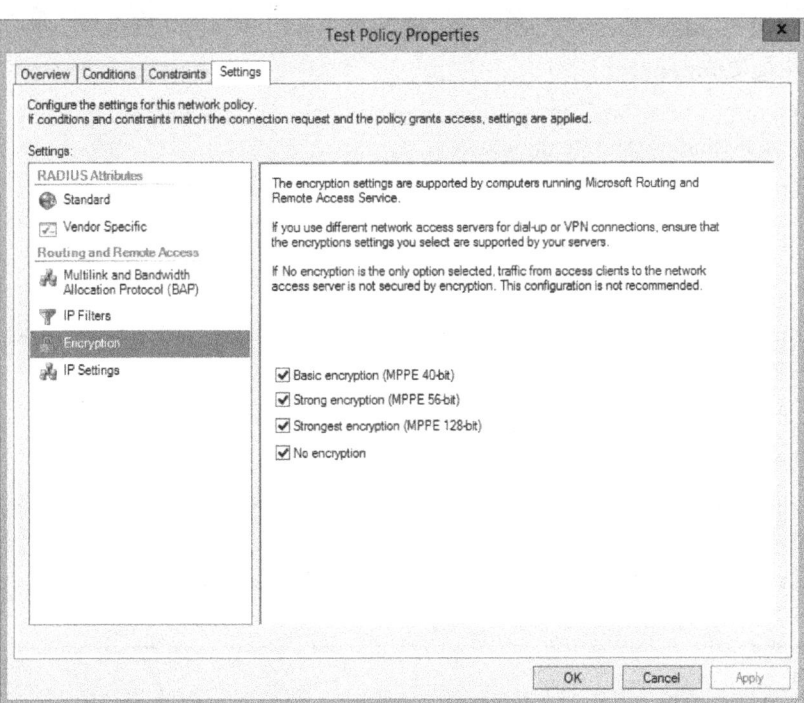

The following radio buttons are on the Encryption pane:

- Basic Encryption (MPPE 40-Bit) means single Data Encryption Standard (DES) for IPsec or 40-bit Microsoft Point-to-Point Encryption (MPPE) for Point-to-Point Tunneling Protocol (PPTP).

- Strong Encryption (MPPE 56-Bit) means 56-bit encryption (single DES for IPsec; 56-bit MPPE for PPTP).

- Strongest Encryption (MPPE 128-Bit) means triple DES for IPsec or 128-bit MPPE for PPTP connections.

- No Encryption allows users to connect using no encryption at all. Unless this button is selected, a remote connection must be encrypted, or it'll be rejected.

In Exercise 5.3, you'll force all connections to your server to use encryption. Any client that can't use encryption will be dropped. You must complete Exercise 5.1 before you do this exercise.

WARNING   Don't do this exercise on your production RRAS server unless you're sure that all of your clients are encryption-capable.

EXERCISE 5.3

Configuring Encryption

1. Open the RRAS MMC snap-in by pressing the Windows key and selecting Administrative Tools ➢ Routing And Remote Access.

2. Expand the server you want to configure in the left pane of the MMC.

3. Right-click the Remote Access Logging & Policies folder.

4. Select Launch NPS.

5. Once the Network Policy Server page appears, click the hours policy you created in Exercise 5.3. (I named mine Test Policy.)

6. Select Action ➢ Properties. The policy's Properties dialog box appears.

7. Click the Settings tab. Select Encryption in the left pane.

8. In the right pane, uncheck the No Encryption check box. Make sure that the Basic, Strong, and Strongest check boxes are all selected.

9. Click the OK button. When the policy Properties dialog box reappears, click the OK button.

Setting Up a VPN Network Access Policy

Earlier in this chapter, you learned how to use the Network Access Policy mechanism on a
Windows Server 2012 R2 domain. Now it's time to apply what you've learned to a virtual
private network (VPN). Recall that you have two ways to control which specific users can
access a remote access server:

■ You can grant and deny dial-up permission to individual users in each user's Properties
dialog box.

■ You can create a network access policy that embodies whatever restrictions you want
to impose.

It turns out that you can do the same thing for VPN connections, but there are a few
additional things to consider.

Granting and Denying Per-User Access

To grant or deny VPN access to individual users, all you have to do is make the appropriate
change on the Dial-In tab of each user's Properties dialog box. Although this is the easiest
method to understand, it gets tedious quickly if you need to change VPN permissions for
more than a few users. Furthermore, this method offers you no way to distinguish between
dial-in and VPN permissions.

Creating a Network Access Policy for VPNs

You may find it helpful to create network access policies that enforce the permissions
that you want end users to have. You can accomplish this result in a number of ways; which
one you use will depend on your overall use of network access policies.

The simplest way is to create a policy that allows all of your users to use a VPN. Earlier in
this chapter, you learned how to create network access policies and specify settings for them;
one thing you may have noticed was that there's a NAS-Port-Type attribute that you can use
in the policy's conditions. That attribute is the cornerstone of building a policy that allows or
denies remote access via VPN because you use it to accept or reject connections arriving over
a particular type of VPN connection. For best results, you'll use the Tunnel-Type attribute in
conjunction with the NAS-Port-Type attribute, as described in Exercise 5.4.

EXERCISE 5.4

Creating a VPN Network Access Policy

1. Open the RRAS MMC snap-in by pressing the Windows key and selecting Administra-
    tive Tools ➤ Routing And Remote Access.

2. Expand the server you want to configure in the left pane of the MMC.

3. Right-click the `Remote Access Logging & Policies` folder.

4. Select Launch NPS.

5.   Once the Network Policy Server page appears, right-click Network Policies and choose New.

6.   The New Network Policy Wizard starts. In the Policy Name box, enter **VPN Network Policy** and click Next (leave the other settings as they are).

7.   On the Specify Conditions page, click the Add button.

8.   On the Select Condition page, scroll down, click NAS-Port-Type Attribute, and click Add. When the NAS Port Type page appears, click Virtual VPN in the Common Dial-Up And VPN Tunnel Types box. Click OK and then click the Next button.

9.   The Specify Conditions page reappears, this time with the new condition listed. Click the Next button.

10.   The Specify Access Permission page appears. Select the Access Granted radio button and click Next to continue.

11.   Next the Configure Authentication Methods page will appear. This page is where you choose which authentication methods will be used for this connection. Make sure that MS-CHAP and MS-CHAPv2 are both checked along with their associated check boxes. Click Next.

12.   The Configure Constraints page appears. Under Constraints, click Session Timeout. On the right side, click the Disconnect After The Following Maximum Session Time box and type **60** in the box (the value specifies minutes). Click Next.

13.   The Configure Settings page appears. This page allows you to configure any additional settings for this network policy. Click Next.

14.   At the Completing New Network Policy page, click Finish.

If you don't want to grant VPN access to everyone, you can make some changes to the process in Exercise 5.6 to fine-tune it. First you'll probably want to move the VPN policy to the top of the list. (When you first add the policy described in the exercise, it is placed at the end of the policy list. Unless you move it, the default policies will take effect before the VPN-specific policy does.)

Next you can create an Active Directory group and put your VPN users in it. You can then create a policy using the two conditions outlined in Exercise 5.6 plus a condition that uses the Windows-Groups attribute to specify the new group. You can also use this process to allow everyone dial-up access and reserve VPN capability for a smaller group.

Connection Manager

To help administrators create and manage remote access connections, Microsoft includes a suite of components called Connection Manager within Windows Server 2012 R2. Connection Manager is not installed by default. You can install the Connection Manager using Server Manager ➢ Add Roles ➢ Network Access Services.

Connection Manager allows an administrator to create remote access connections called *service profiles*. These profiles then appear on client machines as network connections. You can use these network connections to connect client machines to VPNs or remote networks.

Configuring Security

When configuring remote access security, you must consider several aspects, the most fundamental of which involves configuring the types of authentication and encryption that the server will use when accepting client requests. You will look at each of these in the following sections.

Controlling Server Security

The Security tab of the server's Properties dialog box (see Figure 5.7) allows you to specify which authentication and accounting methods RRAS uses. You can choose one of two authentication providers by using the Authentication Provider drop-down list.

FIGURE 5.7   The Security tab of the RRAS server's Properties dialog box

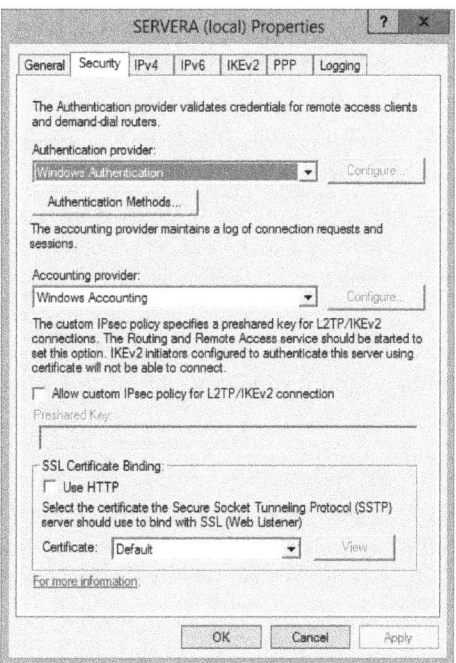

Your choices include the following:

Windows Authentication   This is a built-in authentication suite included with Windows Server 2012 R2.

RADIUS Authentication   This authentication allows you to send all authentication requests heard by your server to a RADIUS server for approval or denial.

You can also use the Accounting Provider drop-down list on the Security tab to choose between the following:

Microsoft-Developed Accounting   With this type of accounting, connection requests are maintained in the event log.

RADIUS Accounting   In this type of accounting, all accounting events, such as call start and call stop, are sent to a RADIUS server for action.

RADIUS Authentication Settings

When you select the RADIUS Authentication option from the Authentication Provider drop-down menu, you are enabling a RADIUS client that passes authentication duties to a RADIUS server. This communication is sent via UDP on port 1645 or 1812, depending on the version of RADIUS being used.

Click the Configure button to open the RADIUS Authentication dialog box. From here, you can set the following options:

- Click the Add button to add the name or address of a RADIUS server to which the RAS server will pass authentication duties.

- You must also enter the correct secret, which is initially set by the RADIUS server.

- The Time-Out option determines how long the RRAS server will attempt to authenticate the remote user before giving up.

- The Initial Score option is similar to the cost value used by routers. The RAS server will attempt to authenticate users on the RADIUS server with the highest score first. If that attempt fails, the RAS server will use the RADIUS server with the next highest score, and so on.

- Although the Port option can be changed, the default setting is part of RFC 2866, "RADIUS Accounting," and it should not be altered unless extraordinary circumstances call for it.

The Internet Assigned Numbers Authority (IANA) is the official source for port number assignment. You can view current port number assignments and other valuable information at www.iana.org/assignments/port-numbers.

Windows Authentication Settings

Select the Windows Authentication option from the Authentication Provider drop-down menu if you want the local machine to authenticate your remote access users. To configure the server by telling it which authentication methods you want it to use, click the Authentication Methods button, which displays the Authentication Methods dialog box. If you look at the list of authentication protocols earlier in the chapter, you'll find that each one has a corresponding check box here: EAP, MS-CHAPv2, CHAP, and PAP. You can also turn on unauthenticated access by checking the Allow Remote Systems To Connect Without Authentication box, but that is not recommended because it allows anyone to connect to, and use, your server (and thus by extension your network).

There's actually a special set of requirements for using CHAP because it requires access to each user's encrypted password. Windows Server 2012 R2 normally doesn't store user passwords in a format that CHAP can use, so you have to take some additional steps if you want to use CHAP:

1. Enable CHAP at the server and policy levels.
2. Edit the default domain GPO's Password Policy object to turn on the Store Password Using Reversible Encryption policy setting.
3. Change or reset each user's password, which forces Windows Server 2012 R2 to store the password using reversible encryption.

After these steps are completed for an account, that account can be used with CHAP.

 These steps aren't required for MS-CHAPv2; for that protocol, you just enable MS-CHAPv2 at the server and policy levels.

Configuring Network Access Protection

Another way that you can have security is to allow users to access resources based on the identity of the client computer. This new security solution is called *Network Access Protection*. Determined by the client needs, network administrators now have the ability to define granular levels of network access using NAP. NAP also allows administrators to determine client access based on compliancy with corporate governance policies. The following are some of the NAP features:

Network Layer Protection   *Network layer protection* is the ability to secure communications at the Network layer of the OSI model.

All communications travel through the seven layers of the OSI model. Starting at the top (layer 7), the seven layers are the Application, Presentation, Session, Transport, Network, Data-Link, and Physical layers.

DHCP Enforcement   If a computer wants to receive unlimited IPv4 network access, the computer must be compliant with corporate governance policies. *DHCP enforcement* verifies that a computer is compliant before granting unlimited access. If a computer is noncompliant, the computer receives an IPv4 address that has limited network access and a default user profile. One advantage of using DHCP is that you can set up user classes so that specific machines (for example, noncompliant DHCP systems) can get specific rules or limited access to the network.

When a client computer attempts to receive an IP address from DHCP, the DHCP enforcement checks the health policy requirements of the system to make sure they meet the compliancy.

VPN Enforcement   *VPN enforcement* works a lot like DHCP enforcement, except that VPN enforcement verifies the compliancy of the system before the VPN connection is given full access to the network.

IPsec Enforcement   *IPsec enforcement* will allow a computer to communicate with other computers as long as the computers are IPsec compliant. You have the ability to configure the requirements for secure communications between the two compliant computer systems. You can configure the IPsec communications based on IP address or TCP/UDP port numbers.

802.1X Enforcement   For a computer system to have 802.1X unlimited access to network connections (Ethernet 802.11 or wireless access point), the computer system must be 802.1X compliant. *802.1X enforcement* verifies that the connecting system is 802.1X connection compliant. Noncompliant computers will obtain only limited access to network connections.

Flexible Host Isolation   *Flexible host isolation* allows a server and domain to isolate computers to help make it possible to design a layer of security between computers or networks. Even if a hacker gains access to your network using an authorized username and password, the server and domain isolation can stop the attack because the computer is not an authorized domain computer.

Multiconfiguration System Health Validator   This feature allows you to specify multiple configurations of a *system health validator (SHV)*. When an administrator configures a network policy for health evaluation, the administrator will select a specific health policy. Using this feature allows you to specify different network policies for different sets of health requirements based on a specific configuration of the SHV. For example, an administrator can create a network policy that specifies that all internal computers must have antivirus software enabled and a different network policy that specifies that VPN-connected computers must have their antivirus software enabled and signature files up-to-date.

NAP Monitoring

There may be many times when you will need to monitor how NAP is running and what NAP policies are being enforced. There are multiple ways that you can monitor NAP. You can use the Network Access Protection MMC snap-in to look at how things are running.

But there is another tool that you can use called Logman. Logman creates and manages Event Trace Session and Performance logs and allows an administrator to monitor many different applications through the use of the command line. Table 5.2 shows some of the different Logman switches you can use.

TABLE 5.2   Logman switches

Switch	Description
Logman create	Creates a counter, trace, configuration data collector, or API
Logman query	Queries data collector properties
Logman start | stop	Starts or stops data collection
Logman delete	Deletes an existing data collector
Logman update	Updates the properties of an existing data collector
Logman import | export	Imports a data collector set from an XML file or exports a data collector set to an XML file

Summary

In this chapter, I talked about the different ways that you can secure your remote access connections. You learned how to configure appropriate security settings so that communication between the client and server is secure because of NAP and NPS settings.

I talked about how to verify that client machines meet the minimum requirements in order to gain either full or limited access to your network.

I also discussed wireless networking and what types of security encryption you can use to help support your wireless network. You learned about the different components of wireless access and using group policies to configure wireless clients.

Exam Essentials

Understand what NAP can do for your network.   Understand that NAP allows administrators to determine client access based on compliancy with corporate governance policies. Some of the settings are Network Layer Protection, DHCP Enforcement, VPN Enforcement, IPsec Enforcement, 802.1X Enforcement, Flexible Host Isolation, and Multi-configuration System Health Validator.

Understand what NPS can do for your network.   Understand how to use NPS to manage network access centrally through a variety of network access servers, including RADIUS-compliant 802.1X-capable wireless access points, VPN servers, dial-up servers, and 802.1X-capable Ethernet switches.

Review Questions

1. You are the network administrator for a large Active Directory domain named Panek.com. The domain contains a server named Saturn that runs Windows Server 2012 R2. Saturn has the DHCP Server role installed. The network contains 400 client computers that run Windows 7 and Windows 8. All of the client computers are joined to the domain and are configured DHCP clients. You install a new server named Jupiter that runs Windows Server 2012 R2. On Jupiter, you install the Network Policy Server (NPS) role service, and you configure Network Access Protection (NAP) to use the DHCP enforcement method. You need to ensure that Saturn provides a valid default gateway only to computers that pass the system health validation. Which two actions should you perform? (Each correct answer presents part of the solution. Choose two.)

   A. From the DHCP console, configure the 016 Swap Server option.

   B. From the DHCP console, enable NAP on all scopes.

   C. From the NAP Client Configuration console, enable the DHCP Quarantine Enforcement client.

   D. From the DHCP console, create a new policy.

   E. From Server Manager, install the Network Policy Server role service.

2. Your network contains an Active Directory domain named Panek.com. The domain contains a server named Server1 that runs Windows Server 2012 R2. Server1 has the Network Policy Server (NPS) role service installed. You plan to configure Server1 as a Network Access Protection (NAP) health policy server for VPN enforcement by using the Configure NAP Wizard. You need to ensure that you can configure the VPN enforcement method on Server1 successfully. What should you install on Server1 before you run the Configure NAP Wizard?

   A. The Host Credential Authorization Protocol (HCAP)

   B. A system health validator (SHV)

   C. The Remote Access server role

   D. A computer certificate

3. You are a network administrator of an Active Directory domain named Stellacon.com. You have a server named Earth that runs Windows Server 2012 R2. Earth has the DHCP Server role and the Network Policy Server (NPS) role service installed. You enable Network Access Protection (NAP) on all of the DHCP scopes on Earth. You need to create a DHCP policy that will apply to all of the NAP noncompliant DHCP clients. Which criteria should you specify when you create the DHCP policy?

   A. The relay agent information

   B. The user class

   C. The vendor class

   D. The client identifier

4. Your network contains an Active Directory domain named contoso.com. Network Access Protection (NAP) is deployed to the domain. You need to create NAP event trace log files on a client computer. What should you run?

   A. Register-ObjectEvent

   B. Register-EngineEvent

   C. tracert

   D. logman

5. Your network contains four Network Policy Server (NPS) servers named ServerA, ServerB, ServerC, and ServerD. Server1 is configured as a RADIUS proxy that forwards connection requests to a remote RADIUS server group named Group1. You need to ensure that ServerB and ServerC receive connection requests. ServerD should receive connection requests only if both ServerB and ServerC are unavailable. How should you configure Group1?

   A. Change the weight of ServerB and ServerC to 10.

   B. Change the weight of ServerD to 10.

   C. Change the priority of ServerB and ServerC to 10.

   D. Change the priority of ServerD to 10.

6. Your network contains an Active Directory domain named Stellacon.com. The domain contains a RADIUS server named Server1 that runs Windows Server 2012 R2. You add a VPN server named Server2 to the network. On Server1, you create several network policies. You need to configure Server1 to accept authentication requests from Server2. Which tool should you use on Server1?

   A. Set-RemoteAccessRadius

   B. CMAK

   C. NPS

   D. Routing and Remote Access

7. Your network contains an Active Directory domain named Panek.com. The domain contains a server named Server1 that runs Windows Server 2012 R2. Server1 has the following role services installed:

   - DirectAccess and VPN (RRAS)

   - Network Policy Server

   Remote users have client computers that run either Windows XP, Windows 7, or Windows 8. You need to ensure that only the client computers that run Windows 7 or Windows 8 can establish VPN connections to Server1. What should you configure on Server1?

   A. A vendor-specific RADIUS attribute of a Network Policy Server (NPS) connection request policy

   B. A condition of a Network Policy Server (NPS) network policy

C. A condition of a Network Policy Server (NPS) connection request policy

D. A constraint of a Network Policy Server (NPS) network policy

8. You are the network administrator for a large organization that contains an Active Directory domain named Stellacon.com. The domain contains a server named Server1 that runs Windows Server 2012 R2. Server1 has the Network Policy and Access Services server role installed. You plan to deploy 802.1X authentication to secure the wireless network. You need to identify which Network Policy Server (NPS) authentication method supports certificate-based mutual authentication for the 802.1X deployment. Which authentication method should you identify?

A. PEAP-MS-CHAP v2

B. MS-CHAP v2

C. EAP-TLS

D. MS-CHAP

9. You are the administrator of a large organization that contains an Active Directory domain named Stellacon.com. The domain contains a server named ServerA that runs Windows Server 2012 R2. ServerA has the Network Policy and Access Services server role installed. Your company's security policy requires that certificate-based authentication be used by some network services. You need to identify which Network Policy Server (NPS) authentication methods comply with the security policy. Which two authentication methods should you identify? (Choose two.)

A. MS-CHAP

B. PEAP-MS-CHAP v2

C. CHAP

D. EAP-TLS

E. MS-CHAP v2

10. You are the network administrator, and you have been asked to set up an accounting system so each department is responsible for their cost of using network services. Your network contains a Network Policy Server (NPS) server named ServerA. The network contains a server named Database1 that has Microsoft SQL server installed. All servers run Windows Server 2012 R2. You configure NPS on ServerA to log accounting data to a database on Database1. You need to ensure that the accounting data is captured if Database1 fails. The solution must minimize cost. What should you do?

A. Implement Failover Clustering.

B. Implement database mirroring.

C. Run the Accounting Configuration Wizard.

D. Modify the SQL Server Logging properties.

Configure and Manage Active Directory

THE FOLLOWING 70-411 EXAM OBJECTIVES ARE COVERED IN THIS CHAPTER:

✓ **Configure service authentication**

- Create and configure Service Accounts

- Create and configure Group Managed Service Accounts

- Configure Kerberos delegation

- Manage Service Principal Names (SPNS)

- Configure virtual accounts

✓ **Configure Domain Controllers**

- Transfer and seize operations master roles

- Install and configure a read-only domain controller (RODC)

- Configure domain controller cloning

✓ **Maintain Active Directory**

- Back up Active Directory and SYSVOL

- Manage Active Directory offline

- Optimize an Active Directory database

- Clean up metadata

- Configure Active Directory snapshots

- Perform object- and container-level recovery

- Perform Active Directory restore

- Configure and restore objects by using the Active Directory Recycle Bin

✓ **Configure account policies**

- Configure domain and local user password policy settings

- Configure and apply Password Settings Objects (PSOs)

- Delegate password settings management

- Configure account lockout policy settings

- Configure Kerberos policy settings

In this chapter, we will dive deeper into the Active Directory realm.

I have covered many important aspects of Active Directory. The most important aspect of any network, including Active Directory, is security. If your network is not secure, then hackers (internal or external) can make your life as a member of an IT department a living nightmare.

In this chapter, you'll learn how to implement security within Active Directory. By using Active Directory tools, you can quickly and easily configure the settings that you require in order to protect information.

Proper planning for security permissions is an important prerequisite of setting up Active Directory. Security is always one of the greatest concerns for an IT administrator.

You should have a security policy that states what is expected of every computer user in your company. Fine-tuning Active Directory to comply with your security policy and allowing end users to function without any issues should be your goals.

You should know how to use Active Directory to apply permissions to resources on the network, and you should pay particular attention to the evaluation of permissions when applied to different groups and the flow of permissions through the organizational units (OUs) via group policies. With all of this in mind, let's start looking at how you can manage security within Active Directory.

Active Directory Security Overview

One of the fundamental design goals for Active Directory is to define a single, centralized repository of users and information resources. Active Directory records information about all of the users, computers, and resources on your network. Each domain acts as a logical boundary, and members of the domain (including workstations, servers, and domain controllers) share information about the objects within them.

The information stored within Active Directory determines which resources are accessible to which users. Through the use of permissions that are assigned to Active Directory objects, you can control all aspects of network security.

Throughout this chapter, you'll learn the details of security as it pertains to Active Directory. Note, however, that Active Directory security is only one aspect of overall network security. You should also be sure that you have implemented appropriate access control settings for the file system, network devices, and other resources. Let's start by looking at the various components of network security, which include working with security principals and managing security and permissions, access control lists (ACLs), and access control entries (ACEs).

 When you are setting up a network, you should always keep in mind that 90 percent of all hacks on a network are internal. This means internal permissions and security (as well as external security) need to be as strong as possible while still allowing users to do their jobs.

Understanding Active Directory Features

Let's take a look at some of the Active Directory features and what each feature can do for you as an administrator.

Active Directory is the heart and soul of a Microsoft domain, and I can never talk enough about the roles and features included with Active Directory. Many of these features have already been discussed, but what follows will be a good review for the 70-411 exam:

Active Directory Certificate Services   Active Directory Certificate Services (AD CS) provides a customizable set of services that allows you to issue and manage public key infrastructure (PKI) certificates. These certificates can be used in software security systems that employ public key technologies.

Active Directory Domain Services   Active Directory Domain Services (AD DS) includes new features that make deploying domain controllers simpler and lets you implement them faster. AD DS also makes the domain controllers more flexible, both to audit and to authorize access to files. Moreover, AD DS has been designed to make performing administrative tasks easier through consistent graphical and scripted management experiences.

Active Directory Rights Management Services   Active Directory Rights Management Services (AD RMS) provides management and development tools that let you work with industry security technologies, including encryption, certificates, and authentication. Using these technologies allows organizations to create reliable information protection solutions.

Hyper-V   Hyper-V is one of the most changed features in Windows Server 2012 R2. Microsoft's new slogan is "Windows Server 2012 R2, built from the cloud up," and this has a lot to do with Hyper-V. It allows an organization to consolidate servers by creating and managing a virtualized computing environment. It does this by using virtualization technology that is built into Windows Server 2012 R2.

IPAM   IP Address Management (IPAM) was one of the new features introduced with Windows Server 2012. IPAM allows an administrator to customize and monitor the IP address infrastructure on a corporate network.

Kerberos Authentication   Windows Server 2012 R2 uses the Kerberos authentication (version 5) protocol and extensions for password-based and public-key authentication. The Kerberos client is installed as a security support provider (SSP), and it can be accessed through the Security Support Provider Interface (SSPI).

Managed Service Accounts   Stand-alone managed service accounts, originally created for Windows Server 2008 R2 and Windows 7, are configured domain accounts that allow automatic password management and service principal names (SPNs) management, including the ability to delegate management to other administrators.

Security Auditing   Security auditing gives an organization the ability to help maintain the security of an enterprise. By using security audits, you can verify authorized or unauthorized access to machines, resources, applications, and services. One of the best advantages of security audits is to verify regulatory compliance.

TLS/SSL (Schannel SSP)   Schannel is a security support provider (SSP) that uses the Secure Sockets Layer (SSL) and Transport Layer Security (TLS) Internet standard authentication protocols together. The Security Support Provider Interface (SSPI) is an API used by Windows systems to allow security-related functionality, including authentication.

Windows Deployment Services   Windows Deployment Services allows an administrator to install Windows operating systems remotely. Administrators can use Windows Deployment Services to set up new computers by using a network-based installation.

Understanding Security Principals

Security principals are Active Directory objects that are assigned *security identifiers (SIDs)*. An SID is a unique identifier that is used to manage any object to which permissions can be assigned. Security principals are assigned permissions to perform certain actions and access certain network resources.

The following basic types of Active Directory objects serve as security principals:

User Accounts   User accounts identify individual users on your network by including information such as the user's name and their password. User accounts are the fundamental unit of security administration.

Groups   There are two main types of groups: security groups and distribution groups. Both types can contain user accounts. System administrators use security groups to ease the management of security permissions. They use distribution groups, on the other hand, solely to send email. Distribution groups are not security principals. You'll see the details of groups in the next section.

Computer Accounts   Computer accounts identify which client computers are members of particular domains. Because these computers participate in the Active Directory database, system administrators can manage security settings that affect the computer.

They use computer accounts to determine whether a computer can join a domain and for authentication purposes. As you'll see later in this chapter, system administrators can also place restrictions on certain computer settings to increase security. These settings apply to the computer and, therefore, also apply to any user who is using it (regardless of the permissions granted to the user account).

Note that other objects—such as OUs—do not function as security principals. What this means is that you can apply certain settings (such as Group Policy) on all of the objects within an OU; however, you cannot specifically set permissions with respect to the OU itself. The purpose of OUs is to organize other Active Directory objects logically based on business needs, add a needed level of control for security, and create an easier way to delegate.

You can manage security by performing the following actions with security principals:

- You can assign them permissions to access various network resources.

- You can give them user rights.

- You can track their actions through auditing (covered later in this chapter).

The major types of security principals—user accounts, groups, and computer accounts—form the basis of the Active Directory security architecture. As a system administrator, you will likely spend a portion of your time managing permissions for these objects.

It is important to understand that, since a unique SID defines each security principal, deleting a security principal is an irreversible process. For example, if you delete a user account and then later re-create one with the same name, you'll need to reassign permissions and group membership settings for the new account. Once a user account is deleted, its SID is deleted.

Users and groups are two types of fundamental security principals employed for security administration. In the following sections, you'll learn how users and groups interact and about the different types of groups you can create.

Types of Groups

When dealing with groups, you should make the distinction between local security principals and domain security principals:

Local Users and Groups   You use local users and groups to assign the permissions necessary to access the local machine. For example, you may assign the permissions you need to reboot a domain controller to a specific domain local group.

Domain Users and Groups   Domain users and groups, on the other hand, are used throughout the domain. These objects are available on any of the computers within the Active Directory domain and between domains that have a trust relationship.

Here are the two main types of groups used in Active Directory:

Security Groups   Security groups are considered security principals. They can contain user accounts, computers, or groups. To make administration simpler, system administrators usually grant permissions to groups. This allows you to change permissions easily at the Active Directory level (instead of at the level of the resource on which the permissions are assigned).

You can also place Active Directory contact objects within security groups, but security permissions will not apply to them.

Distribution Groups   Distribution groups are not considered security principals because they do not have SIDs. As mentioned earlier, they are used only for the purpose of sending email messages. You can add users to distribution groups just as you would add them to security groups. You can also place distribution groups within OUs so that they are easier to manage. You will find them useful, for example, if you need to send email messages to an entire department or business unit within Active Directory.

Understanding the differences between security and distribution groups is important in an Active Directory environment. For the most part, system administrators use security groups for the daily administration of permissions. On the other hand, system administrators who are responsible for maintaining email distribution lists generally use distribution groups to group members of departments and business units logically. (A system administrator can also email all of the users within a security group, but to do so, they would have to specify the email addresses for the accounts.)

When you are working in Windows Server 2003, Server 2008, Server 2008 R2, or Server 2012 functional-level domains, you can convert security groups to or from distribution groups. When group types are running in a Windows 2000 mixed domain functional level, you cannot change them.

> It is vital that you understand group types when you are getting ready to take the Microsoft exams. Microsoft likes to include trick questions about putting permissions on distribution groups. Remember, only security groups can have permissions assigned to them.

Group Scope

In addition to being classified by type, each group is given a specific scope. The scope of a group defines two characteristics. First, it determines the level of security that applies to a group. Second, it determines which users can be added to the group. Group scope is an important concept in network environments because it ultimately defines which resources users are able to access.

The three types of group scope are as follows:

Domain Local   The scope of domain local groups extends as far as the local domain. When you're using the Active Directory Users and Computers tool, domain local accounts apply to the computer for which you are viewing information. Domain local groups are used to assign permissions to local resources, such as files and printers. They can contain domain locals, global groups, universal groups, and user accounts.

Global   The scope of global groups is limited to a single domain. Global groups may contain any of the users that are part of the Active Directory domain in which the global groups reside or may contain other global groups. Global groups are often used for managing domain security permissions based on job functions. For example, if you need to specify permissions for the Engineering department, you could create one or more global groups (such as EngineeringManagers and EngineeringDevelopers). You could then assign security permissions to each group.

Universal   Universal groups can contain accounts or other universal groups from any domains within an Active Directory forest. Therefore, system administrators use them to manage security across domains. When you are managing multiple domains, it often helps to group global groups within universal groups. For instance, if you have an Engineering global group in the research.stellacon.com domain and an Engineering global group in the asia.stellacon.com domain, you can create a universal AllEngineers group that contains both of the global groups. Now whenever you must assign security permissions to all engineers within the organization, you need only assign permissions to the AllEngineers universal group.

For domain controllers to process authentication between domains, information about the membership of universal groups is stored in the global catalog (GC). Keep this in mind if you ever plan to place users directly into universal groups and bypass global groups because all of the users will be enumerated in the GC, which will impact size and performance.

Fortunately, universal group credentials are cached on domain controllers that universal group members use to log on. This process is called *universal group membership caching*. The domain controller obtains the cached data whenever universal group members log on, and then it is retained on the domain controller for eight hours by default. This is especially useful for smaller locations, such as branch offices, which run less-expensive domain controllers. Most domain controllers at these locations cannot store a copy of the entire GC, and frequent calls to the nearest GC would require an inordinate amount of network traffic.

When you create a new group using the Active Directory Users and Computers tool, you must specify the scope of the group. Figure 6.1 shows the New Object – Group dialog box and the available options for the group scope.

However, changing group scope can be helpful when your security administration or business needs change. You can change group scope easily using the Active Directory Users and Computers tool. To do so, access the properties of the group. As shown in Figure 6.2, you can make a group scope change by clicking one of the options.

FIGURE 6.1   The New Object – Group dialog box

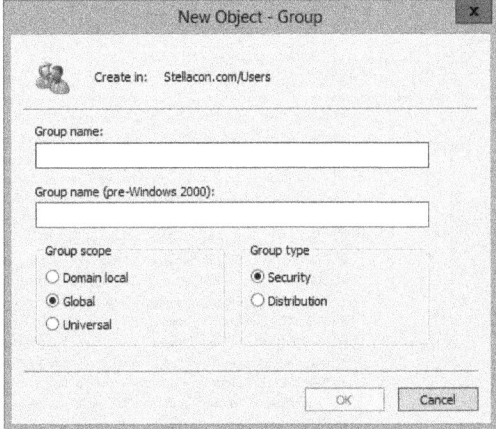

FIGURE 6.2   The Domain Admins Security Group's Properties dialog box

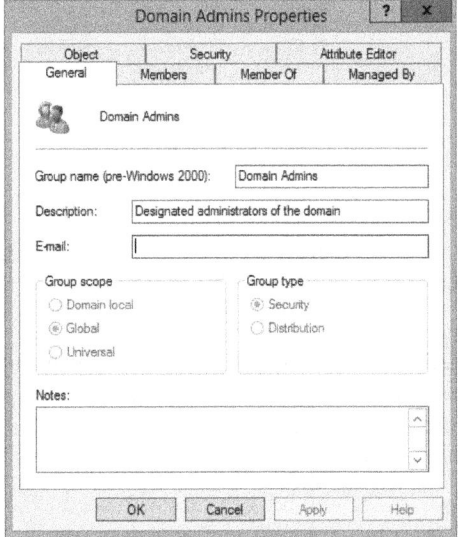

Built-in Service Account Groups

System administrators use built-in domain local groups to perform administrative functions on the local server. Because these have pre-assigned permissions and privileges, they allow system administrators to assign common management functions easily. Figure 6.3 shows the default built-in groups that are available on a Windows Server 2012 domain controller.

FIGURE 6.3   Default built-in local groups

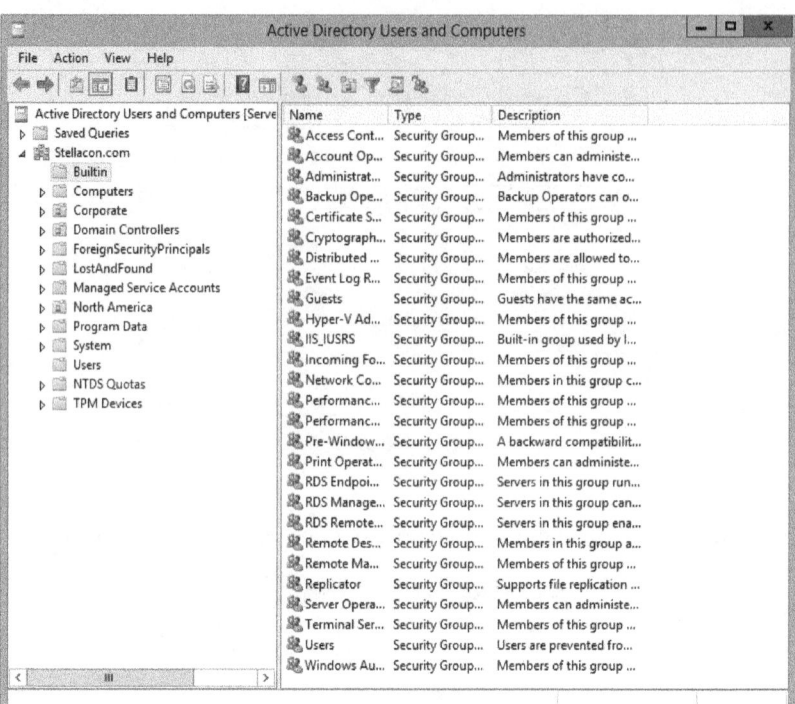

The list of built-in local groups includes some of the following:

Account Operators   These users can create and modify domain user and group accounts. Members of this group are generally responsible for the daily administration of Active Directory.

Administrators   By default, members of the Administrators group are given full permissions to perform any functions within the Active Directory domain and on the local computer. This means they can access all files and resources that reside on any server within the domain. As you can see, this is a powerful account.

In general, you should restrict the number of users who are included in this group because most common administration functions do not require this level of access.

Backup Operators   One of the problems associated with backing up data in a secure network environment is that you need to provide a way to bypass standard file system security so that you can copy files. Although you could place users in the Administrators group, doing so usually provides more permissions than necessary. Members of the Backup Operators group can bypass standard file system security for the purpose of backup and recovery only. They cannot, however, directly access or open files within the file system.

Generally, backup software applications and data use the permissions assigned to the Backup Operators group.

Certificate Service DCOM Access   Members of the Certificate Service DCOM Access group can connect to certificate authority servers in the enterprise.

Cryptographic Operators   Members of the Cryptographic Operators group are authorized to perform cryptographic operations. Cryptography allows the use of codes to convert data, which then allows a specific recipient to read it using a key.

Guests   Typically, you use the Guests group to provide access to resources that generally do not require security. For example, if you have a network share that provides files that should be made available to all network users, you can assign permissions to allow members of the Guests group to access those files.

Print Operators   By default, members of the Print Operators group are given permissions to administer all of the printers within a domain. This includes common functions such as changing the priority of print jobs and deleting items from the print queue.

Replicator   The Replicator group allows files to be replicated among the computers in a domain. You can add accounts used for replication-related tasks to this group to provide those accounts with the permissions they need to keep files synchronized across multiple computers.

Server Operators   A common administrative task is managing server configuration. Members of the Server Operators group are granted the permissions they need to manage services, shares, and other system settings.

Users   The Users built-in domain local group is used to administer security for most network accounts. Usually, you don't give this group many permissions, and you use it to apply security settings for most employees within an organization.

Windows Server 2012 also includes many different default groups, which you can find in the Users folder. As shown in Figure 6.4, these groups are of varying scopes, including domain local, global, and universal groups. You'll see the details of these groups in the next section.

Three important user accounts are created during the promotion of a domain controller:

- The *Administrator account* is assigned the password a system administrator provides during the promotion process, and it has full permissions to perform all actions within the domain.

- The Guest account is disabled by default. The purpose of the *Guest account* is to provide anonymous access to users who do not have an individual logon and password to use within the domain. Although the Guest account might be useful in some situations, it is generally recommended that this account be disabled to increase security.

- Only the operating system uses the *krbtgt*, or *Key Distribution Center Service account*, for Kerberos authentication. This account is disabled by default. Unlike other user accounts, the krbtgt account cannot be used to log on to the domain, and therefore it does not need to be enabled. Since only the operating system uses this account, you do not need to worry about hackers gaining access by using this account.

FIGURE 6.4   Contents of the default Users folder

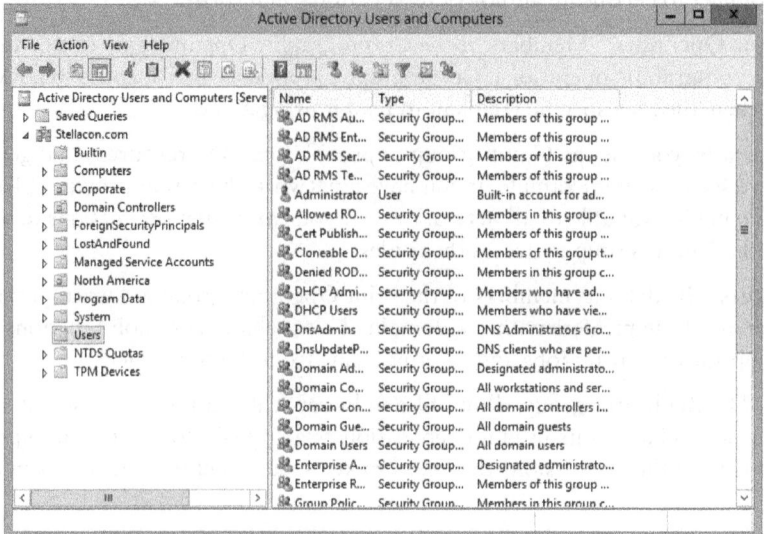

Managed Service Account and Virtual Accounts

One issue that many administrators run into is how to handle application accounts. What I mean by this is, what type of account and what permissions are needed when installing an application such as Microsoft Exchange?

If you were the administrator for the local system, you could just configure Exchange to run as a Local Service. The problem with using these types of accounts is that they are normally used multiple times among different applications.

Another option that you could have is just to create a domain account for each application. For example, an administrator can create a specific domain account that Exchange could use. The problem with this option is that you have to remember to change the password frequency, and once you change that password, you have to remember which services you configured to use that account and change the passwords for each service. This is not an ideal way to set up an application service.

The two types of accounts available in Windows Server 2012 R2 are the managed service account and the virtual account. These two accounts were originally created in Windows Server 2008 R2 and Windows 7. These accounts are specifically designed for use with applications, and an administrator does not need to change the credentials manually every few months. These two domain accounts provide automatic password management and simplified service principal names management.

Virtual accounts even take it a step further because no password management is needed, and they can access the network using a computer identity from the domain environment.

To use the managed service account and the virtual account, your server needs to be running at least Windows Server 2008 R2 or Windows 7/8. When you are using managed service accounts, a managed service account can be used only for services on a single computer. You are not allowed to share managed service accounts between multiple computers. This also means you can't use managed service accounts in a server that is going to be part of a cluster.

To configure or manipulate your managed service account or virtual account on a server, you need to use Windows PowerShell cmdlets or any utility that allows you to work with these types of accounts (`Dsacls.exe`, Services snap-in mmc, `SetSPN.exe`, and so forth).

Predefined Global Groups

As mentioned earlier in this chapter, you use global groups to manage permissions at the domain level. Members of each of these groups can perform specific tasks related to managing Active Directory.

The following predefined global groups are installed in the Users folder:

Cert Publishers   Certificates are used to increase security by allowing for strong authentication methods. User accounts are placed within the *Cert Publishers group* if they must publish security certificates. Generally, Active Directory security services use these accounts.

Domain Computers   All of the computers that are members of the domain are generally members of the *Domain Computers group*. This includes any workstations or servers that have joined the domain, but it does not include the domain controllers.

Domain Admins   Members of the *Domain Admins group* have full permissions to manage all of the Active Directory objects for this domain. This is a powerful account; therefore, you should restrict its membership only to those users who require full permissions.

Domain Controllers   All of the domain controllers for a given domain are generally included within the *Domain Controllers group*.

Domain Guests   Generally, by default, members of the *Domain Guests group* are given minimal permissions with respect to resources. System administrators may place user accounts in this group if they require only basic access or temporary permissions within the domain.

Domain Users   The *Domain Users group* usually contains all of the user accounts for the given domain. This group is generally given basic permissions to resources that do not require higher levels of security. A common example is a public file share.

Enterprise Admins   Members of the *Enterprise Admins group* are given full permissions to perform actions within the entire forest. This includes functions such as managing trust relationships and adding new domains to trees and forests.

Group Policy Creator Owners   Members of the *Group Policy Creator Owners group* are able to create and modify Group Policy settings for objects within the domain. This allows them to enable security settings on OUs (and the objects that they contain).

Schema Admins   Members of the *Schema Admins group* are given permissions to modify the Active Directory schema. As a member of Schema Admins, you can create additional fields of information for user accounts. This is a powerful function because any changes to the schema will be propagated to all of the domains and domain controllers within an

Active Directory forest. Furthermore, you cannot undo changes to the schema (although you can disable some).

In addition to these groups, you can create new ones for specific services and applications that are installed on the server. (You'll notice that the list in Figure 6.4 includes more than just the ones in the preceding list.) Specifically, services that run on domain controllers and servers will be created as security groups with domain local scope. For example, if a domain controller is running the DNS service, the DnsAdmins and DnsUpdateProxy groups become available. In addition, there are two read-only domain controller (RODC) local groups: the Allowed RODC Password Replication and the Denied RODC Password Replication groups. Similarly, if you install the DHCP service, it automatically creates the DHCP Users and DHCP Administrators groups. The purpose of these groups depends on the functionality of the applications being installed.

Foreign Security Principals

In environments that have more than one domain, you may need to grant permissions to users who reside in multiple domains. Generally, you manage this using Active Directory trees and forests. However, in some cases, you may want to provide resources to users who belong to domains that are not part of the forest.

Active Directory uses the concept of *foreign security principals* to allow permissions to be assigned to users who are not part of an Active Directory forest. This process is automatic and does not require the intervention of system administrators. You can then add the foreign security principals to domain local groups for which, in turn, you can grant permissions for resources within the domain. You can view a list of foreign security principals by using the Active Directory Users and Computers tool. Figure 6.5 shows the contents of the ForeignSecurityPrincipals folder.

FIGURE 6.5 The ForeignSecurityPrincipals folder

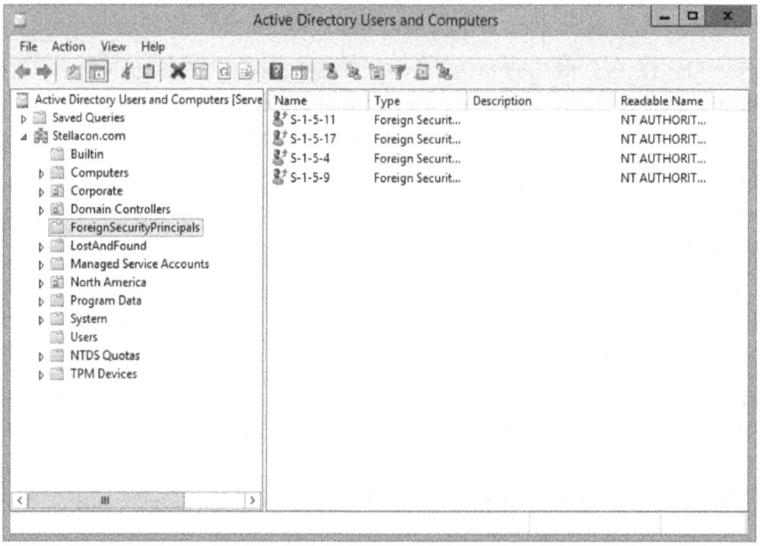

Managing Security and Permissions

Now that you understand the basic issues, terms, and Active Directory objects that pertain to security, it's time to look at how you can apply this information to secure your network resources. The general practice for managing security is to assign users to groups and then grant permissions and logon parameters to the groups so that they can access certain resources.

For management ease and to implement a hierarchical structure, you can place groups within OUs. You can also assign Group Policy settings to all of the objects contained within an OU. By using this method, you can combine the benefits of a hierarchical structure (through OUs) with the use of security principals. Figure 6.6 provides a diagram of this process.

FIGURE 6.6   An overview of security management

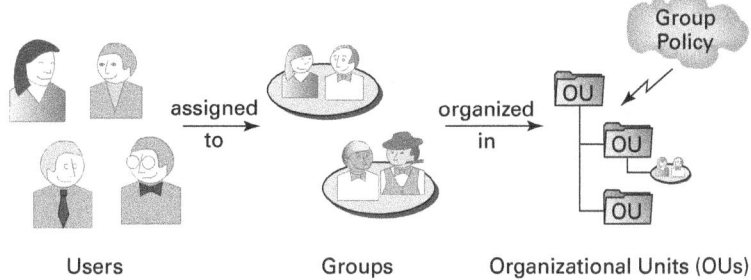

| Users | Groups | Organizational Units (OUs) |

The primary tool you use to manage security permissions for users, groups, and computers is the Active Directory Users and Computers tool. Using this tool, you can create and manage Active Directory objects and organize them based on your business needs. Common tasks for many system administrators might include the following:

- Resetting a user's password (for example, in cases where they forget their password)

- Creating new user accounts (when, for instance, a new employee joins the company)

- Modifying group memberships based on changes in job requirements and functions

- Disabling user accounts (when, for example, users will be out of the office for long periods of time and will not require network resource access)

Once you've properly grouped your users, you need to set the actual permissions that affect the objects within Active Directory. The actual permissions available vary based on the type of object. Table 6.1 provides an example of some of the permissions that you can apply to various Active Directory objects and an explanation of what each permission does.

TABLE 6.1   Permissions of Active Directory objects

Permission	Explanation
Control Access	Changes security permissions on the object
Create Child	Creates objects within an OU (such as other OUs)
Delete Child	Deletes child objects within an OU
Delete Tree	Deletes an OU and the objects within it
List Contents	Views objects within an OU
List Object	Views a list of the objects within an OU
Read	Views properties of an object (such as a username)
Write	Modifies properties of an object

Using ACLs and ACEs

Each object in Active Directory has an *access control list*. The ACL is a list of user accounts and groups that are allowed to access the resource. For each ACL, there is an access control entry that defines what a user or a group can actually do with the resource. Deny permissions are always listed first. This means that if users have Deny permissions through user or group membership, they will not be allowed to access the object, even if they have explicit Allow permissions through other user or group permissions. Figure 6.7 shows an ACL for the Sales OU.

FIGURE 6.7   The ACL for an OU named Sales

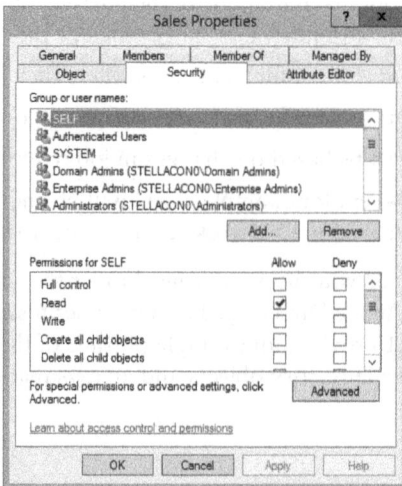

The Security tab is enabled only if you selected the Advanced Features option from the View menu in the Active Directory Users and Computers tool.

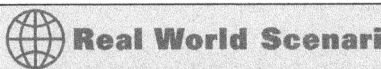

Using Groups Effectively

You are a new system administrator for a medium-sized organization, and your network spans a single campus environment. The previous administrator had migrated the network from Windows 2003 to Windows Server 2012 R2, and everyone seems fine with the network and new workstations. As you familiarize yourself with the network, you realize that the previous administrator applied a very ad hoc approach. Many of the permissions to resources had been given to individual accounts on request. It seems that there was no particular strategy with regard to administration.

Management tells you that the company has acquired another company, ideally the first of several acquisitions. They tell you about these plans because they do not want any hiccups in the information system as necessary changes ensue.

You immediately realize that management practices of the past must be replaced with the best practices that have been developed for networks over the years. One of the fundamental practices that you need to establish for this environment is the use of groups to apply permissions and give privileges to users throughout the network.

It is quite simple to give permissions individually, and in some cases, it seems like overkill to create a group, give permissions to the group, and then add a user to the group. Using group-based permissions really pays off in the long run, however, regardless of how small your network is today.

One constant in the networking world is that networks grow. When they grow, it is much easier to add users to a well-thought-out system of groups and consistently applied policies and permissions than it is to patch these elements together for each individual user.

Don't get caught up in the "easy" way of dealing with each request as it comes down the pike. Take the time to figure out how the system will benefit from a more structured approach. Visualize your network as already large with numerous accounts, even if it is still small; this way, when it grows, you will be well positioned to manage the network as smoothly as possible.

Implementing Active Directory Security

So far, you have looked at many different concepts that are related to security within Active Directory. You began by exploring security principals and how they form the basis for administering Active Directory security. Then you considered the purpose and function of groups, how group scopes can affect how these groups work, and how to create a list of the predefined users and groups for new domains and domain controllers. Based on all of this information, it's time to see how you can implement Active Directory security.

In this section, you'll take a look at how you can create and manage users and groups. The most commonly used tool for working with these objects is the Active Directory Users and Computers tool. Using this tool, you can create new user and group objects within the relevant OUs of your domain, and you can modify group membership and group scope.

In addition to these basic operations, you can use some additional techniques to simplify the administration of users and groups. One method involves using user templates. Additionally, you'll want be able to specify who can make changes to user and group objects. That's the purpose of delegation. Both of these topics are covered later in this section.

Let's start with the basics. In Exercise 6.1, you learn how to create and manage users and groups.

WARNING   This exercise involves creating new OUs and user accounts within an Active Directory domain. Be sure that you are working in a test environment to avoid any problems that might occur because of the changes you make.

EXERCISE 6.1

Creating and Managing Users and Groups

1. Open the Active Directory Users and Computers MMC snap-in by pressing the Windows key (on the keyboard) and choosing Administrative Tools ➤ Active Directory Users And Computers.

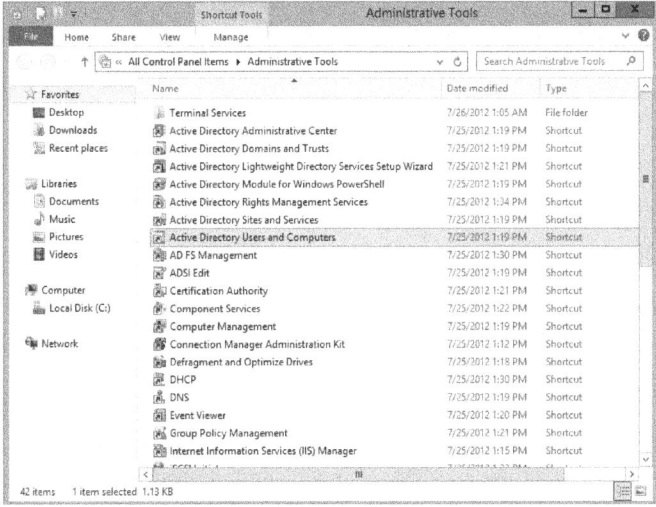

2. Create the following top-level OUs:

   Sales

   Marketing

   Engineering

   HR

3. Create the following User objects within the Sales container (use the defaults for all fields not listed):

   a. First Name: **John**

   Last Name: **Sales**

   User Logon Name: **JSales**

   b. First Name: **Linda**

   Last Name: **Manager**

   User Logon Name: **LManager**

4. Create the following User objects within the Marketing container (use the defaults for all fields not listed):

   a. First Name: **Jane**

   Last Name: **Marketing**

   User Logon Name: **JMarketing**

   b. First Name: **Monica**

   Last Name: **Manager**

   User Logon Name: **MManager**

5. Create the following User object within the Engineering container (use the defaults for all fields not listed):

    First Name: **Bob**

    Last Name: **Engineer**

    User Logon Name: **BEngineer**

6. Right-click the HR container, and select New ➢ Group. Use the name **Managers** for the group and specify Global for the group scope and Security for the group type. Click OK to create the group.

7. To assign users to the Managers group, right-click the Group object and select Properties. Change to the Members tab and click Add. Enter **Linda Manager** and **Monica Manager** and then click OK. You will see the group membership list. Click OK to finish adding the users to the group.

8. When you have finished creating users and groups, close the Active Directory Users and Computers tool.

Notice that you can add users to groups regardless of the OU in which they're contained. In Exercise 6.1, for example, you added two user accounts from different OUs into a group that was created in a third OU. This type of flexibility allows you to manage user and group accounts easily based on your business organization.

The Active Directory Users and Computers tool also allows you to perform common functions simply by right-clicking an object and selecting actions from the context menu. For example, you could right-click a user account and select Add Members To Group to change group membership quickly. You even have the ability in Active Directory Users and Computers to drag users from one OU and drop them into another.

You may have noticed that creating multiple users can be a fairly laborious and a potentially error-prone process. As a result, you are probably ready to take a look at a better way to create multiple users—by using user templates, which is discussed in the next section.

Using User Templates

Sometimes you will need to add several users with the same security settings. Rather than creating each user from scratch and making configuration changes to each one manually, you can create one user template, configure it, and copy it as many times as necessary. Each copy retains the configuration, group membership, and permissions of the original, but you must specify a new username, password, and full name to make the new user unique.

In Exercise 6.2, you create a user template, make configuration changes, and create a new user based on the template. This exercise shows you that the new user you create will belong to the same group as the user template you copied it from. You must have completed Exercise 6.1 first before you begin this one.

EXERCISE 6.2

Creating and Using User Templates

1. Open the Active Directory Users and Computers tool.

2. Create the following User object within the Sales container (use the defaults for all fields not listed):

    First Name: **Sales User**

    Last Name: **Template**

    User Logon Name: **SalesUserTemplate**

3. Create a new global security group called Sales Users and add SalesUserTemplate to the group membership.

4. Right-click the SalesUserTemplate User object and select Copy from the context menu.

5. Enter the username, first name, and last name for the new user.

6. Click the Next button to move on to the password screen and enter the new user's password information. Close the Copy Object—User dialog box when you've finished.

7. Right-click the user that you created in step 5, select Properties, and click the Member Of tab.

8. Verify that the new user is a member of the Sales Users group.

Delegating Control of Users and Groups

A common administrative function related to the use of Active Directory involves managing users and groups. You can use OUs to group objects logically so that you can easily manage them. Once you have placed the appropriate Active Directory objects within OUs, you are ready to delegate control of these objects.

Delegation is the process by which a higher-level security administrator assigns permissions to other users. For example, if Admin A is a member of the Domain Admins group, Admin A is able to delegate control of any OU within the domain to Admin B. You can access the Delegation Of Control Wizard through the Active Directory Users and Computers tool. You can use it to perform common delegation tasks quickly and easily. The wizard walks you through the steps of selecting the objects for which you want to perform delegation, what permission you want to allow, and which users will have those permissions.

Exercise 6.3 walks through the steps required to delegate control of OUs. To complete the steps in this exercise, you must first have completed Exercise 6.1.

EXERCISE 6.3

Delegating Control of Active Directory Objects

1. Open the Active Directory Users and Computers tool.

2. Create a new user within the Engineering OU using the following information (use the default settings for any fields not specified):

    First Name: **Robert**

    Last Name: **Admin**

    User Logon Name: **radmin**

    Password: **P@ssw0rd**

3. Right-click the Sales OU and select Delegate Control. This starts the Delegation Of Control Wizard. Click Next.

4. To add users and groups to whom you want to delegate control, click the Add button. In the Add dialog box, enter **Robert Admin** for the name of the user to add. Note that you can specify multiple users or groups using this option.

5. Click OK to add the account to the delegation list, which is shown in the Users Or Groups page. Click Next to continue.

6. On the Tasks To Delegate page, you must specify which actions you want to allow the selected user to perform within this OU. Select the Delegate The Following Common Tasks option and place a check mark next to the following options:

    Create, Delete, And Manage User Accounts

    Reset User Passwords And Force Password Change At Next Logon

    Read All User Information

    Create, Delete And Manage Groups

    Modify The Membership Of A Group

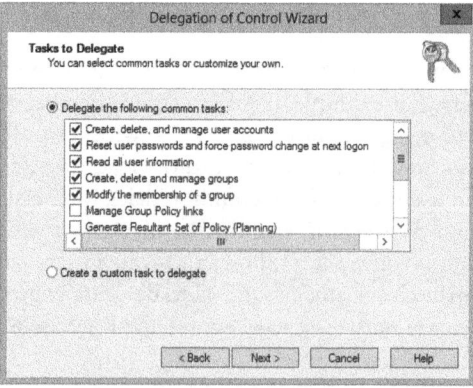

7. Click Next to continue. The wizard summarizes the selections that you have made on the Completing The Delegation Of Control Wizard page. To complete the process, click Finish to have the wizard commit the changes.

Now when the user Robert Admin logs on (using *radmin* as his logon name), he will be able to perform common administrative functions for all of the objects contained within the Sales OU.

8. When you have finished, close the Active Directory Users and Computers tool.

Understanding Dynamic Access Control

One of the advantages of Windows Server 2012 R2 is the ability to apply data governance to your file server. This will help control who has access to information and auditing. You get these advantages through the use of *Dynamic Access Control (DAC)*. Dynamic Access Control allows you to identify data by using data classifications (both automatic and manual) and then control access to these files based on these classifications.

DAC also gives administrators the ability to control file access by using a central access policy. This central access policy will also allow an administrator to set up audit access to files for reporting and forensic investigation.

DAC allows an administrator to set up Active Directory Rights Management Service encryption for Microsoft Office documents. For example, you can set up encryption for any documents that contain financial information.

Dynamic Access Control gives an administrator the flexibility to configure file access and auditing to domain-based file servers. To do this, DAC controls claims in the authentication token, resource properties, and conditional expressions within permission and auditing entries.

Administrators have the ability to give users access to files and folders based on Active Directory attributes. For example, a user named Dana is given access to the file server share because in the user's Active Directory (department attribute) properties, the value contains the value Sales.

 For DAC to function properly, an administrator must enable Windows 8 computers and Windows Server 2012 R2 file servers to support claims and compound authentication.

Using Group Policy for Security

A useful and powerful feature of Active Directory is a technology known as a *Group Policy*. Through the use of Group Policy settings, system administrators can assign thousands of different settings and options for users, groups, and OUs. Specifically, in relation to security, you can use many different options to control how important features such as password policies, user rights, and account lockout settings can be configured.

The general process for making these settings is to create a *Group Policy object (GPO)* with the settings you want and then link it to an OU or other Active Directory object.

Table 6.2 lists many Group Policy settings, which are relevant to creating a secure Active Directory environment. Note that this list is not comprehensive—many other options are available through Windows Server 2012's administrative tools.

TABLE 6.2 Group Policy settings used for security purposes

Setting section	Setting name	Purpose
Account Policies ➢ Password Policy	Enforce Password History	Specifies how many passwords will be remembered. This option prevents users from reusing the same passwords whenever they're changed.
Account Policies ➢ Password Policy	Minimum Password Length	Prevents users from using short, weak passwords by specifying the minimum number of characters that the password must include.
Account Policies ➢ Account Lockout Policy	Account Lockout Threshold	Specifies how many bad password attempts can be entered before the account gets locked out.
Account Policies ➢ Account Lockout Policy	Account Lockout Duration	Specifies how long an account will remain locked out after too many bad password attempts have been entered. By setting this option to a reasonable value (such as 30 minutes), you can reduce administrative overhead while still maintaining fairly strong security.
Account Policies ➢ Account Lockout Policy	Reset Account Lockout Counter After	Specifies how long the Account Lockout Threshold counter will hold failed logon attempts before resetting to 0.
Local Policies ➢ Security Options	Accounts: Rename Administrator Account	Often, when trying to gain unauthorized access to a computer, individuals attempt to guess the administrator password. One method for increasing security is to rename this account so that no password allows entry using this logon.

Setting section	Setting name	Purpose
Local Policies ➤ Security Options	Domain Controller: Allow Server Operators To Schedule Tasks	This option specifies whether members of the built-in Server Operators group are allowed to schedule tasks on the server.
Local Policies ➤ Security Options	Interactive Logon: Do Not Display Last User Name	Increases security by not displaying the name of the last user who logged onto the system.
Local Policies ➤ Security Options	Shutdown: Allow System To Be Shut Down Without Having To Log On	Allows system administrators to perform remote shutdown operations without logging on to the server.

You can use several different methods to configure Group Policy settings using the tools included with Windows Server 2012. Exercise 6.4 walks through the steps required to create a basic group policy for the purpose of enforcing security settings. To complete the steps of this exercise, you must have completed Exercise 6.1.

EXERCISE 6.4

Applying Security Policies by Using Group Policy

1. Open the Group Policy Management Console tool.

2. Expand Domains and then click the domain name.

3. In the right pane, right-click the Default Domain Policy and choose Edit.

4. In the Group Policy Management Editor window, expand Computer Configuration ➤ Policies ➤ Windows Settings ➤ Security Settings ➤ Account Policies ➤ Password Policy.

5. In the right pane, double-click the Minimum Password Length setting.

6. In the Security Policy Setting dialog box, make sure the box labeled Define This Policy Setting Option is checked. Increase the Password Must Be At Least value to eight characters.

7. Click OK to return to the Group Policy Management Editor window.

EXERCISE 6.4 *(continued)*

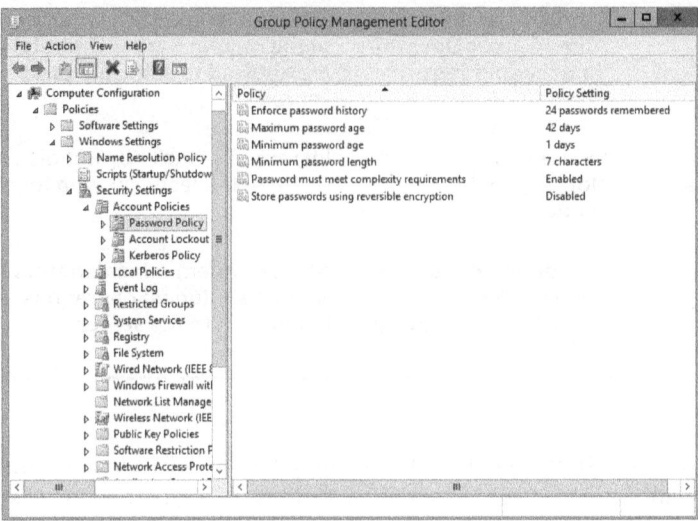

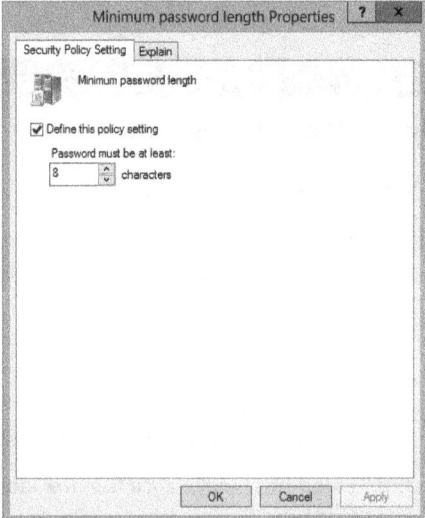

8. Expand User Configuration ➢ Policies ➢ Administrative Templates ➢ Control Panel. Double-click Prohibit Access To The Control Panel And PC settings, select Enabled, and then click OK.

9. Close the Group Policy window.

Fine-Grained Password Policies

The Windows 2012 R2 operating systems allow an organization to have different password and account lockout policies for different sets of users in a domain. In versions of Active Directory before 2008, an administrator could set up only one password policy and account lockout policy per domain.

The Default Domain policy for the domain is where these policy settings were configured. Because domains could have only one password and account lockout policy, organizations that wanted multiple password and account lockout settings had to either create a password filter or deploy multiple domains.

Fine-grained password policies allow you to specify multiple password policies within a single domain. Let's say you want administrators not to have to change their password as frequently as salespeople. Fine-grained password policies allow you to do just that.

Password Settings objects (PSOs) are created so that you can create fine-grained password policies. You create PSOs using the ADSI editor and then you can use those PSOs to create your fine-grained password policies.

Exercise 6.5 walks through the creation of a custom password policy using the ADSI Edit tool, and then you will link that policy to a group using Active Directory Users and Computers. Before completing this exercise, create a new global group named Passgroup in Active Directory Users and Computers.

EXERCISE 6.5

Fine-Grained Password Policy

1. Open ADSI Edit by pressing the Windows key and choosing ADSI Edit.

2. Right-click ADSI Edit and then choose Connect To.

3. When the Connection Settings dialog box appears, click OK.

4. In the window on the left, expand Default Naming Context ➢ DC=yourdomainname,DC=com ➢ CN=System ➢ CN=Password Settings Container.

5. Right-click CN=Password Settings Container and choose New ➢ Object.

6. In the Select A Class box, choose msDS-PasswordSettings and click Next.

7. At the Common Name screen, type **CustomPolicy** and click Next.

8. At the Password Settings Precedence screen, enter **10** as the value. This works as a cost value. The lowest priority takes precedence.

9. At the Password Reversible Encryption Status For Users Accounts screen, set the value to False (recommended by Microsoft).

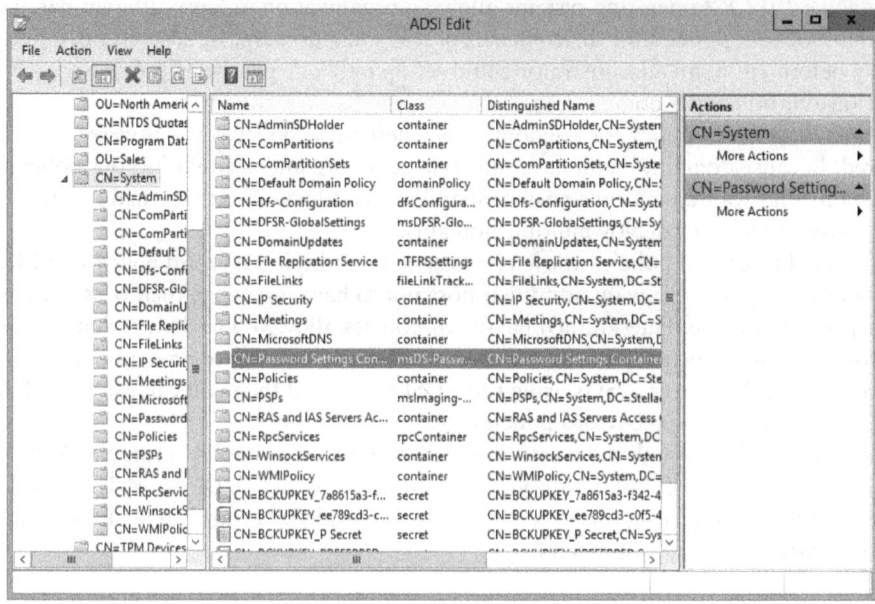

10. The Password History Length screen shows how many passwords are remembered before a password can be used again. You can set this for up to 1,024 remembered passwords. Set the value to **12**. Click Next.

11. At the Password Complexity screen, set the value to True.

12. The next screen will be the Minimum Password Length screen. Set the value to **8** and click Next.

13. At the Minimum Password Age screen, you must enter a value for the amount of time you want the password to be used at a minimum. Time is done in the I8 format, like so:

    −600000000 = 1 minute

    −36000000000 = 1 hour

    −864000000000 = 1 day

    So if you want the minimum to be 10 days, you must calculate −864000000000 × 10 (equaling −8640000000000).

    Enter **−8640000000000** (10 zeros) as your value for 10 days and click Next. You must put the − (minus) sign in the front of the value.

14. At the Maximum Password Age screen, set the value as **–51840000000000** (10 zeros). This value equals 60 days. Click Next.

15. At the Lockout Threshold screen, enter **3** and click Next.

16. At the Observation Window screen, enter **–3000000000** (5 minutes) and click Next.

17. At the Lockout Duration screen, enter **–18000000000** (30 minutes) and click Next.

18. Click Finished. If you received any errors, check all of your times to be sure the – (minus) sign appears in front of the number.

19. Close ADSI Edit.

20. Open the Active Directory Users and Computers snap-in.

21. On the View menu along the top, make sure Advanced Features is checked.

22. In the window on the left, expand Active Directory Users and Computers ➢ *yourdomain* ➢ System ➢ Password Settings Container.

23. In the details pane on the right side, right-click CustomPolicy and choose Properties.

24. Click the Attribute Editor tab.

25. Scroll down and select the msDS-PsoAppliesTo attribute. Click Edit.

26. In the Multi-valued Distinguished Name dialog box, click Add Windows Account.

27. Type in **Passgroup** (this is the group you created before the exercise) and click the Check Name button. Click OK.

28. Click OK twice more, and then you are finished. Close the Active Directory Users and Computers snap-in.

Managing Multiple Domains

You can easily manage most of the operations that must occur *between* domains by using the Active Directory Domains and Trusts administrative tool. On the other hand, if you want to configure settings *within* a domain, you should use the Active Directory MMC tools. In the following sections, you'll look at managing *single-master operations* (FSMO) roles.

Managing Single-Master Operations

For the most part, Active Directory functions in what is known as *multimaster replication*. That is, every domain controller within the environment contains a copy of the Active

Directory database that is both readable and writable. This works well for most types of information. For example, if you want to modify the password of a user, you can easily do this on *any* of the domain controllers within a domain. The change is then automatically propagated to the other domain controllers.

However, some functions are not managed in a multimaster fashion. These operations are known as *operations masters*. You must perform single-master operations on specially designated domain controllers within the Active Directory forest. There are five main single-master functions: two that apply to an entire Active Directory forest and three that apply to each domain.

Forest Operations Masters

You use the Active Directory Domains and Trusts tool to configure forest-wide roles. The following single-master operations apply to the entire forest:

Schema Master   Earlier you learned that all of the domain controllers within a single Active Directory environment share the same schema. This ensures information consistency. However, developers and system administrators can modify the Active Directory schema by adding custom information. A trivial example might involve adding a field to employee information that specifies a user's favorite color.

When you need to make these types of changes, you must perform them on the domain controller that serves as the *Schema Master* for the environment. The Schema Master is then responsible for propagating all of the changes to all the other domain controllers within the forest.

Domain Naming Master   The purpose of the *Domain Naming Master* is to keep track of all the domains within an Active Directory forest. You access this domain controller whenever you need to add/remove new domains to a tree or forest.

Domain Operations Masters

You use the Active Directory Users and Computers snap-in to administer roles within a domain. Within each domain, at least one domain controller must fulfill each of the following roles:

Relative ID (RID) Master   Every security object within Active Directory must be assigned a unique identifier so that it is distinguishable from other objects. For example, if you have two OUs named IT that reside in different domains, you must have some way to distinguish easily between them. Furthermore, if you delete one of the IT OUs and then later re-create it, the system must be able to determine that it is not the same object as the other IT OU. The unique identifier for each object is made up of a domain identifier and a relative identifier (RID). RIDs are always unique within an Active Directory domain and are used for managing security information and authenticating users. The *RID Master* is responsible for creating these values within a domain whenever new Active Directory objects are created.

PDC Emulator Master   Within a domain, the *PDC Emulator Master* is responsible for maintaining backward compatibility with Windows 95, 98, and NT clients. The PDC emulator is also responsible for processing password changes between a domain user account and all of the domain controllers throughout the domain.

The PDC emulator is also the default time server for all of the domain controllers in the domain. This is why it's a good practice to make sure that your PDC emulator has the proper time. It's the system that all others will rely on for time accuracy.

The PDC Emulator Master serves as the default domain controller to process authentication requests if another domain controller is unable to do so. The PDC Emulator Master also receives preferential treatment whenever domain security changes are made. PDC emulators are also the preferred point of contact for many services and applications that run on the domain.

Infrastructure Master   Whenever a user is added to or removed from a group, all of the other domain controllers should be made aware of this change. The role of the domain controller that acts as an *Infrastructure Master* is to ensure that group membership information stays synchronized within an Active Directory domain.

Unless there is only one domain controller, you should not place the Infrastructure Master on a global catalog server. If the Infrastructure Master and global catalog are on the same domain controller, the Infrastructure Master will not function.

Another service that a server can control for the network is the Windows Time service. The Windows Time service uses a suite of algorithms in the Network Time Protocol (NTP). This helps ensure that the time on all computers throughout a network is as accurate as possible. All client computers within a Windows Server 2012 R2 domain are synchronized with the time of an authoritative computer.

Assigning Single-Master Roles

Now that you are familiar with the different types of single-master operations, take a look at Exercise 6.6. This exercise shows you how to assign these roles to servers within the Active Directory environment. In this exercise, you will assign single-master operations roles to various domain controllers within the environment. To complete the steps in this exercise, you need one Active Directory domain controller.

EXERCISE 6.6

Assigning Single-Master Operations

1. Open the Active Directory Domains and Trusts administrative tool.

2. Right-click Active Directory Domains And Trusts and choose Operations Masters.

3. In the Operations Masters dialog box, note that you can change the operations master by clicking the Change button. If you want to move this assignment to another computer, first you need to connect to that computer and then make the change. Click Close to continue without making any changes.

4. Close the Active Directory Domains and Trusts administrative tool.

5. Open the Active Directory Users and Computers administrative tool.

6. Right-click the name of a domain and select Operations Masters. This brings up the RID tab of the Operations Masters dialog box.

    Notice that you can change the computer that is assigned to the role. To change the role, first you need to connect to the appropriate domain controller. Notice that the PDC and Infrastructure roles have similar tabs. Click Close to continue without making any changes.

7. When you have finished, close the Active Directory Users and Computers tool.

Remember that you manage single-master operations with three different tools. You use the Active Directory Domains and Trusts tool to configure the Domain Name Master role, while you use the Active Directory Users and Computers snap-in to administer roles within a domain. Although this might not seem intuitive at first, it can help you remember which roles apply to domains and which apply to the whole forest. The third tool, the Schema Master role, is a bit different than these other two. To change the Schema Master role, you must install the Active Directory Schema MMS snap-in and change it there.

Seizing Roles

Changing roles from one domain controller to another is really simple. An administrator goes into Active Directory or PowerShell and changes an FSMO role from one machine to another. The problem happens when a machine with one of the roles crashes and goes down. You can't just switch the role from a machine that is not working.

So, what is an administrator to do? Well, at that point, what you need to do is seize control of the role. You do this through the use of PowerShell. Let's look at how to seize a role using PowerShell.

You may be familiar with seizing FSMO roles from previous versions of Windows Server. In previous versions, you would use the NTDSUtil.exe command-line utility, but in Windows Server 2012 R2 it needs to be done in PowerShell.

Normally, I would show you how to seize control of an FSMO role using an exercise, but since you probably don't have dozens of Microsoft Windows Server 2012 R2 domain controllers just lying around, I will show you how to seize control through a step-by-step process.

To show you how to set up a step-by-step process, you first have to know what FSMO roles are assigned to what FSMO numbers. The following roles each have a corresponding number:

FSMO role	Number
PDCEmulator	0
RIDMaster	1
InfrastructureMaster	2
SchemaMaster	3
DomainNamingMaster	4

Now that you know the role and the number associated to it, you just need to know the PowerShell commands to seize control of the role. The following is an example of how to use PowerShell commands to seize control of one of the FSMO roles.

I am using the -Identity switch to specify the target domain controller (I am calling my target domain controller DC1) and the -OperationMasterRole to specify which role to transfer. I've also used the -Force command because my current FSMO holder is offline. I will be moving all of the roles to the target domain controller, DC1.

1. On a domain controller, log in as an administrator and start PowerShell with elevated privileges.

2. In PowerShell, type the following command:

   ```
   Move-ADDirectoryServerOperationMasterRole -Identity DC1
   -OperationMasterRole 0,1,2,3,4 -Force
   ```

3. Either type **Y** on each role move prompt or type **A** to accept all prompts.

4. After a few minutes, all of the FSMO roles should be successfully moved.

Finally, I want to show you a couple of useful PowerShell commands so that you can view which domain controller owns which FSMO role.

```
Get-ADForest DomainName | FT SchemaMaster,DomainNamingMaster
Get-ADDomain DomainName | FT PDCEmulator,RIDMaster,InfrastructureMaster
```

Maintain Active Directory

If you have deployed Active Directory in your network environment, your users now depend on it to function properly in order to do their jobs. From network authentications to file access to print and web services, Active Directory has become a mission-critical component of your business. Therefore, the importance of backing up the Active Directory data store should be evident.

As I discussed in earlier chapters, it is important to have multiple domain controllers available to provide backup in case of a problem. The same goes for Active Directory itself—it too should be backed up by being saved. This way, if a massive disaster occurs in which you need to restore your directory services, you will have that option available to you.

Backups are just good common sense, but here are several specific reasons to back up data:

Protect Against Hardware Failures   Computer hardware devices have finite lifetimes, and all hardware eventually fails. We discussed this when we mentioned *Mean Time Between Failures (MTBF)* earlier. MBTF is the average time a device will function before it actually fails. There is also a rating derived from benchmark testing of hard disk devices that tells you when you may be at risk for an unavoidable disaster. Some types of failures, such as corrupted hard disk drives, can result in significant data loss.

Protect Against Accidental Deletion or Modification of Data   Although the threat of hardware failures is very real, in most environments, mistakes in modifying or deleting data are much more common. For example, suppose a systems administrator accidentally deletes all of the objects within a specific OU. Clearly, it's very important to be able to retrieve this information from a backup.

Keep Historical Information   Users and systems administrators sometimes modify files and then later find out that they require access to an older version of the file. Or a file is accidentally deleted, and a user does not discover that fact until much later. By keeping multiple backups over time, you can recover information from prior backups when necessary.

Protect Against Malicious Deletion or Modification of Data   Even in the most secure environments, it is conceivable that unauthorized users (or authorized ones with malicious intent!) could delete or modify information. In such cases, the loss of data might require valid backups from which to restore critical information.

Windows Server 2012 R2 includes a Backup utility that is designed to back up operating system files and the Active Directory data store. It allows for basic backup functionality, such as scheduling backup jobs and selecting which files to back up. Figure 6.8 shows the main screen of the Windows Server 2012 R2 Backup utility.

In the following sections, we'll look at the details of using the Windows Server 2012 R2 Backup utility and how you can restore Active Directory when problems do occur.

FIGURE 6.8   The main screen of the Windows Server 2012 Backup utility

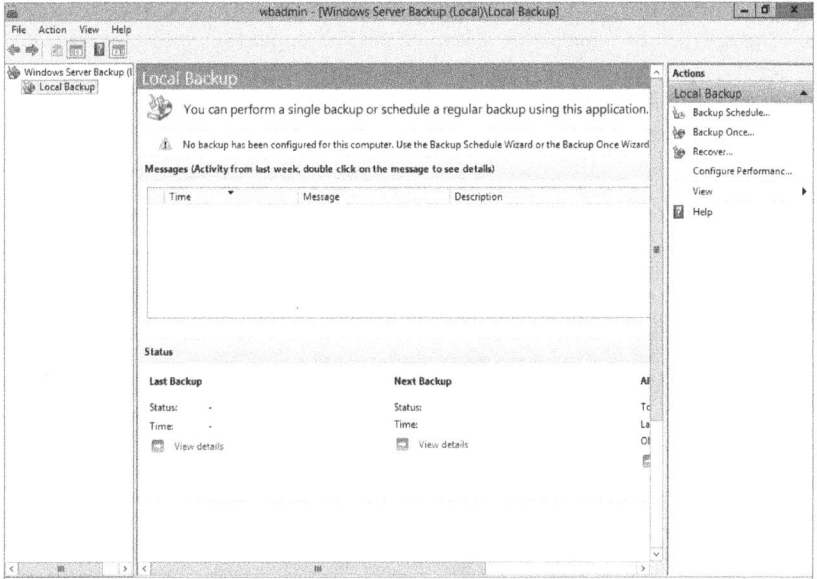

Overview of the Windows Server 2012 R2 Backup Utility

Although the general purpose behind performing backup operations—protecting information—is straightforward, system administrators must consider many options when determining the optimal backup-and-recovery scenario for their environment. Factors include what to back up, how often to back up, and when the backups should be performed.

In this section, you'll see how the Windows Server 2012 R2 Backup utility makes it easy to implement a backup plan for many network environments.

Although the Windows Server 2012 R2 Backup utility provides the basic functionality required to back up your files, you may want to investigate third-party products that provide additional functionality. These applications can provide options for specific types of backups (such as those for Exchange Server and SQL Server) as well as disaster recovery options, networking functionality, centralized management, and support for more advanced hardware.

Backup Types

One of the most important issues you will have to deal with when you are performing backups is keeping track of which files you have backed up and which files you need to back up. Whenever a backup of a file is made, the archive bit for the file is set. You can view the attributes of system files by right-clicking them and selecting Properties. By clicking the Advanced button in the Properties dialog box, you will access the Advanced Attributes dialog box. Here you will see the option Folder Is Ready For Archiving. Figure 6.9 shows an example of the attributes for a folder.

FIGURE 6.9   Viewing the Archive attributes for a folder

Although it is possible to back up all of the files in the file system during each backup operation, it's sometimes more convenient to back up only selected files (such as those that have changed since the last backup operation). When performing backups, you can back up to removable media (DVD) or to a network location.

It is recommended by Microsoft to do a backup to a network location. The reason for this is that if your company suffers from a disaster (fire, hurricane, and so forth), your data can all still be lost—including the backup. If you back up to a removable media source, a copy of the backup can be taken off-site. This protects against a major disaster. Several types of backups can be performed:

Although Windows Server 2012 R2 does not support all of these backup types, it's very important that you understand the most common backup types. Most Administrators use third-party software for their backups. That's why it's important to know all of the different types.

Normal   Normal backups (also referred to as *system* or *full backups*) back up all of the selected files and then mark them as backed up. This option is usually used when a full system backup is made. Windows Server 2012 R2 supports this backup.

Copy   *Copy backups* back up all of the selected files but do not mark them as backed up. This is useful when you want to make additional backups of files for moving files offsite or you want to make multiple copies of the same data for archival purposes.

Incremental   *Incremental backups* copy any selected files that are marked as ready for backup (typically because they have not been backed up or they have been changed since the last backup) and then mark the files as backed up. When the next incremental backup is run, only the files that are not marked as having been backed up are stored. Incremental backups are used in conjunction with normal (full) backups.

The most common backup process is to make a full backup and then make subsequent incremental backups. The benefit to this method is that only files that have changed since the last full or incremental backup will be stored. This can reduce backup times and disk or tape storage space requirements.

When recovering information from this type of backup method, a system administrator must first restore the full backup and then restore each of the incremental backups.

Differential   *Differential backups* are similar in purpose to incremental backups with one important exception: Differential backups copy all of the files that are marked for backup but do not mark the files as backed up. When restoring files in a situation that uses normal and differential backups, you need only restore the normal backup and the latest differential backup.

Daily   *Daily backups* back up all of the files that have changed during a single day. This operation uses the file time/date stamps to determine which files should be backed up and does not mark the files as having been backed up.

Backing Up System State Data

When you are planning to back up and restore Active Directory, be aware that the most important component is known as the *System State data*. System State data includes the components upon which the Windows Server 2012 R2 operating system relies for normal operations. The Windows Server 2012 R2 Backup utility offers you the ability to back up the System State data to another type of media (such as a hard disk or network share). Specifically, it will back up the following components for a Windows Server 2012 R2 domain controller:

Active Directory   The *Active Directory data store* is at the heart of Active Directory. It contains all of the information necessary to create and manage network resources, such as users and computers. In most environments that use Active Directory, users and system administrators rely on the proper functioning of these services in order to do their jobs.

Boot Files   *Boot files* are the files required for booting the Windows Server 2012 R2 operating system and can be used in the case of boot file corruption.

COM+ Class Registration Database   The *COM+ Class Registration database* is a listing of all of the COM+ Class registrations stored on the computer. Applications that run on a Windows Server 2012 R2 computer might require the registration of various share code components. As part of the System State backup process, Windows Server 2012 R2 stores all of the information related to Component Object Model+ (COM+) components so that it can be quickly and easily restored.

Registry   The Windows Server 2012 R2 *Registry* is a central repository of information related to the operating system configuration (such as desktop and network settings), user settings, and application settings. Therefore, the Registry is absolutely vital to the proper functioning of Windows Server 2012 R2.

Sysvol **Directory**   The *Sysvol directory* includes data and files that are shared between the domain controllers within an Active Directory domain. Many operating system services rely on this information in order to function properly.

Bare Metal Backups and Restores

One of the options you have in Windows Server 2012 R2 is to do a *Bare Metal Restore (BMR)*. This is a restore of a machine after the machine has been completely wiped out and formatted. This type of restore is done usually after a catastrophic machine failure or crash.

Windows Server 2012 R2 gives you the ability to backup all of the files needed for a Bare Metal Restore by choosing the Bare Metal Recovery checkbox (see Figure 6.10).

FIGURE 6.10   Bare Metal Option

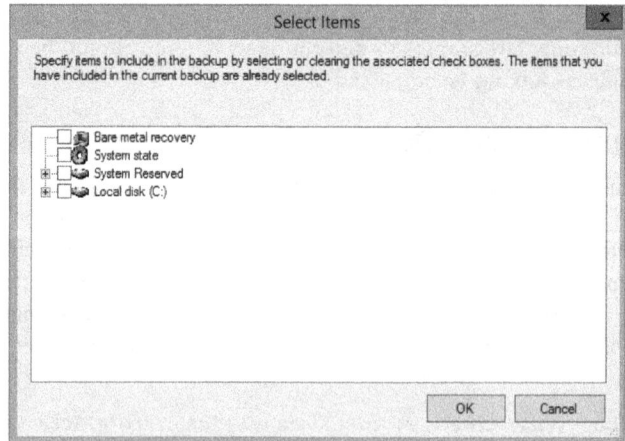

When you choose the Bare Metal Restore option in Windows Server 2012 R2, all of the sub-options (System State, System Reserved, and Local disk) automatically get checked.

When preparing your network for a Bare Metal Backup, you want to make sure that you have everything you need on hand to complete this type of restore. You may want to keep a copy of the server software, server drivers, and so forth on hand and ready to go, just in case you have to do a full restore.

Scheduling Backups

In addition to specifying which files to back up, you can schedule backup jobs to occur at specific times. Planning *when* to perform backups is just as important as deciding *what* to back up. Performing backup operations can reduce overall system performance; therefore, you should plan to back up information during times of minimal activity on your servers.

To add a backup operation to the schedule, you can simply click the Add button on the Specify Backup Time window.

Restoring System State Data

In some cases, the Active Directory data store or other System State data may become corrupt or unavailable. This could be due to many different reasons. A hard disk failure might, for example, result in the loss of data. Or the accidental deletion of an OU and all of its objects might require a restore operation to be performed.

The actual steps involved in restoring System State data are based on the details of what has caused the data loss and what effect this data loss has had on the system. In the best-case scenario, the System State data is corrupt or inaccurate but the operating system can still boot. If this is the case, all you must do is boot into a special *Directory Services Restore Mode (DSRM)* and then restore the System State data from a backup. This process will replace the current System State data with that from the backup. Therefore, any changes that have been made since the last backup will be completely lost and must be redone.

In a worst-case scenario, all of the information on a server has been lost or a hardware failure is preventing the machine from properly booting. If this is the case, here are several steps that you must take in order to recover System State data:

1. Fix any hardware problem that might prevent the computer from booting (for example, replace any failed hard disks).

2. Reinstall the Windows Server 2012 R2 operating system. This should be performed like a regular installation on a new system.

3. Reinstall any device drivers that may be required by your backup device. If you backed up information to the file system, this will not apply.

4. Restore the System State data using the Windows Server 2012 Backup utility.

I'll cover the technical details of performing restores later in this section. For now, however, you should understand the importance of backing up information and, whenever possible, testing the validity of backups.

Backing Up and Restoring Group Policy Objects

Group Policy Objects (GPOs) are a major part of Active Directory. When you back up Active Directory, GPOs can also get backed up. You also have the ability to back up GPOs through the Group Policy Management Console (GPMC). This gives you the ability to back up and restore individual GPOs.

To back up all GPOs, open the GPMC and right-click the Group Policy Objects container. You will see the option Back Up All. After you choose this option, a wizard will start asking you for the backup location. Choose a location and click Backup.

To back up an individual GPO, right-click the GPO (in the Group Policy Objects container) and choose Backup. Again, after you choose this option, a wizard will start asking you for the backup location. Choose a location and click Backup.

To restore a GPO, it's the same process as above except, instead of choosing Backup, you will either choose Manage Backups (to restore all GPOs) or Restore (for an individual GPO).

Setting Up an Active Directory Backup

The Windows Server 2012 R2 Backup utility makes it easy to back up the System data (including Active Directory) as part of a normal backup operation. We've already covered the ideas behind the different backup types and why and when they are used.

Exercise 6.7 walks you through the process of backing up the domain controller. In order to complete this exercise, the local machine must be a domain controller, and you must have a DVD burner or network location to back up the System State.

 The Windows Server 2012 R2 Backup utility is not installed by default. If you have already installed the Windows Server 2012 R2 Backup utility, skip to step 9.

EXERCISE 6.7

Backing Up Active Directory

1. To install the Windows Server 2012 R2 Backup utility, click the Start Key ➤ Administrative Tools ➤ Server Manager.

2. In the center console, click the link for Add Roles And Features.

3. At the Select Installation Type screen, choose role-based or feature-based installation and click Next.

4. The Select Destination Server screen appears. Choose Select A Server From The Server Pool, and choose your server under Server Pool. Click Next.

5. Click Next at the Select Server Roles screen.

6. At the Select Features screen, scroll down and check the box next to Windows Server Backup. Click Next.

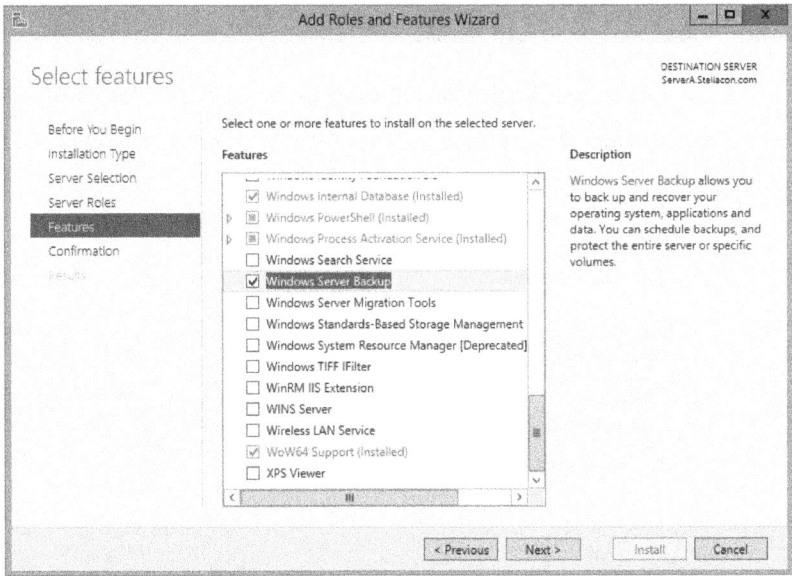

7. At the Confirmation screen, click the checkbox to Restart the destination server auto-
    matically. This will bring up a dialog box. Click Yes, and then click the Install button.

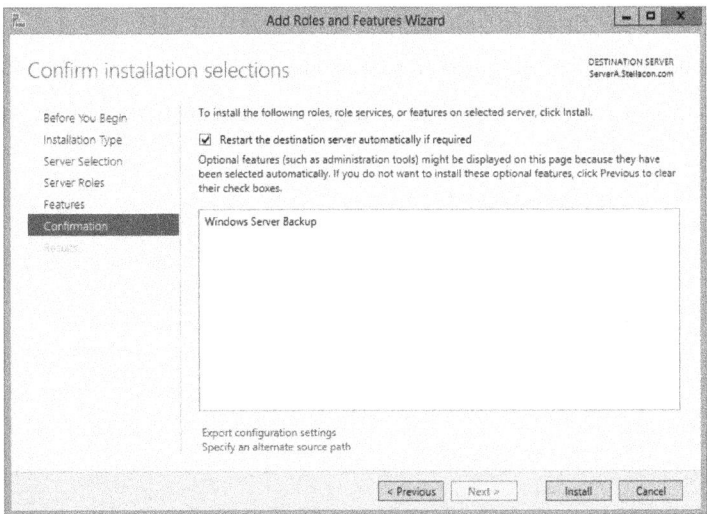

8. Click the Close button when finished. Close Server Manager.

9. Open Windows Backup by clicking the Windows Key ➢ Administrative Tools ➢
    Windows Server Backup.

EXERCISE 6.7 *(continued)*

10. On the left-hand side, click Local Backup. Then, under Actions, click Backup Once.

11. When the Backup Once Wizard appears, click Different Options and click Next.

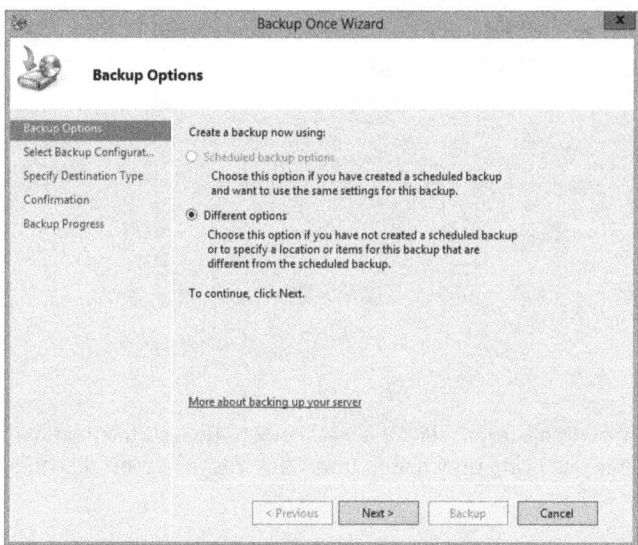

12. At the Select Backup Configuration screen, choose Custom and click Next.

13. Click the Add Items button. Choose System State and click OK. Click Next.

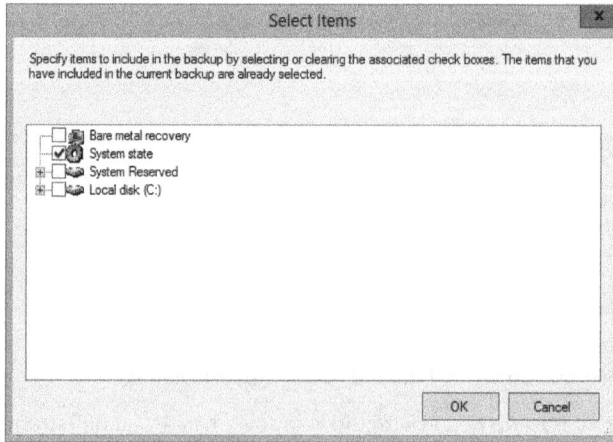

14. At the Specify Destination Type, choose Remote Shared Folder. Click Next.

15. Put in the shared path you want to use and click Next.

16. At the Confirmation screen, click the Backup button.

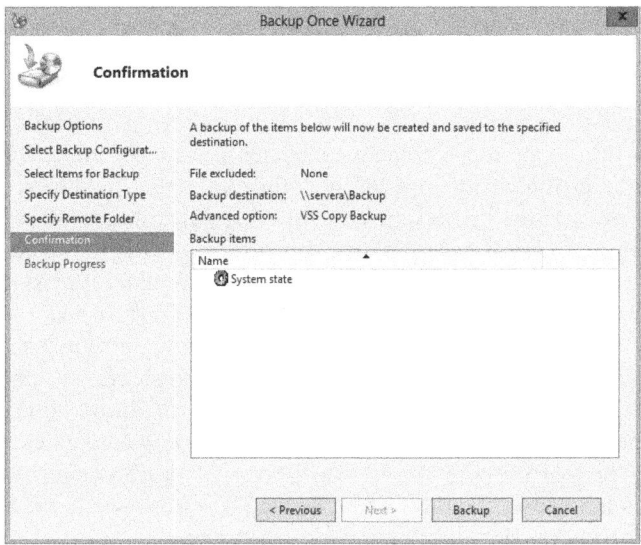

17. Once the backup is complete, close the Windows Server Backup utility.

Restoring Active Directory

Active Directory has been designed with fault tolerance in mind. For example, it is highly recommended by Microsoft that each domain have at least two domain controllers. Each of these domain controllers contains a copy of the Active Directory data store. Should one of the domain controllers fail, the available one can take over the failed server's functionality. When the failed server is repaired, it can then be promoted to a domain controller in the existing environment. This process effectively restores the failed domain controller without incurring any downtime for end users because all of the Active Directory data is replicated to the repaired server in the next scheduled replication.

In some cases, you might need to restore Active Directory from a backup. For example, suppose a system administrator accidentally deletes several hundred users from the domain and does not realize it until the change has been propagated to all of the other domain controllers. Manually re-creating the accounts is not an option because the objects' security identifiers will be different (and all permissions must be reset). Clearly, a method for restoring from backup is the best solution. You can elect to make the Active Directory restore authoritative or nonauthoritative, as described in the following sections.

Overview of Authoritative Restore

Restoring Active Directory and other System State data is an important process should system files or the Active Directory data store become corrupt or otherwise unavailable. Fortunately, the Windows Server 2012 R2 Backup utility allows you to restore data easily from a backup, should the need arise.

I mentioned earlier that in the case of the accidental deletion of information from Active Directory, you might need to restore the Active Directory from a recent backup. But what happens if there is more than one domain controller in the environment? Even if you did perform a restore, the information on this domain controller would be seen as outdated and it would be overwritten by the data from another domain controller. This data from the older domain controller is exactly the information you want to replace. The domain controller that was reloaded using a backup would have an older time stamp, and the other domain controllers would re-delete the information from the backup.

Fortunately, Windows Server 2012 R2 and Active Directory allow you to perform what is called an *authoritative restore*. The authoritative restore process specifies a domain controller as having the authoritative (or master) copy of the Active Directory data store. When other domain controllers communicate with this domain controller, their information will be overwritten with Active Directory data stored on the local machine.

Now that you have an idea of how an authoritative restore is supposed to work, let's move on to looking at the details of performing the process.

Performing an Authoritative Restore

When you are restoring Active Directory information on a Windows Server 2012 R2 domain controller, make sure that Active Directory services are not running. This is because the restore of System State data requires full access to system files and the Active Directory data store. If you attempt to restore System State data while the domain controller is active, you will see an error message.

In general, restoring data and operating system files is a straightforward process. It is important to note that restoring a System State backup will replace the existing Registry, Sysvol, and Active Directory files, so that any changes you made since the last backup will be lost.

In addition to restoring the entire Active Directory database, you can also restore only specific subtrees within Active Directory using the restoresubtree command in the ntdsutil utility. This allows you to restore specific information, and it is useful in case of accidental deletion of isolated material.

Following the authoritative restore process, Active Directory should be updated to the time of the last backup. Furthermore, all of the other domain controllers for this domain will have their Active Directory information overwritten by the results of the restore operation. The result is an Active Directory environment that has been recovered from media.

Overview of Nonauthoritative Restore

Now that you understand why you would use an authoritative restore and how it is performed, it's an easy conceptual jump to understand a *nonauthoritative restore*. Remember that by making a restore authoritative, you are simply telling other domain controllers in the domain to recognize the restored machine as the newest copy of Active Directory for replication purposes. If you only have one domain controller, the authoritative restore process becomes moot; you can simply skip the steps required to make the restore authoritative and begin using the domain controller immediately after the normal restore is complete.

If you have more than one domain controller in the domain and you need to perform a nonauthoritative restore, simply allow the domain controller to receive Active Directory database information from other domain controllers in the domain using normal replication methods.

Active Directory Recycle Bin

The Active Directory Recycle Bin is a great feature that allows an administrator to restore an active directory object that has been deleted.

Let's say that you have a junior administrator who has been making changes to Active Directory for hours. The junior admin then deletes an OU from Active Directory. You would then have to reload the OU from a tape backup, or even worse, you may have to reload the entire Active Directory (depending on your backup software), thus losing the hours of work the junior admin has completed.

The problem here is that when you delete a security object from Active Directory, the object's Security ID (SID) gets removed. All users' rights and permissions are associated with the users' SID number and not their account name. This is where the AD Recycle Bin can help.

The *Active Directory Recycle Bin* allows you to preserve and restore accidentally deleted Active Directory objects without the need of using a backup.

The Active Directory Recycle Bin works for both the Active Directory Domain Services (AD DS) and the Active Directory Lightweight Directory Services (AD LDS) environments.

By enabling (disabled by default) the Active Directory Recycle Bin, any deleted Active Directory objects are preserved and Active Directory objects can be restored, in their entirety, to the same condition that they were in immediately before deletion. This means that all group memberships and access rights that the object had before deletion will remain intact.

To enable the Active Directory Recycle Bin, you must do the following (you must be a member of the Schema Admins group):

- Run the `adprep /forestprep` command to prepare the forest on the server that holds the schema master to update the schema.

- Run the `adprep /domainprep /gpprep` command to prepare the domain on the server that holds the infrastructure operations master role.

- If a read-only domain controller (RODC) is present in your environment, you must also run the adprep /rodcprep command.

- Make sure that all domain controllers in your Active Directory forest are running Windows Server 2012 R2, Windows Server 2012, or Windows Server 2008 R2.

- Make sure that the forest functional level is set to Windows Server 2012 R2, Windows Server 2012, or Windows Server 2008 R2.

Restartable Active Directory

Administrators have the ability to stop and restart Active Directory in the Windows Server 2012 operating system without the need to reboot the entire system. Administrators can perform these actions either by using the Microsoft Management Console (MMC) snap-ins or the command line.

With *Restartable Active Directory Services*, an administrator has the ability to stop Active Directory Services so that updates and other tasks can be applied to a domain controller. One task that an administrator can perform while Active Directory is stopped is an offline defragmentation of the database.

One of the advantages of a Restartable Active Directory is that other services running on the same server do not depend on Active Directory to continue to function properly while Active Directory is stopped. An administrator has the ability to stop and restart the Active Directory Domain Services in the Local Services MMC snap-in.

Offline Maintenance

As you learned in the preceding section, there are times when you have to be offline to do maintenance. For example, you need to perform authoritative and nonauthoritative restores while the domain controller is offline. The main utility we use for offline maintenance is ntdsutil.

Ntdsutil.exe

The primary method by which system administrators can do offline maintenance is through the ntdsutil command-line tool. You can launch this tool by simply entering **ntdsutil** at a command prompt. For the commands to work properly, you must start the command prompt with elevated privileges. The ntdsutil command is both interactive and context sensitive. That is, once you launch the utility, you'll see an ntdsutil command prompt. At this prompt, you can enter various commands that set your context within the application. For example, if you enter **domain management**, you'll be able to enter domain-related commands. Several operations also require you to connect to a domain, a domain controller, or an Active Directory object before you perform a command.

Table 6.3 provides a list of some of the domain-management commands supported by the ntdsutil tool. You can access this functionality by typing the command at an elevated command prompt. Once you are in the ntdsutil prompt, you can use the question mark to see all of the commands available.

TABLE 6.3 Ntdsutil offline maintenance commands

Ntdsutil **Domain Management Command**	Purpose
Help or ?	Displays information about the commands that are available within the Domain Management menu of the ntdsutil utility.
Activate instance %s	Sets NTDS or a specific AD LDS instance as the active instance.
Authoritative restore	Sets the domain controller for the Authoritative restore of the Active Directory database.
Change service account	This allows an administrator to change the AD LDS service account to user name and password. You can use a "NULL" for a blank password, and you can use * to prompt the user to enter a password.
configurable settings	Allows an administrator to manage configurable settings.
DS behavior	Allows an administrator to view and modify AD DS or AD LDS behavior.
files	This command allows an administrator to manage the AD DS or AD LDS database files.
Group Membership Evaluation	Allows an administrator to evaluate the security IDs (SIDs) in a token for a given user or group.
LDAP policies	Administrators can manage the Lightweight Directory Access Protocol (LDAP) protocol policies.
metadata cleanup	Removes metadata from decommissioned domain controllers.
security account management	This command allows an administrator to manage SIDs.
Set DSRM Password	Resets the Directory Service Restore mode administrator account password.

Active Directory Database Mounting Tool

One issue that an administrator may run into when trying to restore Active Directory is the need to restore several backups to compare the Active Directory data that each backup contains. Windows Server 2012 R2 has a utility called the Active Directory database mounting tool (Dsamain.exe), which can resolve this issue.

The Dsamain.exe tool can help the recovery processes by giving you a way to compare data as it exists in snapshots (taken at different times) so that you have the ability to decide which Active Directory database to restore.

Creating snapshots on a regular basis will allow you to have enough data so that you can keep accurate records of how the Active Directory database changes over time. The ntdsutil utility allows you to take snapshots by using the ntdsutil snapshot operation.

> You are not required to run the ntdsutil snapshot operation to use Dsamain.exe. You have the ability to use a backup of the Active Directory database.

You must be a member of the Domain Admins group or the Enterprise Admins group to view any snapshots taken due to the fact that these snapshots contain sensitive Active Directory data.

Compact the Directory Database File (Offline Defragmentation)

One task that all of us having been doing for years is the process of defragging the operating systems that we run. We have used the defragmentation utility since Windows NT. Defragging a system helps return free space from data to the hard drive.

You can also use the defragmentation process to compact the Active Directory database while it's offline. Offline defragmentation helps return free disk space and check Active Directory database integrity.

To perform an offline defragmentation, you would use the ntdsutil command. When you perform a defragmentation of the Active Directory database, a new compacted version of the database is created. This new database file can be created on the same machine (if space permits) or on a network location. After the new file is created, copy the compacted Ntds.dit file back to the original location.

It is a good practice, if space allows, to maintain a copy of the older, original database file. You can either rename the older database file and keep it in its current location or copy the older database file to an alternate location.

Monitoring Replication

At times you may need to keep an eye on how your replication traffic is working on your domain controllers. We are going to examine the replication utility that you can use to help determine if there are problems on your domain.

Repadmin Utility

The Repadmin utility is included when you install Windows Server 2012 R2. This command-line tool helps administrators diagnose replication problems between Windows domain controllers.

Repadmin allows administrators to view the replication topology of each domain controller as seen from the domain controller's perspective. Administrators can also use Repadmin to create the replication topology manually. By manually creating the replication topology, administrators can force replication events between domain controllers and view the replication metadata vectors.

To access the Repadmin utility, open a command prompt using an elevated privilege (Run ➢ CMD). At the command prompt, type **Repadmin.exe**, and all of the available options will appear.

Using the ADSI Editor

Another utility (explained earlier in the chapter) that allows you to manage objects and attributes in Active Directory is the Active Directory Service Interfaces Editor (ADSI Edit). Earlier we used ADSI Edit (Adsiedit.msc) to create multiple password policies to allow for fine-grained password policies. ADSI Edit allows you to view every object and attribute in an Active Directory forest.

One advantage to using the Adsiedit.msc MMC snap-in is that this tool allows you to query, view, create, and edit attributes that are not exposed through other Active Directory Microsoft Management Console (MMC) snap-ins.

ADSI Edit allows you to administer an AD LDS instance. To do this, you must first connect and bind to the instance. After you connect and bind to the instance, you can administer the containers and objects within the instance by browsing to the containers or objects and then right-clicking them. To complete this task, you must be a member of the Administrators group for the AD LDS instance.

Wbadmin Command Line Utility

The wbadmin command allows you to back up and restore your operating system, volumes, files, folders, and applications from a command prompt.

You must be a member of the Administrators group to configure a backup schedule. You must be a member of the Backup Operators or the Administrators group (or you must have been delegated the appropriate permissions) to perform all other tasks using the wbadmin command.

To use the wbadmin command, you must run wbadmin from an elevated command prompt (to open an elevated command prompt, click Start, right-click Command Prompt, and then click Run As Administrator). Table 6.4 shows some of the wbadmin commands.

TABLE 6.4 Wbadmin commands

Command	Description
Wbadmin enable backup	Configures and enables a daily backup schedule.
Wbadmin disable backup	Disables your daily backups.
Wbadmin start backup	Runs a one-time backup.
Wbadmin stop job	Stops the currently running backup or recovery operation.
Wbadmin get items	Lists the items included in a specific backup.
Wbadmin start recovery	Runs a recovery of the volumes, applications, files, or folders specified.
Wbadmin get status	Shows the status of the currently running backup or recovery operation.
Wbadmin start systemstaterecovery	Runs a system state recovery.
Wbadmin start systemstatebackup	Runs a system state backup.
Wbadmin start sysrecovery	Runs a recovery of the full system state.

Summary

In this chapter, I talked about important items that pertain to security, such as which default groups are available after a base install of the operating system and how to secure the most vulnerable accounts.

I then covered how passwords and tokens work within Windows Server 2012 R2 and also how to create a separate password policy using the ADSI Edit utility. I discussed the different Operation Master roles (FSMO) and how to change or seize the role to another domain controller.

Finally, in this chapter, you also learned about how important it is to back up and restore a Windows Server 2012 R2 domain controller machine in the event of a hardware or software failure. I also explained how some of the features such as the Active Directory Recycle Bin and ntdsutil are part of Windows Server 2012 R2 domain controller and how these utilities make an administrator's life easier.

Exam Essentials

Understand the various backup types available with the Windows Server 2012 Backup utility.   The Windows Server 2012 R2 Backup utility can perform full and incremental backup operations. Some third-party backup utilities also support differential and daily backups. You can use each of these operations as part of an efficient backup strategy.

Know how to back up Active Directory.   The data within the Active Directory database on a domain controller is part of the system state data. You can back up the system state data to a file using the Windows Server 2012 R2 Backup utility.

Know how to restore Active Directory.   Restoring the Active Directory database is considerably different from other restore operations. To restore some or the entire Active Directory database, you must first boot the machine into Directory Services Restore mode.

Understand the importance of an authoritative restore process.   You use an authoritative restore when you want to restore earlier information from an Active Directory backup, and you want the older information to be propagated to other domain controllers in the environment.

Understand offline maintenance using ntdsutil.   The ntdsutil command-line tool is a primary method by which system administrators perform offline maintenance. Understand how to launch this tool by entering **ntdsutil** at a command prompt.

Review Questions

1. You are the administrator of a large company, and you need to ensure that you can recover your Windows Server 2012 R2 Active Directory configuration and data if the computer's hard disk fails. What should you do?

   A. Create a complete PC Backup and Restore image.

   B. Create a backup of all file categories.

   C. Perform an automated system recovery (ASR) backup.

   D. Create a system restore point.

2. You need to back up the existing data on a computer before you install a new application. You also need to ensure that you are able to recover individual user files that are replaced or deleted during the installation. What should you do?

   A. Create a system restore point.

   B. Perform an automated system recovery (ASR) backup and restore.

   C. In the Windows Server Backup utility, click the Backup Once link.

   D. In the Backup And Restore Center window, click the Back Up Computer button.

3. You are the administrator of a large organization. While setting up your Windows Server 2012 R2 domain controller, you are creating a data recovery strategy that must meet the following requirements:

   - Back up all data files and folders in C:\Data.

   - Restore individual files and folders in C:\Data.

   - Ensure that data is backed up to and restored from external media.

   What should you do?

   A. Use the Previous Versions feature to restore the files and folders.

   B. Use the System Restore feature to perform backup and restore operations.

   C. Use the NTBackup utility to back up and restore individual files and folders.

   D. Use the Windows Server Backup to back up and restore files.

4. You are a network administrator, and you want to create multiple password policies for the users in your domain. What utility do you use to complete this task?

   A. MMC

   B. Schema Editor

   C. ADSI Edit

   D. Secedit.exe

5. You are the system administrator for a large organization with multiple Active Directory domain controllers. Currently, the environment supports many different domain controllers, some of which are running Windows 2008 and Windows Server 2012 R2. When you are running domain controllers in this type of environment, which of the following types of groups can you *not* use? (Choose all that apply.)

   A. Universal security groups

   B. Global groups

   C. Domain local groups

   D. None—you can use all group types

6. You are the network administrator for your organization. A new company policy has been released wherein if a user enters their password incorrectly three times within 5 minutes, they are locked out for 30 minutes. What three actions do you need to set to comply with this policy? (Choose all that apply.)

   A. Set Account Lockout Duration to 5 minutes.

   B. Set Account Lockout Duration to 30 minutes.

   C. Set the Account Lockout Threshold setting to 3 invalid logon attempts.

   D. Set the Account Lockout Threshold setting to 30 minutes.

   E. Set the Reset Account Lockout Counter setting to 5 minutes.

   F. Set the Reset Account Lockout Counter setting to 3 times.

7. You are teaching a Microsoft Active Directory class, and one of your students asks you which of the following folders in the Active Directory Users and Computers tool is used when users from outside the forest are granted access to resources within a domain? What answer would you give your student?

   A. Users

   B. Computers

   C. Domain Controllers

   D. Foreign Security Principals

8. Your manager has decided that your organization needs to use an Active Directory application data partition. Which command can you use to create and manage application data partitions?

   A. DCPromo.exe

   B. NTDSUtil.exe

   C. ADUtil.exe

   D. ADSI.exe

9. Robert is a system administrator who is responsible for performing backups on several servers. Recently, he has been asked to take over the operations of several new servers, including backup operations. He has the following requirements:

    ▪ The backup must finish as quickly as possible.

    ▪ The backup must use the absolute minimum amount of storage space.

    ▪ He must perform backup operations at least daily with a full backup at least weekly.

    Robert decides to use the Windows Server 2012 R2 Windows Server Backup utility to perform the backups. He wants to choose a set of backup types that will meet all of these requirements. He decides to back up all files on each of these servers every week. Then he decides to store only the files that have changed since the last backup operation (regardless of type) during the weekdays. Which of the following types of backup operations should he use to implement this solution? (Choose two.)

    A. Normal

    B. Daily

    C. Copy

    D. Differential

    E. Incremental

10. You are removing a domain controller from your network. This domain controller holds the forestwide operations master roles. Which roles would you need to transfer to another machine before you remove the domain controller? (Choose all that apply.)

    A. PDC Emulator Master

    B. Schema Master

    C. RID Master

    D. Domain Naming Master

    E. Infrastructure Master

Chapter

7

Configure and Manage Group Policy

THE FOLLOWING 70-411 EXAM OBJECTIVES ARE COVERED IN THIS CHAPTER:

✓ **Configure Group Policy processing**

- Configure processing order and precedence
- Configure blocking of inheritance
- Configure enforced policies
- Configure security filtering and wmi filtering
- Configure loopback processing
- Configure and manage slow-link processing and group policy caching
- Configure client-side extension (CSE) behavior
- Force group policy update

✓ **Configure Group Policy settings**

- Configure settings including software installation, folder redirection, scripts, and administrative template settings
- Import security templates
- Import custom administrative template file
- Convert administrative templates using admx migrator
- Configure property filters for administrative templates

✓ **Manage Group Policy objects (GPOs)**

- Back up, import, copy, and restore GPOs
- Create and configure Migration Table
- Reset default GPOs
- Delegate Group Policy management

✓ **Configure Group Policy Preferences (GPP)**

- Configure GPP settings including printers, network drive mappings, power options, custom registry settings, Control Panel settings, Internet Explorer settings, file and folder deployment, and shortcut deployment

- Configure item-level targeting

One of the most important system administration features in Windows Server 2012 R2 and Active Directory is administering *Group Policy objects (GPOs)*. By using GPOs, administrators can quickly and easily define restrictions on common actions and then apply them at the site, domain, or organizational unit (OU) level. In this chapter, you will see how group policies work, and then you will look at how to implement them within an Active Directory environment.

This chapter will show Windows Server 2012 R2 administrators how to build, link, and deploy GPOs. GPOs are a great way to set policies throughout your entire forest. GPOs are one of the tools that many administrators never use, but once you start using them, you won't be able to stop. Not only can GPOs help you set policies for your users and computers, you can also install software and updates using GPOs.

If you have already taken and passed exam 70-410, then this chapter will be a good refresher with some added material and tips; this material will be on the 70-411 exam, so it will be best to take the extra time and go through the content again.

Introducing Group Policy Objects

Just like everything else, there are always pros and cons to whatever you are working on. Microsoft Windows-based operating systems have an advantage because of their flexibility and manageability. Administrators have the ability to lock down the Microsoft operating systems by placing some rules or policies onto the domain.

Administrators can configure many different options to suit the network environment and help follow corporate policies. However, having the flexibility to configure the network and the Windows operating system comes at a price—generally, end users on a network have the ability to configure many options that they should not be changing. For example, TCP/IP configuration and security policies should remain consistent for all client computers. In fact, end users really don't need to be able to change these types of settings in the first place because many end users do not understand the purpose of these settings.

Windows Server 2012 R2 *group policies* are designed to provide system administrators with the ability to customize end-user settings and to place restrictions on the types of actions those users can perform. Group policies can be easily created by system administrators and then later applied to one or more users or computers within the environment. Although they ultimately do affect registry settings, it is much easier to configure and apply settings through the use of Group Policy than it is to make changes to the registry manually. To make management easy, Microsoft has given administrators the ability to change all Group Policy settings from within one Microsoft Management Console (MMC) snap-in called the Group Policy Management Console (GPMC).

Group policies have several potential uses. I'll cover the use of group policies for software deployment, and I'll also focus on the technical background of group policies and how they apply to general configuration management.

Let's begin by looking at how group policies function.

Understanding Group Policy Settings

Group Policy settings are based on *Group Policy administrative templates*. These templates provide a list of user-friendly configuration options and specify the system settings to which they apply. For example, an option for a user or computer that reads Require A Specific Desktop Wallpaper Setting would map to a key in the registry that maintains this value. When the option is set, the appropriate change is made in the registry of the affected users and computers.

By default, Windows Server 2012 R2 comes with several administrative template files that you can use to manage common settings. Additionally, system administrators and applications developers can create their own administrative template files to set options for specific functionality.

Most Group Policy items have three different settings options:

Enabled Specifies that a setting for this GPO has been configured. Some settings require values or options to be set.

Disabled Specifies that this option is disabled for client computers. Note that disabling an option *is* a setting. That is, it specifies that the system administrator wants to disallow certain functionality.

Not Configured Specifies that these settings have been neither enabled nor disabled. Not Configured is the default option for most settings. It simply states that this group policy will not specify an option and that other policy settings may take precedence.

The specific options available (and their effects) will depend on the setting. Often, you will need additional information. For example, when setting the Account Lockout policy, you must specify how many bad login attempts may be made before the account is locked out. With this in mind, let's look at the types of user and computer settings that can be managed.

Group Policy settings can apply to two types of Active Directory objects: User objects and Computer objects. Because both users and computers can be placed into groups and organized within OUs, this type of configuration simplifies the management of hundreds, or even thousands, of computers.

The main options you can configure within user and computer group policies are as follows:

Software Settings *Software Settings* options apply to specific applications and software that might be installed on the computer. System administrators can use these settings to make new applications available to end users and to control the default configuration for these applications.

Windows Settings   *Windows Settings* options allow system administrators to customize the behavior of the Windows operating system. The specific options that are available here are divided into two types: user and computer. User-specific settings let you configure Internet Explorer (including the default home page and other settings). Computer settings include security options, such as Account Policy and Event Log options.

Administrative Templates   *Administrative Templates* options are used to configure user and computer settings further. In addition to the default options available, system administrators can create their own administrative templates with custom options.

Group Policy Preferences   The Windows Server 2012 R2 operating system includes *Group Policy Preferences (GPPs)* options, which give you more than 20 new Group Policy extensions. These extensions, in turn, give you a vast range of configurable settings within a Group Policy object. Included in the new Group Policy preference extensions are settings for folder options, mapped drives, printers, the registry, local users and groups, scheduled tasks, services, and the Start menu.

Besides providing easier management, Group Policy preferences give an administrator the ability to deploy settings for client computers without restricting the users from changing the settings. This gives an administrator the flexibility needed to decide which settings to enforce and which not to enforce.

Figure 7.1 shows some of the options that you can configure with Group Policy.

FIGURE 7.1   Group Policy configuration options

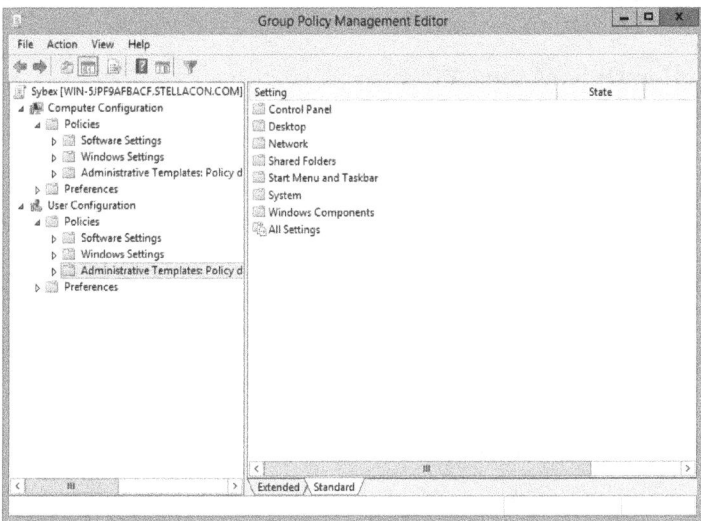

ADMX Central Store Another consideration in GPO settings is whether to set up an *ADMX Central Store*. GPO administrative template files are saved as ADMX (.admx) files and AMXL (.amxl) for the supported languages. To get the most benefit out of using administrative templates, you should create an ADMX Central Store.

You create the Central Store in the SYSVOL folder on a domain controller. The Central Store is a repository for all of your administrative templates, and the Group Policy tools checks it. The Group Policy tools then use any ADMX files that they find in the Central Store. These files then replicate to all domain controllers in the domain.

If you want your clients to be able to edit domain-based GPOs by using the ADMX files that are stored in the ADMX Central Store, you must be using Windows Vista, Windows 7, Windows 8, Server 2008, Server 2008 R2, Server 2012, or Server 2012 R2.

Security Template *Security templates* are used to configure security settings through a GPO. Some of the security settings that can be configured are settings for account policies, local policies, event logs, restricted groups, system services, and the registry.

Starter GPOs *Starter Group Policy objects* give administrators the ability to store a collection of Administrative Template policy settings in a single object. Administrators then have the ability to import and export Starter GPOs to distribute the GPOs easily to other environments. When a GPO is created from a Starter GPO, as with any template, the new GPO receives the settings and values that were defined from the Administrative Template policy in the Starter GPO.

The Security Settings Section of the GPO

One of the most important sections of a GPO is the Security Settings section. The Security Settings section, under the Windows Settings section, allows an administrator to secure many aspects of the computer and user policies. The following are some of the configurable options for the Security Settings section:

Computer Section Only of the GPO

- Account Policies
- Local Policies
- Event Policies
- Restricted Groups
- System Services
- Registry
- File System
- Wired Network
- Windows Firewall with Advanced Security
- Network List Manager Policies

- Wireless Networks
- Network Access Protection
- Application Control Policies
- IP Security Policies
- Advanced Audit Policy Configuration

Computer and User Sections of the GPO

- Public Key Policies
- Software Restriction Policy

Restricted Groups   *Restricted Groups* allows you to control group membership by using a GPO. The group membership to which I am referring is the normal Active Directory groups (domain local, global, and universal). Restricted Groups offers two configurable properties: Members and Members Of.

The users on the Members list do not belong to the restricted group. The users on the Members Of list do belong to the restricted group. When you configure a Restricted Group policy, members of the restricted group that are not on the Members list are removed. Users who are on the Members list who are not currently a member of the restricted group are added.

Software Restriction Policy   *Software restriction policies* allow administrators to identify software and to control its ability to run on the user's local computer, organizational unit, domain, or site. This prevents users from installing unauthorized software. Software Restriction Policy is discussed in greater detail in this chapter in the "Implementing Software Deployment" section.

Group Policy Objects

So far, I have discussed what group policies are designed to do. Now it's time to drill down to determine exactly how you can set up and configure them.

To make them easier to manage, group policies may be placed in items called *Group Policy Objects (GPOs)*. GPOs act as containers for the settings made within Group Policy files, which simplifies the management of settings. For example, as a system administrator, you might have different policies for users and computers in different departments. Based on these requirements, you could create a GPO for members of the Sales department and another for members of the Engineering department. Then you could apply the GPOs to the OU for each department. Another important concept you need to understand is that Group Policy settings are hierarchical; that is, system administrators can apply Group Policy settings at four different levels. These levels determine the GPO processing priority:

Local   Every Windows operating system computer has one Group Policy object that is stored locally. This GPO functions for both the computer and user Group Policy processing.

Sites   At the highest level, system administrators can configure GPOs to apply to entire sites within an Active Directory environment. These settings apply to all of the domains and servers that are part of a site. Group Policy settings managed at the site level may apply to more than one domain within the same forest. Therefore, they are useful when you want to make settings that apply to all of the domains within an Active Directory tree or forest.

Domains   Domains are the third level to which system administrators can assign GPOs. GPO settings placed at the domain level will apply to all of the User and Computer objects within the domain. Usually, system administrators make master settings at the domain level.

Organizational Units   The most granular level of settings for GPOs is the OU level. By configuring Group Policy options for OUs, system administrators can take advantage of the hierarchical structure of Active Directory. If the OU structure is planned well, you will find it easy to make logical GPO assignments for various business units at the OU level.

Based on the business needs and the organization of the Active Directory environment, system administrators might decide to set up Group Policy settings at any of these four levels. Because the settings are cumulative by default, a User object might receive policy settings from the site level, from the domain level, and from the OUs in which it is contained.

You can also apply Group Policy settings to the local computer (in which case Active Directory is not used at all), but this limits the manageability of the Group Policy settings.

Group Policy Inheritance

In most cases, Group Policy settings are cumulative. For example, a GPO at the domain level might specify that all users within the domain must change their password every 60 days, and a GPO at the OU level might specify the default desktop background for all users and computers within that OU. In this case, both settings apply, and users within the OU are forced to change their password every 60 days and have the default desktop setting.

So, what happens if there's a conflict in the settings? For example, suppose you create a scenario where a GPO at the site level specifies that users are to use red wallpaper and another GPO at the OU level specifies that they must use green wallpaper. The users at the OU layer would have green wallpaper by default. Although hypothetical, this raises an important point about *inheritance*. By default, the settings at the most specific level (in this case, the OU that contains the User object) override those at more general levels. As a friend of mine from Microsoft always says, "Last one to apply wins."

Although the default behavior is for settings to be cumulative and inherited, system administrators can modify this behavior. They can set two main options at the various levels to which GPOs might apply:

Block Policy Inheritance   The *Block Policy Inheritance* option specifies that Group Policy settings for an object are not inherited from its parents. You might use this, for example, when a child OU requires completely different settings from a parent OU. Note, however, that you should manage blocking policy inheritance carefully because this option allows other system administrators to override the settings made at higher levels.

Force Policy Inheritance   The *Enforced option* (sometimes referred as the *No Override*) can be placed on a parent object and ensures that all lower-level objects inherit these settings. In some cases, system administrators want to ensure that Group Policy inheritance is not blocked at other levels. For example, suppose it is corporate policy that all network accounts are locked out after five incorrect password attempts. In this case, you would not want lower-level system administrators to override the option with other settings.

System administrators generally use this option when they want to enforce a specific setting globally. For example, if a password expiration policy should apply to all users and computers within a domain, a GPO with the *Force Policy Inheritance* option enabled could be created at the domain level.

You must consider one final case: If a conflict exists between the computer and user settings, the user settings take effect. If, for instance, a system administrator applies a default Desktop setting for the Computer policy and a different default Desktop setting for the User policy, the one they specify in the User policy takes effect. This is because the user settings are more specific, and they allow system administrators to make changes for individual users regardless of the computer that they're using.

Planning a Group Policy Strategy

Through the use of Group Policy settings, system administrators can control many different aspects of their network environment. As you'll see throughout this chapter, system administrators can use GPOs to configure user settings and computer configurations. Windows Server 2012 R2 includes many different administrative tools for performing these tasks. However, it's important to keep in mind that, as with many aspects of using Active Directory, a successful Group Policy strategy involves planning.

Because there are hundreds of possible Group Policy settings and many different ways to implement them, you should start by determining the business and technical needs of your organization. For example, you should first group your users based on their work functions. You might find, for example, that users in remote branch offices require particular network configuration options. In that case, you might implement Group Policy settings best at the site level. In another instance, you might find that certain departments have varying requirements for disk quota settings. In this case, it would probably make the most sense to apply GPOs to the appropriate department OUs within the domain.

The overall goal should be to reduce complexity (for example, by reducing the overall number of GPOs and GPO links) while still meeting the needs of your users. By taking into account the various needs of your users and the parts of your organization, you can often determine a logical and efficient method of creating and applying GPOs. Although it's rare that you'll come across a right or wrong method of implementing Group Policy settings, you will usually encounter some that are either better or worse than others.

By implementing a logical and consistent set of policies, you'll also be well prepared to troubleshoot any problems that might come up or to adapt to your organization's changing requirements. Later in this chapter, you'll learn about some specific methods for determining effective Group Policy settings before you apply them.

Implementing Group Policy

Now that I've covered the basic layout and structure of group policies and how they work, let's look at how you can implement them in an Active Directory environment. In the following sections, you'll start by creating GPOs. Then you'll apply these GPOs to specific Active Directory objects, and you'll take a look at how to use administrative templates.

Creating GPOs

In Windows Server 2000 and 2003, you could create GPOs from many different locations. For example, in Windows Server 2003, you could use Active Directory Users and Computers to create GPOs on your OUs along with other GPO tools. In Windows Server 2012 R2, things are simpler. You can create GPOs for OUs in only one location: the Group Policy Management Console (GPMC). You have your choice of three applications for setting up policies on your Windows Server 2012 R2 computers:

Local Computer Policy Tool   This administrative tool allows you to access quickly the Group Policy settings that are available for the local computer. These options apply to the local machine and to users who access it. You must be a member of the local administrators group to access and make changes to these settings.

Group Policy Management Console   You must use the GPMC to manage Group Policy deployment. The GPMC provides a single solution for managing all Group Policy–related tasks, and it is also best suited to handle enterprise-level tasks, such as forest-related work.

The GPMC allows administrators to manage Group Policy and GPOs all from one easy-to-use console whether their enterprise solution spans multiple domains and sites within one or more forests or it is local to one site. The GPMC adds flexibility, manageability, and functionality. Using this console, you can also perform other functions, such as backup and restore, importing, and copying.

Auditpol.exe   Auditpol.exe is a command-line utility that works with Windows Vista, Windows 7, Windows 8, Windows Server 2008, Windows Server 2008 R2, Windows Server 2012, and Windows Server 2012 R2. An administrator has the ability to display information about policies and also to perform some functions to manipulate audit policies. Table 7.1 shows some of the switches available for auditpol.exe.

TABLE 7.1 Auditpol.exe switches

Switch	Explanation
/?	This is the auditpol.exe help command.
/get	Allows you to display the current audit policy.
/set	Allows you to set a policy.
/list	Displays selectable policy elements.
/backup	Allows you to save the audit policy to a file.
/restore	Restores a policy from previous backup.
/clear	Clears the audit policy.
/remove	Removes all per-user audit policy settings and disables all system audit policy settings.
/ResourceSACL	Configures the Global Resource SACL.

Exercise 7.1 walks you through the process of installing the Group Policy Management MMC snap-in for editing Group Policy settings and creating a GPO.

WARNING

You should be careful when making Group Policy settings because certain options might prevent the proper use of systems on your network. Always test Group Policy settings on a small group of users before you deploy them throughout your organization. You'll probably find that some settings need to be changed to be effective.

EXERCISE 7.1

Creating a Group Policy Object Using the GPMC

1. Press the Windows button and choose Administrative Tools ➢ Group Policy Management. The Group Policy Management tool opens.

2. Expand the Forest, Domains, *your domain name,* and North America containers. Right-click the Corporate OU and then choose Create A GPO In This Domain, And Link It Here.

EXERCISE 7.1 *(continued)*

3. When the New GPO dialog box appears, type **Logon Message** in the Name field. Click OK.

4. The New GPO will be listed on the right side of the Group Policy Management window. Right-click the GPO and choose Edit.

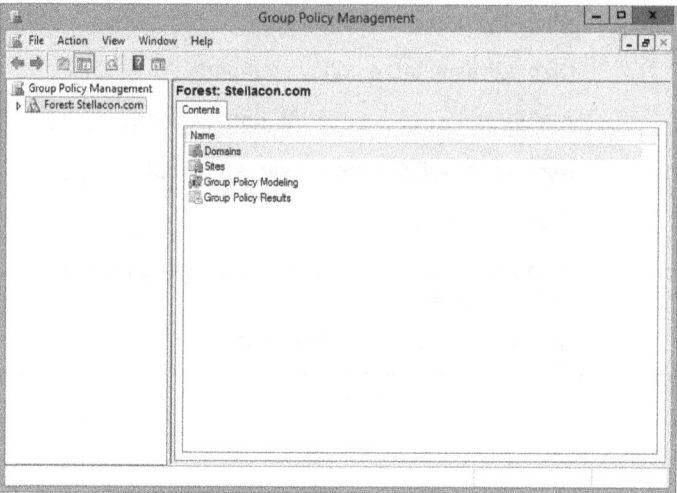

5. In the Group Policy Management Editor, expand the following: Computer Configuration ➢ Policies ➢ Windows Settings ➢ Security Settings ➢ Local Policies ➢ Security Options. On the right side, scroll down and double-click Interactive Logon: Message Text For Users Attempting To Log On.

6. Click the box labeled Define This Policy Setting In The Template. In the text box, type **Welcome to the domain. Domain members only are welcome** and then click OK. Close the GPO and return to the GPMC main screen.

7. Under the domain name (in the GPMC), right-click Group Policy Objects and choose New.

8. When the New GPO dialog box appears, type **Unlinked Test GPO** in the Name field. Click OK.

9. On the right side, the new GPO will appear. Right-click Unlinked Test GPO and choose Edit.

10. In the User Configuration section, click Policies ➢ Administrative Templates ➢ Desktop. On the right side, double-click Hide And Disable All Items On The Desktop and then click Enabled. Click OK and then close the GPMC.

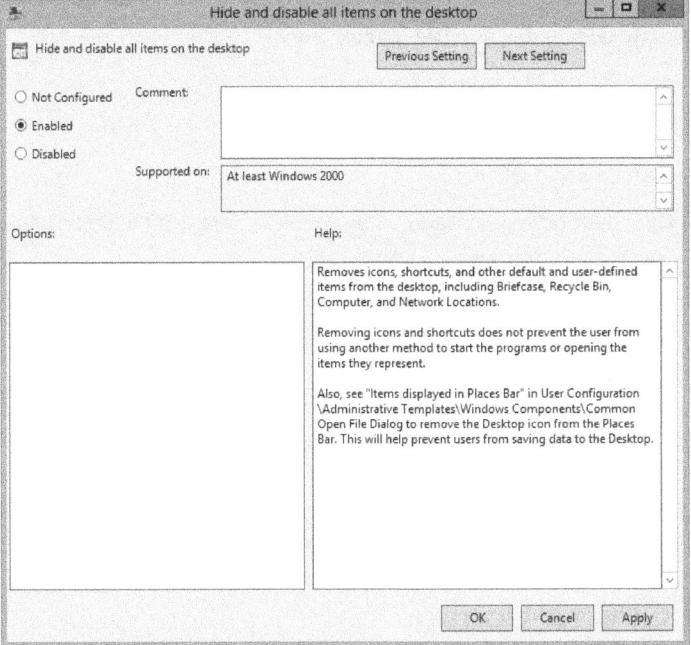

 Note that Group Policy changes may not take effect until the next user logs in (some settings may even require that the machine be rebooted). That is, users who are currently working on the system will not see the effects of the changes until they log off and log in again. GPOs are reapplied every 90 minutes with a 30-minute offset. In other words, users who are logged in will have their policies reapplied every 60 to 120 minutes. Not all settings are reapplied (for example, software settings and password policies).

Linking Existing GPOs to Active Directory

Creating a GPO is the first step in assigning group policies. The second step is to link the GPO to a specific Active Directory object. As mentioned earlier in this chapter, GPOs can be linked to sites, domains, and OUs.

Exercise 7.2 walks you through the steps you must take to assign an existing GPO to an OU within the local domain. In this exercise, you will link the Test Domain Policy GPO to an OU. To complete the steps in this exercise, you must have completed Exercise 7.1.

EXERCISE 7.2

Linking Existing GPOs to Active Directory

1. Open the Group Policy Management Console.

2. Expand the Forest and Domain containers and right-click the Africa OU.

3. Choose Link An Existing GPO.

4. The Select GPO dialog box appears. Click Unlinked Test GPO and click OK.

5. Close the Group Policy Management Console.

Note that the GPMC tool offers a lot of flexibility in assigning GPOs. You can create new GPOs, add multiple GPOs, edit them directly, change priority settings, remove links, and delete GPOs all from within this interface. In general, creating new GPOs using the GPMC tool is the quickest and easiest way to create the settings you need.

To test the Group Policy settings, you can simply create a user account within the Africa OU that you used in Exercise 7.2. Then, using another computer that is a member of the same domain, you can log on as the newly created user.

Forcing a GPO to Update

There will be times when you need a GPO to get processed immediately. If you are testing a GPO, you will not want to wait for the GPO to process in its own time or you may not want to have to log off the domain and log back onto the domain just to get the GPO processed.

Windows Server 2012 R2 has changed how GPOs get processed. In a Windows Server 2012 R2 domain, when a user logs onto the domain, the latest version of the Group Policy gets downloaded from the domain controller, and it writes that policy to the local store.

If you have your GPOs set up and running in synchronous mode, then the next time the computer restarts, it will use the most recently downloaded GPO from the local store and not download the GPO from the domain. This is a new feature in Windows Server 2012 R2, and it helps to reduce the time it takes to log onto the domain because the GPO policy doesn't need to be downloaded each time.

So, now that you understand how GPOs get processed in Windows Server 2012 R2, let's look at a few different ways that you can force a GPO to get processed immediately.

Forcing the GPO from the Server

Windows Server 2012 R2 has an MMC called Group Policy Management Console (GPMC), and by using this MMC, you can remotely refresh an organizational unit (OU) and force the GPO on all users and computers within that OU. The GPMC remote refresh automatically updates all settings, including security settings, which are configured in the GPO that is linked to the OU. In the OU's context menu, you can choose to refresh remotely the OU and the GPOs associated with that OU. When you remotely refresh an OU, the following steps occur:

1. Windows Server 2012 R2 does an Active Directory query, and that query returns a list of all users and computers that belong to the OU.

2. Windows Management Instrumentation (WMI) queries all users and computers that are currently logged into the domain and creates a list that will be used.

3. Using the list that was created in step 2, a remote scheduled task is created, and a GPUpdate.exe /force is executed on all of the users and computers that are logged into the domain. The remote scheduled task is then scheduled to execute with a 10-minute random delay to help decrease the load on network traffic.

 When you are using the GPMC to force a GPO update, you do not have the ability to change the 10-minute random delay, but if you force the GPO through the use of PowerShell, you have the ability to set the delay.

Another way that you can force a GPO to update immediately is to use Windows PowerShell. By using the PowerShell command Invoke-GPUpdate cmdlet, you cannot only force the GPO but also set the parameters to be more granular.

Forcing the GPO from the Client

As an administrator, you have the ability also to force a GPO onto a client machine on which you may be working. The GPUpdate.exe command allows you to run a GPO on a client machine. The GPUpdate command will run on all Windows client machines from Windows Vista to Windows Server 2012 R2. Table 7.2 shows some of the GPUpdate switches you can use.

TABLE 7.2   GPUpdate.exe switches

Switch	Description
/target:{Computer | User}	Updates only the User or Computer policy settings for the computer or user specified.
/force	Forces the GPO to reapply all policy settings. By default, only policy settings that have changed are applied.
/wait:<VALUE>	Determines the number of seconds that the system will wait after a policy is processed before returning to the command prompt.
/logoff	The domain user account will automatically log off the computer after the Group Policy settings are updated.
/boot	The computer will automatically restart after the Group Policy settings are applied.
/sync	This switch forces the next available foreground policy application to be done synchronously. Foreground policies are applied when the computer boots up and the user logs in.
/?	Displays help at the command prompt.

Managing Group Policy

Now that you have implemented GPOs and applied them to sites, domains, and OUs within Active Directory, it's time to look at some ways to manage them. In the following sections, you'll look at how multiple GPOs can interact with one another and ways that you can provide security for GPO management. Using these features is an important part of working with Active Directory, and if you properly plan Group Policy, you can greatly reduce the time the help desk spends troubleshooting common problems.

Managing GPOs

One of the benefits of GPOs is that they're modular and can apply to many different objects and levels within Active Directory. This can also be one of the drawbacks of GPOs if they're not managed properly. A common administrative function related to using GPOs is finding all of the Active Directory links for each of these objects. You can do this when you are viewing the Linked Group Policy Objects tab of the site, domain, or OU in the GPMC (shown in Figure 7.2).

FIGURE 7.2   Viewing GPO links to an Active Directory OU

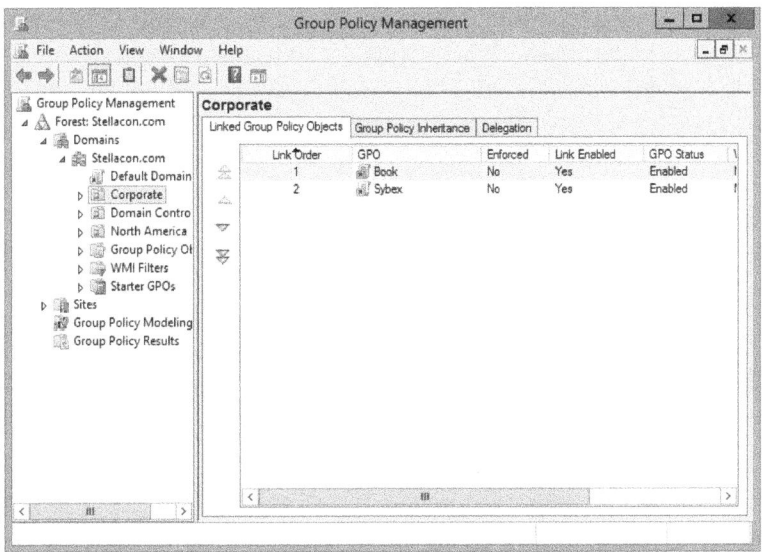

In addition to the common action of delegating permissions on OUs, you can set permissions regarding the modification of GPOs. The best way to accomplish this is to add users to the Group Policy Creator/Owners built-in security group. The members of this group are able to modify security policy.

Windows Management Instrumentation

Windows Management Instrumentation (WMI) scripts are used to gather information or to help GPOs deploy better. The best way to explain this is to give an example. Let's say you wanted to deploy Microsoft Office 2013 to everyone in the company. You would first set up a GPO to deploy the Office package (explained later in the section "Deploying Software Through a GPO").

You can then place a WMI script on the GPO stating that only computers with 10GB of hard disk space actually deploy Office. Now if a computer has 10GB of free space, the Office GPO would get installed. If the computer does not have the 10GB of hard disk space, the GPO will not deploy. You can use WMI scripts to check for computer information such as MAC addresses. WMI is a powerful tool because if you know how to write scripts, the possibilities are endless. The following script is a sample of a WMI that is checking for at least 10GB of free space on the C: partition/volume:

```
Select * from Win32_LogicalDisk where FreeSpace > 10737418240 AND
Caption = "C:"
```

Security Filtering of a Group Policy

Another method of securing access to GPOs is to set permissions on the GPOs themselves. You can do this by opening the GPMC, selecting the GPO, and clicking the Advanced button in the Delegation tab. The Unlinked Test GPO Security Settings dialog box appears (see Figure 7.3).

FIGURE 7.3   A GPO's Security Settings dialog box

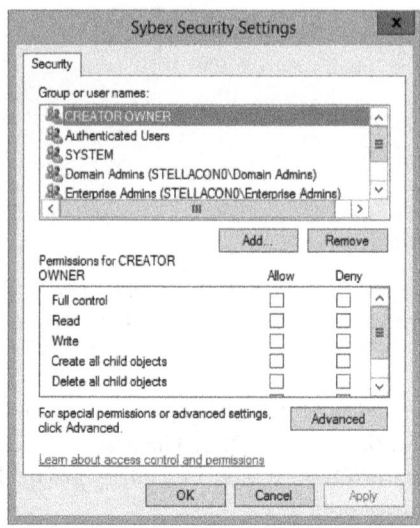

The following permissions options are available:

- Full Control

- Read

- Write

- Create All Child Objects

- Delete All Child Objects

- Apply Group Policy

You might have to scroll the Permissions window to see the Apply Group Policy item. Of these, the Apply Group Policy setting is particularly important because you use it to filter the scope of the GPO. *Filtering* is the process by which selected security groups are included or excluded from the effects of the GPOs. To specify that the settings should apply to a GPO, you should select the Allow check box for both the Apply Group Policy setting and the Read setting. These settings will be applied only if the security group is also contained within a site, domain, or OU to which the GPO is linked. To disable GPO access for a group, choose Deny for both of these settings. Finally, if you do not want to specify either Allow or Deny, leave both boxes blank. This is effectively the same as having no setting.

In Exercise 7.3, you will filter Group Policy using security groups. To complete the steps in this exercise, you must have completed Exercises 7.1 and 7.2.

EXERCISE 7.3

Filtering Group Policy Using Security Groups

1. Open the Active Directory Users and Computers administrative tool.

2. Create a new OU called **Group Policy Test**.

3. Create two new global security groups within the Group Policy Test OU, and name them **PolicyEnabled** and **PolicyDisabled**.

4. Exit Active Directory Users and Computers and open the GPMC.

5. Right-click the Group Policy Test OU and select Link An Existing GPO.

6. Choose Unlinked Test GPO and click OK.

7. Expand the Group Policy Test OU so that you can see the GPO (Unlinked Test GPO) underneath the OU.

8. Click the Delegation tab and then click the Advanced button in the lower-right corner of the window.

9. Click the Add button and type **PolicyEnabled** in the Enter The Object Names To Select field. Click the Check Names button. Then click OK.

10. Add a group named **PolicyDisabled** in the same way.

11. Highlight the PolicyEnabled group and select Allow for the Read and Apply Group Policy permissions. This ensures that users in the PolicyEnabled group will be affected by this policy.

12. Highlight the PolicyDisabled group and select Deny for the Read and Apply Group Policy permissions. This ensures that users in the PolicyDisabled group will not be affected by this policy.

13. Click OK. You will see a message stating that you are choosing to use the Deny permission and that the Deny permission takes precedence over the Allow entries. Click the Yes button to continue.

14. When you have finished, close the GPMC tool.

Delegating Administrative Control of GPOs

So far, you have learned about how to use Group Policy to manage user and computer settings. What you haven't done yet is to determine who can modify GPOs. It's important to establish the appropriate security on GPOs themselves for two reasons:

- If the security settings aren't set properly, users and system administrators can easily override them. This defeats the purpose of having the GPOs in the first place.

- Having many different system administrators creating and modifying GPOs can become extremely difficult to manage. When problems arise, the hierarchical nature of GPO inheritance can make it difficult to pinpoint the problem.

Fortunately, through the use of delegation, determining security permissions for GPOs is a simple task. Exercise 7.4 walks you through the steps you must take to grant the appropriate permissions to a user account. Specifically, the process involves delegating the ability to manage Group Policy links on an Active Directory object (such as an OU). To complete this exercise, you must have completed Exercises 7.1 and 7.2.

Delegating Administrative Control of Group Policy

1. Open the Active Directory Users and Computers tool.

2. Expand the local domain, and create a user named **Policy Admin** within the Group Policy Test OU.

3. Exit Active Directory Users and Computers and open the GPMC.

4. Click the Group Policy Test OU and select the Delegation tab.

5. Click the Add button. In the field labeled Enter The Object Name To Select, type **Policy Admin** and click the Check Names button.

6. The Add Group Or User dialog box appears. In the Permissions drop-down list, make sure that the item labeled Edit Settings, Delete, Modify Security is chosen. Click OK.

7. At this point, you should be looking at the Group Policy Test Delegation window. Click the Advanced button in the lower-right corner.

8. Highlight the Policy Admin account and check the Allow Full Control box. This user now has full control of these OUs and all child OUs and GPOs for these OUs. Click OK.

If you just want to give individual rights to this user, then in the Properties window (step 8), click the Advanced button and then the Effective Permissions tab. This is where you can also choose a user and give them only the rights that you want them to have.

9. When you have finished, close the GPMC tool.

Understanding Delegation

Although I have talked about delegation throughout the book, it's important to discuss it again in the context of OUs, Group Policy, and Active Directory.

Once configured, Active Directory administrative delegation allows an administrator to delegate tasks (usually administration related) to specific user accounts or groups. What this means is that if you don't manage it all, the user accounts (or groups) you choose will be able to manage their portions of the tree.

It's important to be aware of the benefits of Active Directory Delegation (AD Delegation). *AD Delegation* will help you manage the assigning of administrative control over objects in Active Directory, such as users, groups, computers, printers, domains, and sites. AD Delegation is used to create more administrators, which essentially saves time.

For example, let's say you have a company whose IT department is small and situated in a central location. The central location connects three other smaller remote sites. These sites do not each warrant a full-time IT person, but the manager on staff (for example) at each remote site can become an administrator for their portion of the tree. If the user accounts for the staff at the remote site are managed by that manager, this reduces the burden on the system administrator of trivial administrative work, such as unlocking user accounts or changing passwords, and thus it reduces costs.

Controlling Inheritance and Filtering Group Policy

Controlling inheritance is an important function when you are managing GPOs. Earlier in this chapter, you learned that, by default, GPO settings flow from higher-level Active Directory objects to lower-level ones. For example, the effective set of Group Policy settings for a user might be based on GPOs assigned at the site level, at the domain level, and in the OU hierarchy. In general, this is probably the behavior you would want.

In some cases, however, you might want to block Group Policy inheritance. You can accomplish this easily by selecting the object to which a GPO has been linked. Right-click the object and choose Block Inheritance (see Figure 7.4). By enabling this option, you are

FIGURE 7.4 Blocking GPO inheritance

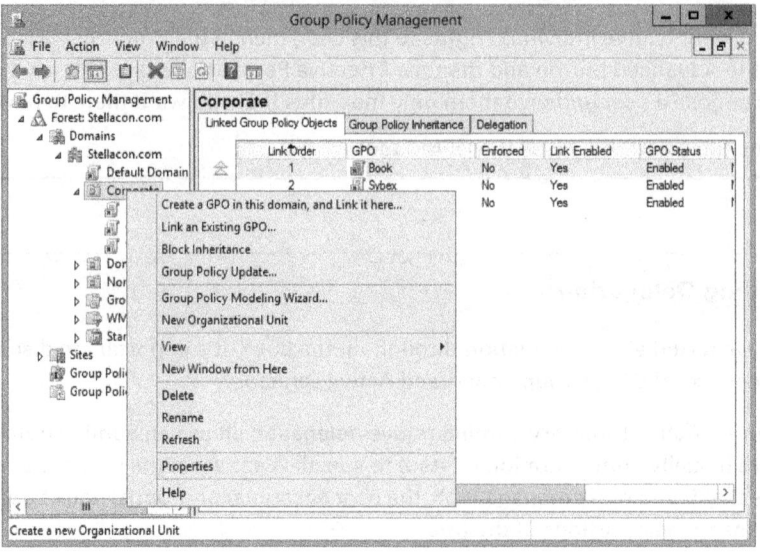

effectively specifying that this object starts with a clean slate; that is, no other Group Policy settings will apply to the contents of this Active Directory site, domain, or OU.

System administrators can also force inheritance. By setting the Enforced option, they can prevent other system administrators from making changes to default policies. You can set the Enforced option by right-clicking the GPO and choosing the Enforced item (see Figure 7.5).

FIGURE 7.5 Setting the Enforced GPO option

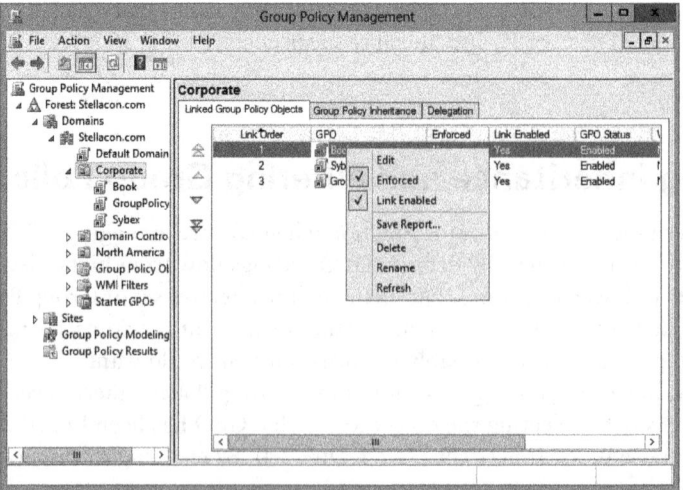

Assigning Script Policies

System administrators might want to make several changes and implement certain settings that would apply while the computer is starting up or the user is logging on. Perhaps the most common operation that logon scripts perform is mapping network drives. Although users can manually map network drives, providing this functionality within login scripts ensures that mappings stay consistent and that users only need to remember the drive letters for their resources.

Script policies are specific options that are part of Group Policy settings for users and computers. These settings direct the operating system to the specific files that should be processed during the startup/shutdown or logon/logoff processes. You can create the scripts by using the *Windows Script Host (WSH)* or with standard batch file commands. WSH allows developers and system administrators to create scripts quickly and easily using Visual Basic Scripting Edition (VBScript) or JScript (Microsoft's implementation of JavaScript). Additionally, WSH can be expanded to accommodate other common scripting languages.

To set script policy options, you simply edit the Group Policy settings. As shown in Figure 7.6, there are two main areas for setting script policy settings.

FIGURE 7.6   Viewing Startup/Shutdown script policy settings

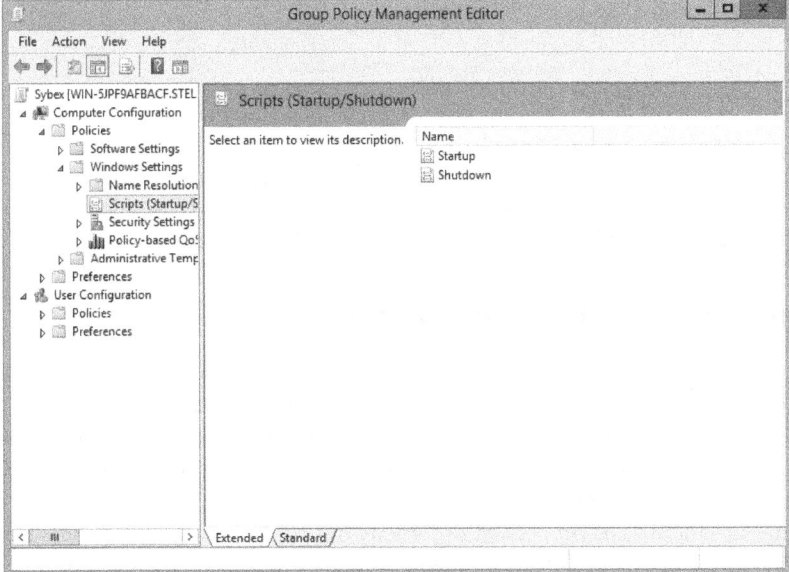

Startup/Shutdown Scripts   These settings are located within the Computer Configuration ➢ Windows Settings ➢ Scripts (Startup/Shutdown) object.

Logon/Logoff Scripts   These settings are located within the User Configuration ➢ Windows Settings ➢ Scripts (Logon/Logoff) object.

To assign scripts, simply double-click the setting and its Properties dialog box appears. For instance, if you double-click the Startup setting, the Startup Properties dialog box appears (see Figure 7.7). To add a script filename, click the Add button. When you do, you will be asked to provide the name of the script file (such as `MapNetworkDrives.vbs` or `ResetEnvironment.bat`).

FIGURE 7.7 Setting scripting options

Note that you can change the order in which the scripts are run by using the Up and Down buttons. The Show Files button opens the directory folder in which you should store the Logon script files. To ensure that the files are replicated to all domain controllers, you should be sure that you place the files within the SYSVOL share.

Understanding the Loopback Policy

There may be times when the user settings of a Group Policy object should be applied to a computer based on its location instead of the user object. Usually, the user Group Policy processing dictates that the GPOs be applied in order during computer startup based on the computers located in their organizational unit. User GPOs, on the other hand, are applied in order during logon, regardless of the computer to which they log on.

In some situations, this processing order may not be appropriate. A good example is a kiosk machine. You would not want applications that have been assigned or published to a user to be installed when the user is logged on to the kiosk machine. *Loopback Policy* allows two ways to retrieve the list of GPOs for any user when they are using a specific computer in an OU:

Merge Mode   The GPOs for the computer are added to the end of the GPOs for the user. Because of this, the computer's GPOs have higher precedence than the user's GPOs.

Replace Mode   In Replace mode, the user's GPOs are not used. Only the GPOs of the Computer object are used.

Managing Network Configuration

Group policies are also useful in network configuration. Although administrators can handle network settings at the protocol level using many different methods, such as Dynamic Host Configuration Protocol (DHCP), Group Policy allows them to set which functions and operations are available to users and computers.

Figure 7.8 shows some of the features that are available for managing Group Policy settings. The paths to these settings are as follows:

Computer Network Options   These settings are located within Computer Configuration ➢ Administrative Templates ➢ Network ➢ Network Connections folder.

User Network Options   These settings are located within User Configuration ➢ Administrative Templates ➢ Network.

FIGURE 7.8   Viewing Group Policy User network configuration options

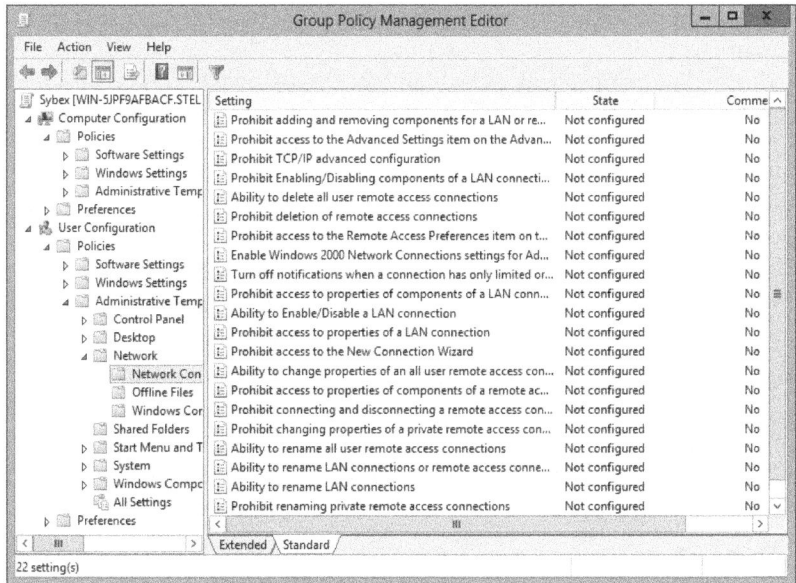

Here are some examples of the types of settings available:

- The ability to allow or disallow the modification of network settings.

  In many environments, the improper changing of network configurations and protocol settings is a common cause of help desk calls.

- The ability to allow or disallow the creation of Remote Access Service (RAS) connections.

    This option is very useful, especially in larger networked environments, because the use of modems and other WAN devices can pose a security threat to the network.

- The ability to set offline files and folders options.

    This is especially useful for keeping files synchronized for traveling users, and it is commonly configured for laptops.

Each setting includes detailed instructions in the description area of the GPO Editor window. By using these configuration options, system administrators can maintain consistency for users and computers and avoid many of the most common troubleshooting calls.

Automatically Enrolling User and Computer Certificates in Group Policy

You can also use Group Policy to enroll user and computer certificates automatically, making the entire certificate process transparent to your end users. Before proceeding further, you should understand what certificates are and why they are an important part of network security.

Think of a digital certificate as a carrying case for a public key. A certificate contains the public key and a set of attributes, including the key holder's name and email address. These attributes specify something about the holder: their identity, what they're allowed to do with the certificate, and so on. The attributes and the public key are bound together because the certificate is digitally signed by the entity that issued it. Anyone who wants to verify the certificate's contents can verify the issuer's signature.

Certificates are one part of what security experts call a *public-key infrastructure (PKI)*. A PKI has several components that you can mix and match to achieve the desired results. Microsoft's PKI implementation offers the following functions:

Certificate Authorities   CAs issue certificates, revoke certificates they've issued, and publish certificates for their clients. Big CAs like Thawte and VeriSign do this for millions of users. If you want, you can also set up your own CA for each department or workgroup in your organization. Each CA is responsible for choosing which attributes it will include in a certificate and what mechanism it will use to verify those attributes before it issues the certificate.

Certificate Publishers   They make certificates publicly available, inside or outside an organization. This allows widespread availability of the critical material needed to support the entire PKI.

PKI-Savvy Applications   These allow you and your users to do useful things with certificates, such as encrypt email or network connections. Ideally, the user shouldn't have to know (or even be aware of) what the application is doing—everything should work seamlessly and automatically. The best-known examples of PKI-savvy applications are web browsers such as Internet Explorer and Firefox and email applications such as Outlook and Outlook Express.

Certificate Templates   These act like rubber stamps. By specifying a particular template as the model you want to use for a newly issued certificate, you're actually telling the CA which optional attributes to add to the certificate as well as implicitly telling it how to fill some of the mandatory attributes. Templates greatly simplify the process of issuing certificates because they keep you from having to memorize the names of all the attributes that you may potentially want to put in a certificate.

Learn More About PKI

When discussing certificates, it's also important to mention PKI and its definition. The exam doesn't go deeply into PKI, but I recommend you do some extra research on your own because it is an important technology and shouldn't be overlooked. PKI is actually a simple concept with a lot of moving parts. When broken down to its bare essentials, PKI is nothing more than a server and workstations utilizing a software service to add security to your infrastructure. When you use PKI, you are adding a layer of protection. The auto-enrollment Settings policy determines whether users and/or computers are automatically enrolled for the appropriate certificates when necessary. By default, this policy is enabled if a certificate server is installed, but you can make changes to the settings, as shown in Exercise 7.5.

In Exercise 7.5, you will learn how to configure automatic certificate enrollment in Group Policy. You must have first completed the other exercises in this chapter in order to proceed with Exercise 7.5.

EXERCISE 7.5

Configuring Automatic Certificate Enrollment in Group Policy

1. Open the Group Policy Management Console tool.

2. Right-click the North America OU that you created in the previous exercises in this book.

3. Choose Create A GPO In This Domain And Link It Here and name it **Test CA**. Click OK.

4. Right-click the Test CA GPO and choose Edit.

5. Open Computer Configuration ➢ Policies ➢ Windows Settings ➢ Security Settings ➢ Public Key Policies.

6. Double-click Certificate Services Client – Auto-Enrollment in the right pane.

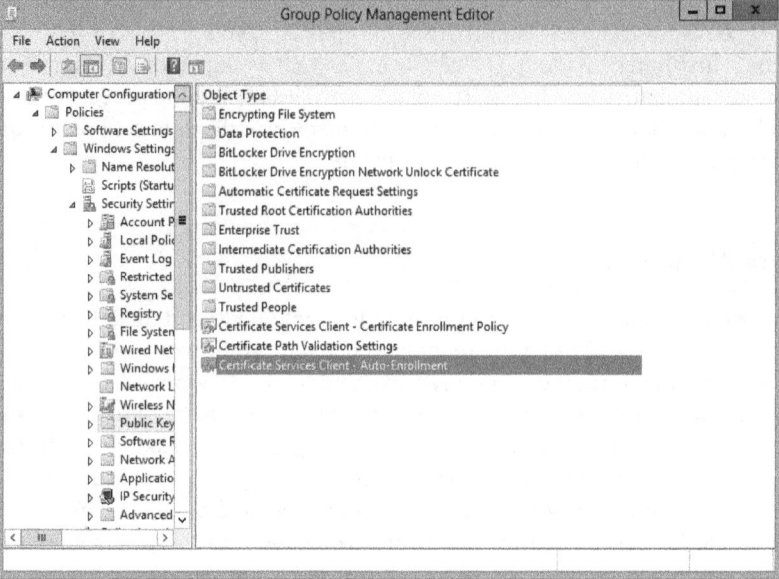

7. The Certificate Services Client – Auto-Enrollment Properties dialog box will appear.

8. For now, don't change anything. Just become familiar with the settings in this dialog box. Click OK to close it.

Redirecting Folders

Another set of Group Policy settings that you will learn about are the *folder redirection settings*. Group Policy provides a means for redirecting the Documents, Desktop, and Start Menu folders, as well as cached application data, to network locations. Folder redirection is particularly useful for the following reasons:

- When they are using roaming user profiles, a user's Documents folder is copied to the local machine each time they log on. This requires high-bandwidth consumption and time if the Documents folder is large. If you redirect the Documents folder, it stays in the redirected location, and the user opens and saves files directly to that location.

- Documents are always available no matter where the user logs on.

- Data in the shared location can be backed up during the normal backup cycle without user intervention.

- Data can be redirected to a more robust server-side administered disk that is less prone to physical and user errors.

When you decide to redirect folders, you have two options, basic and advanced:

- Basic redirection redirects everyone's folders to the same location (but each user gets their own folder within that location).

- Advanced redirection redirects folders to different locations based on group membership. For instance, you could configure the Engineers group to redirect their folders to //Engineering1/Documents/ and the Marketing group to //Marketing1/ Documents/. Again, individual users still get their own folder within the redirected location.

To configure folder redirection, follow the steps in Exercise 7.6. You must have completed the other exercises in this chapter to proceed with this exercise.

EXERCISE 7.6

Configuring Folder Redirection in Group Policy

1. Open the GPMC tool.

2. Open the North America OU and then edit the Test CA GPO.

3. Open User Configuration ➢ Policies ➢ Windows Settings ➢ Folder Redirection ➢ Documents.

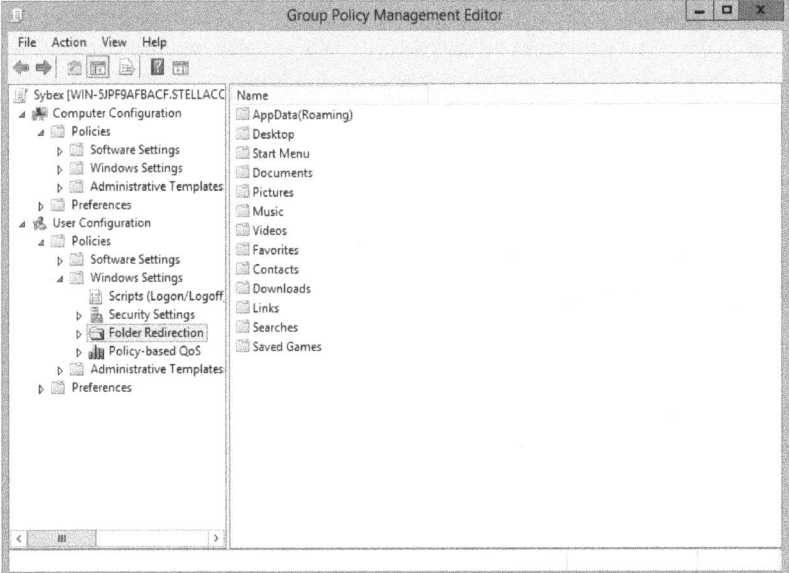

4. Right-click Documents and select Properties.

5. On the Target tab of the Documents Properties dialog box, choose the Basic – Redirect Everyone's Folder To The Same Location selection from the Settings drop-down list.

EXERCISE 7.6 *(continued)*

6. Leave the default option for the Target Folder Location drop-down list and specify a network path in the Root Path field.

7. Click the Settings tab. All of the default settings are self-explanatory and should typically be left at the defaults. Click OK when you have finished.

> **Folder Redirection Facts**
>
> Try not to mix up the concepts of *folder redirection* and *offline folders,* especially in a world with ever-increasing numbers of mobile users. Folder redirection and offline folders are different features.
>
> Windows Server 2012 R2 folder redirection works as follows: The system uses a pointer that moves the folders you want to a location that you specify. Users do not see any of this—it is transparent to them. One problem with folder redirection is that it does not work for mobile users (users who will be offline and who will not have access to files that they may need).
>
> Offline folders, however, are copies of folders that were local to you. Files are now available locally to you on the system you have with you. They are also located back on the server where they are stored. The next time you log in, the folders are synchronized so that both folders contain the latest data. This is a perfect feature for mobile users, whereas folder redirection provides no benefit for the mobile user.

Managing GPOs with Windows PowerShell Group Policy Cmdlets

As stated earlier in this book, *Windows PowerShell* is a Windows command-line shell and scripting language. Windows PowerShell can also help an administrator automate many of the same tasks that you perform using the Group Policy Management Console.

Windows Server 2012 R2 helps you perform many of the Group Policy tasks by providing more than 25 cmdlets. Each of these cmdlets is a simple, single-function command-line tool.

The Windows PowerShell Group Policy cmdlets can help you perform some of the following tasks for domain-based Group Policy objects:

- Maintain, create, remove, back up, and import GPOs.
- Create, update, and remove GPO links to Active Directory containers.
- Set Active Directory OUs and domain permissions and inheritance flags.

- Configure Group Policy registry settings.
- Create and edit Starter GPOs.

The requirement for Windows PowerShell Group Policy cmdlets is Windows Server 2012 R2 on either a domain controller or a member server that has the GPMC installed. Windows 7 and Windows 8 also have the ability to use Windows PowerShell Group Policy cmdlets if it has Remote Server Administration Tools (RSAT) installed. RSAT includes the GPMC and its cmdlets. PowerShell is also a requirement.

Item-Level Targeting

Administrators have the ability to apply individual preference items only to selected users or computers using a GPO feature called item-level targeting. *Item-level targeting* allows an administrator to select specific items that the GPO will look at and then apply that GPO only to the specific users or computers. Administrators have the ability to include multiple preference items, and each item can be customized for specific users or computers to use.

The target item has a value that belongs to it, and the value can be either true or false. Administrators can get even more granular by using the operation command of AND or OR while building this GPO, and this will allow an administrator to combine the targeted items with the preceding one. Once all of the conditions are executed, if the final value is false, then the GPO is not applied. If the final value is true, the GPO is applied to the users or computers that were previously determined. Administrators have the ability to item-target the following items:

- Battery Present Targeting
- Computer Name Targeting
- CPU Speed Targeting
- Date Match Targeting
- Disk Space Targeting
- Domain Targeting
- Environment Variable Targeting
- File Match Targeting
- IP Address Range Targeting
- Language Targeting
- LDAP Query Targeting
- MAC Address Range Targeting
- MSI Query Targeting
- Network Connection Targeting
- Operating System Targeting
- Organizational Unit Targeting

- PCMCIA Present Targeting
- Portable Computer Targeting
- Processing Mode Targeting
- RAM Targeting
- Registry Match Targeting
- Security Group Targeting
- Site Targeting
- Terminal Session Targeting
- Time Range Targeting
- User Targeting
- WMI Query Targeting

Administrators can easily set up item-level targeting by following these steps:

1. Open the Group Policy Management Console. Select the GPO that will contain the new preferences by right-clicking the GPO and then choose Edit.

2. In the console tree under Computer Configuration or User Configuration, expand the Preferences folder and then browse to the preference extension.

3. Double-click the node for the preference extension and then right-click the preference item and click Properties.

4. In the Properties dialog box, click the Common tab.

5. Select Item-Level Targeting and then click Targeting.

6. Click New Item. If you are configuring multiple targeted items, on the Item Option menu, click the logical operation (AND or OR). Then click OK when finished.

7. Click the OK button on the Properties dialog box, and you are all set.

Backup, Restore, Import, Copy, and Migration Tables

One of the biggest advantages of using the Group Policy Management Console is that it is a one-stop shopping utility. You can do everything you need to do for GPOs in one location. The GPMC not only allows you to create and link a GPO but also lets you backup, restore, import, copy, and use migration tables.

Backing Up a GPO

Since this book is about Windows Server 2012 R2 and everything you should do to set up the server properly, then you most likely already understand what backups can do for you.

The reason we back up data as an administrator is in the event of a crash or major error that requires us to reload data to the server. Backups should be done daily on all data that is important to your organization. Backups can be done either by using Windows Server 2012 R2's backup utility, or you can purchase third party software/hardware to back up your data.

I am an IT Director, and data recoverability is one of the most critical items that I deal with on a daily basis. I use a third-party hardware device from a company called Unitrends. This is just one of many companies that helps protect an organization's data.

This hardware device does hourly backups for all of my servers. One of the nice features of the Unitrends box is that it backs up onto the hardware device and then sends my data up to the cloud automatically for an offsite backup. This way, if I need to recover just one piece of data, I can grab it off the hardware device. But if I have a major issue, such as a fire that destroys the entire server room, I have an offsite backup from which I can retrieve my data.

It's the same for GPOs. You need to make sure you back up your GPOs in the event of an issue that requires you to do a reload. To back up your GPOs manually, you can go into the GPMC MMC and, under Group Policy Objects, you can right click and choose Backup All or right click on the specific GPO and choose Backup.

Restoring a GPO

There may be times when you have to restore a GPO that was previously backed up. There are normally two reasons why you have to restore a GPO—you accidently deleted the GPO, or you need to restore the GPO to a previous state. (This normally happens if you make changes and it causes an issue.) Restoring a GPO is simple.

1. Open the Group Policy Management Console.

2. In the console tree, right-click Group Policy Objects and choose Manage Backups.

3. Choose the backup you want to restore and click the Restore button.

Importing or Copying GPOs

As an administrator, there may be times when you need to import or copy a GPO from one domain to another domain. Administrators do this so that the second domain has the same settings as the first domain.

An administrator can use the import or copy-to-transfer settings from one GPO to another GPO within the same domain, to a GPO in another domain in the same forest, or to a GPO in a domain in a different forest.

Importing or copying a GPO is an easy process. To do this, an administrator completes the following steps:

1. Open the Group Policy Management Console.

2. In the console tree, right-click Group Policy Objects and choose either Import Settings or Copy.

Migration Tables

One issue that we run into when copying or moving a GPO from one system to another is that when some GPOs are built, they are domain specific. This can be a problem when they are moved to a system in another domain. This is where migration tables can help you out.

Migration tables will tell you how domain specific settings should be treated when the GPO is moved from the domain in which it was created to another domain.

Migration tables are files that are used to map previous domain information (such as users and groups) to the new domain's object-specific data. Migration tables have mapping entries that map the old data to the new data.

Migration tables store their mapping data in an XML format, and the migration tables have their own extension name, .migtable. If you want to create your own migration table, you can use the *Migration Table Editor (MTE)*. The MTE is an easy-to-use utility for configuring or just viewing migration tables.

It does not matter if you decide to copy or import a GPO, migration tables apply to any of the settings within the GPO. However, if you copy a GPO instead of move it, you have the option of bringing the Discretionary Access Control List (DACL) option over with the copy.

If you are looking at using migration tables, there are three settings that can be used:

Do Not Use A Migration Table   If an administrator chooses this option, the GPO is copied over exactly as is. All security objects and UNC paths are copied over without any modification.

Use A Migration Table   If an administrator chooses this option, the GPO has all of the options that can be in the migration table mapped.

Use A Migration Table Exclusively   If an administrator chooses this option, all security principals and UNC path information in the GPO are chosen. If any of this information is not included in the migration table, the operation will fail.

To open the Migration Table Editor, perform the following steps:

1. Open the Group Policy Management Console.

2. In the console tree, right-click Group Policy Objects and choose Open Migration Table Editor.

Resetting the Default GPO

There may be a time when you need to reset the default GPO to its original settings. This is easy to do as long as you understand how to use the DCGPOFix command-line utility. This command-line utility is just what it spells—it fixes the domain controller's GPO. To use this command, you would use the following syntax:

```
DCGPOFix [/ignoreschema] [/target: {Domain | DC | Both}] [/?]
```

So, let's take a look at the switches in the previous command. The /ignoreschema switch ignores the current version of the Active Directory Schema. The reason you use this switch is because this command works only on the same schema version as the Windows version in which the command was shipped. By using this switch, you don't need to worry about what schema you have on the system.

The next switch is [/target: {Domain | DC | Both}]. This switch specifies the GPO you are going to restore. An administrator has the ability to restore the Default Domain Policy GPO, the Default Domain Controllers GPO, or both. The final switch, /?, displays the help for this command.

Deploying Software Through a GPO

It's difficult enough to manage applications on a stand-alone computer. It seems that the process of installing, configuring, and uninstalling applications is never finished. Add in the hassle of computer reboots and reinstalling corrupted applications, and the reduction in productivity can be substantial.

Software administrators who manage software in network environments have even more concerns:

- First and foremost, they must determine which applications specific users require.

- Then IT departments must purchase the appropriate licenses for the software and acquire any necessary media.

- Next, the system administrators need to install the applications on users' machines. This process generally involves help desk staff visiting computers, or it requires end users to install the software themselves. Both processes entail several potential problems, including installation inconsistency and lost productivity from downtime experienced when the applications were installed.

- Finally, software administrators still need to manage software updates and remove unused software.

One of the key design goals for Active Directory was to reduce some of the headaches involved in managing software and configurations in a networked environment. To that end, Windows Server 2012 R2 offers several features that can make the task of deploying software easier and less error prone. Before you dive into the technical details, however, you need to examine the issues related to software deployment.

The Software Management Life Cycle

Although it may seem that the use of a new application requires only the installation of the necessary software, the overall process of managing applications involves many more steps. When managing software applications, there are three main phases to their life cycle:

Phase 1: Deploying Software   The first step in using applications is to install them on the appropriate client computers. Generally, some applications are deployed during the initial configuration of a PC, and others are deployed when they are requested. In the latter case, this often meant that system administrators and help desk staffs had to visit client computers and manually walk through the installation process. With Windows Server 2012 R2 and GPOs, the entire process can be automated.

Before You Install, Stop

It is important to understand that just because you can easily deploy software, it does not necessarily mean that you have the right to do so. Before you install software on client computers, you must make sure you have the appropriate licenses for the software. Furthermore, it's important to take the time to track application installations. As many system administrators have discovered, it's much more difficult to inventory software installations after they've been performed. Another issue you may encounter is that you lack available resources (for instance, your system does not meet the minimum hardware requirements) and face problems such as limited hard disk space or memory that may not be able to handle the applications that you want to load and use. You may also find that your user account does not have the permission to install software. It's important to consider not only how you will install software but also whether you can or not.

Phase 2: Maintaining Software   Once an application is installed and in use on client computers, you need to ensure that the software is maintained. You must keep programs up-to-date by applying changes due to bug fixes, enhancements, and other types of updates. This is normally done with service packs, hot fixes, and updates. As with the initial software deployment, software maintenance can be tedious. Some programs require older versions to be uninstalled before updates are added. Others allow for automatically upgrading over existing installations. Managing and deploying software updates can consume a significant amount of the IT staff's time.

Using Windows Update

Make sure you learn about Windows Update, a service that allows you to connect to Microsoft's website and download what your system may need to bring it up to compliance. This tool is helpful if you are running a stand-alone system, but if you want to deploy software across the enterprise, the best way to accomplish this is first to test the updates you are downloading and make sure you can use them and that they are not bug ridden. Then you can use a tool such as the Windows Server Update Service (WSUS), which was formerly called the Software Update Services (SUS).

You can check for updates at Microsoft's website (http://update.microsoft.com). Microsoft likes to ask many types of questions about WSUS on its certification exams. WSUS is described in detail in other Sybex certification series books.

Phase 3: Removing Software   The end of the life cycle for many software products involves the actual removal of unused programs. Removing software is necessary when applications become outdated or when users no longer require their functionality. One of the traditional problems with uninstalling applications is that many of the installed files may not be removed. Furthermore, removing shared components can sometimes cause other programs to stop functioning properly. Also, users often forget to uninstall applications that they no longer need, and these programs continue to occupy disk space and consume valuable system resources.

The Microsoft Windows Installer (MSI) manages each of these three phases of the software maintenance life cycle. Now that you have an overview of the process, let's move forward to look at the steps involved in deploying software using Group Policy.

 The *Microsoft Windows Installer* (sometimes referred to as Microsoft Installer or Windows Installer) is an application installation and configuration service. An instruction file (the Microsoft Installer package) contains information about what needs to be done to install a product. It's common to confuse the two.

The Windows Installer

If you've installed newer application programs (such as Microsoft Office 2013), you've probably noticed the updated setup and installation routines. Applications that comply with the updated standard use the *Windows Installer specification* and MSI software packages for deployment. Each package contains information about various setup options and the files required for installation. Although the benefits may not seem dramatic on the surface, there's a lot of new functionality under the hood.

The Windows Installer was created to solve many of the problems associated with traditional application development. It has several components, including the Installer service (which runs on Windows 2000, XP, Vista, Windows 7, Windows 8, Windows Server 2003, Windows Server 2008, Windows Server 2008 R2, and Windows Server 2012 R2 computers), the Installer program (msiexec.exe) that is responsible for executing the instructions in a *Windows Installer package*, and the specifications third-party developers use to create their own packages. Within each installation package file is a relational structure (similar to the structure of tables in databases) that records information about the programs contained within the package.

To appreciate the true value of the Windows Installer, you'll need to look at some of the problems with traditional software deployment mechanisms and then at how the Windows Installer addresses many of them.

Application Installation Issues

Before the Windows Installer, applications were installed using a setup program that managed the various operations required for a program to operate. These operations included copying files, changing registry settings, and managing any other operating system changes that might be required (such as starting or stopping services). However, this method had several problems:

- The setup process was not robust, and aborting the operation often left many unnecessary files in the file system.

- The process included uninstalling an application (this also often left many unnecessary files in the file system) and remnants in the Windows registry and operating system folders. Over time, these remnants would result in reduced overall system performance and wasted disk space.

- There was no standard method for applying upgrades to applications, and installing a new version often required users to uninstall the old application, reboot, and then install the new program.

- Conflicts between different versions of *dynamic link libraries (DLLs)*—shared program code used across different applications—could cause the installation or removal of one application to break the functionality of another.

Benefits of the Windows Installer

Because of the many problems associated with traditional software installation, Microsoft created the *Windows Installer*. This system provides for better manageability of the software installation process and gives system administrators more control over the deployment process. Specifically, the Windows Installer provides the following benefits:

Improved Software Removal   The process of removing software is an important one because remnants left behind during the uninstall process can eventually clutter up the registry and file system. During the installation process, the Windows Installer keeps track of all of the changes made by a setup package. When it comes time to remove an application, all of these changes can then be rolled back.

More Robust Installation Routines   If a typical setup program is aborted during the software installation process, the results are unpredictable. If the actual installation hasn't yet begun, then the installer generally removes any temporary files that may have been created. However, if the file copy routine starts before the system encounters an error, it is likely that the files will not be removed automatically from the operating system. In contrast, the Windows Installer allows you to roll back any changes when the application setup process is aborted.

Ability to Use Elevated Privileges   Installing applications usually requires the user to have Administrator permissions on the local computer because file system and registry changes are required. When installing software for network users, system administrators have two options. First they can log off of the computer before installing the software and then log back on as a user who has Administrator permissions on the local computer. This method is tedious and time-consuming. The second option is to give users Administrator permissions temporarily on their own machines. This method could cause security problems and requires the attention of a system administrator.

Through the use of the Installer service, the Windows Installer is able to use temporarily elevated privileges to install applications. This allows users, regardless of their security settings, to execute the installation of authorized applications. This saves time and preserves security.

Support for Repairing Corrupted Applications   Regardless of how well a network environment is managed, critical files are sometimes lost or corrupted. Such problems can prevent applications from running properly and can cause crashes. Windows Installer packages provide you with the ability to verify the installation of an application and, if necessary, replace any missing or corrupted files. This support saves time and lessens end-user headaches associated with removing and reinstalling an entire application to replace just a few files.

Prevention of File Conflicts   Generally, different versions of the same files should be compatible with each other. In the real world, however, this isn't always the case. A classic problem in the Windows world is the case of one program replacing DLLs that are used by several other programs. Windows Installer accurately tracks which files are used by certain programs and ensures that any shared files are not improperly deleted or overwritten.

Automated Installations   A typical application setup process requires end users or system administrators to respond to several prompts. For example, a user may be able to choose the program group in which icons will be created and the file system location to which the program will be installed. Additionally, they may be required to choose which options are installed. Although this type of flexibility is useful, it can be tedious when you are rolling out multiple applications. By using features of the Windows Installer, however, users are able to specify setup options before the process begins. This allows system administrators to ensure consistency in installations, and it saves users' time.

Advertising and On-Demand Installations   One of the most powerful features of the Windows Installer is its ability to perform on-demand software installations. Prior to the Windows Installer, application installation options were quite basic—either a program was installed or it was not. When setting up a computer, system administrators would be required to guess which applications the user might need and install all of them.

The Windows Installer supports a function known as advertising. *Advertising* makes applications appear to be available via the Start menu. However, the programs themselves may not actually be installed on the system. When a user attempts to access an advertised application, the Windows Installer automatically downloads the necessary files from a server and installs the program. The result is that applications are installed only when they are needed, and the process requires no intervention from the end user. We'll cover the details of this process later in this chapter.

To anyone who has managed many software applications in a network environment, all of these features of the Windows Installer are likely welcome ones. They also make life easier for end users and applications developers; they can focus on the "real work" that their jobs demand.

Windows Installer File Types

When performing software deployment with the Windows Installer in Windows Server 2012 R2, you may encounter several different file types:

Microsoft Windows Installer Packages   To take full advantage of Windows Installer functionality, applications must include Microsoft Windows Installer (MSI) packages. Third-party application vendors and software developers normally create these packages, and they include the information required to install and configure the application and any supporting files.

Microsoft Transformation Files   *Microsoft Transformation (MST) files* are useful when you are customizing the details of how applications are installed. When a system administrator chooses to assign or publish an application, they may want to specify additional options for the package. For example, if a system administrator wants to allow users to install only the Microsoft Word and Microsoft PowerPoint components of Office 2013, they could specify these options within a transformation file. Then, when users install the application, they will be provided only with the options related to these components.

Microsoft Patches   To maintain software, patches are often required. Patches may make registry and/or file system changes. *Patch files (MSP)* are used for minor system changes and are subject to certain limitations. Specifically, a patch file cannot remove any installed program components and cannot delete or modify any shortcuts created by the user.

Initialization Files   To provide support for publishing non–Windows Installer applications, *initialization files* can be used. These files provide links to a standard executable file that is used to install an application. An example might be \\server1\software\program1\ setup.exe. These files can then be published and advertised, and users can access the *Programs and Features* icon to install them over the network.

Application Assignment Scripts   *Application assignment scripts (AAS)* store information regarding assigning programs and any settings that the system administrator makes. These files are created when Group Policy is used to create software package assignments for users and computers.

Each of these types of files provides functionality that allows the system administrator to customize software deployment. Windows Installer packages have special properties that you can view by right-clicking the file in Windows Explorer and choosing Properties (see Figure 7.9).

FIGURE 7.9 Viewing the properties of an MSI package file

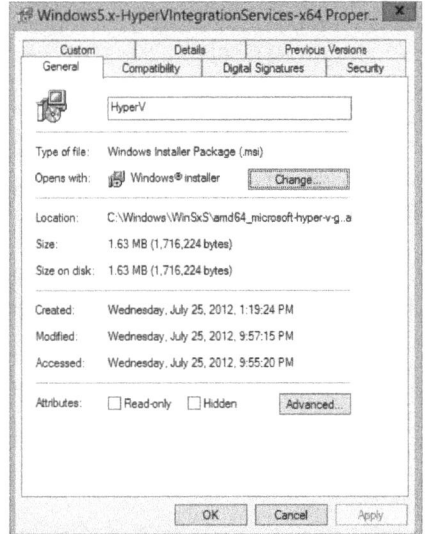

Deploying Applications

The functionality provided by Windows Installer offers many advantages to end users who install their own software. However, that is just the beginning in a networked environment. As you'll see later in this chapter, the various features of Windows Installer and compatible packages allow system administrators to determine centrally which applications users will be able to install.

There are two main methods of making programs available to end users using Active Directory: assigning and publishing. Both assigning and publishing applications greatly ease the process of deploying and managing applications in a network environment.

In the following sections, you'll look at how the processes of assigning and publishing applications can make life easier for IT staff and users alike. The various settings for assigned and published applications are managed through the use of GPOs.

Assigning Applications

Software applications can be assigned to users and computers. *Assigning* a software package makes the program available for automatic installation. The applications advertise their availability to the affected users or computers by placing icons within the Programs folder of the Start menu.

When applications are assigned to a user, programs will be advertised to the user regardless of which computer they are using. That is, icons for the advertised program will appear within the Start menu regardless of whether the program is installed on that computer. If the user clicks an icon for a program that has not yet been installed on the local computer, the application will automatically be accessed from a server and it will be installed.

When an application is assigned to a computer, the program is made available to any users of the computer. For example, all users who log on to a computer that has been assigned Microsoft Office 2013 will have access to the components of the application. If the user did not previously install Microsoft Office 2013, they will be prompted for any required setup information when the program first runs.

Generally, applications that are required by the vast majority of users should be assigned to computers. This reduces the amount of network bandwidth required to install applications on demand and improves the end-user experience by preventing the delay involved when installing an application the first time it is accessed. Any applications that may be used by only a few users (or those with specific job tasks) should be assigned to users.

Publishing Applications

When applications are *published*, they are advertised, but no icons are automatically created. Instead, the applications are made available for installation using the Add Or Remove Programs icon in Control Panel.

 Windows Vista, Windows 7, and Windows 8 do not have the Add Or Remove Programs feature. They use the Programs and Features icon in Control Panel to install the software.

Implementing Software Deployment

So far, you have become familiar with the issues related to software deployment and management from a theoretical level. Now it's time to drill down into the actual steps required to deploy software using the features of Active Directory and the GPMC. In the following sections, you will walk through the steps required to create an application distribution share point, to publish and assign applications, to update previously installed applications, to verify the installation of applications, and to update Windows operating systems.

Preparing for Software Deployment

Before you can install applications on client computers, you must make sure that the necessary files are available to end users. In many network environments, system administrators create shares on file servers that include the installation files for many applications. Based on security permissions, either end users or system administrators can then connect to these shares from a client computer and install the needed software. The efficient organization of these shares can save the help desk from having to carry around a library of CD-ROMs, and it allows you to install applications easily on many computers at once.

 One of the problems in network environments is that users frequently install applications whether or not they really need them. They may stumble upon applications that are stored on common file servers and install them out of curiosity. These actions can often decrease productivity and may violate software licensing agreements. You can help to avoid this by placing all of your application installation files in hidden shares (for example, software$).

Exercise 7.7 walks you through the process of creating a software distribution share point. In this exercise, you will prepare for software deployment by creating a directory share and placing certain types of files in this directory. To complete the steps in this exercise, you must have access to the Microsoft Office 2010 or Microsoft Office 2013 installation files (via CD-ROM or through a network share) and have 2000MB of free disk space. For this exercise, I used Microsoft Office 2010.

EXERCISE 7.7

Creating a Software Deployment Share

1. Using Windows Explorer, create a folder called Software that you can use with application sharing. Be sure that the volume on which you create this folder has at least 2000MB of available disk space.

2. Create a folder called Office 2010 within the Software folder.

3. Copy all the installation files for Microsoft Office 2010 from the CD-ROM or network share containing the files to the Office 2010 folder you created in step 2. If you prefer, you can use switches to install all the Office 2010 installation files. You can find these switches at http://technet.microsoft.com/en-us/library/ff521767.aspx.

4. Right-click the Software folder (created in step 1) and select Share. In the Choose People On Your Network To Share With dialog box, type **Everyone** and click the Add button. Next click the Share button. When you see a message that the sharing process is complete, click Done.

Once you have created an application distribution share, it's time to publish and assign the applications. This topic is covered next.

Software Restriction Policies

One of the biggest problems that we face as IT managers is that of users downloading and installing software. Many software packages don't cause any issues and are completely safe. Unfortunately, many software packages do have viruses and can cause problems. This is where software restriction policies can help. Software restriction policies help to identify software and to control its ability to run on a local computer, organizational unit, domain, or site.

Software restriction policies give administrators the ability to regulate unknown or untrusted software. Software restriction policies allow you to protect your computers from unwanted software by identifying and also specifying what software packages are allowed to be installed.

When configuring software restriction policies, an administrator is able to define a default security level of Unrestricted (software is allowed) or Disallowed (software is not allowed to run) for a GPO. Administrators can make exceptions to this default security level. They can create software restriction policy rules for specific software.

To create a software policy using the Group Policy Management Console, create a new GPO. In the GPO, expand the Windows Settings for either the user or computer configuration section, expand Security, right-click Software Restriction Policy, and choose New Software Restriction Policy. Set the policy for the level of security that you need.

Using AppLocker

AppLocker is a feature in Windows 7, Windows 8, and Windows Server 2012 R2. It is the replacement for Software Restriction Policies. *AppLocker* allows you to configure a Denied list and an Accepted list for applications. Applications that are configured on the Denied list will not run on the system, whereas applications on the Accepted list will operate properly.

The new capabilities and extensions of the AppLocker feature help reduce administrative overhead and help administrators control how users can access and use files, such as EXE files, scripts, Windows Installer files (MSI and MSP files), and DLLs.

Group Policy Slow Link Detection

When setting up GPOs, most of us assume that the connection speeds between servers and clients are going to be fast. In today's world, it is unlikely to see slow connections between locations, but they are still out there. Sometimes connection speeds can cause issues with the deployment of GPOs, specifically ones that are deploying software.

A setting in the Computer and User section of the GPO called *Group Policy Slow Link Detection* defines a slow connection for the purposes of applying and updating GPOs. If the data transfer rate from the domain controller providing the GPO to the computer is slower than what you have specified in this setting, the connection is considered to be a slow connection. If a connection is considered slow, the system response will vary depending on the policy. For example, if a GPO is going to deploy software and the connection is considered slow, the software may not be installed on the client computer. If you configure this option as 0, all connections are considered fast connections.

Publishing and Assigning Applications

As mentioned earlier in this section, system administrators can make software packages available to users by using publishing and assigning operations. Both of these operations allow system administrators to leverage the power of Active Directory and, specifically,

GPOs to determine which applications are available to users. Additionally, OUs can provide the organization that can help group users based on their job functions and software requirements.

The general process involves creating a GPO that includes software deployment settings for users and computers and then linking this GPO to Active Directory objects.

Exercise 7.8 walks you through the steps required to publish and assign applications. In this exercise, you will create applications and assign them to specific Active Directory objects using GPOs. To complete the steps in this exercise, you must have completed Exercise 7.7.

EXERCISE 7.8

Publishing and Assigning Applications Using Group Policy

1. Open the Active Directory Users and Computers tool from the Administrative Tools program group (using the Windows key).

2. Expand the domain and create a new top-level OU called **Software**.

3. Within the Software OU, create a user named **Jane User** with a login name of **juser** (choose the defaults for all other options).

4. Exit Active Directory Users and Computers and open the Group Policy Management Console.

5. Right-click the Software OU and choose Create A GPO In This Domain And Link It Here.

6. For the name of the new GPO, type **Software Deployment**.

7. To edit the Software Deployment GPO, right-click it and choose Edit. Expand the Computer Configuration ➢ Policies ➢ Software Settings object.

8. Right-click the Software Installation item and select New ➢ Package.

9. Navigate to the Software share you created in Exercise 7.7.

10. Within the Software share, double-click the Office 2010 folder and select the appropriate MSI file depending on the version of Office 2010 that you have. Office 2010 Professional is being used in this example, so you'll see that the OFFICEMUI.MSI file is chosen. Click Open.

11. In the Deploy Software dialog box, choose Advanced. (Note that the Published option is unavailable because applications cannot be published to computers.) Click OK to return to the Deploy Software dialog box.

12. To examine the deployment options of this package, click the Deployment tab. Accept the default settings by clicking OK.

13. Within the Group Policy Object Editor, expand the User Configuration ➢ Software Settings object.

EXERCISE 7.8 *(continued)*

14. Right-click the Software Installation item and select New ➢ Package.

15. Navigate to the Software share you created in Exercise 7.7.

16. Within the Software share, double-click the Office 2010 folder and select the appropriate MSI file. Click Open.

17. For the Software Deployment option, select Published in the Deploy Software dialog box and click OK.

18. Close the GPMC.

The overall process involved in deploying software using Active Directory is quite simple. However, you shouldn't let the intuitive graphical interface fool you—there's a lot of power under the hood of these software deployment features! Once you've properly assigned and published applications, it's time to see the effects of your work.

Applying Software Updates

The steps described in the previous section work only when you are installing a new application. However, software companies often release updates that you need to install on top of existing applications. These updates usually consist of bug fixes or other changes that are required to keep the software up-to-date. You can apply software updates in Active Directory by using the Upgrades tab of the software package Properties dialog box found in the Group Policy Object Editor.

In Exercise 7.9, you will apply a software update to an existing application. You should add the upgrade package to the GPO in the same way that you added the original application in steps 8 through 12 of Exercise 7.8. You should also have completed Exercise 7.8 before attempting this exercise.

EXERCISE 7.9

Applying Software Updates

1. Open the Group Policy Management Console from the Administrative Tools program group.

2. Click the Software OU, right-click the Software Deployment GPO, and choose Edit.

3. Expand the Computer Configuration ➢ Policies ➢ Software Settings ➢ Software Installation object.

4. Right-click the software package and select Properties from the context menu to bring up the Properties dialog box.

5. Select the Upgrades tab and click the Add button.

6. Click the Current Group Policy Object (GPO) radio button in the Choose A Package From section of the dialog box or click the Browse button to select the GPO to which you want to apply the upgrade. Consult your application's documentation to see whether you should choose the Uninstall The Existing Package, the Install The Upgrade Package radio button, or the Package Can Upgrade Over The Existing Package radio button.

7. Click Cancel to close the Add Upgrade Package dialog box.

8. Click Cancel and exit the GPMC.

You should understand that not all upgrades make sense in all situations. For instance, if the Stellacon 2010 files are incompatible with the Stellacon 2013 application, then your Stellacon 2012 users might not want you to perform the upgrade without taking additional steps to ensure that they can continue to use their files. In addition, users might have some choice about which version they use when it doesn't affect the support of the network.

Regardless of the underlying reason for allowing this flexibility, you should be aware that there are two basic types of upgrades that are available for administrators to provide to users:

Mandatory Upgrade   Forces everyone who currently has an existing version of the program to upgrade according to the GPO. Users who have never installed the program for whatever reason will be able to install only the new upgraded version.

Nonmandatory Upgrade   Allows users to choose whether they would like to upgrade. This upgrade type also allows users who do not have their application installed to choose which version they would like to use.

Verifying Software Installation

To ensure that the software installation settings you make in a GPO have taken place, you can log into the domain from a Windows 8, Windows 7, or Windows Vista computer that is within the OU to which the software settings apply. When you log in, you will notice two changes. First the application is installed on the computer (if it was not installed already). To access the application, a user needs to click one of the icons within the Program group of the Start menu. Note also that applications are available to any of the users who log on to this machine. Second, the settings apply to any computers that are contained within the OU and to any users who log on to these computers.

If you publish an application to users, the change may not be as evident, but it is equally useful. When you log on to a Windows 8, Windows 7, or Windows Vista computer that is a member of the domain, and when you use a user account from the OU where you published the application, you will be able to install any of the published applications automatically. On a Windows 8 or Windows 7 computer, you can do this by accessing the Programs icon in Control Panel. By clicking Add New Programs, you access a display of the applications available for installation. By clicking the Add button in the Programs and Features section of the Programs dialog box, you will automatically begin the installation of the published application.

Configuring Automatic Updates in Group Policy

So far you've seen the advantages of deploying application software in a group policy. Group policies also provide a way to install operating system updates across the network for Windows 2000, XP, Vista, Windows 7, Windows 8, Windows Server 2003, Windows Server 2008, Windows Server 2008 R2, and Windows Server 2012 R2 machines using Windows Update in conjunction with Windows Server Update Service. WSUS is the newer version of SUS, and it is used on a Windows Server 2012 R2 system to update systems. As you may remember, WSUS and SUS are patch-management tools that help you deploy updates to your systems in a controlled manner.

Windows Update is available through the Microsoft website, and it is used to provide the most current files for Windows operating systems. Examples of updates include security fixes, critical updates, updated help files, and updated drivers. You can access Windows Update by clicking the Windows Update icon in the system tray.

> We will discuss WSUS in greater detail in Chapter 1, "Manage and Maintain Servers."

WSUS is used to leverage the features of Windows Update within a corporate environment by downloading Windows updates to a corporate server, which in turn provides the updates to the internal corporate clients. This allows administrators to test and have full control over what updates are deployed within the corporate environment.

Within an enterprise network that is using Active Directory, you would typically see automatic updates configured through Group Policy. Group policies are used to manage configuration and security settings via Active Directory. Group Policy is also used to specify what server a client will use for automatic updates.

If the WSUS client is part of an enterprise network that is using Active Directory, you would configure the client via a group policy.

Configuring Software Deployment Settings

In addition to the basic operations of assigning and publishing applications, you can use several other options to specify the details of how software is deployed. In the following sections, you will examine the various options that are available and their effects on the software installation process.

The Software Installation Properties Dialog Box

The most important software deployment settings are contained in the Software Installation Properties dialog box, which you can access by right-clicking the Software Installation item and selecting Properties from the context menu. The following sections describe the features contained on the various tabs of the dialog box.

Managing Package Defaults

On the Deployment tab of the Software Installation Properties dialog box, you'll be able to specify some defaults for any packages that you create within this GPO. Figure 7.10 shows the Deployment options for managing software installation settings.

FIGURE 7.10   Deployment tab of the Software Installation Properties dialog box

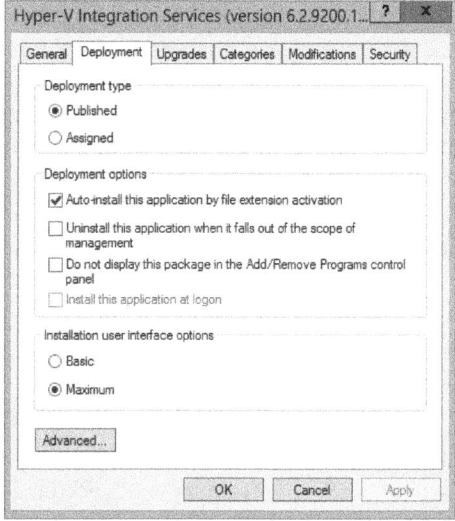

The following options are used for managing software installation settings:

Default Package Location   This setting specifies the default file system or network location for software installation packages. This is useful if you are already using a specific share on a file server for hosting the necessary installation files.

New Packages   These settings specify the default type of package assignment that will be used when you add a new package to either the user or computer settings. If you'll be assigning or publishing multiple packages, you may find it useful to set a default here. Selecting the Advanced option enables Group Policy to display the package's Properties dialog box each time a new package is added (see Figure 7.11).

FIGURE 7.11   Advanced Deployment dialog box

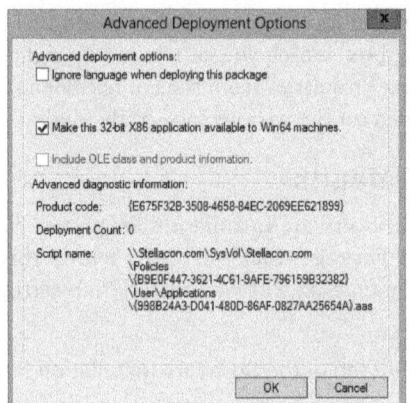

Installation User Interface Options   When installing an application, system administrators may or may not want end users to see all of the advanced installation options. If Basic is chosen, the user will only be able to configure the minimal settings (such as the installation location). If Maximum is chosen, all of the available installation options will be displayed. The specific installation options available will depend on the package itself.

Uninstall Applications When They Fall Out of the Scope of Management   So far, you have seen how applications can be assigned and published to users or computers. But what happens when effective GPOs change? For example, suppose User A is currently located within the Sales OU. A GPO that assigns the Microsoft Office 2013 suite of applications is linked to the Sales OU. You decide to move User A to the Engineering OU, which has no software deployment settings. Should the application be uninstalled, or should it remain?

If the Uninstall This Application When It Falls Out Of The Scope Of Management option is checked, applications will be removed if they are not specifically assigned or published within GPOs. In this example, this means that Office 2013 would be uninstalled for User A. If this box is left unchecked, however, the application will remain installed.

Managing File Extension Mappings

One of the potential problems associated with using many different file types is that it's difficult to keep track of which applications work with which files. For example, if you received a file with the filename extension .abc, you would have no idea which application you would need to view it.

Fortunately, through software deployment settings, system administrators can specify mappings for specific *filename extensions*. For example, you could specify that whenever users attempt to access a file with the extension .vsd, the operating system should attempt to open the file using Visio diagramming software. If Visio is not installed on the user's machine, the computer can automatically download and install it (assuming that the application has been properly advertised).

This method allows users to have applications automatically installed when they are needed. The following is an example of a sequence of events that might occur:

1. A user receives an email message that contains a PDF (.pdf) file attachment.

2. The computer realizes that the PDF file does not have the appropriate viewing application for this type of file installed. However, it also realizes that a filename extension mapping is available within the Active Directory software deployment settings.

3. The client computer automatically requests the PDF software package from the server, and it uses the Microsoft Windows Installer to install the application automatically.

4. The computer opens the attachment for the user.

Notice that all of these steps were carried out without any further interaction with the user.

You can manage filename extension mappings by right-clicking the Software Installation item, selecting Properties, and then clicking the File Extensions tab.

Creating Application Categories

In many network environments, the list of supported applications can include hundreds of items. For users who are looking for only one specific program, searching through a list of all of these programs can be difficult and time-consuming.

Fortunately, methods for categorizing the applications are available on your network. You can easily manage the application categories for users and computers by right-clicking the Software Installation item, selecting Properties, and then clicking the Categories tab.

Figure 7.12 shows you the categories tab of the Software Installation package. When creating categories, it is a good idea to use category names that are meaningful to users because it will make it easier for them to find the programs they're seeking.

FIGURE 7.12 The Categories tab of the Software Installation Properties dialog box

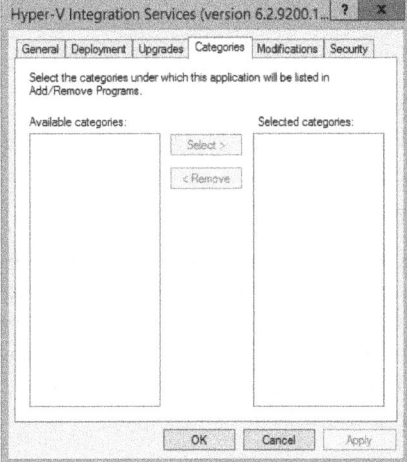

Once the software installation categories have been created, you can view them by clicking the Programs or Programs And Features icon in Control Panel. When you click Add New Programs, you'll see that several options appear in the Category drop-down list. Now when you select the properties for a package, you will be able to assign the application to one or more of the categories.

Removing Programs

As discussed in the beginning of the chapter, an important phase in the software management life cycle is the removal of applications. Fortunately, if you use the GPMC and the Windows Installer packages, the process is simple. To remove an application, you can right-click the package within the Group Policy settings and select All Tasks ➢ Remove (see Figure 7.13).

FIGURE 7.13   Removing a software package

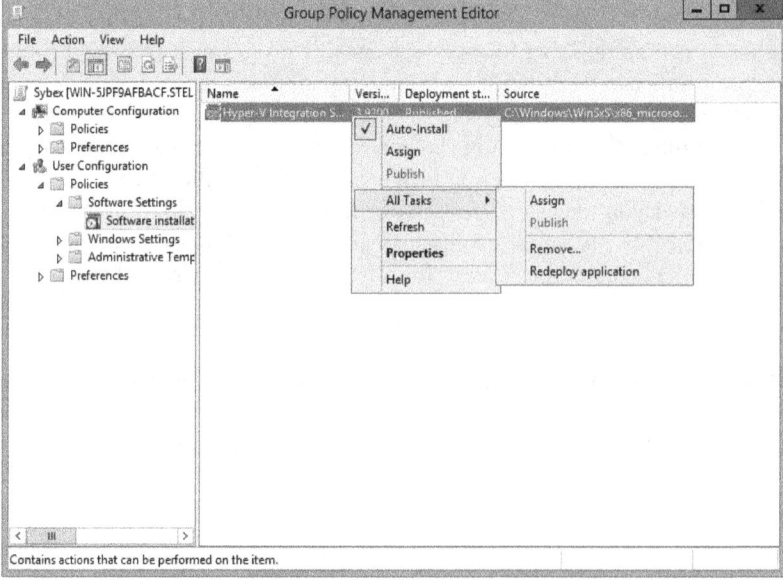

When choosing to remove a software package from a GPO, you have two options:

Immediately Uninstall The Software From Users And Computers   System administrators can choose this option to ensure that an application is no longer available to users who are affected by the GPO. When this option is selected, the program will be uninstalled automatically from users and/or computers that have the package. This option might be useful, for example, if the license for a certain application has expired or if a program is no longer on the approved applications list.

Allow Users To Continue To Use The Software, But Prevent New Installations This option prevents users from making new installations of a package, but it does not remove the software if it has already been installed for users. This is a good option if the company has run out of additional licenses for the software, but the existing licenses are still valid.

Figure 7.14 shows these two removal options.

FIGURE 7.14 Software removal options

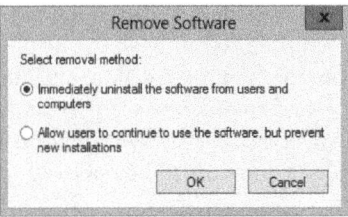

If you no longer require the ability to install or repair an application, you can delete it from your software distribution share point by deleting the appropriate Windows Installer package files. This will free up additional disk space for newer applications.

Microsoft Windows Installer Settings

Several options influence the behavior of the Windows Installer; you can set them within a GPO. You can access these options by navigating to User Configuration ➤ Administrative Templates ➤ Windows Components ➤ Windows Installer (see Figure 7.15). The options are as follows:

FIGURE 7.15 GPO settings for Windows Installer

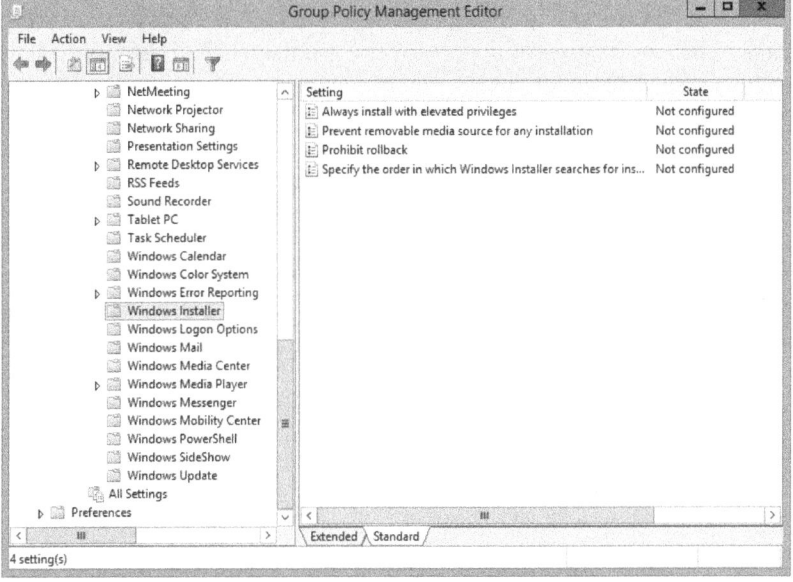

Always Install With Elevated Privileges   This policy allows users to install applications that require elevated privileges. For example, if a user does not have the permissions necessary to modify the registry but the installation program must make registry changes, this policy will allow the process to succeed.

Prevent Removable Media Source For Any Install   This option disallows the installation of software using removable media (such as CD-ROM or DVD-ROM). It is useful for ensuring that users install only approved applications.

Prohibit Rollback   When this option is enabled, the Windows Installer does not store the system state information that is required to roll back the installation of an application. System administrators may choose this option to reduce the amount of temporary disk space required during installation and to increase the performance of the installation operation. However, the drawback is that the system cannot roll back to its original state if the installation fails and the application needs to be removed.

Specify the Order In Which Windows Installer Searches   This setting specifies the order in which the Windows Installer will search for installation files. The options include n (for network shares), m (for searching removal media), and u (for searching the Internet for installation files).

With these options, system administrators can control how the Windows Installer operates for specific users who are affected by the GPO.

Troubleshooting Group Policies

Because of the wide variety of configurations that are possible when you are establishing GPOs, you should be aware of some common troubleshooting methods. These methods will help isolate problems in policy settings or GPO links.

One possible problem with GPO configuration is that logons and system startups may take a long time. This occurs especially in large environments when the Group Policy settings must be transmitted over the network and, in many cases, slow WAN links. In general, the number of GPOs should be limited because of the processing overhead and network requirements during logon. By default, GPOs are processed in a synchronous manner. This means that the processing of one GPO must be completed before another one is applied (as opposed to asynchronous processing, where they can all execute at the same time).

When a group policy gets processed on a Windows-based operating system, client-side extensions are the mechanisms that interpret the stored policy and then make the appropriate changes to the operating system environment. When an administrator is troubleshooting a given extension's application of policy, the administrator can view the configuration parameters for that extension in the operating system's registry. To view the extension in the registry, you would view the following key:

```
HKEY_LOCAL_MACHINE\Software\Microsoft\Windows CA
NT\CurrentVersion\Winlogon\GPExtensions
```

The most common issue associated with Group Policy is the unexpected setting of Group Policy options. In Windows Server 2000, administrators spent countless hours analyzing inheritance hierarchy and individual settings to determine why a particular user or computer was having policy problems. For instance, say a user named wpanek complains that the Run option is missing from his Start menu. The wpanek user account is stored in the New Hampshire OU, and you've applied group policies at the OU, domain, and site levels. To determine the source of the problem, you would have to sift through each GPO manually to find the Start menu policy as well as to figure out the applicable inheritance settings.

Windows Server 2012 R2 has a handy feature called *Resultant Set of Policy (RSoP)* that displays the exact settings that actually apply to individual users, computers, OUs, domains, and sites after inheritance and filtering have taken effect. In the example just described, you could run RSoP on the wpanek account and view a single set of Group Policy settings that represent the settings that apply to the wpanek account. In addition, each setting's Properties dialog box displays the GPO from which the setting is derived as well as the order of priority, the filter status, and other useful information, as you will see a bit later.

RSoP actually runs in two modes:

Logging Mode   *Logging mode* displays the actual settings that apply to users and computers, as shown in the example in the preceding paragraph.

Planning Mode   *Planning mode* can be applied to users, computers, OUs, domains, and sites, and you use it before you apply any settings. As its name implies, planning mode is used to plan GPOs.

Additionally, you can run the command-line utility gpresult.exe to get a quick snapshot of the Group Policy settings that apply to a user and/or computer. Let's take a closer look at the two modes and the gpresult.exe command.

RSoP in Logging Mode

RSoP in logging mode can query policy settings only for users and computers. The easiest way to access RSoP in logging mode is through the Active Directory Users and Computers tool, although you can run it as a stand-alone MMC snap-in if you want.

To analyze the policy settings for wpanek from the earlier example, you would right-click the user icon in Active Directory Users and Computers and select All Tasks ➢ Resultant Set of Policy (Logging). The Group Policy Results Wizard appears. The wizard walks you through the steps necessary to view the RSoP for wpanek.

The Computer Selection page, shown in Figure 7.16, requires you to select a computer for which to display settings. Remember that a GPO contains both user and computer settings, so you must choose a computer to which the user is logged on in order to continue with the wizard. If the user has never logged on to a computer, then you must run RSoP in planning mode because there is no logged policy information yet for that user.

FIGURE 7.16   The Computer Selection page of the Group Policy Results Wizard

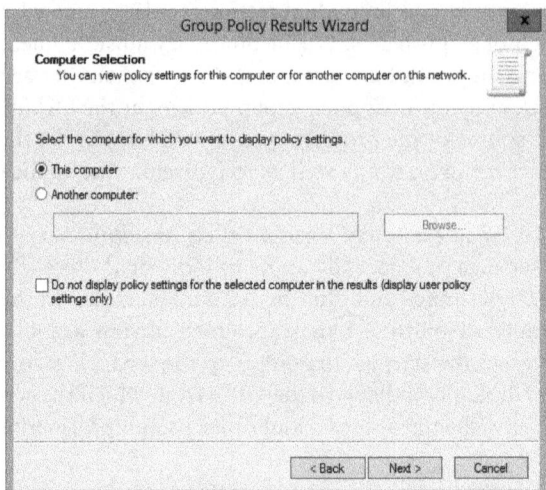

The User Selection page, shown in Figure 7.17, requires you to select a user account to analyze. Because I selected a user from the Active Directory Users and Computers tool, the username is filled in automatically. This page is most useful if you are running RSoP in MMC mode and don't have the luxury of selecting a user contextually.

FIGURE 7.17   The User Selection page of the Group Policy Results Wizard

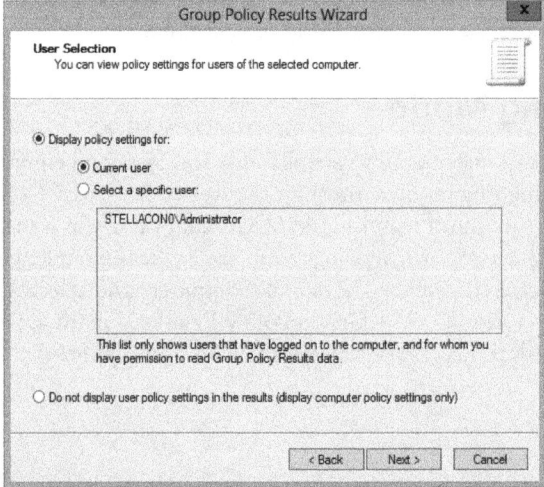

The Summary Of Selections page, shown in Figure 7.18, displays a summary of your choices and provides an option for gathering extended error information. If you need to make any changes before you begin to analyze the policy settings, you should click the Back button on the Summary screen. Otherwise, click Next.

FIGURE 7.18   The Summary Of Selections page of the Group Policy Results Wizard

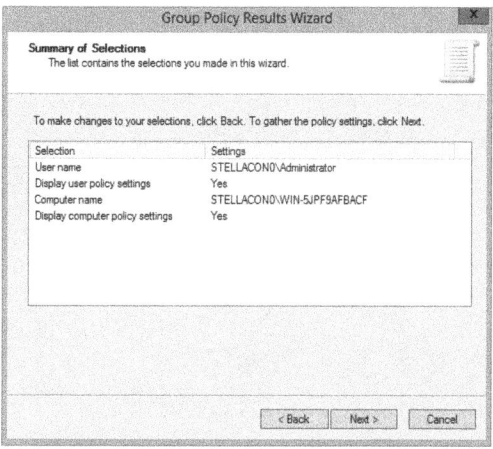

After the wizard is complete, you will see the window shown in Figure 7.19. This window displays only the policy settings that apply to the user and computer that you selected in the wizard. You can see these users and computers at the topmost level of the tree.

FIGURE 7.19   The User Selection page for the administrator on computer SERVER1

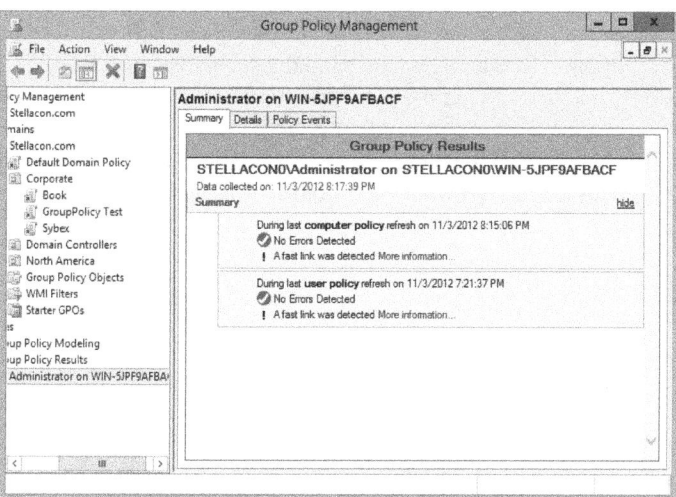

Any warnings or errors appear as a yellow triangle or red *X* over the applicable icon at the level where the warning or error occurred. To view more information about the warning or error, right-click the icon, select Properties, and select the Error Information tab. Figure 7.20 shows an error message.

FIGURE 7.20 Details of event pertaining to the administrator account on computer SERVER1

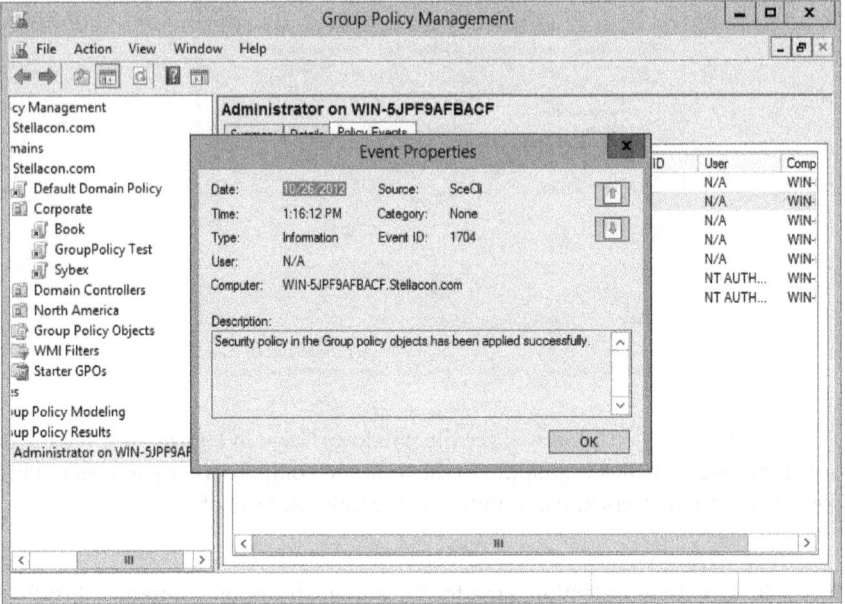

You cannot make changes to any of the individual settings because RSoP is a diagnostic tool and not an editor, but you can get more information about settings by clicking a setting and selecting Properties from the context menu.

The Details tab of the user's Properties window, shown in Figure 7.21, displays the actual setting that applies to the user in question based on GPO inheritance.

FIGURE 7.21   The Details tab of the object's Properties window

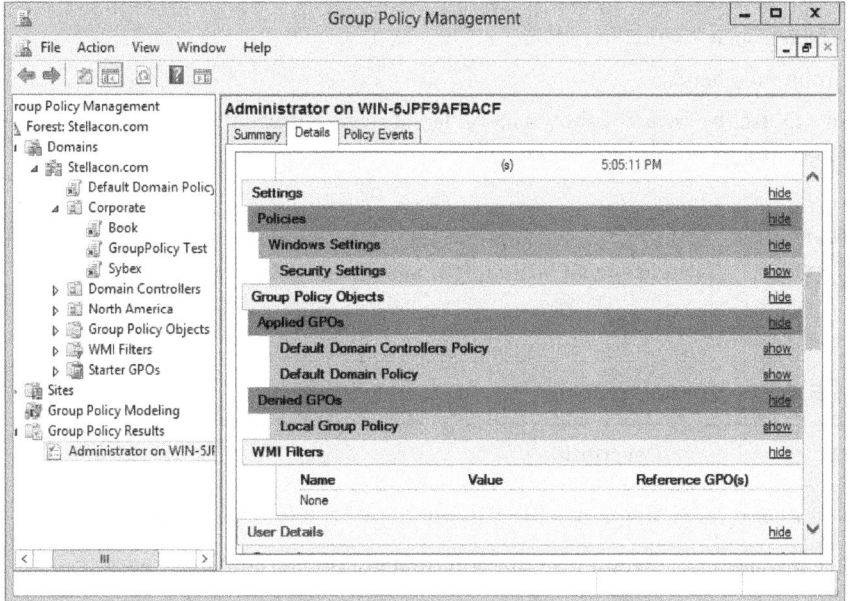

RSoP in Planning Mode

Running RSoP in planning mode isn't much different from running RSoP in logging mode, but the RSoP Wizard asks for a bit more information than you saw earlier.

In the former example, wpanek couldn't see the Run option in the Start menu because the New Hampshire GPO in the San Jose OU affects his user account. As an administrator, you could plan to move his user account to the North America OU. Before doing so, you could verify his new policy settings by running RSoP in planning mode. Run the RSoP on the user wpanek under the scenario that you've already moved him from the San Jose OU to the North America OU. At this point, you haven't actually moved the user, but you can see what his settings would be if you did.

Using the *gpresult.exe* Command

The command-line utility gpresult.exe is included as part of the RSoP tool. Running the command by itself without any switches returns the following Group Policy information about the local user and computer:

- The name of the domain controller from which the local machine retrieved the policy information

- The date and time in which the policies were applied
- Which policies were applied
- Which policies were filtered out
- Group membership

You can use the switches shown in Table 7.3 to get information for remote users and computers and to enable other options.

 Table 7.3 is not a complete list. To see a complete list of the gpresult.exe switches, visit Microsoft at www.microsoft.com.

TABLE 7.3   gpresult switches

Switch	Description
/S *systemname*	Generates RSoP information for a remote computer name.
/USER *username*	Generates RSoP information for a remote username.
/x /h *filename*	Generates a report in either XML (/x) or HTML (/h) format. The filename and location is specified by the *filename* parameter.
/V	Specifies verbose mode, which displays more verbose information such as user rights information.
/Z	Specifies an even greater level of verbose information.
/SCOPE MACHINE	Displays maximum information about the computer policies applied to this system.
/SCOPE USER	Displays maximum information about the user policies applied to this system.
>*textfile.txt*	Writes the output to a text file.

For example, to obtain information about user wpanek in a system called STELLACON, you would use the command gpresult/S STELLACON/USERwpanek.

Through the use of these techniques, you should be able to track down even the most elusive Group Policy problems. Remember, however, that good troubleshooting skills do not replace planning adequately and maintaining GPO settings!

Summary

In this chapter, you examined Active Directory's solution to a common headache for many systems administrators: policy settings. Specifically, I discussed topics that covered Group Policy.

I covered the fundamentals of Group Policy, including its fundamental purpose. You can use Group Policy to enforce granular permissions for users in an Active Directory environment. Group policies can restrict and modify the actions allowed for users and computers within the Active Directory environment.

Certain Group Policy settings may apply to users, computers, or both. Computer settings affect all users who access the machines to which the policy applies. User settings affect users regardless of the machines to which they log on.

You learned that you can link Group Policy objects to Active Directory sites, domains, or OUs. This link determines to which objects the policies apply. GPO links can interact through inheritance and filtering to result in an effective set of policies.

The chapter covered inheritance and how GPOs filter down. I showed you how to use the Enforced option on a GPO issued from a parent and how to block a GPO from a child.

You can also use administrative templates to simplify the creation of GPOs. There are some basic default templates that come with Windows Server 2012 R2.

In addition, administrators can delegate control over GPOs in order to distribute administrative responsibilities. Delegation is an important concept because it allows for distributed administration.

You can also deploy software using GPOs. This feature can save time and increase productivity throughout the entire software management life cycle by automating software installation and removal on client computers. The Windows Installer offers a more robust method for managing installation and removal, and applications that support it can take advantage of new Active Directory features. Make sure you are comfortable using the Windows Installer.

You learned about publishing applications via Active Directory and the difference between publishing and assigning applications. You can assign some applications to users and computers so that they are always available. You can also publish them to users so that the user can install them with minimal effort when required.

You also learned how to prepare for software deployment. Before your users can take advantage of automated software installation, you must set up an installation share and provide the appropriate permissions.

The final portion of the chapter covered the Resultant Set of Policy (RSoP) tool, which you can use in logging mode or planning mode to determine exactly which set of policies apply to users, computers, OUs, domains, and sites.

Exam Essentials

Understand the purpose of Group Policy.   System administrators use Group Policy to enforce granular permissions for users in an Active Directory environment.

Understand user and computer settings.   Certain Group Policy settings may apply to users, computers, or both. Computer settings affect all users who access the machines to which the policy applies. User settings affect users, regardless of the machines to which they log on.

Know the interactions between Group Policy objects and Active Directory.   GPOs can be linked to Active Directory objects. This link determines to which objects the policies apply.

Understand filtering and inheritance interactions between GPOs.   For ease of administration, GPOs can interact via inheritance and filtering. It is important to understand these interactions when you are implementing and troubleshooting Group Policy.

Know how Group Policy settings can affect script policies and network settings.   You can use special sets of GPOs to manage network configuration settings.

Understand how delegation of administration can be used in an Active Directory environment.   Delegation is an important concept because it allows for distributed administration.

Know how to use the Resultant Set of Policy (RSoP) tool to troubleshoot and plan Group Policy.   Windows Server 2012 R2 includes the RSoP feature, which you can run in logging mode or planning mode to determine exactly which set of policies applies to users, computers, OUs, domains, and sites.

Identify common problems with the software life cycle.   IT professionals face many challenges with client applications, including development, deployment, maintenance, and troubleshooting.

Understand the benefits of the Windows Installer.   Using the Windows Installer is an updated way to install applications on Windows-based machines. It offers a more robust method for making the system changes required by applications, and it allows for a cleaner uninstall. Windows Installer–based applications can also take advantage of new Active Directory features.

Understand the difference between publishing and assigning applications.   Some applications can be assigned to users and computers so that they are always available. Applications can be published to users so that the user may install the application with a minimal amount of effort when it is required.

Know how to prepare for software deployment.   Before your users can take advantage of automated software installation, you must set up an installation share and provide the appropriate permissions.

Know how to configure application settings using Active Directory and Group Policy. Using standard Windows Server 2012 R2 administrative tools, you can create an application policy that meets your requirements. You can use automatic, on-demand installation of applications as well as many other features.

Create application categories to simplify the list of published applications. It's important to group applications by functionality or the users to whom they apply, especially in organizations that support a large number of programs.

Review Questions

1. The process of assigning permissions to set Group Policy for objects within an OU is known as:

   A. Promotion

   B. Inheritance

   C. Delegation

   D. Filtering

2. Which of the following statements is true regarding the actions that occur when a software package is removed from a GPO that is linked to an OU?

   A. The application will be automatically uninstalled for all users within the OU.

   B. Current application installations will be unaffected by the change.

   C. The system administrator may determine the effect.

   D. The current user may determine the effect.

3. You are the network administrator for your organization. You are working on creating a new GPO for the sales OU. You want the GPO to take effect immediately. Which command would you use?

   A. GPForce

   B. GPUpdate

   C. GPResult

   D. GPExecute

4. You are the network administrator for your organization. You are working on creating a new GPO for the Marketing OU. You want the GPO to take effect immediately, and you need to use Windows PowerShell. Which PowerShell cmdlet command would you use?

   A. Invoke-GPUpdate

   B. Invoke-GPForce

   C. Invoke-GPResult

   D. Invoke-GPExecute

5. You are the network administrator, and you have decided to set up a GPO with item-level targeting. Which of the following is *not* an option for item-level targeting?

   A. Battery Present Targeting

   B. Computer Name Targeting

   C. CPU Speed Targeting

   D. DVD Present Targeting

6. You are the network administrator for a large organization that uses Windows Server 2012 R2 domain controllers and DNS servers. All of your client machines currently have the Windows XP operating system. You want to be able to have client computers edit the domain-based GPOs by using the ADMX files that are located in the ADMX Central Store. How do you accomplish this task? (Choose all that apply.)

   A. Upgrade your clients to Windows 8.

   B. Upgrade your clients to Windows 7.

   C. Add the client machines to the ADMX edit utility.

   D. In the ADMX store, choose the box Allow All Client Privileges.

7. You work for an organization with a single Windows Server 2012 R2 Active Directory domain. The domain has OUs for Sales, Marketing, Admin, R&D, and Finance. You need the users in the Finance OU only to get Microsoft Office 2010 installed automatically onto their computers. You create a GPO named OfficeApp. What is the next step in getting all of the Finance users Office 2010?

   A. Edit the GPO, and assign the Office application to the user's account. Link the GPO to the Finance OU.

   B. Edit the GPO, and assign the Office application to the user's account. Link the GPO to the domain.

   C. Edit the GPO, and assign the Office application to the computer account. Link the GPO to the domain.

   D. Edit the GPO, and assign the Office application to the computer account. Link the GPO to the Finance OU.

8. You are hired as a consultant to the ABC Company. The owner of the company complains that she continues to have desktop wallpaper that she did not choose. When you speak with the IT team, you find out that a former employee created 20 GPOs and they have not been able to figure out which GPO is changing the owner's desktop wallpaper. How can you resolve this issue?

   A. Run the RSoP utility against all forest computer accounts.

   B. Run the RSoP utility against the owner's computer account.

   C. Run the RSoP utility against the owner's user account.

   D. Run the RSoP utility against all domain computer accounts.

9. You are the network administrator for a large organization that has multiple sites and multiple OUs. You have a site named SalesSite that is for the sales building across the street. In the domain, there is an OU for all salespeople called Sales. You set up a GPO for the SalesSite, and you need to be sure that it applies to the Sales OU. The Sales OU GPOs cannot override the SalesSite GPO. What do you do?

   A. On the GPO, disable the Block Child Inheritance setting.

   B. On the GPO, set the Enforce setting.

   C. On the GPO, set the priorities to 1.

   D. On the Sales OU, set the Inherit Parent Policy settings.

10. You are the administrator for an organization that has multiple locations. You are running Windows Server 2012 R2, and you have only one domain with multiple OUs set up for each location. One of your locations, Boston, is connected to the main location by a 256Kbps ISDN line. You configure a GPO to assign a sales application to all computers in the entire domain. You have to be sure that Boston users receive the GPO properly. What should you do?

A. Disable the Slow Link Detection setting in the GPO.

B. Link the GPO to the Boston OU.

C. Change the properties of the GPO to publish the application to the Boston OU.

D. Have the users in Boston run the GPResult/force command.

Appendix A

Answers to Review Questions

Chapter 1: Manage and Maintain Servers

1. D. All of the applications that are running on the Windows Server 2012 R2 machine will show up on the Details tab. Right-click the application and end the process.

2. A. If you use MBSA from the command-line utility `mdsacli.exe`, you can specify several options. You type **`mdsacli.exe/hf`** (from the folder that contains Mdsacli.exe) and then customize the command execution with an option such as */ixxxx.xxxx.xxxx.xxxx*, which specifies that the computer with the specified IP address should be scanned.

3. B and E. You can set the registry key `HKEY_LOCAL_MACHINE\Software\Policies\Microsoft\Windows\WindowsUpdate\AU\UseWUServer` to 0 to use the public Windows Update server, or you can set it to 1, which means that you will specify the server for Windows Update in the `HKEY_LOCAL_MACHINE\Software\Policies\Microsoft\Windows\WindowsUpdate` key. The `WUServer` key sets the Windows Update server using the server's HTTP name, for example, `http://intranetSUS`.

4. C. Server Manager is the one place where you install all roles and features for a Windows Server 2012 R2 system.

5. C. All options are valid steps to complete the configuration except option C because SERVERB cannot automatically draw updates from whichever sources are on SERVERA.

6. B, D, and F. Option A schedules the updates to occur at a time when the computers are generally not connected to the corporate network. Options C and E require more user interaction than would be considered minimal. By setting updates to occur with no user interaction at noon, you satisfy the requirements.

7. D. You can recover system state data from a backup, which always includes the Active Directory database. In this case, Event Viewer and System Monitor wouldn't help you recover the database, but they might help you determine why the hard drive crashed in the first place.

8. D. By using the Network Monitor, you can view all of the network packets that are being sent to or from the local server. Based on this information, you can determine the source of certain types of traffic, such as pings. The other types of monitoring can provide useful information, but they do not allow you to drill down into the specific details of a network packet, and they don't allow you to filter the data that has been collected based on details about the packet.

9. A. Microsoft Baseline Security Analyzer is a free download that you can get from Microsoft's website.

10. C. The Update Source And Proxy Server option allows you to specify where you will be receiving your updates (from Microsoft or another WSUS server) and your proxy settings if a proxy server is needed.

Chapter 2: Manage File Services

1. C. You need to publish shares in the directory before they are available to the users of the directory. If NetBIOS is still enabled on the network, the shares will be visible to the NetBIOS tools and clients, but you do not have to enable NetBIOS on shares. Although replication must occur before the shares are available in the directory, it is unlikely that the replication will not have occurred by the next day. If this is the case, then you have other problems with the directory as well.

2. A. The Sharing tab contains a check box that you can use to list the printer in Active Directory.

3. B, E, G and H. The Active Directory Users and Computers tool allows system administrators to change auditing options and to choose which actions are audited. At the file system level, Isabel can specify exactly which actions are recorded in the audit log. She can then use Event Viewer to view the recorded information and provide it to the appropriate managers.

4. B. Offline files give you the opportunity to set up files and folders so that users can work on the data while outside the

5. A, B, C and D. Improved security, quotas, compression, and encryption are all advantages of using NTFS over FAT32. These features are not available in FAT32. The only security you have in FAT32 is shared folder permissions.

6. A. Encrypting File System (EFS) allows a user or administrator to secure files or folders by using encryption. Encryption employs the user's security identification (SID) number to secure the file or folder. Encryption is the strongest protection that Windows provides.

7. B. Disk quotas allow you to limit the amount of space on a volume or partition. You can set an umbrella quota for all users and then implement individual users' quotas to bypass the umbrella quota.

8. B. Cipher is a command-line utility that allows you to configure or change EFS files and folders.

9. B. The Distributed File System (DFS) Namespace service in Windows Server 2012 R2 offers a simplified way for users to access geographically dispersed files. DFS allows you to set up a tree structure of virtual directories to allow users to connect to shared folders throughout the entire network.

10. D. File servers are used for storage of data, especially for users' home folders. Home folders are folder locations for your users to store data that is important and that needs to be backed up.

Chapter 3: Configure DNS

1. B. Because of the `.(root)` zone, users will not be able to access the Internet. The DNS forwarding option and DNS root hints will not be configurable. If you want your users to access the Internet, you must remove the `.(root)` zone.

2. C. Active Directory Integrated zones store their records in Active Directory. Because this company has only one Active Directory forest, it's the same Active Directory that both DNS servers are using. This allows ServerA to see all of the records of ServerB and allows ServerB to see all the records of ServerA.

3. D. The Secure Only option is for DNS servers that have an Active Directory Integrated zone. When a computer tries to register with DNS dynamically, the DNS server checks Active Directory to verify that the computer has an Active Directory account. If the computer that is trying to register has an account, DNS adds the host record. If the computer trying to register does not have an account, the record gets tossed away and the database is not updated.

4. A. If you need to complete a zone transfer from Microsoft DNS to a BIND (Unix) DNS server, you need to enable BIND Secondaries on the Microsoft DNS server.

5. B. Conditional forwarding allows you to send a DNS query to different DNS servers based on the request. Conditional forwarding lets a DNS server on a network forward DNS queries according to the DNS domain name in the query.

6. B. On a Windows Server 2012 R2 DNS machine, debug logging is disabled by default. When it is enabled, you have the ability to log DNS server activity, including inbound and outbound queries, packet type, packet content, and transport protocols.

7. D. Active Directory Integrated zones give you many benefits over using primary and secondary zones including less network traffic, secure dynamic updates, encryption, and reliability in the event of a DNS server going down. The Secure Only option is for dynamic updates to a DNS database.

8. A. Windows Server 2012 R2 DNS supports two features called DNS Aging and DNS Scavenging. These features are used to clean up and remove stale resource records. DNS zone or DNS server aging and scavenging flags old resource records that have not been updated in a certain amount of time (determined by the scavenging interval). These stale records will be scavenged at the next cleanup interval.

9. C. The dnscmd /zoneexport command creates a file using the zone resource records. This file can then be given to the Compliance department as a copy.

10. D. Stub zones are useful for slow WAN connections. These zones store only three types of resource records: NS records, glue host (A) records, and SOA records. These three records are used to locate authoritative DNS servers.

Chapter 5: Configure Routing and Remote Access

1. B. The boot threshold for an interface controls how long the relay agent will wait before forwarding DHCP requests it hears on that interface.

2. B. Multilink PPP has nothing to do with encryption of data. Multilink is easy to set up, relatively low in cost, and it makes the connection faster.

3. C and E. MS-CHAPv2 provides encrypted and mutual authentication between the respective RRAS locations. MPPE works with MS-CHAPv2 and provides encryption for all of the data between the locations. CHAP provides encrypted authentication, but MS-CHAPv2 is needed for MPPE to work. PAP is the lowest level of authentication providing passwords, but it sends passwords in cleartext, which is not the most secure solution. L2TP needs to team up with IPsec to provide the data encryption for the secure transfer of information between the locations.

4. B. MS-CHAPv2 authentication allows you to create VPN connections with a stand-alone server using PPTP and MPPE. MPPE employs keys that are created via MS-CHAPv2 or EAP-TLS authentication. EAP-TLS is not the correct answer because only domain controllers or member servers support EAP-TLS. Stand-alone servers support only MPPE. Neither PAP nor CHAP is supported with MPPE.

5. A and C. L2TP connections can be used to authenticate both sides of the VPN. L2TP needs IPsec to provide the encryption for the connection. These two together will provide the secure and authenticated transmission of data across the Internet between the two sites. PPTP connections provide encryption using only MPPE, but they don't provide authentication between the machines. RADIUS is a service that provides dial-in connectivity. MS-CHAPv2 is an authentication protocol for clients accessing the network.

6. B. L2TP and IPsec each has its own negotiation procedure for making a connection. If you remove the IPsec portion of the connection and the problem is alleviated, it is likely that IPsec is the problem, and you can then focus on IPsec. If the problem remains, you can work on the L2TP portion of the connection. IPsec has two modes: tunnel mode and transport mode. But because L2TP is a tunneling protocol, there is no sense in using IPsec tunneling. IPsec transport mode is used with L2TP and should be set aside for troubleshooting, as discussed. The L2TP implementation in Windows Server 2012 R2 doesn't support MPPE.

7. C. The default configuration for RRAS supports 5 PPTP ports and 5 L2TP ports. There are up to 150 sales reps trying to connect to the server, but only the first 10 will be able to connect. You can increase the number of ports available, up to 1,000, by using the Ports Properties dialog box. The Windows 8 clients are, by default, ready to support VPNs; they will first try L2TP and then switch over to PPTP if ports are unavailable.

8. C, E and G. Because the communication is not a continuous or frequent occurrence, it doesn't make sense to have the line always available, so RRAS with demand-dial will be less expensive than ISDN, which is always up. MS-CHAPv2 provides encryption and a mutual authentication process. The MPPE provides the encryption of the actual data that travels across the connection. PAP is a cleartext authentication method, and CHAP provides only one-way authentication. L2TP doesn't provide any encryption by itself.

9. C. When you use Windows accounting, the local Windows account logs are found in the *systemroot*\System32\LogFiles folder. These logs can be stored in one of two formats for later analysis—Open Database Connectivity (ODBC) or Internet Authentication Service. The Performance Monitor utility that came with Windows NT has been replaced with the system event log. This keeps track of global service errors such as initialization failures and service starts and stops. There is no RRAS authentication log. You do have RADIUS logging available; when it's used, the log files are stored on the RADIUS servers. This is useful when you have multiple RRAS servers because you can centralize RRAS authentication requests. Active Directory is not used to log events from the various services in Windows Server 2012 R2.

10. B. The Server Status node in the RRAS snap-in shows you a summary of all the RRAS servers known to the system. Each server entry displays whether the server is up, what kind of server it is, how many ports it has, how many ports are currently in use, and how long the server has been up.

Chapter 6: Configure a Network Policy Server Infrastructure

1. B and E. By setting the Network Policy Server, you can force your DHCP users to use NAP on all of the DHCP scopes. This ensures that client systems meet minimum requirements to connect to a domain network.

2. D. Servers that are running Network Policy Server (NPS) are required to have a certificate installed on the NPS server.

3. B. One advantage of using NAP for DHCP is that you can set up user classes so that specific machines (for example, noncompliant DHCP systems) can get specific rules or limited access to the network.

4.   D. Logman creates and manages Event Trace Session and Performance logs, and it allows an administrator to monitor many different applications through the use of the command line.

5.   D. The higher the RADIUS priority number, the less that the RADIUS server gets used. To make sure that RADIUS ServerD is used only when ServerB and ServerC is unavailable, you would set the RADIUS priority from 1 to 10. This way it will get used only when ServerB and ServerC are having issues or are unresponsive.

6.   C. The NPS snap-in allows you to set up RADIUS servers and specify which RADIUS server would accept authentication from other RADIUS servers. You can do your entire RADIUS configuration through the NPS snap-in.

7.   C. NPS allows you to set up policies on how your users could log into the network. NPS allows you to set up policies that systems needs to follow, and if they don't follow these policies or rules, they will not have access to the full network.

8.   C. Windows Server 2012 R2 comes with Extensible Authentication Protocol with Transport Level Security (EAP-TLS). This EAP type allows you to use public key certificates as an authenticator. TLS is similar to the familiar Secure Sockets Layer (SSL) protocol used for web browsers and 802.1X authentication. When EAP-TLS is turned on, the client and server send TLS-encrypted messages back and forth. EAP-TLS is the strongest authentication method you can use; as a bonus, it supports smart cards. However, EAP-TLS requires your NPS server to be part of the Windows Server 2012 R2 domain.

9.   B and D. PEAP-MS-CHAP v2 is an EAP-type protocol that is easier to deploy than Extensible Authentication Protocol with Transport Level Security (EAP-TLS). It is easier because user authentication is accomplished by using password-based credentials (username and password) instead of digital certificates or smart cards. Both PEAP and EAP both use certificates with their protocols.

10.   C. One advantage of NPS is that you can use the accounting part of NPS so that you can keep track of what each department does on your NPS server. This way, departments pay for the amount of time they use on the SQL server database.

Chapter 7: Configure and Manage Active Directory

1.   A. Using images allows you to back up and restore your entire Windows Server 2012 R2 machine instead of just certain parts of data.

2.   C. The Backup Once link allows you to start a backup on the Windows Server 2012 R2 system.

3. D. If you need to back up and restore your Windows Server 2012 R2 machine, you need to use the Windows Server Backup MMC.

4. C. To create multiple password policies, you would use ADSI Edit (or adsiedit.msc).

5. D. Universal security groups, global groups, and domain local groups are all available when you are running a Windows 2008 and Windows 2012 domain functional level.

6. B, C and E. The Account Lockout Duration setting states how long an account will be locked out if the password is entered incorrectly. The Account Lockout Threshold setting is the number of bad password attempts, and the Account Lockout Counter setting is the time in which the bad password attempts are made. Once Account Lockout Counter reaches 0, the number of bad password attempts returns to 0.

7. D. When resources are made available to users who reside in domains outside the forest, foreign security principal objects are automatically created. These new objects are stored within the Foreign Security Principals folder.

8. B. The primary method by which systems administrators create and manage application data partitions is through the ntdsutil tool.

9. A and E. To meet the requirements, Robert should use the normal backup type to create a full backup every week and the incremental backup type to back up only the data that has been modified since the last full or incremental backup operation.

10. B and D. You would need to transfer the two forestwide operations master roles: Schema Master and Domain Naming Master. This means that there can only be one Schema Master and only one Domain Naming Master per forest. The PDC Emulator Master, RID Master, and Infrastructure Master are all domain-based operations master roles. (Each domain in the forest must have a domain controller with these three roles installed.)

Chapter 8: Configure and Manage Group Policy

1. C. The Delegation of Control Wizard can be used to allow other system administrators permission to add GPO links.

2. C. The system administrator can specify whether the application will be uninstalled or whether future installations will be prevented.

3. B. You would use GPUpdate.exe /force. The /force switch forces the GPO to reapply all policy settings. By default, only policy settings that have changed are applied.

4. A. You would use the Windows PowerShell `Invoke-GPUpdate` cmdlet. This PowerShell cmdlet allows you to force the GPO to reapply the policies immediately.

5. D. DVD Present Targeting is not one of the options that you may consider when using item-level targeting.

6. A and B. If you want your clients to be able to edit domain-based GPOs by using the ADMX files that are stored in the ADMX Central Store, you must be using Windows Vista, Windows 7, Windows 8, or Windows Server 2003/2008/2008 R2/2012/2012 R2.

7. D. If you assign an application to a user, the application does not get automatically installed. To have an application automatically installed, you must assign the application to the computer account. Since Finance is the only OU that should receive this application, you would link the GPO to Finance only.

8. C. The Resultant Set of Policy (RSoP) utility displays the exact settings that apply to individual users, computers, OUs, domains, and sites after inheritance and filtering have taken effect. Desktop wallpaper settings are under the User section of the GPO, so you would run the RSoP against the user account.

9. B. The Enforced option can be placed on a parent GPO, and this option ensures that all lower-level objects inherit these settings. Using this option ensures that Group Policy inheritance is not blocked at other levels.

10. A. If the data transfer rate from the domain controller providing the GPO to the computer is slower than what you have specified in the slow link detection setting, the connection is considered to be a slow connection, and the application will not install properly.

Appendix B

About the Additional Study Tools

IN THIS APPENDIX:

- Additional Study Tools
- System requirements
- Using the Study Tools
- Troubleshooting

Additional Study Tools

The following sections are arranged by category and summarize the software and other goodies you'll find from the companion website. If you need help with installing the items, refer to the installation instructions in the "Using the Study Tools" section of this appendix.

The additional study tools can be found at www.sybex.com/go/mcsawin2012r2admin. Here, you will get instructions on how to download the files to your hard drive.

Sybex Test Engine

The files contain the Sybex test engine, which includes two bonus practice exams, as well as the Assessment Test and the Chapter Review Questions, which are also included in the book itself.

Electronic Flashcards

These handy electronic flashcards are just what they sound like. One side contains a question, and the other side shows the answer.

PDF of Glossary of Terms

We have included an electronic version of the Glossary in .pdf format. You can view the electronic version of the Glossary with Adobe Reader.

Adobe Reader

We've also included a copy of Adobe Reader so you can view PDF files that accompany the book's content. For more information on Adobe Reader or to check for a newer version, visit Adobe's website at www.adobe.com/products/reader/

System Requirements

Make sure your computer meets the minimum system requirements shown in the following list. If your computer doesn't match up to most of these requirements, you may have problems using the software and files. For the latest and greatest information, please refer to the ReadMe file located in the downloads.

- A PC running Microsoft Windows 98, Windows 2000, Windows NT4 (with SP4 or later), Windows Me, Windows XP, Windows Vista, or Windows 7

- An Internet connection

Using the Study Tools

To install the items, follow these steps:

1. Download the .ZIP file to your hard drive, and unzip to an appropriate location. Instructions on where to download this file can be found here: www.sybex.com/go/mcsawin2012r2admin

2. Click the Start.EXE file to open up the study tools file.

3. Read the license agreement, and then click the Accept button if you want to use the study tools.

The main interface appears. The interface allows you to access the content with just one or two clicks.

Troubleshooting

Wiley has attempted to provide programs that work on most computers with the minimum system requirements. Alas, your computer may differ, and some programs may not work properly for some reason.

The two likeliest problems are that you don't have enough memory (RAM) for the programs you want to use or you have other programs running that are affecting installation or running of a program. If you get an error message such as "Not enough memory" or "Setup cannot continue," try one or more of the following suggestions and then try using the software again:

Turn off any antivirus software running on your computer. Installation programs sometimes mimic virus activity and may make your computer incorrectly believe that it's being infected by a virus.

Close all running programs. The more programs you have running, the less memory is available to other programs. Installation programs typically update files and programs; so if you keep other programs running, installation may not work properly.

Have your local computer store add more RAM to your computer. This is, admittedly, a drastic and somewhat expensive step. However, adding more memory can really help the speed of your computer and allow more programs to run at the same time.

Customer Care

If you have trouble with the book's companion study tools, please call the Wiley Product Technical Support phone number at (800) 762-2974. 74, or email them at http://sybex.custhelp.com/

Index

Note to the Reader: Throughout this index **boldfaced** page numbers indicate primary discussions of a topic. *Italicized* page numbers indicate illustrations.

H

S